Unruly Women of Paris

Frédéric Lix, "The Incendiaries: The Pétroleuses and Their Accomplices." *Le Monde Illustré*, June 3, 1871. Bibliothèque Nationale.

UNRULY WOMEN
OF PARIS

*Images of the
Commune*

GAY L. GULLICKSON

Cornell University Press

ITHACA AND LONDON

First published 1996 by Cornell University Press.

Printed in the United States of America

⊗ The paper in this book meets the minimum requirements of the
American National Standard for Information Sciences–Permanence
of Paper for Printed Library Materials, ANSI Z39.48-1984.

Library of Congress Cataloging-in-Publication Data

Gullickson, Gay L.
Unruly women of Paris : images of the commune / Gay L. Gullickson.
p.   cm.
Includes bibliographical references and index.
ISBN 0-8014-3228-6 (cloth : alk. paper). — ISBN 0-8014-8318-2
(paper : alk. paper)
1. Paris (France)—History—Commune, 1871.   2. Women
revolutionaries—France—Paris—History—19th century.   3. Women's
rights—France.   I. Title.
DC317.G85   1996
944.081'2—dc20   96-19780

For my family

Contents

Illustrations

Preface

If I believed in fate, I would believe I was destined to write this book. When I discovered the Commune in graduate school (I made this discovery late since I was not a history major), I was fascinated by it. It did not occur to me, however, that I might write on the Commune. It was, after all, the early 1970s and a wealth of books and articles had just appeared for the centennial celebrations of the Commune's short life.

But the Commune continued to appear in my life. When I was interviewing for my first job teaching history, the University of Louisville asked me (and all the other job candidates) to give a lecture on the Commune. Later, when I was teaching at Skidmore College, I used accounts of the Commune to introduce my students to the politics of history. Finally, in the summer of 1985, while I was working on another topic, I requested a journal at the Bibliothèque Historique de la Ville de Paris, the title of which I have long since forgotten. The issue I had requested was at the end of that journal's run, and it was bound with the first two issues of a journal on the history of medicine. Thumbing through the second journal, I came across an article on Georges Clemenceau, who was a physician as well as a statesman. Illustrating the article was a picture of Louise Michel, the Red Virgin of the Commune. Suddenly I knew I wanted to study the Commune. I dashed across the reading room to ask Joan Scott, who was also working there, if she knew of anyone who was working on the women of the Paris Commune. She said no, and, whether it was serendipity or fate, I was launched on ten years of research and writing.

As I worked on this book, it changed shape and focus. It began as a social history of women's lives and activities and metamorphosed into a study of the female figures that appear in accounts of the Commune. As my interests changed, the book became more complex, and the secondary literatures I needed to understand expanded. I found myself reading about the history of caricature and iconography, Greek goddesses and Amazons, theories of representation, and nineteenth-century psychology.

As I worked, I saw remnants and reminders of the Commune everywhere. In the Bibliothèque Nationale, and the Library of Congress, I was surrounded by statues and paintings of goddesses, muses, and allegories. At the Archives Historiques de la Guerre at Vincennes, I was in the land of the French army. In the world at large, political struggles that drew the attention of the world reminded me of the Commune. Chinese students challenged their government and were killed, as the Communards had been. Russian citizens confronted Soviet tanks and triumphed, as the Communards had believed they could. East German citizens streamed through the wall that had kept them isolated from West Germany and then hacked it down, in a literal and symbolic protest that the Communards who burned the guillotine would surely have understood. Romanian revolutionaries cut the Ceauçescu government's seal out of the national flag, another symbolic gesture the Communards would have cheered. The citizens of Sarajevo and other Bosnian cities endured the same sort of bombardments and food shortages as the Parisians had during the Prussian and French sieges of 1870 and 1871. The Commune began to seem archetypal as well as particular.

In the years I have worked on this book, I have acquired many debts. The University of Maryland supported the book with research grants and a sabbatical leave. My colleagues in French history and women's history listened to conference papers and offered comments and advice. *Feminist Studies* 17 (Summer 1991): 240–65 and *Gendered Domains,* edited by Dorothy Helly and Susan Reverby (Ithaca: Cornell University Press, 1992), pp. 135–53, published earlier versions of Chapter 5. I reuse this material here with the permission of the publisher, *Feminist Studies,* Inc., c/o Women's Studies Department, University of Maryland, College Park, MD 20742.

At an early stage, Joan Scott encouraged my desire to rewrite the Commune's history through its female representations. She and Jim Gilbert, Jim Lehning, and Claire Moses read complete drafts of the manuscript and gave me wise advice and moral support. Jim Lehning discussed ideas and visited the Mur des Fédérés with me. Claire Moses puzzled over obscure French words and phrases and shared her knowledge of French feminism. Jean Joughin welcomed me to the study of the Commune with a wonderful poster of a *communarde*. Joseph Ansell discussed caricature and art history. Jon Sumida answered questions about the French army. Marvin Breslow and Elaine Kruse endured literary and linguistic questions. Carol Mossman helped me with French translations. Elaine Kruse and Leslie Moch read parts of the manuscript and sent references to the Commune as they came across them, including the "fact" that Babette of Isak Dinesen's short story "Babette's Feast" was a pétroleuse. Peggy Darrow and Andrea Tarnowski tracked down a document at the Bibliothèque Nationale. Darlene King cheerfully printed out seemingly endless copies of chapters and helped me prepare the final draft of the manuscript. I am grateful to all of them, and to my friends, family, colleagues, and students who, over the years, offered moral support and asked me how the work was going and not if I was finished yet. I think of this as George's book, since he slept on my desk and reminded me of the here and now while I worked on the past. Like most of the cats of Paris, he did not survive to see the end of the Commune.

GAY L. GULLICKSON

Silver Spring, Maryland

Unruly Women of Paris

Rereading the Commune

In 1862 Jules and Edmond de Goncourt discovered that their devoted servant Rose, who had taken care of them for twenty-five years, had deceived them. They thought she had lived a quiet, chaste life, devoted to their service, but she had not. She had had passionate affairs with men, had stolen money and provisions from the Goncourt brothers to support them, had rented rooms for them, and had borne two children who died. In short, she had "kept men." The discovery of Rose's secret life provoked in the Goncourts "a suspicion of the entire female sex, . . . a horror of the duplicity of woman's soul," which they believed "had entered their minds for the rest of [their] lives."[1] The Goncourts were not alone in their suspicion of women. Male reformers, socialists, and conservative essayists alike debated the question of woman's nature and whether she should have the right to vote or even to work.[2]

Paralleling men's obsession with women in the 1860s was a lively bourgeois fear about the political and social ambitions of the working class. This fear was especially acute in France, which had a history of revolution that stretched back to 1789 and a working class whose desires for a republican form of government had been thwarted in 1830 and 1848. The Revolution of 1848 was a source of especially bitter memories for French workers, since it had resulted in the deaths of fifteen hundred to three thousand men and women and the deportation of four thousand. In the following two decades, as workers' living conditions deteriorated, employment fluctuated, and the building projects of Louis Napoleon and Georges

Haussmann drew more and more workers into Paris, the bourgeoisie watched nervously for signs of revolt.

In 1871 their suspicions of women and fears of the working class were confirmed when Parisians once again defied the French government and launched the revolution known as the Paris Commune. From its beginning on March 18, when the working-class women and men of the Montmartre district faced down the army over control of the city's cannons, to its end ten weeks later, when that same army invaded the city and slaughtered twenty-five thousand to thirty thousand people, the Commune was high drama. The French army bombarded the city, and the National Guard defended it; troops and civilians paraded through the streets; a new government was joyously inaugurated; the archbishop of Paris was taken hostage; a guillotine was burned; the Vendôme Column was pulled to the ground; churches were turned into political clubs; rumors of betrayal and atrocities circulated freely; and once the final battles had begun, the city burst into flame. Foreign correspondents wired reports around Europe and across the Atlantic; editors wrote emotionally of events in Paris; caricaturists produced drawings; and Parisians and foreign residents of the city kept diaries and wrote letters. Some championed the Commune's cause; others denounced it. No one remained neutral.

There is more to the Commune than spectacle and drama, however. People's reactions to it helped to create our political and cultural world. For over a century, the Commune has been a touchstone for political theorists and activists, for conservatives and reformers, and for our understanding of concepts ranging from class and revolution to femininity and masculinity. Conservatives presented the Commune as a dangerous usurpation of power by people who had no respect for property, morality, or the legitimately elected government of France and watched for it to happen again. Radicals saw it as a tragically failed attempt to establish worker democracy and vowed not to make what they regarded as the Communards' mistakes again. From the successful Russian Revolution of 1917, to the failed 1989 revolution in Tiananmen Square, those who have sought political change have seen the world through the lens of the Commune and have looked to it for inspiration, while those who have opposed change have weighed the costs of repression. And everywhere, from the end of the Commune to the end of the cold war, people have oversimplified political complexities and divided the world into irreconcilable political camps that parallel the conflict between the Commune and the French government at Versailles.

The defining importance of the Commune for modern politics has made the writing of its history a compelling but tricky task for historians. Virtually everyone has taken sides in telling its story. Its defenders have condemned the French government; its critics have maligned the revolutionaries. As Stewart Edwards presciently noted in the preface to his centenary history of the Commune, "Objectivity is not to be expected of mortals writing their own story, the history of the events that have constructed the world they live in."[3]

Examples abound, but two should suffice. In his pro-Commune history, Frank Jellinek describes the Versailles troops' actions during the *semaine sanglante,* the final "bloody week" of fighting between the Communards and the army, as a "massacre," an "orgy," and an "uncontrolled slaughter," of the Communards, who "held out bravely" and, if they survived to be arrested, endured "torments."[4] In their college textbook, Paul MacKendrick and his colleagues present a different view. Using the language of the cold war, they refer to "Communards and sympathizers" who went on an "orgy of slaughter and destruction" during the "so-called Bloody Week," and they present a false chronology of events to explain and justify the national government's actions.[5] Two more different views of the Commune are difficult to imagine.

The legacy of the Commune extends well beyond politics, however. As Albert Boime has shown, it was a defining moment for two powerful generations of French artists, the Impressionists and the Post-Impressionists.[6] It was also, as this book seeks to demonstrate, a defining moment for Western conceptualizations of gender, not least because it gave birth to the powerful, evil, and imaginary *pétroleuses* (female incendiaries) who were accused of setting fire to Paris during the semaine sanglante. Exercising a powerful grip on the Western cultural imagination, the pétroleuse became the negative embodiment of the publicly active woman and cast a long shadow over debates about women's rights and proper roles. Although no longer well known by name, versions of the pétroleuse continue to shape our understanding of the past and remain a touchstone for Western notions of gender.

Representations of the Communardes: An Overview

The images or representations of the *communardes** in texts produced during or immediately after the Commune vary widely. Some male Communards and Commune supporters portray them positively. In the eyes of

* In French the female supporters of the Commune are *communardes;* male supporters, *communards.* I use these terms as well as the English phrases "female Communards" and "male Communards" when I am speaking of one or the other group. When I am speaking of women and men together, I use the ungendered English term Communards.

the pro-Commune journalist and historian Prosper-Olivier Lissagaray, they were gallant young women, wounded lionesses, and the bravest of the martyrs who died on the barricades.[7] For former military officer Sébastien Commissaire, they were "idealistic girls"; for revolutionaries Félix Pyat and Benoît Malon, both elected members of the Commune, they were "self-sacrificing mothers" who fought "to make their children free."[8]

Negative views displayed more rhetorical ebullience. Conservative journalists and essayists vied with one another in hyperbole. Writing while the final battles were still being fought in Paris, the anti-Commune journalist Francisque Sarcey suggested that the women had been more ferocious and more evil than the men because "their brains are weaker and their emotions livelier."[9] Maxime Du Camp, whose four volumes on the Commune were designed to dissuade the French government from granting amnesty to the convicted and exiled Communards, thought quite simply that the women who "gave themselves to the Commune" were evil and insane. More than the men, he declared, "the women excel in acts of cruelty that they mistake for acts of courage."[10] Army Captain Beugnot referred to the communardes as "mad dogs,"[11] Edmond Lepelletier likened them to a Greek chorus crying for vengeance and urging on the men,[12] and Jules Claretie, musing on the women's militant speeches and actions, wondered "from what slime the human species is made."[13] Essayist Alexandre Dumas, fils, refused to call the communardes women at all. Instead, he used the term *femelles* (a term ordinarily used for female animals), "out of respect for the women whom they resembled—when they were dead."[14] And writer after writer identified them as megaeras, amazons, furies, viragoes, jackals, hecates, and madwomen, until these figures finally merged into one—the horrific pétroleuse.

Even supporters of the Commune found it difficult to accept all of women's revolutionary actions and could muster only lukewarm support for them. Gaston Da Costa, sentenced to death for his role in the Commune, felt compelled, for example, to distinguish between "good" and "bad" women and to distance himself from the latter whom he, like critics of the Commune, identified as prostitutes.[15] Jules Bergeret, an elected member of the Commune and one of its generals, opined from a slightly different perspective that women were destined "by their physical and moral nature" to remain within the "domestic sphere" and that the furies of the Commune had been driven into action not by a flaw in their nature but by the failures of the French government.[16]

These positive and negative images or representations of women were part of a nineteenth-century discourse about woman's nature and appropriate female behavior. Women had been a subject of discussion for centuries,[17] but industrialization had given the debate new urgency. As work moved out of the home and the scale of production increased in western Europe and America, women found it harder and harder to integrate productive work and child care. For working-class women, the choice between caring for their children and contributing to the family's income usually had to be resolved on the side of paid work. For bourgeois or middle-class women, the dilemma was usually solved by withdrawal from family-run businesses and concentration on domestic and charitable activity. Historians have identified the latter pattern as both the separation of spheres (productive and reproductive, or public and private) and the cult of domesticity.[18]

The separation of the bourgeois home and workplace led to increasingly dichotomized conceptualizations of male and female nature which, in turn, were used to justify the confinement of bourgeois women to domestic roles.[19] Bourgeois gender conceptualizations were never stable or uncontested, but the view that might be labeled normative (or conservative) characterized women as more emotional, nurturing, altruistic, passive, virtuous, and frail than men. These were the characteristics that suited women for a protected life of domesticity and child rearing. Men, in contrast, were fitted for the rigors of work and politics because they were stronger, less virtuous, more rational, more aggressive, and more self-interested.

Confronted with women whose behavior seemed more aggressive than passive, and who refused to remain in the domestic sphere, bourgeois men reflected again on woman's nature. Some viewed it as unified; others saw it as internally flawed; still others, as bifurcated. From the first perspective, women like the communardes were perceived as having violated their nature. The appeal of this theory was that it emphasized the unnaturalness, hence the evilness, of these women's behavior, although the ability of the women to violate their feminine nature, as well as what they became when they did so, was difficult to explain. In the latter two views, either aspects of femininity, such as frailty of mind, made women more susceptible to evil, or their very nature was divided between good and evil. Both theories explained the unruly woman's behavior. She had either succumbed to temptation, or the evil side of her nature had overwhelmed the good. These theories were logically more consistent than the first, but they turned even the most virtuous woman into a potential fury—an unsettling thought for bourgeois men in 1871.

Visible in these bourgeois versions of woman's nature are nineteenth-century Christian depictions of Mary and Eve as the embodiments of good and evil.[20] The iconographical presentation and meaning of Mary has shifted over the centuries, but she remains the unique embodiment of maternity and sinlessness. Eve, in contrast, is one of a host of powerful, dangerous, and sinful women in Western culture, including the Amazons and Sirens of ancient Greece, the biblical Delilah, and the witches of medieval Europe. Mary might mediate for men with her son in heaven, but Eve and her sisters remained a source of temptation and danger in real life. They made it difficult for men to see publicly active, powerful women in nonthreatening terms. Thus, the communardes, who acted in most unladylike ways, were more likely to be represented negatively than positively, especially if the opponents of the revolution got to create the representations.

Gender and Allegory

In Western culture, the representation of governments and philosophical concepts in female form originated in the gender conventions of the Greek language and the goddesses of classical Greek myths. In Greek and other Indo-European languages, abstract nouns of virtue, knowledge, and spirituality are commonly gendered female. When those abstractions are personified, as they regularly have been, the gender of the word has carried over to representation of them in female form. The same is true of countries, cities, and political philosophies. Athena, warrior goddess and patroness of wisdom, and, to a lesser extent, the other Greek goddesses are the models for the personifications of virtues and governments.[21]

Nineteenth-century French painters and sculptors, like other Western artists, followed the Greek pattern and commonly represented countries, cities, and governments, as well as a broad range of political philosophies—liberty, equality, justice, victory, peace, war, fraternity, and glory, to name a few—in female form. (All these concepts bear the feminine grammatical gender in French.) Only artists and other members of the cultural elite were likely to know all the allegorical goddesses by their symbolic paraphernalia, but some figures were commonly recognizable.

The effectiveness of the female allegorical figures depended on gender conventions or stereotypes (positive and negative) and the exclusion of human women from the traits they embodied, conventions and exclusions that would have made it difficult for male figures to convey the same messages even if the gender of abstract nouns had been masculine.[22] Female figures radiated power when real women were presumed, or forced, to be powerless; they represented governments that excluded women from full citizenship; they embodied attributes that were thought to reside more fully, if not entirely, in men than in women.[23]

FIGURE 1. The First Seal of the Republic. Archives Nationales.

Men and women may derive different messages from female representations, as other scholars have noted.[24] Women are said to experience a certain identification with the figures, which "interact with ideas about femaleness and affect the way women act as well as appear"; for men, such figures portray alterity.[25] Parisian women, however, appear to have responded to the allegorical goddesses and female personifications of the French state, French governments (monarchy, empire, and republic), and French cities in much the same way as men did. Indeed, during the Commune and the war with Prussia which immediately preceded it, one of women's favorite rallying places was the female allegorical statue representing the city of Strasbourg in the place de la Concorde. (The rescue of Strasbourg was a Parisian cause célèbre from the time it was captured by

FIGURE 2. Eugène Delacroix, *Liberty Leading the People on the Ramparts*. Musée du Louvre.

the Prussians early in the war to its annexation to the new German state at the end of the war.)

During the French Revolution, Liberty emerged as the most important of the allegorical political figures when she was chosen by the new government to represent the French republic in place of the king. On the first seal of the republic she stood, barefooted (a symbol of freedom from restraint), holding a pike topped with a Phrygian cap (a symbol of freedom since it was identified as the cap worn by freed Roman slaves) in her right hand and a bundle of fasces (a symbol of unity consisting of a sheaf of rods among which is bound a hatchet) in her left hand (fig. 1). Liberty was eventually relieved of her double symbolic duty when a new figure, Marianne, became the symbol of the French republic. Originating among counter-revolutionaries as a symbol of what was wrong with the republic (rule by commoners), Marianne, a girl of common origins, gradually became the positive embodiment of the republic from which, had she been an actual woman, she would have been politically excluded.[26]

In 1831 one of the grandest and most famous examples of the use of female allegory, Eugène Delacroix's painting *Liberty Leading the People on the Ramparts,* was exhibited in Paris (fig. 2). A stirring representation of the Revolution of 1830, Delacroix's Liberty combines features of the classical Liberty and Marianne. This powerful goddess, clad in the garb of the working class and baring her right breast (her left breast is not entirely exposed), is linked representationally to the Greek Amazons and the Virgin Mary, and she can be seen, Anne Hollander observes, as simultaneously "holy, desirable, and fierce."[27] Well-equipped with the symbols of freedom and revolution—a Phrygian cap on her head, the French tricolor flag (in this case, a symbol of the republic, although it was also used by both French empires) in one hand and a flintlock in the other, she strides radiantly forward. For later generations she became the personification not only of the Three Glorious Days of the July Revolution but also of the Revolution of 1848 and of the Paris Commune.

Historians and the Commune

Dispassionate objectivity has often eluded historians of the Commune. Many of the early histories, of course, were written by participants in and eyewitnesses to events in Paris, and we might expect them to take sides. But twentieth-century historians' feelings about the Paris Commune and women's actions have run almost as deep as those of the early chroniclers and polemicists. Many have echoed the judgments of earlier writers, calling the women prostitutes and amazons and finding them to have been mentally more unstable and excitable than the men, their behavior "worse" or "more cruel." Even pro-Commune historians have often repeated the negative female stereotypes and images they found in earlier histories and primary texts.[28] One of the objectives of this book is to discover why this has happened.

The answer lies not only in historians' political convictions but also, we will see, in their failure to examine and understand how their primary texts employ female representations. In uncritically accepting eyewitness descriptions of the communardes and, to a lesser degree, of bourgeois women as objective rather than ideological, historians have perpetuated the cultural biases of their sources. Wittingly or not, they have played the roles of witness and judge of the Commune, of the communardes, and of women in general.

Some recent historians, presumably motivated by a desire to provide a more objective or accurate account of the Commune than earlier writers, have eliminated the stereotypes and largely confined their accounts of women to specific sections of the text.[29] Although this strategy constitutes an important break with the partisan tradition, it has a high cost. It both marginalizes women's roles in the Commune and eliminates the pétroleuses and other female figures who populate the early texts. Representation of the communardes as increasingly demeaned and threatening female figures was not marginal to contemporaries' or subsequent generations' understanding of the Commune. Far from it. Such representations embodied and represented the revolution for generations. Edith Thomas, the author of the only book-length study of the communardes to date, implicitly acknowledged the importance of these images when she titled her 1963 study *Les "Pétroleuses."*[30] The pétroleuse and other female images need to be analyzed, as Thomas began to do, not eliminated, for eliminating them impedes rather than improves our understanding of the Commune.

This History

This history uses many of the same sources as other studies of the Commune—contemporary newspapers; memoirs; letters; diaries; government dossiers; statements of judges, prosecutors, witnesses, defendants, and defense attorneys at the Communards' trials; and the National Assembly's final report on the Commune's origins, participants, and policies. It focuses, however, not on governmental decisions and political philosophies but on representation, meaning, and ideology.

Everyone who has written about, drawn, photographed, or painted the Commune, whether eyewitness or historian, has made decisions, some conscious, some not, about what to include and exclude. All narratives and visual representations interpret as well as report. Historians' judgments are a product of their personal experiences and political philosophies (what we might think of as their context), as well as of the texts with which they work. Their representations and interpretations, like those of the original narratives and images, structure our understanding of the past.

In the lexicon of contemporary cultural history, this book is a study of *mentalités*. It asks questions about how contemporaries and historians construed women's participation in the Commune, the meaning they attached to their activities, and the ideological purposes served by the caricatures, stereotypes, and other representations of women. Answering these questions involves us in a process of rereading the history of the Commune and, ultimately, retelling its story.

Historians may, and often do, regard events differently from each other.

Some of this difference is a product of the questions they ask as readers of texts. This history is a case in point. By asking questions about meaning and representation, it rereads the history and historiography of the Commune and rewrites the story.

The questions of this book grow out of two fundamental premises: first, that the women and men of 1871 lived in a conceptually and politically gendered universe that deeply influenced their choices, actions, and perceptions of themselves and their world; and second, that the verbal and visual representations of women that appear in the texts of the Commune are the key to understanding its meaning for its participants and for subsequent generations.

Like biblical scholars whose analyses include prior interpretations, I have subjected the writings of historians to analysis along with those of contemporaries. I have adopted this somewhat unusual procedure because historians have not only constructed the meaning of the Commune for future generations; they have judged it and proselytized for or against it just as its supporters and opponents did. In this sense, the application of the techniques of biblical exegesis may be peculiarly appropriate to a study of the Commune, however avowedly antireligious it was.[31]

The book advances a series of arguments: Examination of the female imagery in contemporary accounts of the Commune reveals that the struggle between Paris and the French national government operating at Versailles was perceived and understood in gendered terms. As writers and artists created, employed, and manipulated female representations (whether consciously or unconsciously), they assigned meaning to and passed judgment on the Commune and the individuals who supported or opposed it. These images are the most powerful tool writers and artists, contemporaries and historians, conservatives and liberals have had for conveying political and moral judgments. They have structured our understanding of the Commune, continued to provoke emotional responses to it, and created its cultural significance. They have done so by drawing our attention away from complexity and pointing us toward judgment.

Historians have perpetuated the initial judgments of the Commune by repeating the female imagery of the primary texts and drawings. We cannot understand either this historical event called the Commune or its significance in Western politics and culture unless we examine these images directly. When we do, we find that the cultural practice of personifying and identifying revolutions in female form, in combination with bourgeois men's fascination with unruly woman like the communardes, made the invention of the powerful, deeply disturbing (and imaginary) pétroleuse and her historical identification with the Commune all but inevitable. Defeated, the Communards were powerless to dethrone this new negative female allegory or even to temper its ideological messages. As a result, in certain discourses, the pétroleuse came to represent not just the dangerous, uncontrolled woman but a world turned thoroughly upside down.

The book begins with a synopsis, which, like an opera program, provides a brief narrative of the origins, history, and defeat of the Commune for those who are unfamiliar with or have forgotten this period of French history. The chapters that follow might be thought of as exploring the arias and recitatives by and about women that appear in contemporary and historical texts. Each chapter stands alone analytically and might be read separately, but read as a whole, the book proceeds chronologically and is a history of the Commune.

After the synopsis, the curtain rises on Paris in 1871. The opening act (Chapter 1) takes place on March 18. A variety of figures—the working-class women of Montmartre, lower-class prostitutes, street urchins, national guardsmen, soldiers, generals, and the schoolteacher and dedicated revolutionary Louise Michel—take the stage. Through exploration of the actions, motives, and voices given to these characters, this chapter demonstrates how writer after writer attempted to prove that the Commune was either good or evil from its beginning.

The second act (Chapter 2) introduces a new set of characters and issues—those that lived on in popular memory from the time of the first French Revolution in 1789. It examines the gendered and class-based divisions of French society and the "memories" of the French Revolution which colored conservative reactions to the Commune. Central among the figures of the first revolution who appear again in accounts of the Commune are the *tricoteuses*—the women who, according to tradition, knitted at the foot of the guillotine as the enemies of the revolution were executed. As we will see, by associating the *communardes* with the *tricoteuses,* conservatives evoked memories of the Terror and condemned both revolutionary women and the Commune through historical association.

In the third act (Chapter 3), the major female figures of this revolution—the innocent victim, the scandalous orator, the amazon warrior, and the ministering angel—take center stage as we explore the truths about women and revolution that contemporaries and historians have found in the Commune. In contrast to these stereotyped figures, in the fourth act (Chapter 4), a more complex set of characters steps onto the stage— Parisian women who wrote their own accounts of the revolution. In their presentation of themselves and the Commune, four articulate women— two revolutionaries and two conservative bourgeoises—reveal the cultural images and values they used to judge the Commune and its supporters, and to organize, justify, and make sense of their experiences.

The fifth act (Chapter 5) takes place during the final week of the Commune, the semaine sanglante, when the women and men of Paris mounted the barricades to defend their revolution against the French army. In this chapter the most famous and powerful of the figures associated with the Commune take the stage, the pétroleuses, who were accused of maliciously burning Paris to the ground with their little bottles of kerosene.

In the sixth act (Chapter 6), the scene shifts to Versailles where thousands of Communards were taken in May to await trial. With stunning rapidity, the army determined guilt and innocence and handed down sentences to men, women, and children. From the prosecution's perspective, Louise Michel and five working-class pétroleuses were the most important female defendants. Like the other women on trial, they puzzled and angered judges and observers not only because they had participated in the Commune but because they represented aspects of femininity that the bourgeoisie preferred not to see.

The conclusion of the book (Chapter 7) steps outside the narrative to analyze the history that is revealed when we pay attention to the allegorical, stereotypical, and human female figures who have always populated the pages of the Commune's texts but whose meanings and messages have not been clearly seen before.

La Commune de Paris

On July 15, 1870, the Prussian chancelor Otto von Bismarck's two-year-old plan to maneuver the French emperor Napoleon III into declaring war on Prussia finally succeeded over the issue of who would ascend to the vacant Spanish throne. Napoleon's ill-fated decision to challenge Prussia catapulted France into a year of warfare, civil strife, political experimentation, and tragedy. The emperor and a hundred thousand French troops were captured less than two months after the war began. Word of the army's defeat and Napoleon's capture reached the Parisian public on September 3. By the afternoon of the fourth, crowds of Parisians had invaded the Legislative Assembly meeting and then moved on to the Hôtel de Ville, the Parisian city hall, where a new republican government was declared.[1]

A crowd of citizens and national guardsmen greeted the new government with enthusiasm. Here was the peaceful revolution Parisians, consistently more republican than the rural French, had longed for. People sang the "Marseillaise." Crowds circulated in the streets. Vendors sold blue, white, and red tricolor cockades (the colors of the French republics) and red ribbons (the color of revolution). The statues in the place de la Concorde were decorated with small red flags. Red crepe fluttered from the lampposts. The enthusiasm of the Parisians seemed unbounded. Only the supporters of the now-defunct empire and the most radical social revolutionaries found the scene disturbing, the former because it meant the end of their hopes, the latter because they feared that the new republic would be hijacked and betrayed by the Right.

The Parisian deputies to the Legislative Assembly formed a provisional governing body pending new national elections, and General Trochu, who had divorced himself from the fate of the empire when word of its defeat reached Paris, agreed to preside over the new government. Many hoped that the Prussians' quarrel with the emperor would now end and an armistice be established. When this did not happen, Parisians turned to the task of preparing the city to resist the advancing Prussians. Trees were cut down for barricades and fuel, bridges over the Seine were blown up, houses that could shelter the enemy were destroyed, and an army of men trained to defend the city. On September 18 the siege of Paris began. The city was encircled, cut off from the outside world, and its citizens hunkered down to endure what turned out to be five months of bitter cold, hunger, disease, and finally bombardment. While they waited for the provincial armies to come to their aid, virtually every able-bodied Parisian man who was not already a member of the army joined the National Guard and prepared to fight the Prussians.

Paris never did surrender. Indeed, the city held out far longer and through far worse conditions than most had imagined possible while the political leaders and provincial armies tried and failed to come to its rescue. Finally, at the end of January, the Government of National Defense accepted Bismarck's armistice terms and surrendered the city to the Prussians. The French hurriedly held elections for a National Assembly, which in turn selected the elderly conservative statesman Adolphe Thiers to lead the government. On February 26, 1871, Thiers accepted the Prussian peace terms, ceding most of Alsace, one-third of Lorraine, and the city of Metz to the new German state, agreeing to pay 5 billion francs in indemnity, and permitting a triumphal march of Prussian troops through Paris.

Appalled at the government's capitulation to Bismarck's terms and angered that the Prussian troops who had starved and bombarded Paris were to be allowed to humiliate the city with a triumphal march, the Parisians grew daily more suspicious of the government's motives. As the date of the Prussian entry into Paris approached, the city seemed on the verge of hysteria. Armed crowds roamed the streets day and night. Working-class neighborhoods like Montmartre, Belleville, and La Chapelle barricaded themselves. Cannons that had been left in the zone to be occupied by the Prussians were dragged by hand to the hills of Paris for safekeeping. The Parisian newspapers unanimously called for calm and announced on the twenty-eighth that they would not publish again until the Germans had left the city. Many feared that the Prussians were looking for any provocation that would give them an opportunity to impose even harsher peace terms or to pillage the city.

On March 1, the Prussians entered Paris through the Bois de Boulogne, marched up to the Arc de Triomphe and then down the Champs-Elysées to the place de la Concorde and the Louvre. They were greeted with angry silence and closed shops. Well versed in political symbolism, the Parisians shielded the eyes of the statues representing the cities of France in the place de la Concorde with black hoods and flew black flags from the buildings along the parade route. Only a small crowd watched the troops march through the streets. The few shopkeepers who remained open to serve the Prussians were punished afterward with broken windows and furniture. Prostitutes who ventured into the Prussian camps were scolded and whipped. Engaging in their own symbolic theater, the German troops marched directly through the Arc de Triomphe on their way out of the city two days later, celebrating their triumph over the country whose earlier victories on German soil were enshrined on the Arc. The French, in turn, built a massive bonfire at the Arc to purify the soil the Germans had desecrated.

After the Prussians had left the city (but not their encampments around its perimeter), relations between the newly elected National Assembly (composed largely of political conservatives and royalists from the provinces) and working-class, republican Paris deteriorated rapidly. Ignoring the city's precarious economic condition, the assembly lifted the wartime moratorium on the sale of goods being held at the state-run pawnshop; announced that landlords could immediately claim all back rents due them; and made all debts due with interest within the next four months. Working-class Parisians faced the imminent sale of the furniture, clothing, and tools they had pawned during the siege and still could not redeem because they had no jobs and no money and, along with small merchants, were threatened with immediate eviction.

In addition, the national government turned what had been regarded as a patriotic right into a dole by declaring that only those national guardsmen who could demonstrate economic need would continue to receive pay. It also suppressed radical newspapers, sentenced the working-class leaders Auguste Blanqui and Gustave Flourens to death in absentia for their role in a brief flurry of revolutionary activity the previous October during the Prussian siege, and voted to move the National Assembly (which had been meeting in Bordeaux since the siege of Paris began) to Versailles, rather than back to Paris, thereby decapitalizing the city.

Finally, in a poorly planned and subsequently much-debated decision, Thiers sent French army troops in the early hours of March 18, 1871, to remove the cannons and other large guns the National Guard had dragged to the hills of Paris in February. Whether the military operation was simply badly handled or was designed to provoke a revolt so the government could crush and disarm the workers and national guardsmen is unclear. In any case, the predawn raid on the cannons was detected when the government failed to send horses to pull the heavy guns away. While the soldiers at Montmartre and other points waited for horses, they fraternized with the people, and military order was lost. Thiers and the rest of the national government withdrew from Paris to Versailles, and late in the day two French generals were killed. The steps that would lead to the establishment of a separate government in Paris (the Paris Commune) and a second siege of Paris, this time by provincial French troops, had been taken.[2]

With the withdrawal of the army, ministers, and government agencies from Paris, the leaders of the political Left scrambled to catch up with the crowd. Failing to understand that what they faced was civil war, the National Guard Central Committee, arrondissement mayors, and Parisian deputies debated options and then instituted self-rule for Paris, announced citywide elections for March 22, postponed them to Sunday, March 26, and tried to negotiate with the government in Versailles to reach a peaceful solution to the crisis. On March 28 the Paris Commune officially came into existence (although the term is commonly used to refer to the entire period of the revolution from March 18 to May 28) with the inauguration of the newly elected municipal council at the Hôtel de Ville.

The inaugural ceremony demonstrated the Parisians' mastery of political pageantry and symbolism. Civilians hung out of windows and thronged the square to watch the spectacle. Red, the color of revolution, was everywhere. Red sashes draped the shoulders of the newly elected members of the Commune and the outgoing members of the Central Committee, red streamers hung from the windows, a red flag flew from the roof, and a red scarf draped a bust of Marianne, the symbolic representation of the French republic.[3] Bayonets glinted in the sun, drums beat, bands played, and the crowd sang the revolutionary French anthem the "Marseillaise" and the "Chant du départ." Cannons roared a salute along the Seine while the National Guard battalions, and regular army soldiers, artillerists, and marines, who had sworn loyalty to the Commune, marched endlessly across the square and down the streets, two hundred thousand strong, their banners topped by Phrygian caps.

On the surface, the situation looked hopeful. The elections had been a success. There was news of sympathetic uprisings in other cities.[4] The trash had been collected; the streets were cleaner than they had been since the beginning of the Prussian siege; and the city's fountains splashed water. Only the city's cats were missing, as the Reverend Mr. William Gibson observed, having been turned into "rabbit" during the siege.[5] It seemed possible, as the *Cri du Peuple* declared, that "the drums of Santerre will never roll again, nor rifles gleam from the windows of our Communal Hôtel de Ville, nor the Place de Grève be stained with blood."[6] The democratically elected Commune began to undo the decrees of the National Assembly and sought to negotiate with Thiers for Parisian home rule.

Below the surface lay a grimmer reality. Despite the relatively modest Parisian political demands, Thiers and the National Assembly refused to negotiate and prepared to do battle. In the beginning, neither side was well prepared for war and virtually all historians have agreed that if the Commune had marched upon Versailles in the first few days of its existence, it could have defeated the badly demoralized army. The leaders of the National Guard could not be certain of that, however, nor could they be sure that the Prussians, who still ringed the eastern side of Paris, would remain neutral. While the Commune hesitated, Thiers began to build an army that would remain loyal to its officers (as it had not on the eighteenth) and could be used to humiliate the city that had challenged his authority.

Loyalty was not a problem for the National Guard, but preparation and leadership were, and even as talk of a march on Versailles increased in the city, intelligent people worried about the ability of the guard to launch and win an offensive battle. On Palm Sunday, April 2, a scant five days after the elected Communal Council was sworn in, the Versailles troops attacked the suburb of Courbevoie, pushed the National Guard back, and captured the bridge over the Seine into the *faubourg* (suburb) of Neuilly. The war had begun. On April 3 the National Guard marched determinedly toward Versailles, only to fall into a trap set by the Versaillais. Versailles was relieved by its victory; Paris, horrified. People poured into the streets. National guardsmen beat the call to arms and dragged their cannons to the western walls. Thousands of men demanded to march on Versailles; women proposed to march in front of them.

All night long, guardsmen filed spontaneously out of the city, without organization, without provisions, without even forming up in their battalions, convinced that the soldiers would not fire on their fellow countrymen. The great offensive the Parisians had wanted since the beginning of the Prussian attack had come to pass. Women rallied at the place de la Concorde and waited at the city gates for word of the battle.

By evening it was clear that enthusiasm and numbers had not been enough for victory. Carts of dead and dying men trundled into the city. The army had remained loyal to its commanders, fired on the guardsmen, and routed them. Thiers was not inclined to be gracious in victory. On April 6 he increased the pressure on Paris by bombarding the western (ironically, the bourgeois) sections of the city. For the next seven weeks, cannon and artillery fire trapped the residents of Neuilly in their homes, supplied background noise for life in Paris, and provided entertainment for the intrepid who walked up the Champs-Elysées to watch the battle.

In a terrible foreshadowing of things to come, the Versailles troops executed some of their captured prisoners on April 3 and 4, including two National Guard generals, and allowed others to be abused by crowds in Versailles. In retaliation, the Commune took a variety of hostages, including the archbishop of Paris and several priests, and threatened to execute them if Versailles continued to kill its Communard prisoners, a threat it did not carry out until May 24, during the final battle for the control of Paris.

As the war continued, the Commune debated and passed legislation that has earned it a place among the most radical of French governments. Petty fines for rule violations in factories were eliminated; the pay for legislators was set at the daily wage for ordinary workers; and the tools, furniture, and clothing people had pawned during the Prussian siege were returned to their owners free of charge. Night baking was abolished at the request of the bakers. Separation of church and state was declared, and education was secularized. The widows (legally married or not) and children of men who died "defending the rights of Paris" were adopted by the city. Women's work and wages were studied and meetings were held to discuss plans for improving women's education.

Working-class Parisians mourned the dead (by May 8, five hundred had died in the struggle for control of Fort Issy alone), avoided the wealthier areas of the city that were within range of the Versailles artillery, followed the progress of the war, and carried on remarkably normal lives under the circumstances. Following in the footsteps of the revolutionaries of 1789, people attended nightly political debates in churches. Aware of the power of symbolic actions, the Commune signaled its politics by flying the red flag of revolution, burning a guillotine in front of the statue of Voltaire (to disavow the Terror of the first French Revolution), pulling down the Vendôme Column (a symbol of despotism and militarism to republicans like the Communards, since it glorified the imperial aspects of Napoleon I's rule and was the site of an annual parade of Napoleon III's imperial troops),[7] and razing Thiers's house. Freemasons, in the first public demonstration in their history, marched through the city to show their support for the Commune. As the military situation worsened, however, liberal principles were sorely tested, and the Communal Council, like its conservative predecessors, shut down the opposition press.

Relegated to the margins of formal politics by a "universal" suffrage that excluded them, women found their own ways to express their support for the Commune. Neighborhood groups formed vigilance committees and prepared to defend the barricades. Female orators denounced the government and the National Guard for cowardice and ineptitude. Female cooks, water carriers, and medical assistants accompanied the battalions of the National Guard into battle. Wives, sisters, and daughters carried food and drink to the defenders of the city walls. Women workers manufactured gun cartridges, uniforms, and sacks to be filled with sand for the barricades. André Léo (Léodile Champseix), the female editor of the Commune newspaper *La Sociale*, warned the Commune and National Guard leaders about the dangers of alienating women's support. Louise Michel, the Commune's most passionate supporter, joined the National Guard in battle. Elizabeth Dmietrieff, a Russian émigrée, and other members of the International Working Men's Association founded the Union of Women for the Care of the Wounded and the Defense of the Commune.

The wealthier part of the bourgeoisie was unsympathetic to the revolution from the beginning, believing, with Edmond de Goncourt, that when the "men from the very bottom" of the social ladder spoke of liberty, equality, and fraternity, they had "the enslavement or death of the upper classes" in mind.[8] The international and non-Parisian French press consistently but inaccurately referred to the Communards as "Communists." Bourgeois men who had joined the National Guard during the Prussian siege abandoned their units and fled Paris to avoid being forced to serve the Commune. Meanwhile, in Versailles Thiers and his generals continued to train the army and prepared to teach the Parisians "a lesson."[9]

As the war continued, conditions in the isolated city deteriorated, disagreements among its leaders multiplied, and fears of an invasion escalated. The propaganda disseminated by Versailles had convinced people outside of Paris that the Commune, far from being a defense of the republic, was a threat to it. If this revolution were allowed to succeed, the government warned, it would institute a new reign of terror. No one outside Paris, either in the provinces or in other countries, came to the city's assistance. Still, most Parisians found it impossible to believe that French troops would actually invade the city and kill its citizens.

On Sunday evening, May 21, the unthinkable occurred. The Versailles army entered Paris through an unguarded gate. Having been told to take no prisoners, the troops instituted a seemingly endless nightmare of street fighting followed by the surrender and then the execution of the Commune's defenders. Trapped in the city by the Versailles troops on one side and the Prussians on the other, the Communards retreated from barricade to barricade. As they fell back, some set fires to prevent the army's pursuit. Others, in anger and desperation burned the Tuileries Palace, Hôtel de Ville, and other buildings. Still others executed some of the Commune's hostages, including the city's archbishop. Rumors circulated that female incendiaries, called pétroleuses, had set the fires, and the bourgeoisie, angered at the disruption the Commune had caused in their lives and fearful for their property, readily believed them.

Thousands of Parisians died defending the barricades and on the Parisian killing fields of the Parc Monceau, the Luxembourg Gardens, the Ecole Militaire, and the Père-Lachaise Cemetery. Machine guns made the killing fast and easy although the victims did not always die immediately. Women and children as well as adult men met this summary "justice." By the end of the week the conquering Versailles troops had lost fewer than nine hundred; the Communards, more than twenty thousand. At least thirty-eight thousand more were marched to Versailles, exposed to the taunts, insults, and physical assaults of bourgeois women and men. Those who survived the march (and many did not, for soldiers dispatched those who walked too slowly or collapsed from exhaustion, as well as those who displeased them) faced months of incarceration and investigation.

The courts martial that tried the Communards assumed the defendants were guilty and brought them swift judgment. Ten thousand were convicted (a thousand in absentia); twenty-three were executed; forty-five hundred were incarcerated in French prisons; and forty-five hundred more were deported to New Caledonia.[10] Like the prisoners' march to Versailles, the voyage to the South Pacific was deadly for many. On board ship, the prisoners were confined to large cages and guarded by machine guns. Some who survived the journey were incarcerated with common criminals; others were left to fend for themselves in the inhospitable climate, terrain, and culture.

As would be the case a quarter of a century later in the Dreyfus Affair, the justness of the trials and sentences for people who, in many cases, were accused only of political crimes raised questions that could not be permanently ignored. Finally in 1880, when the republicans gained control of the National Assembly and the presidency of France, a general amnesty was granted to the Communards, and they were allowed to return from exile. Greeted enthusiastically by the French Left that had worked for their return for almost a decade, the thousands who had suffered in French prisons, languished in exile in London, Switzerland, or Brussels, or endured the hardships and futility of life in New Caledonia resumed their lives and their political interests.

The Commune's cultural and political significance did not end with its defeat or even with amnesty for its convicted supporters. The deaths of both the Communards and the hostages during the semaine sanglante, the last, bloody week of fighting in May, made the Commune a central refer-

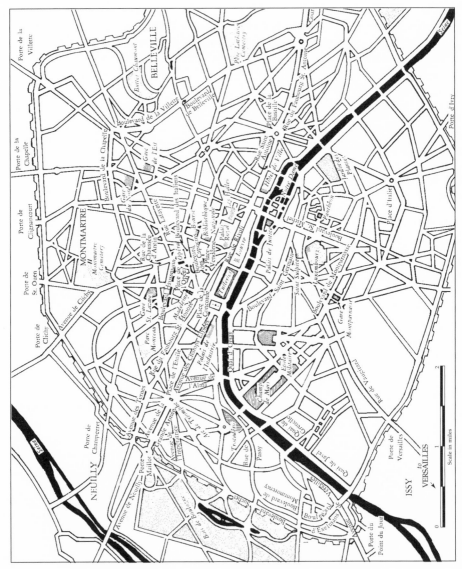

FIGURE 3. Map of Paris, 1871

ence point for both the Left and the Right. For the Right, it provided a warning about the dangers of working-class revolt. For the Left, it provided both a positive and a negative example of how to conduct a revolution. (Lenin studied it carefully.)[11] The Mur des Fédérés (Wall of the Communards) in the Pére-Lachaise Cemetery,[12] where, legend has it, the Commune's last defenders perished, became a place of pilgrimage for admirers of the Commune ranging from French workers to would-be revolutionaries from all over the world (fig. 3).

CHAPTER ONE

The Women of March 18

The revolution known as the Paris Commune began with a day of high drama in the working-class neighborhoods of Paris, and women played leading parts. Street theater seemed to be their métier, and as we will see, they are often credited with the Parisians' success in defeating the army in the morning and blamed for the deaths of two generals in the late afternoon, even though they held no guns and fired no shots. In this chapter, I examine the representations of women that appear in the accounts of March 18 and analyze why they have been so important in the telling of the Commune's story.

None of the chroniclers of these events wanted us, their readers, to remain neutral, and all have employed depictions or representations of women to gain our allegiance. Indeed, such representations have played critical roles in the telling of the Commune's story. As the writers (and their readers) represent women, they pass judgment on them and, by extension, on the Commune, which is, by the laws of metonymy, only as good or as bad as its women. Representations of the street women of Montmartre—the major female actors on March 18—are particularly important since they program us for what is to come. They establish the guilt or innocence of the Commune from the outset.

The Revolution Begins

In the early hours of March 18, soldiers slipped silently through the cold, damp streets of Paris from concentration points on the Champs-Elysécs and the place de la Concorde toward the hills of Paris. Only one incident marred their movement through the night. A National Guard sentry who was standing watch challenged their approach and was shot in one of the small streets of Montmartre. By five o'clock in the morning troops had occupied the heights of Montmartre and taken control of the cannons and machine guns stored there by the National Guard. The men who had been guarding them were locked in the Tour Solférino, while the people of Montmartre slept behind closed shutters and blinds. Meanwhile, other troops had taken control of the city's major squares and the guns parked at the place Puebla, the buttes Chaumont, and Belleville on the eastern side of the city. As dawn broke, the army seemed to have captured the city's cannons and machine guns from its citizens and national guardsmen with a single shot. But the day had barely begun.

From two o'clock to six o'clock that morning the struggle for control of the cannons was a male drama. The actors were soldiers, generals, and a few early-rising guardsmen who were captured as they left their homes and tried to rally their fellows. After six o'clock, however, women and other civilians became central players in the struggle for the cannons and, ultimately, for control of the city.

The most significant events of the day took place at Montmartre. Lying on the northern edge of the city, the steep hill of Montmartre was climbed by narrow, twisting roads and paths. It had been incorporated into the city only in 1860, and the top of the hill was still covered with open fields and only an occasional building. The base and lower part of the hill were populated by working-class men and women. The arrondissement (coincidentally, the eighteenth) was a center of political and economic radicalism. The newly elected conservative national government was suspicious of the republican city in general, but it was especially nervous about areas like Montmartre where workers lived and discussed politics.

To make matters worse, from the government's point of view, Montmartre was also the location of the largest collection of heavy guns—ninety-one cannons, seventy-six machine guns, and four other large guns—which the National Guard had dragged up the hill by hand when it discovered them in the part of Paris that the Prussians were to occupy on March 1.[1] On the night of March 17–18, the guns stood in rows on two open fields, one at the top of the hill, the other on a lower plateau (fig. 4).

Nearly four thousand troops were dispatched to Montmartre in the early hours of March 18. General F. J. Paturel directed his men to occupy the field at the top of the hill; General Claude Lecomte's troops moved to the main gun park on the lower plateau on the east side. Smaller groups of troops occupied the Tour Solférino near the summit (where they would

FIGURE 4. "The National Guard's Cannons on the Butte Montmartre." *L'Illustration,* 1871. Musée Carnavalet.

hold prisoners during the morning), strategic intersections and streets, and the church of Saint-Pierre (to prevent the National Guard from using its bells to raise an alarm) near the base of the hill.[2]

Having successfully taken control of the lightly guarded guns, the troops knocked down the stone walls and filled in the trenches that surrounded the gun parks while they waited for the horses that were to move the heavy guns. For reasons that remain obscure, the horses did not arrive for several hours and then only in inadequate numbers. Lacking horses, soldiers moved several of the guns by hand, but they were heavy and the hill was steep, and the soldiers had gotten no farther than the base of the hill when the residents of Montmartre began to awaken.

Accustomed to rising early to fetch food for breakfast, the women of Montmartre are often credited with being the first to discover the troops in their midst. Around six o'clock as they raised the blinds and opened the shutters of their homes and shops, they peered out onto the scene of the government's triumph. Although the troops had not arrived in utter silence, what noise they had made had failed to alarm the city, which had seen so many troops and so many false alarms in the past six months.

What had been ignored during the night galvanized attention when dawn began to break. As the people of Montmartre filtered out into the streets, staring and gesturing at the troops, the tenor of the day began to change. Already suspicious of the national government, the people concluded almost immediately that they were witnessing a royalist coup. As the soldiers waited for the horses, opposition to the imagined coup d'état developed.

As the people of Montmartre were discovering the soldiers in their streets, Georges Clemenceau, the mayor of the eighteenth arrondissement, was pulling on his clothes and rushing through the dark streets to the butte.[3] Awakened about six by one of his colleagues in the *mairie*, Clemenceau was both alarmed and angry that the national government had decided to act without informing him in advance. For days, he and other arrondissement mayors had been working to arrange the return of the cannons and machine guns to the national government without military action. Now the government's actions would make him look like a duplicitous government accomplice, as indeed the people quickly concluded he was.[4]

When Clemenceau arrived at the butte Montmartre, he found the atmosphere curiously relaxed. On the lower part of the hill, he later reported, "on the doorsteps and in front of all the still-closed shops men in shirt sleeves were chatting and preserving a completely calm attitude." Higher up, "a great many civilians . . . chatted with the soldiers, several of whom had laid their rifles down on the pavement to go into the bakers' shops."[5] So began the fraternization of the troops with the people of Paris and the undoing of the government's plan.

When Clemenceau found General Lecomte on the eastern plateau, he told him that he was "surprised and disappointed" that the government had decided to use force without warning the mayors and urged him to move the guns and leave as quickly as possible. He then proceeded to the house at 6, rue des Rosiers,[6] where about a hundred prisoners, including the wounded guardsman Turpin, were being held. Clemenceau, a physician, examined the critically injured man, dressed his wound, and decided that he should be moved to a hospital where he could be cared for and made more comfortable. At Turpin's side were two women from the quarter, a National Guard *cantinière* and Louise Michel, who would become the most famous of the communardes. (*Cantinières* provided food and water for military groups like the National Guard.)

Michel had climbed the hill to the rue des Rosiers in the evening to deliver a message to the National Guard and had then spent the night. When Clemenceau left to get a stretcher, she ran down the hill, looking for the

Vigilance Committee of the eighteenth arrondissement, her rifle under her coat, yelling, "Treason!"[7] Now, the alarm began to ring throughout Paris, passed from bugler to bugler, warning the people and the National Guard that the enemy was present.[8] Drums beat the general alarm.[9] National guardsmen pulled on their clothes, grabbed their rifles, and made their way toward their staging areas. Ordinary people flowed out into the streets to see what was happening.

By the time Clemenceau returned to the rue des Rosiers with two stretcher bearers, the crowd had grown in size. Sensing the danger that the growing number of people in the streets portended, General Lecomte refused to allow Clemenceau to transport Turpin, lest "the sight of him . . . rouse the mob," and Clemenceau was forced to return to the *mairie* empty handed.[10] It was not yet eight o'clock, and he reported later that he saw no cause for alarm. In his view, the growing crowds were still calm and friendly. Some soldiers were "chatting familiarly with the people of the neighbourhood," who were giving them food. Others were being "reproached in lively fashion . . . for having taken part in this expedition," and Clemenceau was surprised "at the piteous expression" on the face of one of them.[11]

While Clemenceau was returning to the *mairie,* perhaps more worried than he later admitted, Louise Michel and other women were climbing back up the butte to do battle with the soldiers. Now a more dangerous drama began. All over the city as well as throughout Montmartre, crowds of women, children, guardsmen, and male civilians confronted the troops who had captured the cannons and were guarding the streets. In Montmartre the horses had finally arrived and the troops were moving the cannons and artillery from the top of the hill. But it was too late for this maneuver to succeed. By now, the anonymous author of *La vérité sur la Commune* reported, "women and children, a compact mass, mounted the hills like the foam on an ocean wave; the artillery tried in vain to stop its passage; the human wave overran everything, flowing over the gun carriages, over the caissons, under the wheels, under the feet of the horses, paralyzing the attempts of the horse guards who beat their teams in vain."[12]

Following the women up the hill, came the national guardsmen who had finally made their way through the crowd-filled streets. According to the most detailed account of the day, the women, emboldened perhaps by the arrival of the armed guards, screamed furiously, "Unharness the horses! Let's go! We want the cannons! We will have the cannons!" Then, over the noise of the crowd a voice called out, "Cut the traces!" and as the crowd cheered with joy, the women who were closest to the guns "passed a knife that the men gave them from hand to hand" and cut the cords attaching the horses to the guns. Finally, at the direction of the same national guardsman who had suggested cutting the traces, the crowd parted, slapped the horses on their flanks, and the artillerymen seated on their backs were carried away from the cannons into the crowd.[13]

The victory that a couple of hours earlier had seemed assured to the government's troops had become the crowd's. The soldiers, who had left their barracks in the middle of the night without their packs and without breakfast, were hungry and cold, as were the people of Montmartre. A fine rain fell incessantly; only three days earlier, it had snowed.[14] Soon the Montmartrois were offering the soldiers wine and bread.[15] As they accepted, it became clear that these men at least would neither fire upon nor repel the crowd.

A *Times* (of London) reporter who had been awakened at five o'clock by the army's beating of the call to arms, arrived at the boulevard Ornano, to the east of the butte, in time to see the horses arrive and to witness another confrontation turn to fraternization and capitulation as a line regiment encountered a band of national guardsmen. The guardsmen had already picked up some of the defecting soldiers from other places. The correspondent reported:

> As soon as they got within 20 or 30 yards of the Line regiment, the soldiers leading the National Guard, and who acted as a sort of screen of protection, shouted *"Vive la République!"* This seemed to be the signal for the whole of the regular troops to throw the butts of their rifles in the air, a movement which was responded to by the whole of the National Guards by enthusiastic shouts of *"Vive la Ligne!"* and the instantaneous reversal of all their butts. For a moment there was nothing to be seen but the butt-ends of rifles, or to be heard but shouts of *"Vive la Ligne!" "Vive la République!"* The soldiers in the balconies and windows, where, I suppose, they had been placed to shoot the Guards, came down and embraced them instead; women shed tears of joy, and talked about their sons and brothers who were *sous le drapeau* [in the army]; arms were intertwined, hands wrung, cheeks kissed.[16]

Similar scenes were played out around Paris and elsewhere in Montmartre, sometimes with greater tension, sometimes with less.[17] Occasionally the army resisted the crowd and continued to move the guns. In one Montmartre incident, a crowd attacked the troops who had already begun to move some of the guns down the hill. People threw bottles and stones at the soldiers, and women attempted to cut the harnesses of the teams as they had on the upper plateau. In this case, however, the troops managed to keep their horses moving and dragged a few cannons to the Ecole Militaire.[18] For the most part, however, the crowd succeeded in preventing the army from taking the cannons.

While crowds of women and men were overwhelming Paturel's troops and cutting the horses' traces on the western plateau, another group was intermingling with and confronting Lecomte's troops on the eastern plateau. Lecomte ordered the people to move back, and his men to load their rifles. Whether he actually ordered his men to fire is unclear, but many believed that he had, and their belief would have serious consequences before the day was over.[19] Faced with the possibility of firing on the citizens and national guardsmen of Paris, the soldiers balked; they turned up their rifle butts, and as Louise Michel would report, "The Revolution was made."[20]

Confusion about Lecomte's orders in hardly surprising under the circumstances. While the officers had worried that their troops would refuse to fire on the people if commanded to do so, the Parisians feared exactly the opposite. Tension was extremely high. Noise and confusion ran through the streets like water. Clemenceau, back inside the *mairie,* watched the National Guard assemble in the square in front of the building. "Armed National Guards were running about in all directions and in the greatest confusion. . . . they called out, they were shouting; it was all a perfect bedlam."[21] Like the *Times* reporter on the boulevard Ornano, many, probably most, found the morning's confrontations—"the uncertainty for a moment over whether the men were meeting as friends or as enemies, the wild enthusiasm of the shouts of fraternization, the waving of the up-turned muskets, the bold reckless women laughing and exciting the men against their officers"—to be "intensely exciting."[22]

While some citizens reminded the soldiers that they were their brothers and brought them food when they agreed to lay down their arms, others, often apparently women, screamed death threats and threw rocks, paving stones, and vegetables at them.[23] In some accounts, the people stood their ground when soldiers raised their rifles to fire; in others, they screamed and ran, fearing they would be killed.[24] No doubt both reactions occurred. Those who held their ground did so with fear and trepidation. Louise Michel remembered later that the people who climbed the hill with her "in the first light of day" to confront Lecomte's troops "believed they would die."[25]

Whether commanded to fire or not, the soldiers ultimately upended their rifles and the people claimed victory. Lecomte's troops were overrun, and the National Guard took him and several of his officers prisoner before they could be lynched. Now cast in the unusual role of rescuing and protecting the general and his officers, the National Guard marched their prisoners off to the Château-Rouge, a popular dance hall near the base of the hill, which was serving as a National Guard post.[26]

Although little actual violence had occurred, the threat had been very real. When the soldiers did not fire, fear turned to relief and celebration. According to Edmond Lepelletier, the crowd that accompanied Lecomte and his National Guard protectors to the Château-Rouge quickly became a joyous, disorderly mob. "Men, women, children, soldiers, and national guards surrounded the general and descended the rue Muller, in noisy confusion. People cried, jeered, sang the Marseillaise, cheered the Line, and booed Vinoy. All was a disorderly jostling, pierced by the strident sounds of a bugle."[27]

While the victory celebration got under way, the morning's last battle at Montmartre was taking place at the place Pigalle. Here, when the crowd advanced on the square and the army, the command to fire was obeyed. The women and children fled while the National Guard returned fire. Men were wounded on both sides, and an army officer (Saint-James), three gunners, and five horses were killed, one of which was cut up and distributed to the crowd.[28] It was still only nine thirty in the morning.

By now all Paris was in a state of agitation. Throughout the working-class arrondissements, citizens and guardsmen were confronting soldiers and throwing their arms around them. Barricades were going up, army troops were fraternizing with the people or trying to make their way back to the Ecole Militaire,[29] and the government was trying and failing to rouse the bourgeois units of the National Guard to march against the rebels. The national guardsmen who had captured General Lecomte were trying to decide what to do with him and their other prisoners; the National Guard Central Committee, which was later accused of directing the uprising, was in fact trying to figure out what was happening. Thiers, who had initiated the army's action, panicked and fled for Versailles when a National Guard battalion marched noisily down the quai d'Orsay where the government was meeting.[30]

While the government was assessing its losses, Simon Mayer, the National Guard captain in charge of the post at the Château-Rouge, sought advice from Clemenceau and money to feed Lecomte and his other prisoners. Clemenceau complied, apparently still not sensing any great danger to the men. But outside the Château-Rouge another crowd was forming. This group was far more dangerous than the morning crowds had been, perhaps because the composition of the crowd had changed, perhaps because the morning's events had given people a taste for action which the after-noon lull was not satisfying, perhaps because these people had spent much of the morning and afternoon drinking.[31]

Lecomte and the other officers who had been taken prisoner were jus-tifiably nervous and, wishing to deal with someone in authority, asked re-peatedly to be taken to the National Guard Central Committee. Believing the committee to be at the house on the rue des Rosiers and anxious to be free of the responsibility of guarding them, the National Guard officers at the Château-Rouge decided to move the prisoners back up the butte in the midafternoon.[32] The trip was a nightmare for prisoners and guards alike. Captain Beugnot, one of the prisoners, recalled it as "our real agony, our stations of the cross," and credited the guardsmen with saving the prison-ers' lives from the angry crowd.[33]

The Central Committee was not meeting on the rue des Rosiers and the guardsmen now found themselves and their prisoners in an even more dangerous environment than before. The crowd, by this time thoroughly inflamed, struggled to get into the house. Even so, virtually all witnesses and historians have agreed that bloodshed might have been avoided had it not been for the arrival of another prisoner, General Clément Thomas. Clément Thomas was well hated in Paris for his role in the deadly repres-sion of the workers' revolt in June 1848 and for criticism of the National Guard during the Prussian siege.[34] Guardsmen had recognized him when he apparently ventured out of doors to see what was going on, and they had hastened him off to the rue des Rosiers. His arrival reignited the furor that some believed had begun to calm down. Clément Thomas was pushed into the garden behind the house and shot to death. Next Lecomte was led into the garden, where he faltered and asked the men to remember that he had a wife and five children. Mercy was not forthcoming, and he too was exe-cuted.[35]

At this point, Clemenceau reappeared on the scene. Simon Mayer, the National Guard captain who had been in charge of the prisoners at the Château-Rouge, had rushed to find him after escorting the prisoners to the rue des Rosiers, knowing that they were in imminent danger. Grabbing the sash that identified him as a government official, Clemenceau had fol-lowed Mayer back up the butte. As they approached the house at 6, rue des Rosiers, the word that the generals had been shot reached them. Clemenceau was stunned, as were the men accompanying him. Then, he reported, "a terrific noise broke out, and the mob which filled the court-yard of No. 6 burst into the street in the grip of some kind of frenzy."[36]

Fearing for his own life, Clemenceau beat a hasty retreat, hoping, he said later, to save not only himself but also the other prisoners who had been marched away from the rue des Rosiers as he was arriving.[37] The crowd faded away from the scene of the executions, the soldiers who had fraternized with the people began to make their way across Paris, the national government continued to leave the city, and the "leaders" of the people met to decide what to do about the events of the day. It was five o'clock in the afternoon. The revolution known as the Paris Commune had begun.

The Army, the Government, and the Crowd

The deaths of Generals Lecomte and Clément Thomas certainly made it more difficult for the leaders of the national government and of the city to negotiate a settlement in the following weeks, but they were not the reason the government leaders left Paris. Thiers left for Versailles well before the generals were executed. Indeed, he did not learn of their deaths until many hours later. After his departure, the civilian ministers remained in the city and tried to persuade the army to stay as well, but the generals feared losing control of the army, and they issued orders to evacuate the city around two o'clock in the morning of March 19, approximately twenty-four hours after the fiasco had begun.[38]

What is most remarkable about March 18 is not that two generals were killed but that there was not more bloodshed. No doubt there would have been much more had not the Parisians generally found it easy to persuade the soldiers to abandon their orders and join them. After fighting and losing a war to a foreign enemy, French soldiers were not inclined to turn their guns against their fellow countrymen, especially those who had held out the longest against the Prussians. If anything, their own officers appeared villainous for having failed to devise victory against the Prussians. In addition, of course, the government's plan was poorly thought out at best, if not a maneuver designed to provoke an insurrection and to give Thiers an excuse to crush the city.[39]

However one evaluates Thiers's motives, it is clear that the operation was hastily and poorly planned. The soldiers were sent out without their packs, increasing the likelihood that they would join forces with the Parisians if they offered them food. Without horses, moreover, it was impossible for the soldiers to accomplish their mission quickly or at all, and in fact, there may not have been enough horses in the city for the army to pull so many cannons and machine guns.[40] In addition, the troops in the city were young and inexperienced and had billeted with and been befriended by the workers of Paris, further increasing the likelihood that they would break ranks, as their officers knew at the outset.[41] Inadequately organized, the government's maneuver was doomed from the beginning.

The capitulation of the troops is, of course, only half of the story of March 18. The other half belongs to the crowd. That crowds would gather was more than predictable. Parisians have a long history of pouring out into the streets to see what is happening. As recently as September 4, 1870, crowds had precipitated the creation of a Government of National Defense, and at the end of February 1871, when the impending Prussian occupation of the city was announced, people had roamed the streets day and night.[42] That the crowds would take direct action was perhaps less certain. Had people merely watched from a distance, the army would have succeeded in removing the cannons and machine guns.

We have characterizations of the crowd and its actions from a variety of eyewitnesses and a plethora of historians. The most important firsthand accounts are those of Louise Michel, Gaston Da Costa, the anonymous author (the *Ancien Proscrit,* or Former Exile) who wrote *La vérité sur la Commune* (The truth about the Commune), and Edmond Lepelletier, all of whom were active supporters of the Commune;[43] Arthur Chevalier, a member of the National Guard, and Captain Beugnot, who was taken prisoner by the National Guard during the day;[44] Georges Clemenceau, the mayor of the eighteenth arrondissement; and three English journalists—the correspondents for the *Times* and the *Daily News* and Ernest Vizetelly, who later wrote a history of the Commune in which he described his own meanderings and observations. None of these observers and participants witnessed all the day's events. Some wrote immediately; others, many years later. Probably not present that day in Montmartre, but writing very early accounts that are often used as primary sources were the impassioned opponents of the Commune Jules Claretie and Catulle Mendès, and the Commune defenders Prosper-Olivier Lissagaray, Paul Lanjalley, and Paul Corriez.

When the crowds first encountered the troops, they reportedly were passive, if not happy, according to Clemenceau.[45] The first group the *Times* reporter met consisted of "gloomy" women and national guardsmen out of uniform, who were muttering and denouncing everyone, but no one was taking any action.[46] Da Costa, perhaps echoing the other accounts, since he does not seem to have been an eyewitness to the early morning encounters, reported that the crowd at first was curious and "waggish."[47]

At some point, however, virtually all the groups that gathered in the city turned to action, forcing the troops to abandon their efforts and gaining control of the day. In Montmartre the crowd's actions were decisive at three different points: the morning struggle for control of the cannons and the streets, the demonstrations outside the Château-Rouge which led to the transfer of the prisoners to the rue des Rosiers, and the assassinations of the generals. Eyewitnesses and historians have assigned leading roles to women in all these events, although they have disagreed about how to describe, categorize, and judge these roles. These disagreements reveal deeply held (and changing) convictions about the nature of woman and women's proper roles and provide the first of many demonstrations of the use of representations of women to make judgments about the Commune.

Reports of Women's Voices

The women in the morning and afternoon crowds are commonly described as being more vocal than the men. It is they who are credited with chastising the soldiers in the morning and with screaming for the generals' deaths in the afternoon. It is possible that the women were more verbal in their encounters with the male soldiers and officers than the national guardsmen were, either because they were socialized to be more verbal or because they had no guns and their only weapons were words. It is also possible that the women were not more vocal than the men and that the reports reflect male expectations rather than the actual situation. Whatever might be "factually" correct, it is clear that the women's words seemed more memorable and more decisive than the men's to the male observers of the day's events.

The words placed in women's mouths by observers and historians fall roughly into four categories: reproaches, demands, inarticulate sounds, and insults. In many accounts of the morning, the women reproached the troops by reminding them of their common heritage and their "real" enemy—Prussia—and by playing upon accepted gender conventions and asking them if they truly intended to kill women and children. Da Costa, for instance, tells us that the women asked the soldiers, "Are you going to fire on us? On your brothers? On our husbands? On our children?"[48] A woman overheard by the *Times* correspondent asked the soldiers if they were not "ashamed of coming to fire upon us?"[49] Lissagaray in the same vein reported that the women appealed to the soldiers' sense of honor, saying, "This is shameful! What are you doing there?"[50]

Other observers heard women's words as demands. General d'Aurelles de Paladine, for instance, testified before the parliamentary inquest that the women and children told the troops, "You will not fire upon the people."[51] Lepelletier, more vividly, quoted the women as saying, "Don't fire! You are our friends! We are all brothers [*sic*]!"[52] The author of *La vérité sur la Commune* claimed that it was the women, above all, who cried, "Unharness the guns! Go on! We want the cannons! The cannons are ours!"[53] In the afternoon, women, not men, were "credited" with demanding the deaths of the prisoners and generals. Beugnot, for instance, reported that the women "screamed that they were going to kill us."[54]

Women also insulted the officers in the morning, sometimes in conjunction with shaming them. One woman, said the *Times* correspondent, called the troops "sacré gredins (damned scoundrels) and complained loudly that "they can fight against French fathers of families, but not against Prussians."[55] In the eyes of E. B. Washburne, the American minister to France, the women's greatest insult to General Vinoy took not a verbal but a physical form. "He was surrounded by a mob of women," Washburne reported, "who pelted him with stones, and, as the deepest mark of insult, threw at him a cap."[56] Captain Beugnot also claimed that the women who surrounded the prisoners as they were moved from the Château-Rouge to the rue des Rosiers "hurled insults" at the men.[57] Occasionally women's insults were directed toward the National Guard rather than the soldiers. One woman, complaining about the failure of the guardsmen to protect the guns at the outset, observed, "If they had only left them to us [i.e., to women] to guard, they would not have been captured so easily."[58]

Sometimes observers placed inarticulate but nevertheless expressive sounds in women's mouths. Catulle Mendès claimed that women formed a circle around Vinoy's horse in the place Pigalle, and "hooted" at him.[59] In Clemenceau's memory, the women whom he encountered on the rue des Rosiers "utter[ed] raucous cries," while the men, even less articulate, "danced about and jostled one another in a kind of savage fury," and both "shrieked like wild beasts."[60] Washburne reported that the women, "howled like a pack of wolves."[61] Alistair Horne, one of the most colorful and critical of the Commune historians, echoed him, declaring that women "howled for the blood of the captive" on the march back up the hill.[62]

Lepelletier placed the women in a more literary context than most observers, according them the role of the chorus in Greek tragedies. They gave voice to the action, encouraged the protagonists, and provoked the tragedy that was to occur; in short, they controlled and narrated the events of the day.[63]

Men, of course, were not silent on March 18, but eyewitnesses and historians put many fewer words in their mouths. On one of his trips up the butte, Clemenceau reported that he saw "a National Guardsman reproaching in lively fashion a soldier for having taken part in this expedition."[64] The *Times* correspondent also recounted a soldier's forceful defense of himself to the crowd that was accusing him of planning to fire on the people. "Do you think I will fire on a Frenchman?" he asked. "Am I not a Frenchman? Have I not twice been taken prisoner by the Prussians, once at Sedan and once at Dijon? Why, then, should I fire upon my country-men?"[65] The words most frequently attributed to the National Guard, how-ever, are shouts of *Vive la Ligne!* and *Vive la République!*—phrases intended to encourage the soldiers to defect. The soldiers, for their part, join in the chants once they have abandoned their orders and add *Vive le Garde Na-tionale!* as a show of unity.[66]

Some of the words attributed to women and men on March 18 fit cul-tural conceptualizations of appropriate female and male behavior. When women reminded men of their responsibilities and when men criticized other men or declared their solidarity with one another, they were acting in gender-appropriate ways. But some of the words that were said, or that observers imagined were said, were not culturally appropriate, and these portended the decline of civilization to conservative critics of the Com-mune. Women who insulted soldiers, howled like wolves, and declared that they could have defended the guns better than the men were acting against their gender, as were men who plaintively declared that they would not fire on the people. These signs of the instability of gender formulations would trouble observers, especially critics, of the Commune throughout its brief reign.

Women's Actions

Accounts and analyses of the day's events in Montmartre generally di-vide them into two parts, the relatively nonviolent events of the morning and the violent events of the afternoon. This division is made on the basis of what is perceived as a change in the behavior of the women in the crowd. Gaston Da Costa, an official of the Commune, made this distinction in his 1903 memoir. The afternoon violence, he explained, had occurred be-cause the "housewives" of Montmartre had "returned to their homes" and been replaced by the prostitutes of the place Pigalle. According to his read-ing of the crowd, the morning women were "curious, gaping, joking and jeering," "anguished," and "superb and truly humane." The afternoon women were "a horrible phalanx of registered and unregistered prostitutes from the quartier des Martyrs and . . . the hotels, cafés and brothels." The family-loving and self-sacrificing morning women were those who had "stood in the snow for hours, without bread and without heat in their lodg-ings, forming queues for rations at the doors of the butchers and bakers," during the Prussian siege. The afternoon women were self-indulgent; they "got drunk at all the bars, and howled their scoundrel joy at this defeat of the authorities." The morning women were "the true women of the people;" the afternoon women, "true furies . . . the sad froth of prostitution on the revolutionary wave."[67]

Da Costa drew these distinctions to rescue both the women of the morning crowds and the reputation of the Commune from general vilification by conservatives like Jules Claretie. As Da Costa observed, "One of the proceedings of the crazed reaction [to the Commune] was to present the women of Montmartre under the most hideous aspects. Before presenting them as the pétroleuses, they identified them, from the 18th of March, with horrible shrews."[68] No comparable division is made for male participants. With the exception of some references to pimps in the afternoon crowds, the men are universally described as national guardsmen, soldiers who had switched sides, and "blouses" (workers). The consistency with which the men in the crowd are portrayed contrasts sharply with the dichotomized picture of the women and reveals the effect of gender conceptualizations on the "reporting," analyzing, and judging of the day's events.

Men were expected to act in the public arena. Conservatives might question the morality and legality of their actions during the day, and even Commune supporters might condemn those who participated in the executions of the generals, but no one would question the normalcy of their actions. Their presence on the streets conformed to gender expectations in ways that women's did not. The judgments of women that appear in contemporary and historical texts reflect more than gender conventions, however. They are part of a complex intellectual process of alteration, substitution, and judgment which identifies the Commune with its female supporters and judges both. The more critical the observer or historian, the more bloodthirsty the representations of women.

Discovering the Troops

Only a few of the early accounts of the morning events include the discovery of the troops. Lissagaray, Clemenceau, and Lanjalley and Corriez "describe" this scene. Da Costa, Michel, the author of *La vérité sur la Commune,* Claretie, the *Times* reporter, and Lepelletier, all of whom describe other events of the morning, do not. Lissagaray, a pro-Commune journalist who escaped capture and completed his history of the Commune in exile in Brussels in 1876, reported that while the troops waited for the horses to arrive, the faubourgs are awaking and the morning shops opening. Around the milkmaids and before the wine merchants the people talk in low voices; they point at the soldiers, the machine guns leveled at the streets, the walls covered with the still-wet placard signed by M. Thiers and his ministers. . . .

The women set out first, as in the days of the Revolution. Those of March 18, hardened by the siege—they had had a double ration of misery—do not wait for the men. They surround the machine guns and question the men in charge, saying, "This is shameful; what are you doing there?" The soldiers are silent. . . . Suddenly, the call to arms sounds. The national guardsmen have discovered two drums.[69]

Lanjalley and Corriez, in contrast, recounted that

the firing of guns [at the rue des Rosiers] had, in effect, sounded the alarm in the quarter. The warning was given; the national guardsmen descended into the streets where groups of housewives [*ménagères*] were gathered, having left their homes to do their morning shopping. They learned of the retaking of the cannons, and they spread the news in all directions.[70]

Clemenceau, who arrived on the scene before any fighting had taken place between the people and the troops, reported that on his first trip to the top of the butte,

The news of the coup was just beginning to spread. On the doorsteps and in front of all the still closed shops men in shirt sleeves were chatting and preserving a completely calm attitude. Of National Guard, uniforms or arms, not a sign. The nearer I came to the top of the Buttes, the more relaxed seemed to be the attitude of the soldiers. Up there, there were a great many civilians. They chatted with the soldiers, several of whom had laid their rifles down on the pavement to go into the bakers' shops.[71]

The similarities and differences among these texts are interesting. Lanjalley and Corriez and Lissagaray explicitly mention women; Clemenceau does not. Clemenceau sees soldiers and civilians (perhaps men and women, perhaps just men); Lissagaray, people whom he later identifies as national guardsmen and women; Lanjalley and Corriez, national guardsmen and housewives. Clemenceau sees soldiers entering bakeries (again women are not mentioned); Lissagaray's people cluster around milkmaids and wineshops; Lanjalley and Corriez's women have arisen to purchase unspecified goods. In all accounts, the news of the troops spreads quickly. In none of these accounts are any children mentioned.

These three texts form the basis for later accounts of the beginnings of the Commune. Some later histories eliminate all details and with them, women. Stéphane Rials and Georges Bourgin say simply, "the day broke," and move directly to the confrontations over the cannons.[72] Some mention women but, like Clemenceau, assign them no independent roles. William Serman, for instance, tells us, "Paris wakes up," and "men, women and children arise, question each other, and emerge en masse to learn what is happening."[73] Some combine information from the three primary sources, including some details, eliminating others, but not changing the basic sense of the early sources. Some embellish the texts with additional details, sometimes to incorporate their own knowledge about the situation in Paris (such as the resumption of regular milk delivery),[74] sometimes simply to heighten the drama. Some add children. Some increase the size of the crowd. But some exceed simple embellishment of these fairly compatible texts, altering them to establish differences between men's and women's behavior that do not appear in the original versions.

Lepelletier, writing in 1911, combined texts and then embroidered on them:

> Montmartre . . . had awakened, and already it was extraordinarily animated. Blinds and shutters were opened; bewildered people were at the windows and on the thresholds of the shops. Around the milkmaids, the housewives curiously questioned and chattered; groups formed around the wine merchants' counters. Gunfire had been vaguely heard. . . . Soon the alarm began to sound, and the drums beat the general alarm in the chaussée Clignancourt. Rapidly, it was like a change of scene in a theater: all the streets leading to the butte were filled with a trembling crowd. . . . It was *un grand bal populaire,* in vogue during the empire.[75]

Henri Lefebvre, writing a half century later, added children and another set of embellishments, this time about the women.

> But at Montmartre? First the women came out into the streets; they were accustomed to rising early to go in search of milk, whose regular distribution had been restored. They preceded the men. Hair disheveled, dressed in their morning gowns [*négligé matinal*], and at first stunned, they came out. Children followed. And all at once, it was a human sea, among which the women dominated.[76]

In his centenary history, Stewart Edwards followed the primary texts carefully but, like Lefebvre, added children to the scene.

> Slowly the village awakened. Women came out to fetch milk and saw the
> troops everywhere. Astonished, they were joined by their children and men-
> folk. Shops and cafés opened their shutters. The troops were now famished
> and cold, having been up some five hours. Not having their packs with them,
> many laid down their rifles and went off to buy some food from nearby. It was
> the women most noticeably who began to remonstrate with the soldiers, ask-
> ing where they thought they were going to take the cannons: "To Berlin?" At
> the same time the local women offered the troops wine and bread. . . . In the
> streets below the drums were now beating out the *rappel* [call to arms].[77]

Women without children were an apparent impossibility.

These texts, though they remain relatively faithful to the original
sources, adding details to enliven and vivify the scene, create an identification of women with the purchase of milk which does not exist in the primary texts. Wine is either eliminated from the story (Edwards mentions it
only when the women offer food to the soldiers) or is sought by a non-
gendered group. Milk, however, is sought only by women. In these texts a
subtle distinction between male and female behavior in the lull before the
battle, hence between male and female nature, begins to take shape, a distinction that is more complete and less subtle in Georges Bourgin's 1928
text.

> But people were already up in the heavily populated streets where the sound
> of the marching companies, despite the issuing of commands in low voices,
> had risen to the unshuttered windows. The women were clustered in the
> dairy shops, the men in those of the wine merchants or before the govern-
> ment's posters.[78]

Bourgin's version of the early morning events varies in three seemingly
small but ideologically significant ways from the early accounts. First, he
completely separates the women from the men by associating women with
the purchase of milk and men with wine. Second, he places women inside
dairy shops rather than on the street around milkmaids. Third, only men
read the government's posters. Each change plays a role in establishing
separate male and female public places, roles, and character. Women go to
the dairy shops to buy food for their families; men go to the wine shops to
buy wine for themselves. Men read political posters and act politically;
women do not read the posters and hence cannot act politically. The world
of politics is a male world. The world of the family is a female world.
Women go out into public only to secure provisions for their families, not
to act on their own behalf. Believing in the existence of these separate do-

mains for women and men, Bourgin imposes them on the residents of Montmartre even though they do not exist in his sources.

The Struggle for the Cannons

Louise Michel, *La vérité sur la Commune,* the *Times* correspondent, the national guardsman Chevalier, and Lissagaray witnessed and described various episodes in the struggle for the cannons and, one might add, for the hearts and minds of the soldiers. The differences among these descriptions are partially accounted for by the writers having witnessed different scenes. The *Times* reporter saw confrontations at the base of the butte but not those higher up. Michel and the author of *La vérité sur la Commune* witnessed the confrontations on the upper plateaus. Da Costa and Lepelletier were present later at the place Pigalle, but not earlier on the hill. All but one of these accounts place women in the center of the confrontations and assign them leading roles in the struggle.

Only in the confrontation between Lecomte's troops and the crowd are the differences in the accounts clearly contradictory rather than complementary. The most detailed of these "eyewitness" accounts is that of *La vérité sur la Commune,* which gives a dramatic rendition of the scene:

> The general [Lecomte] knew that the disposition of the battalion was poor; that was why he had taken direct command of it.
>
> At that moment, the crowd of women and children, gathered at the mouth of the rue Muller, saw that the general was going to give the command to fire. An involuntary shudder swept them, but instead of fleeing, they threw themselves in front of the soldiers, crying, "Don't fire!"
>
> The general, in a resounding voice that carried above the noise, commanded, "Prepare arms!"
>
> The crowd stopped.
>
> "Aim!"
>
> Rifles were placed on shoulders; muzzles of cannons were lowered. The crowd trembled, but it did not budge. In a short but profound silence, the word resounded, "Fire!"
>
> The agony was piercing. The national guardsmen prepared to avenge the crowd if the troops fired.
>
> They refused to obey. One gun, then ten, then a hundred were turned up, and it seemed that the death that had hovered over this multitude took flight and spared them. . . .

[The general] commanded the men to fire three different times. . . .
Nothing aroused them; nothing convinced the soldiers; they remained un-
moved.[79]

Louise Michel's briefer account is similar:

The women threw themselves on the cannons and machine guns; the soldiers remained immobile. When General Lecomte commanded them to fire
on the crowd, a noncommissioned officer left the ranks, placed himself before his company and yelled, louder than Lecomte: "Turn up your rifle
butts!" The soldiers obeyed. . . . The Revolution was made.[80]

A third account of the same scene is not compatible with those of Michel
and *La vérité sur la Commune*. Arthur Chevalier recalled that when the soldiers knelt and raised their guns,

the women and the children screamed. The men were maddened. A panic
took possession of everyone and they descended the butte in complete disorder. In the shelter of the houses, they reformed immediately into a column, this time without the women and the children. They recommenced the
attack. This time, the foot soldiers were overwhelmed and carried away.[81]

The differences in these accounts are impossible to reconcile. One won-
ders, indeed, if all of them describe the same event. Michel and *La vérité
sur la Commune* give the women decisive roles. No one flees. The women
and guardsmen hold their ground, confront the soldiers, and insinuate
themselves among the cannons and machine guns. Chevalier gives a more
"feminine" (and less significant) role to the women. When threatened,
they, like the children, scream and run away. The men, failing in the beginning to act like soldiers (that is, like men), overcome their fear, regroup,
and return to the fray. In this scenario, written by a national guardsman, it
is the National Guard that plays the decisive role.

Impossible as it is to reconcile these accounts, they share elements with
one another and with the other accounts of the morning's events. The
crowds that confront the soldiers contain women; the confrontations are
tense; people fear for their lives (whether they hold their ground or flee);
and the crowd and National Guard prevail without violence. These elements, as well as Michel's account of women throwing themselves on the
cannons, appear in most histories of the morning's events. In pro-Commune histories, the unarmed women who challenge the troops become

heroines. The Communard Da Costa described them as "superb and truly humane";[82] the English journalist Ernest Vizetelly, as "largely instrumental in prevailing on the soldiers to fraternize with the National Guard."[83] Lepelletier thought the crowd was predominantly women.[84] These were the good "housewives" (*ménagères*) of Montmartre whose potentially sacrificial acts stayed within gender conventions and could be praised by men. Even Jules Claretie, a foe of the Commune, credited women with disarming the soldiers, although his characterization was a bit less flattering. He reported that "women ran up and, climbing up the butte from the place Saint-Pierre where the crowd was gathering, approached the soldiers, now insulting them, now pleading with them not to fire on the people."[85]

In some accounts the use of large inclusive terms obscures the specific roles of women in the confrontations. In some pro-Commune histories, women disappear into the *peuple* (people); in anti-Commune histories, into the *canaille* (rabble) and the *foule* (mob). Still others, following Chevalier, give credit for the reconquest of the cannons to the National Guard.[86]

The Place Pigalle

The morning crowds defeated the soldiers with little or no actual violence. Not until shots were fired in the place Pigalle was anyone killed or wounded. Although Da Costa and some historians have classified the place Pigalle with the more dangerous and violent confrontations of the afternoon, the crowd here seems to have had the same tenor and goal as others during the morning. The difference in outcome was determined by the army, not the crowd. General Susbielle ordered his men to clear the place. The cavalry initially tried to do so by backing their horses across the square—a standard crowd control measure in Paris. Buoyed by their successes on the butte, however, the crowd, instead of retreating, hooted at the cavalry. Captain Saint-James, infuriated by the crowds' taunts, ordered his men to turn their horses and charge the crowd. When his men hung back, he drew his sword and rode into the midst of the people, where he and his horse were killed by shots from the National Guard. The subsequent battle was brief and the number of soldiers killed and wounded was small, but like other generals throughout Paris on this day, Susbielle retreated, and his soldiers fraternized with the people. As Lepelletier, an eyewitness, described the battle, "The women, as earlier on the butte, threw themselves into the midst of the soldiers, linesmen and cavalry. The battle was over. . . . The people, the national guardsmen, the troops fraternized.

Wine and food were passed around. A machine gun, abandoned by the fleeing troops, was reclaimed."[87]

The Horse

The main reason Da Costa and historians want to categorize the battle in the place Pigalle with the afternoon's rather than the morning's events is the occurrence of a seemingly minor event in the aftermath of the fighting: the butchering of Saint-James's horse. Quickly identified as the work of women in the crowd, this act acquired considerable symbolic significance among historians writing as early as 1871. It was an omen of things to come.

Most accounts of the battle in the place Pigalle read as though only one horse was killed in the battle, although the testimony of officers indicates that at least five horses died.[88] The tradition of one horse began early, perhaps because only one horse was cut up. The only published eyewitness account of what happened to the horse was written by Edmond Lepelletier in 1911, in a footnote to his text: "The author saw a band of individuals *of both sexes,* starving and ragged, run up from who knows where, throw themselves on the dead horse of the captain of the chasseurs [light cavalry], abandoned in a sea of blood on the pavement. In an instant, the animal was dismembered. These starving people ran away after having divided the bloody flesh of this unexpected offering."[89] Clemenceau's memoirs, written even later than Lepelletier's history, also contain a dispassionate account of the incident, though Clemenceau himself was not present at the battle: "There were collisions in the Place Pigalle between National Guards and Chasseurs. One officer was killed. . . . An hour later the officer's horse, which had also been killed, had been completely cut up for food by the crowd. Not a trace of it was left. A characteristic detail."[90] Whether Clemenceau thought this "detail" was characteristic of the day's events or of something else is unclear. What is clear and important, given other versions of this "event," is the nonjudgmental character of Clemenceau's and Lepelletier's accounts. Neither man seems horrified at the butchering of the horse, nor does either attribute it solely to women. Both seem to include it (in both cases in a footnote) as a mere oddity.

Lepelletier's and Clemenceau's dispassionate, even sympathetic reportorial styles stand in considerable contrast to most other accounts of this small event. Although many historians, like Lissagaray, fail to mention the dead horse at all, others attribute the dismembering of the animal solely to women.[91] One of the first to identify women as the butchers was Claretie, writing in 1872. He presented the cutting up of the horse as a paradigm of what the Commune had done to France. The horse butchers and the Communards alike had been depraved, uncivilized:

> The poor people [during the Prussian siege], attacked in their guts, became wild, savage. They fought for a little meat. The ruthless desire to gnaw bloody flesh drove them. One saw, in these days of distress and famine, horses dismembered in the middle of the street. Before the Hôtel de Ville, a horse fell down. The crowd raced to it like dogs to a quarry. They cut, divided, sawed, carried off, ate. Human beings returned to primitive brutality. Hunger kindled their sinister passions. The morning of March 18, an artillery officer was killed in the place Pigalle; the same volley felled his horse. Women and children ran forward, knives in their hands. Prostitutes in silk skirts and flying hair, streetwalkers from the local cafés, threw themselves on the horse, and cut up its flesh entirely. This dividing of the spoils took place in broad daylight. We seemed to have returned to the dark days of famine of the Middle Ages.[92]

Claretie's version replaces the hungry and ragged men and women of Lepelletier's account with women and children and then prostitutes—all of whom act upon "sinister passions."[93] Changing the cast of characters changes the meaning of the event. No longer a sign of the hardships of the recently ended siege, the butchering of the horse is a sign of the end of civilization, the return to a "primitive brutality" associated with the dark ages. By analogy, Claretie implies, the leaders of the Commune would be no better than the prostitutes who butchered a horse on the street and Paris would be brutalized.

It was Claretie's account that prompted Da Costa's distinction between the "good" women of the morning and the "bad" women of the afternoon. In the morning, the good women of Montmartre risked their lives to confront the soldiers, and they regained control of the guns without bloodshed. In the afternoon, the bad women of the place Pigalle (whom he described as prostitutes) grew brutal. They harassed the prisoners, called for their deaths, and rejoiced at the executions on the rue des Rosiers. They also dismembered the horse.[94]

Despite his desire to defend the revolutionaries, the university-educated Da Costa could not bring himself to approve the butchering of the horse even though he attributed it to the ravages of the Prussian siege. Unlike Lepelletier who described the butchers as "famished and ragged" (and, one might add, presented them as resourceful), Da Costa saw them as demoralized. "Some poor women," he said, "demoralized by the deleterious effects of poverty . . . cut up the still-warm flesh of the horse of an officer killed some moments earlier."[95]

The addition of the descriptive detail, "still-warm flesh," reveals Da Costa's horror. Civilized people (especially civilized women, meant to give life, not death) would not cut up an animal whose body still retained the warmth of life. Despite his abhorrence of Claretie's politics, Da Costa was not as far from him in his judgment of this particular act, or of women, as he wanted to be. But he did differ from Claretie in the significance he attached to this event. Da Costa condemned the act, but he did not use it to vilify the female supporters of the Commune or, indeed, the Commune in general.

The word that both Claretie and Da Costa seemed to be groping for and not finding was supplied by Frank Jellinek in his 1937 history of the Commune. Subscribing to the theory that it was women who cut up the horse and agreeing with Claretie and Da Costa that this behavior had been learned during the siege, Jellinek, a pro-Commune historian, declared that the horse was "cut to pieces by the women, who had conserved this *jackal trick* from the Prussian Siege."[96] A few pages later, he noted that among the afternoon crowd were "the sinister persons who had mangled the horse in the Place Pigalle."[97]

Two things are interesting about the accounts of the dismembering of the captain's horse: first, its identification with women, and, second, its appearance in so many histories of the Commune. The second is a result of the first. The fascination with and ideological usefulness of the butchering of the horse came only with its attribution to women. Had the butchers been men or even of both sexes as Lepelletier specified, the event would not have seemed so horrifying. Men were and have continued to be the butchers of large animals in western European society. For women to join in, "in broad daylight," as Claretie pointed out, was to act against their nature. Few actions would have been regarded as more unfeminine and hence more disturbing by both liberal and conservative male writers. Symbolically, if not in actual fact, the virtuous, life-giving mothers of the morning had turned into evil, murderous jackals.

Indeed, when the death of the horse is disassociated from women, it becomes merely a picturesque detail, as Edwards's history demonstrates. By using the passive voice and placing the dismembering of the horse in the context of the siege, he attributed the act to no one and eliminated its symbolic significance: "The slain officer's horse was torn to pieces where it lay in the square, a common enough practice dating from the siege."[98] Once it was dissociated from women, the horse began to disappear from histories altogether.[99]

The Assassinations

Having connected the horse butchering to women, historians used it to foreshadow and explain the killing of Generals Lecomte and Clément Thomas later in the day—deaths for which women would largely be held accountable, although they were not literally responsible. Two early accounts describe the crowd that surrounded the Château-Rouge as consisting "chiefly of soldiers" or of "prostitutes . . . on the arms of the soldiers of the line, accompanied by a legion of pimps and bullies [*souteneurs*]."[100] But the account that would attract the most attention focused exclusively on women. Captain Beugnot, one of the captured officers, described the crowd as composed of "mad bitches, [who] raised their fists to us, crushed us with insults, and screamed at us that they were going to kill us."[101] Similarly, Lepelletier likened the women to a "sanguinary antique choir" and to "the plebeians of the Roman arenas . . . [who] gave new life to the cruel desires of the furies of the guillotine, under the Terror."[102] The twentieth-century historian Alistair Horne called them "prostitutes and an appalling group of harpies . . . figures horribly reminiscent of the *tricoteuses* of the Terror . . . [who] howled for the blood of the captive."[103]

The executions of Generals Lecomte and Clément Thomas were condemned by virtually everyone. Versaillais and Parisian newspapers and political leaders decried them. But while contemporaries and historians agreed that the deaths should not have occurred, they agreed on little else about the events on the rue des Rosiers. People alternatively blamed the crowd, the National Guard, the National Guard Central Committee, and the army for the deaths. Even the words they used for the deaths—"assassination," "killing," "execution," and "murder"—depended upon their political position.[104] Everyone connected to the deaths, however tangentially, was tainted. Clemenceau narrowly escaped punishment for failing to save the generals, and in a final injustice, the French national government tried and executed the guardsmen who had tried to prevent the executions.[105]

The autopsy reports establish what we might think of as the facts of the case. Many shots were fired at the generals. Forty bullets were removed from Clément Thomas's body and nine from Lecomte's. Each was shot in the head as well. Clément Thomas's body was more damaged than Lecomte's because it sustained a greater number of wounds. Most of the

bullets removed from the bodies (perhaps all) had been fired from the
type of rifles that the army and not the National Guard possessed, which
means that disaffected soldiers and not the national guardsmen or the
crowd were responsible for the assassinations of the generals.[106] But the
Commune would be blamed.

[handwritten margin note: they would have taken guns from troops]

Contemporaries and historians who admired the Communards often
left women out of the story of the generals' deaths,[107] feeling, perhaps,
that the executions were damaging enough to the Commune without the
participation of women in such an immoral act. Da Costa, so critical of
the women in the place Pigalle, declared that "on the rue des Rosiers, at
the hour of murder, they had for the most part disappeared."[108] Even
Edith Thomas, whose history of the Commune highlights women's actions, noted merely that women were part of the crowd that "escorted and
insulted" the prisoners up the butte from the Château-Rouge. Once the
convoy had reached the rue des Rosiers, she made no further reference to
them.[109]

There is no question that women were present for the deaths of the generals (their disappearance from the crowd at this point would be inexplicable), but exactly where they were and what they did is unclear. Some accounts mention women among the crowd that tried to force its way into
the house.[110] Clemenceau "saw" weeping and shrieking women pouring
out of the house's courtyard (not the garden) when he arrived.[111] The in-
ference that these women knew of, if they had not actually witnessed, the
executions is unmistakable. Lanjalley and Corriez place them around the
garden on the other side of the house: "On all sides, there is an immense
crowd; women are there in large numbers. The walls of the garden are
crowned with spectators. This human throng demands immediate execution."[112]

We will never know exactly what happened in the garden and exactly
what role women played, although it seems safe to assume that they were
not directly responsible for the generals' deaths. No one, neither the
staunchest critics of the Commune nor the guardsmen who were later tried
for the executions, placed guns in their hands or accused them of participating in the firing squads. Aside from this "fact," what we know is that accusations and rumors abounded and they conveyed emotional, if not literal, truths about the meaning of these deaths. On the morning of March
19, the *Journal Officiel*, still in the hands of the national government,
claimed that "the [generals'] bodies were mutilated by blows of bayonets."[113] In 1871 Joanni d'Arsac, citing an unnamed eyewitness, claimed
that "after these unfortunate victims had fallen, the assassins, overexcited
by their crime, defiled the corpses and stripped them of their clothes."[114]

Claretie wrote a little after d'Arsac in a slightly more restrained vein, "The people of the crowd kicked and hit the old man's [Clément Thomas's] body" as it lay on the ground.[115] General Appert repeated this claim in his official report on the Commune, adding that the bodies were "mutilated."[116]

In his memoir, Clemenceau denied having watched "the National Guardsmen executing a sort of *danse macabre* round the bodies." He did not deny that it had happened, merely that he had seen it.[117] By 1928 Georges Bourgin was writing that "they dragged [Lecomte's] body next to that of Thomas, and again fired at the bodies, soon half-naked, and around them cries and chants rose in the bitter twilight."[118] Even what happened next varies from commentator to commentator. Alphonse Daudet believed that the bodies lay "exposed" in the garden for two days, until, d'Arsac added a bit later, doctors finally declared that their decomposition was a health hazard.[119]

In contrast to these versions of the generals' deaths and mistreatment, Vizetelly reported that "at a rather late hour on the evening of March 18," he climbed the hill to the rue des Rosiers to see what was happening. The bodies had been moved inside the house and covered with a sheet. He went into

> a bare room where a tall candle was burning on a box. On the floor beside it, lay two bodies, one that of an elderly man with a full white beard, and the other that of one who had been struck down in the prime of life, and who had a small moustache and imperial [small beard]. I could see that the former wore civilian garb, and the latter the uniform of a brigadier-general; but the bodies were for the most part covered with a large and somewhat blood-stained sheet, which had been thrown over them in order, probably, to hide the traces of the shots with which these men had been despatched in the garden of the house, earlier in the day. . . . They were the bodies of Generals Clément Thomas and Lecomte, the first victims of the Rebellion of the Commune.[120]

Many other sources report that late on the night of the eighteenth, on Clemenceau's order, the bodies were buried in a local cemetery.[121]

Some of the atrocity stories seem more plausible than others. It is possible that some of the soldiers, national guardsmen, and crowd kicked the bodies of the dead generals, and someone might have poked at them with a bayonet. People might have grabbed at torn pieces of clothing or other souvenirs. It seems less likely that the bodies were stripped half naked (Vizetelly reportedly saw clothing on the bodies later that night), or that the corpses were defiled or surrounded by singing, chanting people. But we will never know for sure.

Women and children are prominent in some accounts. Claretie emphasized their role in precipitating the deaths: "The women and the children, outside, screaming aloud, broke the windows. . . . It was a fever of massacre, a desire for blood which had taken hold of this mob, of these thousands of spectators or anonymous actors who have appeared, unleashed in their fury at certain dates in history. They want to kill and to see killing."[122] E. B. Washburne, the American minister to France, who was not an eyewitness to any of the events in Montmartre but wrote as though he were, declared: "It was a strange sight to see the women and children all coming into the streets, taking part with the insurrectionary forces and howling like a pack of wolves."[123] The pro-Commune author of *La vérité sur la Commune,* in contrast, saw the departing crowd as "pursued by remorse."[124]

On April 3 Edmond de Goncourt recorded one of the most lurid rumors in his diary. Someone had told him that "after the execution of Clément Thomas two women began to piss on the corpse, which was still warm." Revealing some uneasiness about the veracity of the story, as well as about journalists, he added that "this terrible story was told [to my friend] the very day of the execution, which removes the suspicion that it was made up by a journalist."[125]

Some twentieth-century historians embellished even these accounts. In 1940, for instance, D. W. Brogan, building implicitly on Clemenceau's and d'Arsac's texts (he does not cite his sources) claimed that "women [not national guardsmen, whom Clemenceau was accused of watching,] danced obscenely round their bodies."[126] In 1965 Alistair Horne, embroidering (again implicitly) on Appert's report and Goncourt's rumor, declared that "some hideous scenes now ensued. The men continued to discharge their rifles into the dead and mutilated bodies, while maenads from the mob squatted and urinated upon them. Small urchins fought one another for a view of the corpses from the garden wall."[127]

What is most noteworthy about the contemporary rumors and the historians' repetition and exaggeration of them is the intensifying focus on women. The identification of the Commune with the unruly woman had begun. As historians and eyewitnesses alike sought to win allegiance to their views of the Commune, depictions or representations of women became crucial. Those who judged the Commune negatively, ascribed obscene, immoral, and nefarious deeds to the women in the crowd. Those who supported the Commune could only minimize their roles or ascribe them to bad women, since they too were troubled by the presence of women in these crowds.

The Pathological Crowd

The nineteenth-century explanation for the generals' executions was that the crowd was in a pathological state when it accompanied the officers up the hill, tried to break its way into the house, and urged the soldiers and national guardsmen to kill the prisoners. The concept of the pathological crowd was not particularly precise or clinical in the 1870s.[128] Judging by its usage in the early literature on the Commune, it was a way of both understanding and discrediting the crowd's actions. A mob in the grip of a pathology could hardly have had rational political goals.

In a letter written to the press on March 30, 1871, to defend himself against accusations of having allowed the executions to take place, Clemenceau described the crowd as "overexcited."[129] Later, when he had to defend himself against accusations of complicity in the generals' deaths, his assessment of the crowd's condition went well beyond overexcited. Indeed, he said it was in the grip of

> some kind of frenzy. . . . All were shrieking like wild beasts without realising what they were doing. I observed then that pathological phenomenon which might be called blood lust. A breath of madness seemed to have passed over this mob. . . . women, dishevelled and emaciated, flung their arms about while uttering raucous cries, having apparently taken leave of their senses. . . . Men were dancing about and jostling one another in a kind of savage fury. It was one of those extraordinary nervous outbursts, so frequent in the Middle Ages, which still occur amongst masses of human beings under the stress of some primeval emotion.[130]

Clemenceau's references to "wild beasts," "blood lust," "madness" and "primeval emotion" echoed the writings of Claretie and other conservatives. Claretie believed the crowd's desire "to kill and to see killing" had been unleashed by the food shortages of the siege. Starvation had turned poor men into "beasts." "Human nature has these hours of crisis," he said, "where all that remains of bestiality in the human becomes nakedly visible."[131]

The construction of the crowd as bloodthirsty began with eyewitnesses like Beugnot. His brief description contained elements that would be emphasized later. "The crowd of beasts," he said, "savage and unchained, wanted blood."[132] Soon the beasts became wolves. Alphonse Daudet, who did not see the executions but visited the rue des Rosiers a few days later, likened the crowd to "wolves who smelled blood."[133] Washburne who similarly was not present on the 18th, said the crowd was "howling like a pack of wolves."[134]

The notion of the pathological crowd runs through nineteenth-century histories, whether favorable to the Commune or not. Da Costa, for instance, who abhorred Claretie's politics, told his readers that they were "going to be present at one of the pathological crises common in crowds over which the shadow of revolution has passed. . . . the crowd was that day in an undefinable pathological state."[135]

These rudimentary psychological analyses also took into account what was widely believed to be the crowd's subsequent behavior. Bad as the killing of the generals was, according to Claretie (who certainly did not exonerate the crowd), it had had the salutary effect of satiating the crowds' bloodlust. As soon as the generals were dead, the crowd was overwhelmed by "a strange stupor. Montmartre fell silent. Fear set in and they set the other prisoners free. The deaths in the rue des Rosiers saved the life of the other [prisoners]."[136] Others echoed this view. Paraphrasing Claretie, General Appert declared that "after this double crime, a kind of stupor took hold of the crowd. It drifted away silently and as though it were afraid."[137] The Communard author of *La vérité sur la Commune* agreed: "When the two bodies were on the ground, two soldiers again exasperatedly discharged their rifles into Lecomte; then suddenly a great silence fell; the exaltation of the murders plunged abruptly; there was a moment of stupor."[138] These accounts of the crowd's lassitude after the generals' deaths, written by men who were not present at the time, may express the magnitude of the event better than they do the facts, since they are contradicted by the statements of others who were at the rue des Rosiers. Both Beugnot and Clemenceau, who arrived immediately afterward, wrote later of their certainty that they, too, were in grave danger.[139] Clemenceau, in fact, thought the situation he encountered outside the house on the rue des Rosiers was becoming "more and more dangerous." "This crazed mob," he wrote, "was looking at me suspiciously while uttering the cry of 'Down with the traitors!' Several fists were raised." Explaining why he did not enter the house, he said that he had "a profound conviction that I should not come out of it alive."[140]]

Adolphe Thiers, whose desire to wrest control of the cannons from the Parisians precipitated the revolt, used a version of the pathological crowd to defend his decision to withdraw from the city in the early afternoon. Unlike Claretie, who viewed the crowd's madness as dissipating rapidly once the generals were dead, Thiers saw it as an insidious and contagious disease from which his troops must be protected. "Were we to stay in Paris," he explained, "the moral infection would lay hold of the army, which would not be long before abandoning us."[141]

Women and Children

Street children who appeared wherever there was trouble or excitement were a standard feature of Parisian life. They were the *gamins* of France earlier immortalized in Victor Hugo's novel *Les Miserables* and in Delacroix's painting *Liberty Guiding the People on the Ramparts* (see fig. 2). Virtually every description of a crowd and every encounter between people and police in the nineteenth century mentions them. March 18 is no exception. In the primary accounts, children swarm up the hill with the women in the morning, throw stones and caps and vegetables at the officers, brandish "indescribable trophies" after the execution, and struggle "to obtain a view of the bodies" late that night.[142] In later histories they also sit on top of the garden wall at 6, rue des Rosiers "with their legs swinging" and their fingers pointing at the generals' bodies.[143]

Children are most important in these texts, however, not as *gamins* or independent actors but in their connection to women. On the butte in the morning, women and children are commonly linked together. A standard assumption of eyewitnesses and historians is that the psychological difficulty the soldiers faced when they were commanded to hold their ground and perhaps to fire upon their fellow countrymen was compounded by the fact that the "enemy" was not simply other Frenchmen. Those who believed that Lecomte had given the order to fire on the crowd stated his "crime" most forcefully when they pointed out that he had asked them to fire on women and children. Others believed that Lecomte did not give the order to fire, precisely because there were women and children in the crowd.[144] The message of both versions is clear. Women and children were defined as innocents in a way that men, even unarmed civilians, were not. Firing upon them was a worse crime, in everyone's eyes, than firing upon men, and it helped determine the outcome of the conflict.

In most accounts, both women and children forfeited this innocence later in the day when they called for and reveled in the murder of the generals. During the Versaillais killing spree that ended the Commune in May, the army would exact expiation. Three women, four children, and forty-two men would be forced to kneel by the garden wall at 6, rue des Rosiers where they would be executed in retaliation for the deaths of the generals.[145] That these women, men, and children could not be identified as participants in the events of March 18, or even as having watched or encouraged the executions, was irrelevant to the government.

The working-class women of Montmartre are only the first of many women to act on the stage of the Commune. They, like their sisters who appear in later acts, reveal the gender conceptualizations of their creators and beckon to us to watch and listen and pass judgment on the Commune. They appear in three guises. The positive representations are nonviolent women who confront armed troops. In their most virtuous incarnation, they risk death, appeal to the soldiers' sense of right and wrong, and entreat them not to fire on their fellow citizens. Their actions are not so much political as moral, and their goodness is confirmed by references to the presence of children. These women are mothers, sisters, and wives. In a less virtuous but still acceptable incarnation, women confront the soldiers more angrily and criticize them for their very presence in the streets, but they too act out of a moral sense with which no one takes issue. In their most negative incarnation, women are no longer calm and brave mothers but a horrible phalanx of drunken prostitutes who thirst for blood, howl for death, shriek and dance raucously when it has been achieved, and defile the bodies of murdered men. The positive images portray what were perceived as the natural and saintly virtues of women; the negative, their frightening, unnatural (although the extent to which their actions were natural or unnatural was always in question, given perceptions of their nature as dichotomous), sexual, and by implication, evil side.

Whether they believed that the women in the morning and afternoon crowds were the same or different, contemporaries and historians presented them in dichotomous good-and-evil terms. Either the good women of the morning crowds were overcome by a pathological bloodlust that turned them into bad women, or the good housewives were replaced by bad prostitutes. In both cases, the array of complex, hardworking, poor, resourceful, angry, frightened, and sometimes politically committed women, whose actions helped defeat the government's plan to remove the cannons from Montmartre and who would suffer enormous losses in April and May 1871 is missing. Instead, we have a set of binarily opposed images—good/bad, calm/agitated, food-giving/death-desiring, brave/bloodthirsty, and maternal/sexual.

Through these portrayals of women, writers have made, and have wished us to make, moral judgments about the Commune. Making "proper" judgments depends upon understanding their symbolic content. Allegory works only as long as observers share the cultural assumptions of its cre-

ators. That twentieth-century histories repeat and even magnify the horrific constructions of the women in the Montmartre crowds is evidence that
the gender assumptions that gave these representations meaning continued well after the Commune's short life had ended. Their disappearance
from more recent histories is evidence that these assumptions have begun
to change. Ironically, that change has made women less rather than more
visible in histories of the Commune.

CHAPTER TWO

Remembering and Representing

B y the morning of March 19, Paris was calm. A red flag flew over the Hôtel de Ville. Inside the famous city hall of Paris, the National Guard Central Committee made plans. In the hallways, exhausted guardsmen leaned against the walls and slept. Across the city, others took possession of the ministries, the telegraph office, the *Journal Officiel,* and the Prefecture of Police. Soldiers continued to leave the city. The "riot and confusion" that the *Daily News* correspondent and others had gone to bed expecting were nowhere to be seen.[1] Neighborhood shops were open as usual and everyday life continued unabated, albeit with some new distractions: the Central Committee posters decorated the walls of Paris, barricades blocked streets, and national guardsmen posed proudly for photographers. The revolution had succeeded, at least for the moment.[2]

While conservatives and foreigners were surprised by how quickly order had been reestablished in Paris, they were "surprised" by virtually nothing else that the revolutionaries did or that they imagined they had done. Unable to shed their "memories" of other revolutions or their fear of the working class, whose motives and intelligence they viewed with profound suspicion, bourgeois observers of the Commune identified the men and women of 1871 with those of the revolution that began in 1789 and expected them to act as they "remembered" the Jacobins and sans-culottes had acted then.[3] Expecting mayhem, pillage, and class war, they saw it everywhere.

The soon-to-be Communards' view of themselves and their cause differed radically from that of the conservatives. Their "memories" of the French Revolution were positive rather than negative, and they saw their struggle in political rather than class terms. They sought accommodation rather than confrontation with the government in Versailles, although the *communardes* occasionally hoped to repeat their ancestors' march to Versailles and to capture Thiers as they had captured the king. No matter what the revolutionaries did or said, however, most bourgeois could see only what they expected to see. These differences of perception and representation, combined with Thiers's and the army's desire to reverse the humiliation they had just suffered, made compromise and negotiation impossible.

Communard women provoked a special measure of fear. The working-class National Guard and the men elected to office during the Commune, seen as jealous and vengeful proletarians who wanted to steal the bourgeoisie's property and power, were dangerous enough. But women posed even greater threats to the social order. Rumors that they had been present at the deaths of Generals Lecomte and Clément Thomas and perhaps had even demanded their deaths and defiled their bodies, recalled the specter of the Terror and the *tricoteuses*. Enshrined in popular lore, the latter were said to have knitted at the foot of the guillotine while heads rolled. These "memories," combined with the bourgeois distrust of the working class, meant the battle joined on the eighteenth was far from over on the nineteenth.

The Struggle Takes Shape

The hopes, fears, memories, and representations that would plague the Commune throughout its short life were present, at least in embryo, on March 19. The workers were ebullient. They had won. The cannons had been saved. The government had fled. The army had refused to fire on the people. The republic had been protected from the monarchists in the National Assembly. Paris would receive self-government. The Commune, revered by the workers of Paris since the Revolution of 1789, would be reestablished. Several observers described the celebratory mood of the Parisians. The Reverend Mr. Gibson, for instance, recorded that "the square in front of the Hôtel de Ville was filled with National Guards, who seemed to have nothing to do but to enjoy themselves in the bright sun," and the *Daily News* reported that it was a "fête day."[4]

The bourgeoisie feared that the workers were right. They were incredulous that the government had been so easily defeated, and normalcy so quickly reestablished. Catulle Mendès was pained that the Central Committee's announcements appeared on white paper, the color reserved for government use and a sign that there was indeed a new government in

Paris.[5] The names on the posters were similarly distressing. Most of these men were completely unknown to the general public. Edmond de Goncourt thought the list must be "a joke." "After Assi's name the least unknown is that of Lullier," he wrote in his diary, "[and he] is notoriously mad."[6] More important for the future, Goncourt was overcome "with disgust" at the national guardsmen's "stupid and abject faces, where triumph and drunkenness have implanted a radiant debauchery," and he and his friends worried about where this left-wing revolution "made with men from the very bottom" would ultimately lead.[7] This distrust of and disdain for the working class and its political leaders would not abate in the coming weeks.

At least one observer, the *Times* correspondent, focused his suspicion and memories of dark deeds on the women in the crowds that strolled around the city, examining the barricades and posters. "The women," he declared, "especially seem[ed] in their element," adding that they went about "with babies wherever barricades are to be built, or police agents drowned."[8] The latter reference was to the killing of a police spy, Vincenzoni, on January 28. A group of Parisians had tied him up, thrown him into the canal near the place de la Bastille, and stoned him as his body floated downstream. As on March 18, both men and women were involved,[9] but women's actions were more memorable. The men's behavior had crossed moral lines, but the women's had crossed gender lines as well and it was thus more alarming. It was more effective in generating unease, even though the bulk of the revolutionaries, in both instances, probably were men.

Inside the Hôtel de Ville indecision reigned. The members of the National Guard Central Committee, who had spent the previous day trying to catch up with the revolt, found themselves thrust into power by the national government's flight, but they had too little political experience to know how to consolidate the people's victory.[10] Some argued for direct action: the National Guard had won; it should now take control of the city and march on Versailles. Others urged caution, pointing out that the committee had no legitimate power to govern (or to send the National Guard outside the city). Some believed the committee should organize elections to a municipal council (the Commune), which could negotiate with Versailles as the people's representatives; others (the mayors of the twenty arrondissements of Paris, led by Georges Clemenceau) disputed the right of the Committee to govern at all and urged negotiation rather than elections. The Central Committee, for its part, feared negotiation would lead to capitulation as it had in 1830 and 1848.

On March 19, before the Central Committee could seize control of the official government newspaper, the *Journal Officiel*, the national government produced one final issue, in which it positioned itself as the defender of morality and order. "A Committee, calling itself the Central Committee, . . . has shot the defenders of order," it announced. It "has taken prisoners, [and] has cold-bloodedly murdered General Clément Thomas and a general of the French army, General Lecomte."[11] The accusation was untrue. The Central Committee had had nothing to do with the killing of the generals, and national guardsmen had protected them as long as they could from the mob that clamored for their deaths and the soldiers who finally shot them.

The Central Committee denied the accusation in the next edition, but sought to explain rather than to condemn "the regrettable facts" of the generals' deaths so as not to disavow the Parisians who had led the revolt against the government. Lecomte, they pointed out, had ordered his troops to fire on the "inoffensive crowd of women and children" and had been shot by soldiers of the line. Clément Thomas had been "spying" on the defenses of Montmartre, and had been executed by national guardsmen.[12] Even if these statements were absolutely accurate, and the Central Committee believed they were, they did not alter the fundamental problem that the generals' deaths had created. The fledgling Communards had lost the moral high ground. Now Versailles and the conservatives viewed them as villains, not victims.

The outcome of the dispute between Versailles and Paris could not be foreseen on the nineteenth. How long the revolution would last was as unpredictable as the exodus of the government from Paris had been the day before. What the city's new leaders might achieve was unknown. That the revolt would end in a slaughter that would sicken even the Commune's most ardent critics was unimaginable. Those who knew Thiers well and those with experience of earlier repressions in France worried about what he would do next, but no one believed the government of France would lay siege to the city as the Prussians had, much less that the army would invade it and kill Parisians by the thousands. More worrisome at the outset was the possibility of Prussian action if the national government with which it had signed a peace treaty were attacked by Paris.

Unable to persuade Thiers to negotiate a settlement, the Central Committee turned to governing and organizing the election of a municipal council. It took control of the *mairies* and ministries, lifted martial law, reestablished the freedom of the press, granted amnesty to political prisoners, and negotiated loans with Baron Rothschild and the governor of the Bank of France so it could pay the National Guard. Thousands of guardsmen camped out at the Hôtel de Ville and moved around the city, staff officers on horseback in full uniforms, the rank and file on foot.[13] Feeling it had done no wrong, indeed, feeling it had *been* wronged, both when Thiers allowed the Prussians to march triumphally through the streets of Paris,[14] and when Thiers and the army attempted to take its guns by force, the National Guard had no intention of surrendering the city or its cannons to Versailles and the army.

Representing the Conflict

While Thiers and the National Assembly repeatedly accused the Central Committee (and subsequently the Commune) of assassinating Generals Lecomte and Clément Thomas, the conflict between Paris and the national government in Versailles had little to do with the generals' deaths. The accusations were simply a convenient and effective means of putting the committee on the moral defensive. The clash was about political philosophies, class interests, and political conflicts that had led to Thiers's attempt to seize the cannons.

How each side saw and presented the dispute depended to a large extent on what it thought the men on the other side were doing or would do. When the conflict was perceived as class war or as a battle for Parisian self-rule, women were irrelevant. They were not members of the Central Committee, Communal Council, or National Guard. They were not leaders of the International or among the "scum of Europe" that the bourgeoisie believed had gathered in Paris to fight for the Commune. Nor were they considered true members of the proletariat, even though they worked in factories alongside men. Reformers like the Communards tended to agree. They, too, believed the problems of the working-class family could be solved by getting the wife and mother out of the labor force and into the home. If they were workers, they should not be. Or to put it as Jules Simon had in 1860, "The woman who becomes a worker is no longer a woman."[15] True workers (those who did not violate their nature by working) were men.[16] Similarly, the leaders of the Commune gave little or no thought to extending political self-determination to women, and its political and military enemy in Versailles was clearly male.

When the conflict was seen in terms of the past, however, women were central. Then bourgeois fears identified the communardes with the tricoteuses of the French Revolution, and the Commune's threat was represented in female form.

Class War versus Self-Rule

The leaders of the revolt (and their followers) espoused a variety of democratic and socialist philosophies, but they generally agreed that the re-

volt was about who would govern Paris. In the list of demands it presented
to the National Assembly, the Central Committee placed municipal liberties for the city first.[17] The revolutionaries wanted the right to select the
arrondissement mayors and to elect a Parisian municipal council with the
power to make and enforce laws without the intervention of the National
Assembly, a right that Paris alone among French cities did not have. Second, it wanted the Prefecture of Police and its gendarmes, repressors of the
working class, suppressed. Third, the Committee wanted autonomy for the
National Guard, that is, the right to name its own chiefs, rather than have
them chosen and imposed upon them by the government, and the right to
reorganize itself, as it already had, in a relatively democratic fashion.
Fourth, it wanted the army forbidden to enter Paris. If the city were attacked, the National Guard would defend it (hence the desire to retain
control of the cannons). Fifth, it wanted the recently passed laws on rents
and overdue bills changed. And finally, it wanted the National Assembly to
proclaim the republic as the legitimate government of France, and to assure the people that it would not be undermined and overthrown as the
Second Republic had been by Louis Napoleon at the end of 1851.[18]

To concede to these political demands would have been to transfer considerable power from the hands of the conservative and monarchist-lean-
ing national government to working-class and republican Parisians. This
Thiers and other conservatives were unwilling to do. For them, the conflict was not about self-government for Paris but about who—what class—
would govern France. The controlling figure in this struggle was Adolphe
Thiers, whose conflict with the workers of Paris was of long standing. As
Louis-Philippe's minister of the interior, he had approved the July Monarchy's 1834 Law on Associations, which made it possible for the government
to repress workers' organizations and prosecute their leaders. That same
year, he had organized the violent repression of the workers' revolts in
Paris and Lyons, and he had been one of the architects of the September
Laws, which closed down the Republican and Legitimist press. By 1848 he
had come to believe that the working class would "ruin the country from
top to bottom" if its socialist tendencies were not restrained. In 1850 he
supported a new electoral law that excluded about one-third of the voters,
among them the militant Left and workers. The attempt to wrest the cannons out of the hands of the working-class units of the National Guard and
to place them under the army's control was only the latest in this series of
repressive actions by the man who now was the head of the national government.[19]

While the National Guard Central Committee was drawing up its political platform, the national government was denouncing them as *criminels*

artisans, and enumerating their past and anticipated future "crimes." Suggesting nefarious allegiances, the government asked, "Who are the members of this committee? . . . Are they Communists, Bonapartists, or Prussians? Are they the agents of a triple coalition? Whatever they are, they are the enemies of Paris which they will deliver up to pillage; of France which they will deliver to the Prussians; of the republic which they will deliver up to despotism."[20]

These insinuations made good reading and placed the Central Committee on the defensive, but they were hardly accurate. Parisians in general, including the National Guard (from which the Central Committee was derived) had opposed the peace treaty with Prussia and its triumphal parade through Paris, and only an odd twist of logic could now make them collaborators with the Prussians. Nor were the Communards Bonapartists or despots. Whatever else they were, the men and women who led and supported the Commune were republicans; they had opposed the Second Empire and cheered its demise in September. These accusations would quickly fade.

The references to criminals, communists, and pillaging would recur continually, however. According to the dominant perception at Versailles, the male revolutionaries were workers whose class and self-interests had run amok (i.e., they were communists), who envied the bourgeoisie's wealth and property and intended to pillage it (i.e., they were criminals). This view and the emotions it evoked were widely shared among the bourgeois. It underlay Goncourt's remark on the nineteenth about the "radiant debauchery" of the guardsmen and his fuller expression on March 28. "What is happening," he wrote then, "is very simply the conquest of France by the workers and the enslavement under their despotism of the nobles, the bourgeois, and the peasants. The government is passing from the hands of those who have to those who have not, from those who have a material interest in the conservation of society to those who are completely uninterested in order, stability, or conservation." Perhaps, he mused, "the workers are for modern civilization what the barbarians were for ancient societies, convulsive agents of dissolution and destruction."[21]

That the Central Committee and Commune reopened the stock exchange, negotiated loans from the Bank of France, and established a schedule for the repayment of debts, rather than simply expropriating the bank's funds, meant little in the intellectual and emotional climate of 1871. What mattered to the bourgeoisie was that the people of Montmartre whose actions had precipitated the revolution and the battalions of the National Guard that had supported it, as well as the elected members of the Central Committee and the Commune, were themselves either workers (loosely defined) or allies of the working class. If the rebels were workers, the rebellion could only be a class war.

The support of labor unionists, the International Working Men's Association, various groups of socialists, and the authors of *The Communist Manifesto* (Karl Marx and Friedrich Engels) for the Commune further reinforced the bourgeois notion of class war. Journalists regularly referred to the "Reds" in Paris and used "communist" as a synonym for "communard," even though the Communards made no attack on private property (aside from that of Thiers) and did not even take control of the Bank of France's assets.

The varied political views of the elected members of the Commune, as well as the workers of Paris—ranging from neo-Jacobinism to Proudhonism to Blanquism to communism—were similarly irrelevant to conservatives.[22] From their perspective, the similarities in these positions outweighed the differences. Even the mildest socialist measures taken by the Commune, such as the abolition of fines for carelessness in factories, the reopening of abandoned factories as cooperatives, and the fixing of the salary of elected representatives at "the ordinary wages of a skilled workman," were enough to convince conservatives that its intentions were communistic.[23] The same was true of the laws that benefited the workers and codified the working-class view of right and wrong, such as the remission of back rent from the period of the Prussian siege, a three-year moratorium on the repayment of debts, and the release of all household goods and work tools valued at less than twenty francs from the state-run pawnshop.[24]

Such laws convinced Maxime Du Camp and other conservatives that "what the Commune stood for—continues to stand for—is instant substitution . . . of the proletariat for all other classes of society, in property ownership, in administration, in the exercise of power."[25] Like Thiers, whose views were enshrined in the national government's initial proclamations about the criminal nature of the rebellion, Du Camp, writing in 1881, attributed the rebellion to the envy that led Cain to kill Abel, the envy of those who "hate to work" and prefer "warfare to daily travail."[26] It was a significant revision of the Cain and Abel story, but it fit the common notion that the national guardsmen preferred playing at soldiering to working for a living.

Some bourgeois who viewed the rebellion as class struggle were sympathic to the workers. William Gibson, a British Methodist minister with a small congregation in Paris, combined parts of the government's and the Communards' views on the revolt, regarding it both as a working-class struggle for social justice and as an attempt to obtain municipal liberties for Parisians. He reported in a letter on April 7 that he had just read a "significant paragraph" in the newspapers which showed that "for the same room occupied by a workman the rent has been *trebled* within the last eighteen years." For this and other reasons, he concluded, "the notion, right or wrong, that the workmen are spending muscle and brain to enrich capitalists, without getting a corresponding increase in wages in proportion to the increasing value of their labour, is laying hold of the whole class of workers." He concluded not unsympathetically that "this 'proletariat' controversy which is at the bottom of all, is the great question for the next generation to settle."[27]

As the weeks passed and Versailles propaganda made its way into Paris, bourgeois sympathy for the Commune was undermined, and men like Gibson moved closer and closer to the Versailles perspective. On April 18, for instance, Gibson observed, "The more I get to know about this insurrectionary movement the more I am convinced that it is a great effort of the Red Republican party in Europe to gain their ends. . . . The 'word of order' to these people is said to come from the International Society in London! . . . The scum of Europe has been collected in Paris to fight out this battle."[28]

Caricaturists took a different tack. Instead of representing the Communards as criminals, they presented them as drunkards, playing up another widespread belief.[29] Less villainous than the "scum of Europe" Gibson imagined, the national guardsmen and elected officials of the caricaturists' imagination were depicted lying across benches and tables with drinks in their hands, alternately leering and staring vacantly, clearly incapable of either defending or governing the Commune (see fig. 8). Though unquestionably critical of the Commune, the caricatures resembled comic opera more than a life-and-death struggle between good and evil.

More serious was the French bourgeoisie's conviction that the Communards would turn to theft now that they had political power. Throughout the rebellion, the bourgeoisie accused the Communards of pillaging homes, churches, and government buildings, beginning on the morning of March 19, when the national government warned that the revolutionaries, regardless of their political sentiments, would "deliver Paris up to pillaging."[30] Fear for their property soon turned the warning to conviction and accusation.

Articles in pro-Commune newspapers condemning pillaging, decrees of the Communal Council that pillaging would be punished, and the statements of sympathetic (or at least somewhat sympathetic) observers that remarkably little pillaging was taking place had little or no effect on conservative convictions.[31] What the government proclaimed against, the bourgeoisie believed. Gibson reported on April 13, for instance, "What makes everyone so full of fear in these troublesome times is that numbers of men under the name of the Commune go about to pillage."[32] A few days later, he noted: "A young Englishman residing in Paris . . . said that the current opinion was that a great attack by the Versailles troops was expected within the next week, and at the same time by the insurgents a blow-up of some of the streets, and a general pillage!"[33] In the same vein, Philibert Audebrand, writing in the immediate aftermath of the semaine sanglante, accused the Commune of having "organized pillaging" and even of having "raised it to a civic virtue."[34]

General Appert's final report to the National Assembly as well as conservatives' memoirs and histories included pillaging in their litanies of the Commune's "crimes."[35] Appert's list was detailed. Once the war between Paris and Versailles resumed in early April, he wrote, "countless pillages . . . desolated the city"; churches were "invaded, profaned, and looted"; when priests were arrested, their personal property was "stolen"; "armoires were broken open and emptied"; national guardsmen who were billeted in private homes "took things at their convenience"; the National Guard refused to allow servants to stay behind to guard their masters' homes when Neuilly was evacuated, so they could act on their "secret desires . . . [and] pillage the abandoned buildings. . . . gowns of silk and velvet, shawls, lace, linens, curtains, clocks, paintings, curios and objets d'art, everything that could be carried was selected, packed up, and sent back to Paris." Finally, in a flight of what appears to be complete fantasy, Appert reported that the looters held "hideous balls where the thieves wore the spoils of their victims, accompanied by their concubines and wives."[36] Women certainly were not innocent in this presentation of the Commune's crimes, but their guilt was by association.

Reign of Terror

In contrast, another bourgeois conviction—that the Commune would institute a reign of terror—drew much of its inspiration from bourgeois representations of revolutionary women. The exact content of the reign-of-terror accusation was often vague, but its origins were clear. They lay in the bourgeoisie's memories of the French Revolution. Any law passed or action taken by the Commune or the National Guard, as well as rumors about events (or even nonevents), could bring cries of a reign of terror.

British journalists raised the specter first, on March 20. "Last night," a *Times* correspondent in Paris wrote in the chatty style of the day, "many people were half expecting a Reign of Terror, in the best style of the last century, and dire was the consternation of innocent tourists—fathers of families and newly married couples—who had run over to Paris to look for the traces of the bombardment and pick up 'relics of the siege.'"[37]

Events in Paris soon added fuel to the fear. On March 23, opponents of the revolution calling themselves the Friends of Order marched down the rue de la Paix toward the place Vendôme and the National Guard. Confident of success, the Friends of Order (with the tacit support of the Versailles government) insulted the guards and pressed toward them. The guardsmen demanded that the demonstrators stop and disperse. Shots were eventually fired (at whose instigation is unknown). The Friends fled. Ten demonstrators and two national guardsmen lay dead; several more on each side were wounded.[38] Called "the massacre in the rue de la Paix" by the conservative press, the deaths created "agitation and alarm" in Versailles and became further "proof" (along with the deaths of Generals Lecomte and Clément Thomas) of the bloodthirstiness of the revolution to distribute in the provinces.[39]

On April 4 the Commune passed the decree for which it would be most criticized. In response to the executions of Generals Emile Duval and Gustave Flourens by the army, it decided to hold anyone convicted of complicity with the Versailles government hostage and declared that the Commune would respond to all executions of Communard prisoners by shooting triple that number of hostages.[40] In the next few weeks, the Commune took Monsignor Georges Darboy, archbishop of Paris; Judge Louis-Bertrand Bonjean, the former president of the Parisian Supreme Court; and a variety of priests hostage. Versailles took the holding of hostages and the ferocious rhetoric of Raoul Rigault, the delegate to the Prefecture of Police (who was in charge of the prisoners), as further proof that a reign of terror was beginning in Paris. It was not induced, however, to treat its own prisoners more humanely, and the executions of captured soldiers and guardsmen continued. Meanwhile, in Paris the hostages were not harmed until after the Versailles troops invaded the city in May and began wholesale execution of the guardsmen who surrendered to them.

The institution of conscription for the National Guard on April 7 and subsequent attempts to enforce it raised further cries of a reign of terror even from men like Gibson, who was initially sympathetic to the Commune. "We are truly under a 'Reign of Terror,'" he moaned on April 14, when a woman who had worked for him as a servant told him that "her husband had been taken off by some National Guards and forced into a *compagnie de Marche* three days ago, and she had heard nothing from him since."[41]

English observers may have been particularly sensitive to the conscription decree because young Englishmen who spoke French, including Vizetelly, frequently had to produce official identification to avoid being pressed into service. At least one young Englishman who was in the wrong place at the wrong time was forced to serve in the National Guard.[42] Such stories became grist for the Versailles press, which regarded conscription into the National Guard as tantamount to forced labor. Bourgeois Parisians who did not want to serve first hid in the city and then tried to flee. Some escaped easily. Others "let themselves down from the ramparts at night by means of ropes" or "dressed themselves up as girls" and tried to escape by train.[43]

Supporters of the Commune were not above calling for a new reign of terror. On May 7 Goncourt visited the first meeting of the political club at the church of Saint-Eustache, where he heard "a man in pearl-gray trousers . . . in a raging voice declare that Terror is the only way to ensure victory." He demanded, according to Goncourt, the establishment of a revolutionary tribunal, "so the heads of traitors may roll immediately on the square," and his proposal received "frenzied applause."[44] Such statements voiced the worst fears of the bourgeoisie.

For many bourgeois, the anticlerical attitudes of many Communards were linked with the idea of the Terror. The anti-Commune press regularly reported that priests and nuns were being arrested, harassed, and even executed.[45] The *Journal de Bruxelles* reported on April 6, for instance: "A nun, who has hastily fled from Paris, brings us intelligence to the effect that the churches are being sacked and the curés arrested, some of the latter being shamefully mistreated. The Vicar General is also a prisoner in the hands of the insurgents, and the arrest of the Archbishop is confirmed. The convents are being searched, the visits being made during the night. It is asserted that 20 Jesuits have been shot."[46] Much of this statement was untrue, including the deaths of twenty Jesuits. What mattered, however, was not its accuracy but that it was believed to be true.

For their part, the pro-Commune press and the sensationalist *Times* periodically treated their readers to reports of newly discovered atrocities committed by the Catholic church. The most famous involved the nuns of the rue Picpus in the Faubourg Saint-Antoine. The National Guard discovered three madwomen housed in small huts in the convent garden and a variety of objects (a mattress with straps and buckles, iron corsets, an iron skullcap, and a rack turned by a cog-wheel) which led immediately to accusations of imprisonment and torture. (The nuns claimed they were old orthopedic instruments.) To add a note of sexual scandal to the story, the national guardsmen pointed out a subterranean connecting door between the nunnery and the adjacent monastery.[47]

As the war worsened, disagreements among the elected members of the Commune intensified and decisions were made that once again fed fears of a reign of terror. At the end of April men who looked to the past and wanted a strong executive prevailed over those who identified more generically and less historically as socialists, and they established a five-man executive committee to lead the revolution. They then made the symbolically disastrous decision to call this new executive committee the Committee of Public Safety, after the war cabinet created during the French Revolution. In addition to defending the revolution against its European opponents, the Committee of Public Safety had been responsible for the political purges of 1793 and 1794. The painter Gustave Courbet, an elected member of the Commune, understood the emotional response such a name would provoke and warned his fellow Communards that they would be "re-establishing to our own detriment a Terror that is not of our time. Let us employ," he pleaded, "the words suggested by our own revolution."[48]

As Courbet had warned, the name created alarm among both republicans and conservatives. Bourgeois warnings of another Terror gained credence, even though some supporters of the Commune attempted to head them off. Jacques Durand, for instance, impressed Goncourt at the May 7 meeting in Saint-Eustache when he insisted the Commune had had "no idea, no intention, of a Terror," when it set up a Committee of Public Safety.[49]

In April references to revolutionary women also took on a new aspect. No longer identified as the victims of terror, like the nun who "escaped" to Brussels, they began to be seen as the instigators and the enjoyers of terror. Catulle Mendès, foreshadowing the emotions men would experience at the end of the Commune when they watched the pétroleuses being marched to Versailles, was both attracted to and repulsed by the cantiniéres who took up arms. "In their horribleness, they have a kind of savage grandeur," he wrote. And they reminded him of the past. "We have our cantinières, as '93 its tricoteuses."[50]

The appellation *tricoteuse* (knitter) referred to the women of the Parisian sans-culottes who, unlike wealthier women, who were expected to remain at home, participated freely in the popular events of the revolution and knitted while they listened to the debates of the revolutionary assemblies. Largely a creation of the nineteenth century and used exclusively by the opponents of the Revolution, the term replaced the phrase *furies de guillotine* and elided all the female supporters of the revolution with those who supported the terror, simultaneously reflecting and creating a fear of women and a fear of revolution.[51]

Like the Goncourts' maid Rose, whose outward appearance and demeanor had concealed her sexual activity, the tricoteuses concealed their
lust for violence in the feminine activity of knitting. But unlike Rose, whose
secret life seemed to symbolize the duplicity of women to the Goncourt
brothers, the tricoteuses symbolized the "degeneration of the human race"
and its "excesses of depravity and horror" to bourgeois men.[52] E. Lairtullier created a stirring verbal portrait in 1840:

> These women, devoted body and soul to the instrument of corporal punish-
> ment, double the atrocity by their demoniacal vociferations. [They] fling sin-
> ister sarcasm at the blood about to be shed, and sardonic laughter at the lives
> about to end. [They] crowd around the fatal plank so as to savor all the bet-
> ter the livid pallor, the mysterious trembling, and the anguish of the victim.
> [They] rejoice in the cowardly executioner, whose place they would have tak-
> en with delight. [They] stamp their feet with joy at the moment of the bloody
> holocaust; pant impatiently after the victim who, in their frightful lingo, *is go-
> ing to jump like a carp or sneeze in the sack;* and dance hideous revolutionary
> dances in celebration at the very foot of the scaffold.[53]

Identification of the communardes with the tricoteuses gave interpretations of the Commune an ominous tone. Mendès wrote in his journal that
the women of the people were "drunk with hate."[54] On May 5 the *New York
Herald* published letters from its correspondents which juxtaposed "ladies"
who watched the shells fall near the Arc de Triomphe and *vivandières* who
fought like men. (*Vivandières* and cantinières both furnished provisions to
military and National Guard troops. In this context, however, *vivandière*
also connotes a woman who violated gender norms by joining in the fighting.) One of the *Herald*'s correspondents reported that "these Parisiennes
have 'supped so full of horrors' lately that their mental digestion must be
much impaired. The women are very fierce, some of them; they are perhaps reviving the race that watched the guillotine and counted the heads
that fell like autumn leaves."[55]

The association of the Terror, the guillotine, and women was strong in
the nineteenth century and was not offset by the participation of women
in the public burning of a guillotine at the statue of Voltaire at the outset
of the Commune.[56] Any angry or agitated woman could conjure up images
of guillotines in use. On May 5, for instance, Goncourt recorded his impressions of a group of Communards. One animallike woman caught his
attention when she came to the front of the group. "Her paws in the air
making wild gestures," she denounced the men in the group as "cowards!
men who look on while others fight," and professed her desire for combat.

"I'd just like to get my hands on a reactionary, on a royalist, I'd claw his face for him!" she declared. Then, Goncourt reported, "she probes the crowd with an eye avid for the guillotine, then draws away, staggering in a sort of drunken anger." In contrast to the images of wild beasts and the guillotine evoked by the woman's words and demeanor, the men's expression of class sentiments—they wanted "no more rich people"—provoked only condescension and exasperation from Goncourt. The men were foolish and despicable; the women were dangerous.[57]

Goncourt's communarde, like Mendès's cantinières, bears a strong resemblance to Charles Dickens's character Madame Defarge in *A Tale of Two Cities*, first published in 1859. The fictional Madame Defarge, who ruthlessly denounced "traitors" to the Revolution and knitted at the foot of the guillotine as their heads rolled, was, indeed, memorable,

> of a strong and fearless character, of shrewd sense and readiness, of great determination, of that kind of *beauty* which not only seems to impart to its possessor firmness and animosity, but seems to strike into others an instinctive recognition of those qualities; the troubled time would have heaved her up, under any circumstances. But, imbued from her childhood with a brooding sense of wrong, and *an inveterate hatred of a class*, opportunity had developed her into *a tigress*. She was *absolutely without pity*. If she had ever had the virtue in her, it had quite gone out of her.
>
> It was nothing to her that an innocent man was to die for the sins of his forefathers; she saw, not him, but them. It was nothing to her, that his wife was to be made a widow and his daughter an orphan; that was insufficient punishment, because *they were her natural enemies and her prey*, and as such had no right to live. To appeal to her, was made hopeless by her *having no sense of pity*.[58]

The tricoteuse embodied in Madame Defarge had become *the* image of the female revolutionary by 1871. This new French revolution brought her back to life. She appears not only in Goncourt's vision of the communarde on May 5 but throughout the memoirs, reports, editorials, and histories that have been written about the Commune. The sight of women knitting was enough to arrest the attention of virtually any bourgeois. E. B. Washburne reported in his memoirs that "the great feature which attracted my attention was the large number of women who were present with their knitting-work,—*'tricoteuses'* they were called," when he visited a political gathering at Saint-Eustache. He needed to say no more for bourgeois readers. Even though he reported that the knitters appeared "motherly, plain and serious women, and very well behaved," the seed of doubt about their character had been planted.[59]

The same is true of American journalist John Russell Young's reflections on the Commune. Writing at the end of the semaine sanglante, he, too, re-called a visit to a club, where he saw "a number of women, some of whom were knitting, recalling the Tricoteurs [*sic*] who were wont in the other days to sit all day near the guillotine."[60] In case the allusion to the trico-teuses left any doubts about his views of the Commune, he then noted that although he heard only peaceful speeches, he was certain that if he "had remained long enough, I might have heard an address or two upon the di-vision of property and the duty of general pillage."[61] For bourgeois ob-servers, the Commune was like the knitting woman. Both appeared be-nign, but they knew the appearances were false.

Images of unnatural, violent, and bloodthirsty women became even more prominent at the end of the Commune when women defended the barricades and were accused of being incendiaries. Equations of the pétroleuses with the tricoteuses of the first Revolution abounded. Among the most misogynist of them came from English writers. In 1873 the anony-mous author of the text in the English edition of Charles Bertall's draw-ings of the Communards, for instance, abandoned the image of the tigress, a noble beast in Western imagination, and likened the women of the Com-mune to "the thirsty Hyaena" that has "tasted Blood."[62] Denis Arthur Bing-ham, who wrote for a variety of British newspapers in the 1870s, was still so agitated about the pétroleuses when his memoirs were published in 1896 that he likened them to "the *lécheuses* [female gourmands—from the verb *lécher*, to lick] of the First Revolution [who were] intoxicated with the fumes of wine and blood." Completing the connection, he concluded that they deserved the guillotine as a punishment.[63] This spine-tingling image of women swooning at the smell of blood and Bingham's explanation that the *lécheuses* "used to lick the blood as it trickled down the guillotine"[64] are unparalleled, but similar sentiments lived on for a long time. Almost a cen-tury after the Commune, Alistair Horne could still present the women of March 18 as "figures horribly reminiscent of the *tricoteuses* of the Terror, . . . [who] howled for the blood of the captive."[65]

On the other side of the political divide, Communards and their sup-porters also identified angry, vengeful women with the Terror, the guillo-tine, and blood. The pro-Commune journalist Lissagaray called the women of Versailles who attacked the Communard prisoners in the streets of Versailles hyenas and jackals, and he was appalled to hear them scream for the prisoners to be taken "to the guillotine!"[66] What the bourgeoises of Versailles did and said is not entirely clear, although their words and ac-tions were widely reported and discussed. Other journalists and witnesses heard the women insult the prisoners and call for their deaths, but only

Lissagaray "heard" them call for the guillotine.[67] Like the Versaillais, he saw the Commune through the lens of the French Revolution and conveyed his judgment of women's behavior through his association of them with the guillotine and, by implication, the Terror.

Like Lissagaray, Louise Michel turned the bloodthirsty imagery that was so often used against the Communards against the women of Versailles, although she made no explicit allusions to the past. Writing about the attacks on the dead and the prisoners who were taken to Versailles in April, she did not mince words. "These creatures, hideous with ferocity, dressed in luxury and coming from who knows where, . . . insulted the prisoners and dug out the eyes of the dead with the ends of their umbrellas. . . . *Thirsting for blood,* like ghouls, they were . . . monstrous and irresponsible like she-wolves [*louves*]."[68]

Although imagery from the French Revolution was available to both sides in this conflict, it never worked as well for the Communards as it did for the bourgeoisie, since the historical reference point was to revolutionaries, not counterrevolutionaries. The image of the tricoteuse, in fact, was used only by the Commune's opponents, as it had been used earlier in the century by the opponents of the French Revolution. But references to and representations of the present in terms of the past, and in female form, allowed both sides to tell themselves and the world that their opponents were unnatural, inhuman, immoral, and without pity. These images from the Revolution of 1789 were only the beginning of the process of representation that would take place during and after the Commune, however. Many more female figures were about to be born.

CHAPTER THREE

The Symbolic Female Figure

Composite or stereotyped female figures are liberally sprinkled through the newspapers, histories, and memoirs of the Commune. Among the most prominently displayed are widows and mothers who mourned the dead; cantinières and ambulancières (female cooks and nurses), who brought food, drink, and medical assistance to the National Guard; "amazons" who volunteered to fight against the Versaillais; female orators (also amazons) who appeared nightly at political clubs; and, during the final week of fighting, pétroleuses who were accused of setting the fires that burned the city. Each figure reflects late nineteenth-century notions of appropriate and inappropriate, natural and unnatural, acceptable and unacceptable female behavior, and each tells us about her creators' perceptions of the differences between women and men. These figures do more than reflect cultural assumptions about woman's nature and appropriate behavior, however. They also assign meaning to women's actions, and embody judgments of them and of the Commune.

The meaning of these representations of communardes (the term is itself a representation, for it identifies women in terms of their political activities and beliefs) were not stable even in 1871. Each figure had more than one persona, and as her personas changed, so did the judgments behind the presentation of her. The cantinière appeared alternately as silly, saintly, and devious. The female warrior and female orator were heroic, dangerous, foolish, and irrational, depending upon their creators' political positions. The grieving widow was usually an innocent victim, but in the hands of caricaturists even she could become a duplicitous figure. The pétroleuse was more often evil than good, but she, too, had various representations, ranging from the alluring to the hideous and from victim to villain. This chapter explores the female victims and villains that appeared before the Versailles invasion of Paris in late May, and the ideological roles they played in the texts of the Commune. The pétroleuses of the semaine sanglante will appear in Chapter 5.

Female Victims

Men were the major defenders of the city and bore the brunt of the casualties once the war between Paris and Versailles began in early April. By May 21, four thousand Parisian men as well as a goodly number of women and children had been killed, and thirty-five hundred men had been taken prisoner.[1] Many other men had joined the ranks of the *blessés* (wounded) who could be seen around the city and in the hospitals. *Blessées* (injured women) also existed, but the term was never used. Wounded women either were not part of the public scene or, for some reason, were unmentionable. Other female and child victims of the war appear regularly in the Commune's texts, however, and their symbolic significance extended well beyond their actual numbers.

Even though wounded men appeared in public and were buried daily in the cemeteries of Paris, culturally it was easier to portray women as victims. Generally speaking, war was supposed to be a situation in which men demonstrated their manhood.[2] To die in combat might be tragic, but it was to be expected in wartime, and neither side wanted to view its fallen men as victims. Instead, political leaders and journalists referred to them as martyrs,[3] placing them in a related but more heroic cultural category. In contrast, women and children were not combatants (at least in theory), and their deaths were not considered a normal consequence of war. Indeed, men fought, at least in part, to protect them. The military commanders of the Commune understood this impulse and used it when they needed to rally their troops.[4] When women and children were injured or killed or when they lost their male protectors, they could be used to symbolize the horrors of war and the villainy of the enemy.

The cultural availability of women and children to represent the horrors of war was not new in 1871, but one of its most memorable uses appeared in that year when Honoré Daumier, the foremost caricaturist in France, reacted to the carnage of the Franco-Prussian War. He made powerful use of female allegory in his drawing *Appalled by the Heritage* (fig. 5). A grieving figure representing France dominates the drawing. She stands in the fore-

FIGURE 5. Honoré Daumier, *Appalled by the Heritage*. The Metropolitan Museum of Art, Bequest of Edwin T. Bechtel, 1957. (57.650.108.) All rights reserved. The Metropolitan Museum of Art.

ground, turned to the side, shrouded in black from head to foot, with her face buried in her hands. She is the symbolic opposite of Delacroix's Liberty. Instead of leading the French into glorious battle, she mourns the dead men whose bodies stretch out to the horizon. She is contained within the picture's frame, but they are not, and neither, Daumier seems to suggest, is her despair. It, like the dead, is unmeasurable, reaching to the horizon and beyond.[5]

The assignment of killing to men and grieving to women was part of a long-standing Western conceptualization of sex roles and traits, although the understanding of gender differences evolved over time. In general, men were seen as strong, women as weak; men as independent, women as dependent; men as protectors, women as the protected. Mothers might protect their children in peacetime (or might at least try to protect them), but only men could protect them in times of war.[6]

The power of these dichotomies to structure the representation and meaning of events was demonstrated at the outset of the revolution when women and children confronted General Lecomte's troops on the slopes of Montmartre. As the story was told and retold, unarmed women faced down armed men. Whether the women were literally unarmed or not is unclear (Louise Michel, who was part of the crowd, claimed that she was carrying a gun under her cloak),[7] but the meaning of the event depended upon the representation of them as unarmed, that is, powerless. They were the weak and the innocent who could inflict no physical harm on the men they confronted. In the eyes of the people, Lecomte's crime, for which he would pay with his life, was ordering his troops to fire on these innocents. The symbolic, if not the literal, truth of the scene on Montmartre lay in this clash between the powerful and the weak. For Communard supporters, it was *the* (acceptable) explanation for Lecomte's execution, even though the soldiers who were held prisoner with him and who escaped execution saw the women of Montmartre as anything but powerless.[8]

The Women of Neuilly

The terrible irony of an urban war fought to protect women and children is that the fighting endangers the very people who are being defended. This irony was brought home bitterly to the village of Neuilly, a bourgeois faubourg, when, on April 2, Versailles aimed its guns toward Paris and opened fire. Most of the shells landed in Neuilly. The heinousness of Versailles's crime was symbolized by the news that a group of schoolgirls had been "littéralement hachée" (literally cut up) by machine-gun fire as they came out of a church, a story that was carried in every Communard newspaper.[9] This shelling on the second was just the beginning of the attack on the western side of the city. The bombardment continued night and day for the next two months. Some managed to escape from Neuilly, others were trapped for weeks.[10]

The victimization of women and children by war became a popular story in the American press. On May 5 the *New York Herald* published a chatty, first-person account of the shelling of Neuilly under the headline, "Dreadful Suffering of Women and Children." The story recounted a correspondent's "stroll" through Neuilly while bullets flew about "in every direction." Stopping for a moment in a doorway, he reported,

> I heard a sound as of sobbing apparently beneath me and I made bold to enter, a thing not hard to do, although the door was supposed to be shut and fastened. The room on the ground floor was in the greatest disorder and the furniture which evidently belonged to a family in humble circumstances, was in the wildest confusion. Bits of clay and mortar were scattered over the floor, and one corner of the house was almost knocked out. Finding my way to the cellar, I peered down, and there I saw a women trying to pacify two crying children, and crying herself more than they. The shell in question had come crashing in the day before, and they had not left the cellar for a moment since, having passed the night in it, and were still afraid to go out to get anything to eat or to seek an asylum elsewhere. I consoled them with the assurance that shells were like lightning—that they never strike twice in the same place, and that they were therefore perfectly safe. It was rather cold comfort, however, the more so as it was not by any means safe to go out in the street, and they would be obliged to stay within doors for the present at least or run the risk of being overtaken by a bullet in case they went out to procure anything to eat, even if they had money to get anything with, which seemed more than doubtful. Her husband, she said, was away in the south of France, at work, but she had not heard from him for weeks.[11]

The story uses a variety of gender conventions to convey the honorableness of the woman and hence the horror of war. The house/home, which should be orderly, has been violated and is in disarray; the mother and her two children are frightened, crying, impoverished, and incapable of rescuing themselves; and the natural protector of the family is absent (increasing their helplessness), but for an honorable reason, working in the south of France. This family was not unique, however, as the writer pointed out. "When you think that there are hundreds in the villages of Neuilly, Courbevois and Asnières in just the same situation," he concluded, "you may form some idea of the misery which this fratricidal war is entailing upon the inhabitants of the villages where it is raging."[12]

What the story did not say was that the conditions in Neuilly were the fault of Versailles. The *New York Herald* was not a pro-Commune newspaper. It regularly referred to the Communards as communists, and the day before it had carried a report from a *Times* special dispatch claiming that "the insurgents at Neuilly [not the Versailles troops] are themselves throwing petroleum shells into Paris, to keep up the indignation of the populace against the Versailles Government."[13] The villain was war, and the helpless woman and child were the irresistible symbol of its horrors.

On April 25 both sides agreed to a one-day cease-fire, so the remaining residents of Neuilly could be evacuated. When the shelling stopped, ambulances (mobile field hospitals or aid stations), guardsmen, and journalists rushed into the faubourg. Spectators gathered near the bridge to watch the evacuation as they had watched bombs fall in the preceding weeks. Among those present was the English journalist Ernest Vizetelly who recalled the scene in picturesque detail—the crowd that gathered to watch, the "great branches of trees" lying on the ground, the broken streetlamps and ruined houses, the dead bodies "over which flies were constantly hovering and buzzing," and the "woeful procession of the victims" with their goods and chattels.[14]

Everyone reported on the female evacuees, but the displacement of able-bodied women alone could not adequately convey the pathos of the situation and the evils of war. Vizetelly and others created catalogs of even more helpless victims, including "unhappy, dazed-looking septuagenarian sisters," "crippled girls," "sick children," "paralyzed old men," and children "no more than six years old."[15] Varied as the members of the category might be, they all occupied the same symbolic position. In relation to the male combatants, they were like the women of Montmartre on March 18: they were powerless.

The Cartridge Workers

A more ambiguous group of female victims was created in the waning days of the Commune when the cartridge factory near the Champs-Elysées exploded. Around the city, as many as three thousand women were employed in the manufacture of gun cartridges. Little was recorded about them, but they did not escape the notice and censure of the English journalist D. A. Bingham, who recorded in his memoirs that the women who worked in a cartridge manufactory near the Palais Royal "belonged to that class of women called 'bad,' and their faces were covered with a thick layer of flour." He noted that "there were a number of similar establishments scattered about Paris, and close to the church of St. Augustin was a market-place in which some hundreds of well-floured unfortunates were to be seen at work."[16] Bingham does not explain why he assumed that the munitions workers were prostitutes. Perhaps he accepted the bourgeois disapproval of paid work for women and, therefore, assumed that only women who were willing to accept pay for other (immoral) purposes would take such jobs. Or perhaps he simply wanted to titillate his readers.

In stark contrast to Bingham's unsavory verbal portrait, a drawing in the collection of the Bibliothèque Nationale depicts the cartridge makers as well-dressed, pretty young women who seem to be more bourgeois than working class. Both portraits contain large doses of fiction. Munitions workers, like the women who sewed uniforms for national guardsmen and sandbags for stopping up the chinks in the barricades, were ordinary working-class women who had worked before the revolution and who would work after it because they and their families needed the money they earned. They were as unlikely to be bourgeoises as they were to be prostitutes.

When the cartridge factory on the avenue Rapp exploded on May 17 at 5:45 P.M., panic swept the city and rumors flew. Some thought the Issy fortress had blown up; others, Montrouge. People thought the Versaillais had launched a massive attack or that the Ecole Militaire, or the artillery museum, or the tobacco factory, or a barricade had blown up. Some raced for their homes; others streamed toward the explosion.[17]

Those who arrived quickly were stunned by what they saw. For a considerable radius houses were damaged beyond habitation, and the factory itself was razed to the ground.[18] The *New York Times* correspondent who arrived on the scene early enough to help with "placing stretchers for the heads and limbs and mutilated trunks of the killed," reported that "homes were burning, and there was an incessant rattle of exploding cartridges. A brilliant blaze shot up. . . . Hundreds of thousands of cartridges, cracking and rattling one after another, mingled with the shrieks of the wounded, frightened the people terribly. . . . Mutilated forms of humanity were on every side, groaning and writhing in agony."[19] The correspondent from the *Times* of London, who arrived a bit later, reported that he saw "half a body taken down from the roof of one of the tallest houses in the neighbourhood." Gibson, too, said that bodies were "thrown . . . to the roofs of neighbouring houses" and added that "fragments of bodies and mangled limbs were to be seen in all directions."[20] Edwin Child, a young Englishman in Paris, focused on the physical destruction, writing to his family that he "could hardly believe [his] ears and eyes. Roofs torn off, not a window to be seen, sunblinds hanging by a broken hinge, fronts of shops smashed in and 4 houses of 5 stories thrown to the ground. The cafés even had the glasses and decanters splintered to pieces by the shock."[21] Edmond de Goncourt described walking on powdered glass when he went to view the disaster the next day.[22]

The number of women employed in the Rapp factory is unclear, as is the number killed. The *Times's* first dispatch reported that "six hundred *employés,* chiefly women, are said to have been killed."[23] This estimate, though it may reflect the actual number of women who worked in the factory, was much too high, for the employees had been sent home two hours early that day, at five o'clock. On May 18, the *Journal Officiel* reported that a hundred persons had been killed.[24] Lissagaray, writing later in the decade, estimated the number of deaths at "more than forty."[25]

In addition to workers who were still in the factory, the explosion killed passersby and national guardsmen on duty outside.[26] The *Times* correspondent saw a woman searching for her husband, who had been seen near the building earlier, and a mother, "carrying about a little child's straw hat, with pretty pink rosettes," asking people if they had "seen a child in a similar hat." People, he said, treated her kindly and told her that "the only children they had seen about wore no such hat."[27]

Women figured prominently in the early reports not because most of the cartridge workers were women, a fact that was missing from many reports, but to emphasize the horror of the scene. The *New York Times* correspondent played up the melodrama: "To one body clung the scorched fragments of a hoop-skirt, and on the remaining finger of one hand was the wedding ring." Other newspapers repeated the story verbatim.[28] Others focused on frightened and distraught relatives, sometimes critically. Lewis Wingfield, assistant surgeon to the American Ambulance during the Prussian siege, reported, not unsympathetically, that "poor women were crying and searching for the remains of their daughters."[29] The *New York Times* correspondent, by contrast, faulted "aged women, wringing their hands in despair at the uncertainty of the situation of kindred," for increasing "the terror which everywhere prevailed."[30] The *New York Tribune* reported that, "women and children rushed frantically hither and thither, not knowing what they did or whither they went, for some of them would have actually dashed into the flaming ruins had they not been prevented by the firemen," and then underscored the irrationality of women with a detail missing from other reports: "One woman, mad with terror, flung herself from a third-story window, and was dashed to pieces on the pavements."[31]

Who or what was responsible for the explosion was widely debated. The discovery that the workers had been sent home early rapidly convinced many Parisians that agents of Versailles had conspired to blow up the factory. The Committee of Public Safety issued a statement blaming Versailles "agents" for the deaths.[32] The police arrested four men for sabotage and treason. Their guilt or innocence, as well as their fate, is unknown, but Lissagaray, among others, remained convinced in 1876 "that a serious inquest would probably have revealed a crime."[33] British observers and journalists, however, believed that the explosion was "a pure accident,"[34] although Vizetelly, in a classic instance of blaming the victim, attributed the "accident" to "the carelessness of one or another of the scores of women who were employed in the works."[35]

The presentation of the innocent victim (in hoop skirt and wedding ring), the worried mother (with her child's bonnet), and the mad old woman (spreading panic in her wake) in the early accounts demonstrates the ease with which female stereotypes replaced the complex women of the Commune in contemporary texts. How much political advantage might have been won from the mangled bodies, grieving survivors, and conspiracy theories if the Commune had lasted longer is impossible to tell. Four days later, the Versailles troops invaded the city, and the cause of the explosion and pity for its female victims were overshadowed by the far greater bloodshed of the semaine sanglante.

Grieving Widows and Mothers

Akin to the literal victims of the fighting but even more important symbolically, since they posed no challenges to gender norms, were the widows and mothers of dead guardsmen. Whether they were overwhelmed by grief or able to act nobly, their public presence, both in the city and in sympathetic texts, served as a reminder of the dead (and thus absent) young men for whom they mourned. During the Commune, these noble, grieving figures were used to spur the city to renewed efforts; after its defeat, they symbolized the nobility of the cause and the crimes of Versailles.

Early memoirs, diaries, and newspaper accounts repeatedly mentioned the women who waited anxiously by the city gates after every battle and the "heart-rending scenes" when "near relations and friends" were recognized among the dead and wounded.[36] These scenes began with the fighting on April 3 and 4. The newspaper and memoir accounts of the day described the crowds of women clustered together, waiting for the return of their husbands and apprehensively searching the wagons of dead and wounded soldiers as they entered the city. Indeed, the distress of these women was so great that some of the foreign correspondents in the city (writing out of their own political hopes) believed that they would now turn against the Commune.[37]

On the sixth, the city held the first of what became daily funerals for fallen guardsmen. Three enormous horse-drawn hearses, flying the Commune's red flags, moved slowly through the streets, followed by the elected leaders of the Commune, their heads bared, red sashes over their shoulders. Next came the families of the dead men, national guardsmen with their guns reversed, and an immense silent crowd that had joined the procession. Muffled drums beat the pace for the marching throng. Thousands watched from windows and sidewalks. At Père-Lachaise Cemetery, Charles Delescluze, the hero of the Revolution of 1848 and a member of the Communal Council, himself a dying man, moved forward to speak. "These [deaths] have already cost us too dearly," he said in a speech reminiscent of Lincoln's Gettysburg address in its somberness and inspiration. But "this *grande ville* . . . holds the future of humanity in its hands. . . . Cry not for our brothers who have fallen heroically, but swear to continue their work, and to save Liberty, the Commune, and the Republic!"[38]

The newspaper and early memoir accounts of the funeral noted the presence of the grieving women without emphasis. But as time passed, pro-Commune writers gave the women more prominence, as they attempted to counterbalance the Versailles portraits of the communards as unfeeling assassins and of the communardes as unnatural, fire-setting furies. Lanjalley and Corriez, writing in the immediate aftermath of the Commune, emphasized the grief of the women—"the relatives of the dead, *their crying wives and mothers*"—who followed the hearses behind the members of the Commune.[39] Lissagaray's account of the procession begins with a scene of weeping women, "bending over the bodies" and uttering "cries of fury and vows of vengeance for the deaths of their sons and husbands, many of whom they knew had been executed after they were captured."[40]

Pro-Commune caricaturists, too, were drawn to the grieving mother and widow to symbolize the horrors of war and the evils of Versailles. New piétas, maternal figures holding dead soldiers in their arms, appeared, some in drawings that are generically pacifist, others with such pro-Commune messages as *The Triumph of the Monarchy:* "Among the dead and the dying, look for your sons, poor mothers," to represent the sins of the Versailles government (fig. 6). *The Triumph of the Monarchy* depends on the gendered roles and iconography of the period to make its point. Thiers, holding a phallic cannon barrel, stands atop a mountain of dead men. Death, holding a scythe, crowns him with a laurel wreath, while vultures and bats descend upon the scene and women grieve. Two hold men in the posture of

FIGURE 6. *The Triumph of the Monarchy:* "Among the dead and the dying, look for your sons, poor mothers." Bibliothèque Nationale.

the piéta; a third clutches her children to her. The woman who buries her face in her hands resembles several iconographic figures (see fig. 2). Like Daumier's representation of a grieving France (see fig. 5), she is turned away from the viewer and holds her face in her hands. Like that of Delacroix's Liberty (see fig. 2), her bodice has slipped down from her shoulders to her arms, leaving her back bare. But her dark skirt differs from Liberty's traditional white clothing and her hair flows down her back, likening her also to representations of Marianne (the Republic). In any case, the message is clear: Thiers has triumphed over the Commune, the Republic, Paris, and Liberty at the cost of many French lives. Thiers, the artist assumes (as did the Communards), having proven his manhood, will reinstitute the monarchy.

In political acts as symbolic as they were practical, the Commune organized fund-raising concerts and events for the widows and children of the dead. It adopted children who were completely orphaned by the death of their fathers and undertook to provide for their care and education. It established pensions of 600 francs for the widows and 365 francs per year for each child of the men who died in battle. Enshrining a working-class notion of marriage that did not require legal sanction, the Commune made all widows and orphans eligible for aid, regardless of the formal marital status of the man and woman. While the claims were being verified, needy widows and orphans could apply for an immediate fifty francs.[41] Seen as sanctioning illegitimacy, the law provoked an outcry from conservatives and provided a field day for anti-Commune caricaturists, who reversed the image of the widow from victim to villain and quickly produced cartoons of women urging their men to go and fight and complaining when they returned alive.

Dangerous Women

Symbolically the opposite of the women who bore witness to the evils of Versailles and the toll of war in Communard texts were the Parisian women who fought for the Commune in one way or another, and conservative and anti-Commune writers paid them considerable attention. The willingness of theses "amazons" to participate in the taking of life violated bourgeois conceptualizations of woman's nature and called into question a basic assumption of nineteenth-century Western civilization—that aggression, bellicosity, and courage were masculine, not feminine, attributes. Particularly disturbing was that men found many of these woman to be physically attractive. For conservatives, the combination of violence and beauty was both evil and compelling, and when they wrote about the female warriors of Paris, though the tone varied from outright denunciation to sarcasm, the condemnation was always clear.

In contrast, pro-Commune writers were ambivalent. Only the truly radical Parisian journalists who welcomed any challenge to the status quo praised them wholeheartedly. Most did not know quite what to do with these champions of the Commune whose words and deeds challenged patriarchal culture. When they could, they ignored the women. When they could not, as was particularly the case when they wrote about the final week of fighting when women defended the barricades, they presented them as women of the people whose actions would save the revolution. But male commentators were not entirely comfortable with this portrayal.

"Amazon" was the word most commonly applied to the female defenders of the Commune. They were known as the amazons of the Seine, the amazons of Paris, the amazons of the Commune, the amazons of the rabble, and there was talk of forming a battalion of amazons.[42] Although other terms were also used, including virago, fury, harpy, and *vivandière,* the primary reference point was the Amazons of ancient Greece, the world's most enduring representation of the powerful woman.

More malleable, perhaps, than most images, the female warriors of Greek mythology have appeared over time as everything from free spirits who created their own society and desired only brief encounters with men in order to beget children to powerful, man-hating demons, willing to sacrifice their right breasts in the pursuit of a straight shot in archery. Literate and literary French, English, and American men in the nineteenth century were well acquainted with the amazons of antiquity as their scattered references to Queen Penthesilea attest. This familiarity had many sources—an education in the classics; the popularity of Heinrich von Kleist's 1808 poetic drama *Penthesilea;* and warrior-maiden representations of the French national heroine Jeanne d'Arc.

In the writings of Herodotus, Homer, Hippocrates, and Aristophanes, the Amazons were a society of skilled and fierce warriors who lived without men, rode horses, fought ferociously in battle, and eventually were defeated by the Athenians. Sculptors created scenes of these battles for the Parthenon and other civic buildings, and carved statues of individual amazons dressed in short tunics that left one breast uncovered. This artistic convention entered into Roman portrayals of the Amazons as riding into battle with one breast exposed.[43] The belief that Amazons cut or burned off one of their breasts in childhood is a later tradition.[44]

In myth, the beauty and strength of the Amazons, despite their warlike ways, exercise considerable appeal among the Greeks. The strength and steadfastness of more than one young man is tested by sending him on a quest to capture something from the Amazons. And more than one falls in love with an Amazon. When Heracles captures the sacred girdle of Queen Antiope (also called Hippolyta), he gives her to Theseus, the king of Athens, who falls in love with her and marries her. In another history, written by the fourth-century Greek poet Quintus, Achilles falls tragically in love with the beautiful queen Penthesilea after he has fatally wounded her in the battle of Troy.[45]

In Kleist's play Penthesilea leads her forces into battle against the Greeks during the siege of Troy, to capture young men who will become their lovers and the fathers of their children. During the battle, Penthesilea falls in love with Achilles. Aroused by passion, she pursues him in battle only to be conquered by him. Achilles, for his part, overwhelmed by her courage and beauty, becomes emotionally enslaved to her. When she discovers that she is a prisoner, she goes mad and tears Achilles limb from limb. When she comes to her senses and discovers Achilles is dead, she kills herself.[46]

Elements of these stories are interlaced with the legend of Jeanne d'Arc. In 1429 the seventeen-year-old Jeanne, from a village in the duchy of Lorraine, inspired the young Charles, heir to the throne of France, to victory over the English at Orleans. Jeanne said she had been inspired by the divine voices she heard. Some time after the victory, Charles's enemies, the Burgundians, captured Jeanne and sold her to the English; they turned her over to the Inquisition, and she was tried for heresy and burned at the stake in the marketplace in Rouen.

A variety of circumstances led to the association of this young martyred heroine with the Amazons, the other maiden warriors of legend. The association begins with her independence from men, symbolized by her virginity, cropped hair, male clothing, and direct communication with God. It continues, of course, with her role as a warrior at the battle of Orleans, where she inspired victory, and it concludes in the alteration of her name. Jeanne herself said that her family name was Darc. Over time Darc was transformed into d'Arc. The *de* awarded noble birth to the peasant girl, and the *Arc*, meaning "bow," "arch," and "curve," associated her with the Amazons of antiquity whose weapon was the bow. Enhancing the connection were Renaissance texts, engravings, and statues that presented Jeanne as an armed classical warrior and sometimes explicitly compared her with Penthesilea.[47]

Like the men of ancient Greece, bourgeois journalists, essayists, and historians were drawn to the fierce, beautiful female warriors of the Commune and were convinced that they were man-hating, independent, dangerous, and mad. Anti-Commune writers left Jeanne d'Arc out of their

FIGURE 7. H. Nérac, "The Virgin . . . Mad: The Joan of Arc of the Commune, S.G.D.G." *Les signes du Zodiaque.* Bibliothèque Nationale.

representations of the communardes, since she represented valor, good-ness, and purity and the female warriors of the commune represented evil, but her legend and image hovered somewhere in the background, com-plicating their representations and reactions.

   The one place where the communardes were explicitly identified with Jeanne d'Arc was in a drawing by the anti-Commune caricaturist Nérac representing Virgo or the Virgin (La Vierge) in his series on the signs of the zodiac (fig. 7). The frame of the picture includes a bit of doggerel: "On the field of battle as on the boulevard, / I can shoot a man at a thousand meters without mistake."

Like most unflattering representations of the communardes, Nérac's caricature reveals what conservative men found disturbing. The title, "La Vierge... Folle" (The mad virgin), is not meant to be read ironically, but the allusion to Jeanne d'Arc is. This cold-blooded, cigarette-smoking woman with the Medusa-like curly hair and phallic shotgun is no androgynous, virginal Jeanne d'Arc. But neither is she a true warrior. Only men (and the saintly Jeanne) can be warriors. In thinking she is one, and in taking on the outward appearance of a man, the communarde has violated her female nature and become mad.

Cantinières and Ambulancières

The cantinières and ambulancières, who provided food and drink to the National Guard and cared for the wounded, were the least controversial of the Commune's female warriors. These women were a customary part of the nineteenth-century warfare and were easily identified. Cantinières wore uniforms and often carried small casks at their waists. Ambulancières were less likely to wear uniforms, but they carried red crosses and medical supplies. Both groups braved the battle alongside the men in their battalions.

Some cantinières and ambulancières regarded their work as a job; others were volunteers who wanted to be near their husbands or to defend the Commune. Like the guardsmen who were ordinary workers and had little training in the art of warfare, these women were often ill prepared for battle. Cantinières were simply women who knew how to cook. Ambulancières had little if any real training to guide them, since nursing had yet to be established as a profession. They purchased their own supplies and did what they could to aid wounded men. Women (not the government or physicians) organized permanent and mobile ambulance stations in Montmartre and Issy, and the Union des Femmes pour la Défense de Paris et les Soins aux Blessés (Union of Women for the Defense of Paris and the Care of the Wounded) recruited ambulancières and cantinières to support the battalions.[48]

As early as March 19, cantinières could be seen marching through the streets with their battalions. In April and May they accompanied them into battle. The Commune newspapers carried accounts of their bravery throughout April and May. In Neuilly, a cantinière who was "wounded in the head bound up her wound and returned to the combat post." On the Châtillon plateau, a cantinière fought with the National Guard, "loading her weapon, firing, and reloading without stopping." The cantinière of the

68th Battalion was "struck and killed by an artillery shell." The body of a young cantinière, "riddled with bullets," was taken to the Vaugirard *mairie* for identification.[49] Like the references to grieving widows, reports about the cantinières in the Commune press better demonstrated the treachery of Versailles than did the more numerous deaths of men, which were to be expected. In addition, of course, they represented the zeal and selflessness of the Commune's troops.

Because they wore uniforms, the cantinières attracted more attention than the ambulancières. Outsiders and critics of the Commune were inclined to see them as objects of curiosity and ridicule. Gibson described their attire as early as March 19: "Preceding most of the battalions" that marched through the streets "were young women (one to each battalion) dressed in kepi and Bloomer costumes, with a small cask suspended by a strap flung over the shoulders."[50] Another Englishman provided more detail: "Very trim and neat they looked in their pretty costume; a black jacket trimmed with red, fitting tightly to the figure, black trousers with a broad red stripe, covered to the knees with a petticoat of the same stuff, and a broad red band running round it, —all this, together with a Tyrolese hat and feathers, and the little barrel slung across the left shoulder."[51]

The cantinière in her distinctive uniform was easily and frequently caricatured, her representations used to ridicule the National Guard, the Commune, and of course, cantinières themselves. Typical of these drawings is Léonce Shérer's depiction of a cantinière handing out liquor to already drunk guardsmen (fig. 8). Juxtaposing the cantinière's naive cheerfulness to the slovenliness of the men, Shérer simultaneously ridicules the working-class guardsmen and the women who supported them. Paris, not Versailles, would have to worry about a city that was defended by men such as these. Maxine Du Camp played with the same themes of alcohol and stupidity but singled out the ambulancière instead of the cantinière for attention. In his portrayal, "under the pretext of 'reviving' them," she kills the wounded by giving them eau-de-vie instead of the "simple medication that would have healed."[52]

Although the cantinière was most often caricatured as a young, silly, perky girl, other images were also used. The same anonymous Englishman who described the cantinière's costume in such detail, created a maternal image. He reported that he "struck up a great acquaintance with the *cantinière* of the battalion, a kind, motherly woman, who lived in the canteen with her husband and children; . . . [during] the past siege [she provided] her services in the double capacity of *ambulancière* and *cantinière*. She had been decorated, and wore her scrap of red ribbon on her breast. . . . her

FIGURE 8. Léonce Schérer, "The Defenders of the Sector." The verse reads: "Let's go, friends, have courage, / Here is the ray of sunshine that chases away the clouds." *Souvenirs de la Commune.* Bibliothèque Nationale.

only wish was for peace and quietness, to enable her to gain her living honestly.[53]

Charles Bertall, for his part, created three cantinières, foregrounding a forbidding-looking, solid, older woman (fig. 9). Behind her, sketched in lighter tones, are two other figures whom we are presumably supposed to see as other cantinières, inasmuch as the one-word title of the drawing is in the plural. One of the other figures is a young, slim, stylish woman carrying a small basket; the other is a working-class *femme agée*, clothed in the long dress and kerchief of her class and sex and carrying a large market basket. Whatever Bertall's intent may have been, the harshness of the foregrounded figure makes the cantinière look ominous rather than nurturing. The anonymous English editor of Bertall's caricatures declared that "there were *some* among [the citoyennes] perhaps . . . who had Sincerity and Faith in the Cause they espoused. . . . Such as these however were not *Cantinières*, on whom the Men depended for their hot Coffee and Brandy, and to be useful in the thousand and one odd jobs, scarcely suitable for any not already half or wholly unsexed." He went on to blame them for "much of the prolongation of the Strife, and of the wilful destruction of Life and Property in the last days."[54]

Cantinières' and ambulancières' presentations of themselves and their experiences differ markedly from those of the caricaturists. Some, perhaps many, women who adopted these roles were following their husbands. Alix Milliet Payen, the daughter of a republican family and the young wife of a national guardsman, was one. When her husband's battalion was sent to the Issy front in April, she purchased medical supplies, outfitted herself as an ambulancière, and persuaded the authorities to let her follow the men. Like other women who accompanied the troops, she shared their dangerous and primitive conditions. We know something about her experiences from letters she wrote to her mother.[55]

At Issy, Payen and the men camped in a cemetery, without tents or blankets, sheltering when they could in the damaged mausoleums. It rained constantly. At night, she reported, the Versailles bombardment continued unabated and she could not sleep. One man was wounded in the leg and she assisted a doctor in amputating it. She and the doctor then spent the night in a trench, the only safe place available. She worried about her husband, Henri, who had been wounded in the eye by his own gun when it misfired (a common accident). "I assure you," she told her mother, "that I have never heard the shells, balls and bullets so well; the shells from the ramparts are especially fearsome. Our campsite is very picturesque, but the men are very tired. They will be relieved tomorrow morning."[56]

Victorine Brocher, who was also at the battle for Issy, reported that the

FIGURE 9. Bertall, "Cantinières." *Les communeux, 1871: Types, caractères, costumes* (Paris: Gotschalk, 1871). Bibliothèque Nationale.

ambulancières "lacked everything," even bandages and cups for water. "We had to make those wretched men drink from little cartridge boxes." It was harrowing to watch the wounded die during the night, and she reflected, "If I were to live a hundred years, I could not forget that terrible slaughter."[57]

Conditions varied slightly but rarely improved from one part of the front to another. When the men could, they found shelter and blankets for the cantinières and ambulancières, but that was not always possible.[58] On April 24, Payen reported from the Vanves fort, "What a ruin the poor fort is. There are not even two rooms in the barracks where water does not fall. No candles, no straw. The blankets are too wet to use, so the night was scarcely better than in the trenches." Medical supplies were also in short supply.[59]

The work was not for the fainthearted. Some could not tolerate the suffering; others, the battle. The first cantinière Payen met had also volunteered her services so she could be near her husband, but the war was too much for her, and she quickly gave up any attempt at helping the troops and stayed in the village. The captain's wife who was with the guardsmen at their first battle at Issy left early on. Two new ambulancières who arrived in May were very frightened and wanted to leave.[60] In addition to the dangerous and difficult living and working conditions and the injuries and deaths of strangers, which Louise Michel described as the worst she had ever seen,[61] women often had to cope with the injury or death of their own husbands. When Henri Payen, wounded in mid-May, died of infection at the end of the month, Alix was left distraught and exhausted.[62]

Some of the women who accompanied the Commune's troops did not survive. On May 6 the diary of two National Guard officers at the Issy fortress reported, "The battery at Fleury is sending us regularly six shots every five minutes. —They have just brought into the first-aid post a cantinière who has been hit by a bullet in the left side of the groin. For four days, three women have gone under the most severe fire to succor the wounded. Now this one is dying and begs us to look after her two small children."[63] Victorine Brocher was one of the two cantinières who survived.[64]

Capture by the Versailles troops could have gender-specific consequences. The geographer Elisée Reclus, who was captured in the early April fighting, later recorded how a cantinière who was being marched to Versailles with him and other men was threatened. "The poor woman was in the row in front of mine," he wrote, "alongside of her husband. She was not at all pretty, nor was she young: rather [she was] a poor, middle-aged proletarian, small, marching with difficulty. Insults rained down upon her, all from officers prancing on horseback along the road." A young officer volunteered, "You know what we're going to do with her? We're going to screw her with a red-hot iron."[65] In mid-May reports circulated that five Versailles soldiers had raped and killed an ambulancière as she tried to aid a wounded man.[66]

The Communard press, like the letters and diaries of some guardsmen, resisted the silly and sinister caricatures of the cantinières and ambulancières and presented them as brave, self-sacrificing heroines, but the attitude of the Commune leaders and generals toward the woman who risked their lives for the Commune was not always supportive. On May 6, André Léo, the only known female journalist of the Commune, wrote a searing article for *La Sociale* about the experiences of nine ambulancières who risked their lives on the front line, only to be insulted by National Guard officers and forced to return to Paris.

Carrying a red cross to identify themselves as aid workers, the women set out for the front on May 2. Four of them stayed with the 34th Battalion when they reached it, and five continued on to Levallois where the fighting was taking place. The officer in charge there declared that he knew nothing about "the ambulances or the wounded" and told them to find them themselves. Unable to do so, the women continued on to the headquarters of General Jaroslav Dombrowski at Neuilly, where they were misled by a physician, rebuffed by a superior officer, and insulted by a young officer who, "encouraged by the curtness of his superior [officers]," made a "jest in bad taste."[67]

Finally befriended by an enlisted man, the women were taken to three women who were already attached to these troops, including Louise Michel who had left Issy when the attack had shifted to Neuilly. Michel, who had fought with the National Guard at Issy, was now unarmed and dressed in "feminine clothing." When someone pointedly asked if the National Guard "could not provide a gun for the woman who, they say, was the best combattant at Issy," Louise Michel responded, "If only they would let me care for the wounded. You would not believe the obstacles, the jokes, the hostility!" Then, as if to demonstrate the truth of her remarks, the officers placed the nine ambulancières under guard and escorted them back to Paris as though they were the enemy, despite the fighting and the likelihood that casualties would need medical aid.[68]

The heroes, villains, and victims in Léo's article are clear, as is her political message. The ordinary, working-class guardsmen, who treated the women with "respect, fraternity and sincerity," were the true revolutionaries. The officers and physicians attached to the troops who harassed and rebuffed the women, displayed a "bourgeois and authoritarian spirit," more in keeping with Versailles than with the Commune. The women, whom Léo represents as naively feeling "humiliated by the treatment they received," were both victims and heroines. They had bravely tried to help the guardsmen and had been mistreated by officers and physicians.[69]

Léo's criticism of the officer corps led to a speedy response by Louis Rossel, the Commune's delegate of war, who publicly asked her for advice on how best to use the assistance of women and denounced the May 1 order of the Committee of Public Safety (proscribing the presence of women in the aid stations at the front) which had fueled the incident.[70] However ready Rossel may have been to accept the women's help, the insolence with which they were treated suggests that the military commanders were more than happy to comply with the Committee of Public Safety's order, despite the need for the women's services. The commander's reactions to the women who accompanied the guardsmen to the front were at odds with the image of the ambulancières and cantinières to be seen in the writings of guardsmen and journalists. Alphonse Freye, for instance, asked the *Cri du Peuple* in early May for "a small corner" in which to thank the ambulancière with the 169th Battalion who had saved his life when he was wounded in the fighting.[71] His portrait of the angel of mercy is directly opposed to the meddlesome, troublesome female who provoked the hostility of the officers.

Female Demonstrators

When open warfare between Paris and Versailles began in early April, women sought ways to support the National Guard. The Commune press reported on demonstrations and marches of women eager either to participate in the struggle or to end it. On April 5 newspapers carried stories about one or more demonstrations of citoyennes. Groups, ranging in size from seven hundred to twenty, reportedly gathered at the statue personifying the city of Strasbourg in the place de la Concorde and marched around the city with red flags. (Thiers's identification with the Franco-Prussian peace treaty that ceded Strasbourg to Germany made the statue a popular gathering place during the Commune.) The demonstrators proposed to march to Versailles to present the Commune's case or else to join the men who were fighting. In one account the women wanted to protect the men from the enemy by literally placing their bodies in front of them, in another to help them fight. In one account, they carried guns; in others, they did not. In one, they were critical of men who did not want to fight; in another, they prepared to emulate their female ancestors who had "saved the revolution of '89" by marching to Versailles.[72]

One rally was announced in advance in the *Cri du Peuple*. An anonymous woman (*une veritable citoyenne*) called for women to make a final attempt at reconciliation with Versailles before more blood was shed. Women, the announcement suggested, should meet at the Strasbourg statue, march to Versailles, and explain the Parisians' goal ("to remain free") and the city's grievances (Paris had been "slandered, betrayed, and a secret attempt made to disarm her").[73]

Beatrix Excoffons, a young working-class woman, reported that she went to the announced meeting at the place de la Concorde where she joined a procession of seven hundred to eight hundred women. Some talked of "explaining to Versailles what Paris wanted," and "others talked about how things were a hundred years ago when the women of Paris had once before gone to Versailles to carry off the baker and the baker's wife and the baker's little boy, as they said then."[74] (The reference is to the women's march to Versailles in October 1789 which resulted in the return of Louis XVI (the baker), Marie Antoinette (the baker's wife), and the dauphin (the baker's little boy) to Paris.)

In Belleville, a group of women whose husbands were fighting on the Versailles side reportedly proposed to march at the head of the Parisian forces to see "if the *ex–sergents de ville* [their husbands] would also kill their wives."[75] Augustine-Melvine Blanchecotte, a bourgeois woman who kept a diary during these months, similarly reported that she had heard a young woman propose to a group of national guardsmen (perhaps in Belleville) that they should "have the wives of the *sergents de ville* stationed in Paris march before them, so the army of Versailles will not fire."[76]

Despite their intentions, most of these groups never left the city. Some were stopped by the National Guard; others may have had only a demonstration in mind. A small group led by Beatrix Excoffons when the larger demonstration splintered may have been the sole exception. Excoffons suggested to her group that "while there were not enough of [them] to go to Versailles, there were enough to go tend the injured in the Commune's marching companies." They purchased medical supplies, persuaded the National Guard to let them leave the city, crossed the Seine, and made their way to the Issy fortress, where they joined the ranks of the ambulancières.[77]

The Commune newspapers reported briefly but sympathetically on the women's demonstrations, presenting the marchers as women of the people engaged in appropriate female activity on behalf of the Commune. Not everyone agreed with this view. Foreign correspondents, bourgeois Parisians, and even some supporters of the Commune were critical of the women, although the content of their criticisms varied. The mildest came from Commune supporters. Paul Lanjalley and Paul Corriez, for instance, writing in 1871, disingenuously declared that they were not going "to ridicule the slightly theatrical enthusiasm" of the female demonstrators who wanted to "join their husbands"—a statement reminiscent of Marc Anthony's disingenuous declaration that he had "come to bury Caesar, not to praise him."[78]

The *Times* correspondent was more direct. He reported that an appeal had been made to "the 'manliness' of the women." "They have been told to go and conquer Versailles, like their grandmothers in former times," he wrote. "Three or four hundred presented themselves for this office, and it is not stated whether they were mothers of families. They placed a trumpeter at their head; but there was no Maillard to lead them, and the 'manifestation' failed miserably."[79]

The innuendo, images, contrasts, and tone of the *Times* report reveal the hostility that politically active women could evoke from men who disagreed with their politics and regarded them as crossing gender lines. In stark contrast to the *Cri du Peuple,* which emphasized the femininity of the demonstrators by commenting on their "very proper clothing," "serious and grave" demeanor, "simple and natural" voices, and desire to join their "husbands," the *Times* correspondent questioned their femininity by claiming that an appeal had been made to their "manliness" and asked whether they were really "mothers of families."[80] As was often the case in references to amazons or manly women, what the *Times* reporter raised with one hand— the specter of the unnatural woman warrior—he took away with the other. Manly as these women might have been, they were incapable of success without a real man (Maillard) to lead them. Like Nérac's Jeanne d'Arc (see fig. 7), they were imposters, not real amazons.

"Real women," women who acted within the gender conventions of the day, appear in the next paragraph of the *Times* article, where they stand in explicit contrast to the manly warriors of the demonstrations. As wounded men were brought into the city, "women, this time really wives and mothers, flew to the ramparts, besieged doors, waited, despaired." They deplored the war ("I said so. He would go and fight for the Commune.") and criticized the Commune ("And what is the Commune? I don't know, nor he either. What is certain, however, is that it will not give us back our sons, our husbands, our brothers; and if they do come back, it is not from the Commune that we shall get work. . . . A curse on the Commune, and all who are in office at the Hôtel de Ville!"). The reporter believed that these "real (pacifist) women" were turning against the war, and their reaction would be "irresistible."[81] Whether an abrupt end might have been preferable to the prolonged warfare between Versailles and Paris and the bloody final week is unclear. What is clear is that the *Times* correspondent's perception of the women who supported the Commune did not correspond to his conceptualization of femininity.

Women Warriors

As the war with Versailles continued, the spontaneous demonstrations of early April gave way to serious organizing. On April 11 and 12 a new "Appeal to the Citizenesses of Paris" appeared in Parisian newspapers. This one, unlike that published on the fourth, called the women "to arms" and appealed to the example of their heroic ancestors. "Citoyennes," it asked, "where are our children, our brothers, our husbands? Do you hear the cannons that roar and the tocsin that sounds the sacred call? To arms! The country is in danger! . . . the decisive hour has arrived."[82]

This appeal went considerably farther than had the attempts to mobilize women on April 4. It called for women to join their male kin in battle, to "prepare to defend and to revenge our brothers!" Passive resistance was not the goal, although unarmed self-sacrifice could be tried if all else failed: "If the infamous ones who shoot the prisoners and assassinate our leaders turn their machine guns against a crowd of unarmed women, so much the better! The cry of horror and indignation from France and the world will achieve what we have wanted!" But armed resistance was more desirable than martyrdom, no matter what form it might have to take: "If the guns and bayonets are all being used by our brothers, there will still be paving stones with which to crush the traitors."[83]

An announcement that women who were "ready to die for the triumph of the Revolution" would meet to form committees in each arrondissement for the defense of Paris followed the appeal.[84] The organization that emerged was the Union des Femmes pour la Défense de Paris et les Soins aux Blessés, led by a central organizing committee of eight women and presided over by Elizabeth Dmitrieff. The leaders of the Union des Femmes publicly announced that "the success of the present conflict . . . is as important to the women as it is to the men of Paris" and declared their resolve to "fight until we win or die in defense of our common rights," if the enemy should enter Paris.[85]

When a group of citoyennes pleaded in their capacity as wives and mothers for an armistice so brothers could recognize each other and come to a peaceful solution, the Union des Femmes responded quickly to the "shameful proclamation." "It is not peace but all-out war that the women workers of Paris demand! Conciliation today amounts to betrayal!" they declared. "Paris will not give in. . . . The women of Paris will prove to France and to the world that . . . they are as capable as their brothers of giving up their lives in the cause of the Commune, the cause of the People!"[86]

Public declarations like these, combined with the reactivation of women's vigilance committees (originally created during the Prussian siege), worried conservatives. This was not the way women were supposed to act. Even more alarming, however, were the public appearances of women who spurred on the men and declared their own willingness to fight by their words, their uniforms, and their weapons. Women marching through the streets, clad in various uniforms, carrying weapons, and proposing, at the very least, to join the fighting became a common sight. Conservatives took them and other "exotic" groups as evidence of the Parisian penchant for flamboyant theatricality. D. A. Bingham reported with typical British condescension that "the streets were filled with swash-bucklers who indulged in fanciful uniforms and quaint denominations, and appeared to be under no control." For those who desired more detail, he added a footnote that listed the swashbucklers: "Mohicans of Marseilles, Desperadoes of Tarascon, Outlaws of Carcasson [sic], Amazones [sic] of the Seine, etc."[87] It is true that a variety of military groups, each with its own distinctive uniform, had companies in Paris. Nevertheless, Bingham's statement should be read as caricature not fact.

There probably were not many armed and uniformed women in Paris in 1871, but there had been a proposal to create some female battalions during the Prussian siege, and the ridicule that it had attracted lingered in the public imagination and vocabulary. The proposed battalions, to be called Amazons of the Seine had been the idea of Félix Belly. On October 3, 1870, he had suggested that ten battalions of women, composed of eight companies of 150 women each, should be trained and armed to help defend the barricades against the Prussians. Green posters had broadcast the idea around the city. Women who wished to volunteer were urged to bring a member of the National Guard who could vouch for their good character to 36, rue Turbigo. Belly reported later that fifteen hundred women had signed up, but the National Guard had not been interested in such a battalion.[88]

Belly's views on women were rooted in the gender conceptions of his day, although he combined them in an unusual way. He believed that women would make "model soldiers" not because of their similarities to men but because of their differences. Women, he asserted, "like military uniforms, have an instinct for the war of ambush . . . drink little and above all do not smoke."[89] He also, as Edith Thomas wryly noted, thought of everything. The battalions would be funded by the donations of wealthy women whose jewelry would be confiscated anyway if the Prussians invaded the city. The

FIGURE 10. *The Amazons of the Seine.* "Reviewing recruits." Bibliothèque Nationale.

pay would be 1.5 francs per day (half what the men earned in the National Guard). A female doctor would be attached to each battalion. Appropriate weapons would be selected for the women. And special uniforms with black and orange jackets, pants, and hats would be created for them.[90]

The battalions came into existence only in the public imagination and the drawings of caricaturists,[91] where they lived on well past the end of the war with Prussia. One anonymous caricature was particularly popular (fig. 10). It depicts a small but fully clothed Napoleon III reviewing a collection of female recruits, clad only in boots. The women range from short and chubby to tall and skinny. Some look rather shyly at the ground, others at Napoleon; one peers down at him as though at a small oddity, while another, chubbiest of them all, looks longingly over her shoulder at a shapely "amazon" clad in the proposed uniform.[92] The messages are multiple. The women themselves are ridiculed, as is the idea of female soldiers. They stand at attention (it is a military review), but their size and shape demonstrate their unfitness—and, by extension, all women's unfitness—for military service. These are no athletic amazons. Their interest in the battalion, the artist suggests, lies not in serious political convictions but in looking attractive in military uniforms. The role model in the group seems more qualified for display than for combat. Napoleon III is also lampooned in the cartoon, although he is not subjected to the indignity of nudity. Not only is he placed in the company of these inappropriate warriors, he is shorter than all but one of them, putting his manhood in question.

Ernest Vizetelly represented the women quite differently, but he was no less focused on their physical attributes. He visited Belly's office on the rue Turbigot one day while women were registering for the battalion. There, he reported later, he saw "a staircase crowded with recruits, who were mostly muscular women from five-and-twenty to forty years of age, the older ones sometimes being unduly stout, and not one of them, in my youthful opinion, at all good-looking."[93]

The ridicule surrounding the proposed battalion of amazons was heightened by Jules Allix's plan to arm them with prussic acid. Allix, mayor of the eighth arrondissement and a member of the Commune, was a genuine supporter of women's causes. During the Prussian siege he founded a Committee of Women whose goals were to advance the work, education, social welfare, and rights of women.[94] He was also an inventor and a bit crazy. In 1870 he proposed that the Amazons of the Seine be armed with *doigts prussiques*, rubber thimbles tipped with a small pointed tube full of prussic acid, which they could use to kill Prussians.[95] "The Prussian advances towards you," Allix said, "you put forth your hand, you prick him—he is dead, and you are pure and tranquil."[96] The hilarity generated by this plan in the grim days of the Prussian siege is easy to imagine. Nor has it escaped historians, who have looked for similar relief in telling the history of the two sieges of Paris. The pro-Commune historian Frank Jellinek, for instance, commenting on Allix's election to the "feminine" club at the Gymnase Triat during the siege, observed that "the tall scraggy figure with the venerable beard and wild glare of the crazy prophet was just the sort of solitary male a women's club *would* elect!"[97] While the meaning of this statement is obscure, Jellinek's attempted humor, like that of the caricaturists, is clearly at the expense of women.

Memory of the proposed battalion lingered to undermine and ridicule women who wanted to participate in the city's defense in April and May. The anonymous caricature continued to appear in the streets.[98] On April 12 André Léo took the press to task for ridiculing the idea of a battalion of amazons. It was particularly offensive that men who had celebrated women's heroism in the past now criticized women's desires to defend the Commune. The case in point was Jeanne Hachette, who, like Jeanne d'Arc, was a fifteenth-century French heroine.[99] In 1472, when Beauvais was losing its battle against the duc de Bourgogne, Hachette climbed a wall, seized the Burgundians' standard, and rallied the city's defenders.[100]

The Commune press may have been persuaded by Léo, but critics of the Commune certainly were not. They knew a good opportunity for ridicule when they saw it. Catulle Mendès's eyewitness description of the caricature is liberally sprinkled with misogynist associations and remarks. Allegedly upset by the caricatures that adorned the walls of Paris, he nevertheless described their contents for his readers. The artists, he likened to "highborn and depraved women [who] wear masks and engage in hideous orgies."[101] Then he turned to the Amazons of the Seine. Whereas the artist made fun of the women, Mendès criticized with a heavy hand. The lampooned but not completely unappealing women of the caricature became "formidable monstrosities," "Himalayan masses of flesh," "pyramids of bone," and "creatures of ugliness and immodesty," as though the objects of the artist's imagination were themselves to blame for their appearance and their nakedness.

> Horror of horrors! "Review of the Amazons of Paris," it is called. Oh formidable monstrosities! if the brave Amazons are like these, it will suffice to place them undressed in the first row in battle, and I am sure that not a soldier of the line, not a guardian of the peace, not a gendarme will hesitate a moment at the sight. But in the field, everyone, without exception, will flee in terrified haste, forgetting in their panic even to turn the butt ends of their rifles in the air. One of these Amazons—but why has my sympathy for the amateurs of collections led me into the description of these hideous creatures without clothing?—one of them... but no, I prefer leaving to your imagination those Himalayan masses of flesh and pyramids of bone, these Penthesileas of the Commune of Paris![102]

The number of women who took up arms to help the National Guard, or wanted to, is unclear. Their existence, however, is not. Women carrying guns, sometimes in uniform, sometimes not, were a fairly common sight in Paris. On May 1, for instance, Edmond de Goncourt saw a woman with a rifle on her shoulder in a group of exhausted national guardsmen returning from Issy.[103] In addition to the women who were injured and killed in early April, the Communard papers reported favorably on several women who fought with the National Guard. A woman with the 61st Battalion fought "energetically," "killing several gendarmes and *gardiens de la paix*." The widow of Colonel Rochebrune fought with the 192d Battalion to revenge the death of her husband. A cantinière was shot in the leg when she led the 208th Battalion into battle, shouting, "Vive la Commune!" Another cantinière, when she killed a gendarme who was pursuing her in Neuilly, won an ovation from the crowd watching from behind the city wall. And Louise Michel, who fought in many battles with the National Guard, received considerable attention from the Parisian newspapers.[104]

By the middle of May, rumors about battalions of women were circulating, although reports about the number and size of these groups are contradictory. Vizetelly had heard the rumors and reported that arms were distributed "to a considerable number of female volunteers, who marched to the Hôtel-de-Ville."[105] Sébastien Commissaire, a pro-Commune republican, reported that "companies of women were organized militarily" toward the end of the Commune.[106] The *Times* reported on May 18 that the twelfth legion of the National Guard had formed a battalion of women, "who in addition to their other military duties are to disarm publically all runaways."[107] Communard Benoît Malon reported similarly in his history of the Commune that "on May 12, a company of women organized and armed voluntarily, marched with the twelfth legion."[108] Jules Simon, a member of Thiers's cabinet in Versailles, reported in his memoirs that the Union des Femmes "turned out a battalion of 2500 women, commanded by men, well armed and equipped, who were reviewed on the 15th May in the courtyard of the Tuileries by two general officers, and a delegate of the Commune."[109] How much fighting these groups were engaged in before the semaine sanglante is unclear, but groups of women armed with rifles did defend the barricades during the final week.

Reactions to the Commune's female defenders varied. André Léo regarded them as perfectly normal. "Great causes excite the same sentiments in all human hearts," she said, and women experience "the same passions as men."[110] Her husband, Malon, echoed her thoughts in his memoir: One sees this revolutionary action by women only in the great days of the people," and then it spurs the men on.[111] Jules Claretie, on the contrary, regarded the women as distinctly abnormal. "When we remember," he moaned in 1872, "squads of women, armed, uniformed, bedecked with scarfs around their waists and red cockades, running through the streets and, like hysterics in politics, preparing for the implacable resistance of the last eight days, we can only wonder from what slime the human species is made and what animalistic instincts, hidden and ineradicable, still crouch in the dark soul of mankind!"[112]

Catulle Mendès was similarly appalled; the women warriors, it seemed to him, had abandoned their female roles and were "drunk with hate." "What are these extraordinary beings who give up the housewife's broom and the seamstress's needle for a rifle," he asked. "Who leave their children, to kill beside their lovers and their husbands? Amazons of the street, magnificent and abject, they take their place between Penthesilea and Théroigne de Méricourt [a flamboyant supporter of the revolution of 1789 who wore a red cape and pistols]. . . . What is this rage that seizes these furies? Do they know what they are doing? Do they understand why they are dying?"[113]

Laid out explicitly in Mendès's text and underlying his and Claretie's hyperbole is a fascination with these female warriors. For Claretie, they raised questions about human nature and the origin of the species. For Mendès, they had a kind of nobility. The Commune "has its cantinières as '93 had its tricoteuses," he wrote, "but the cantinières are preferable. In their hideousness, they have a kind of savage grandeur. Repulsive because they are fighting against fellow Frenchmen, against a foreign enemy, these women would be sublime."[114]

Lest women be attracted to such behavior, Mendès hastened to include a moral tale about the consequences of such passion for women. When one of these "viragoes" entered a shop "with her gun on her shoulder and her bayonet covered with blood," and was challenged by a woman, "she sprang upon her adversary, and bit her violently in the throat," and then, before she could fire her gun, "she suddenly turned pale, dropped her gun, and sank to the floor. She was dead. Her fury had caused a rupture of an aneurism."[115] The wages of sin (and this behavior was sinful in Mendès's eyes) were death.

Like the bourgeois literary men who criticized the Commune, anti-Commune caricaturists were also drawn to the female warriors and barricade fighters. In his zodiac series, Nérac presented the female warrior as Jeanne d'Arc, but only to distinguish between the two (see fig. 7). Bertall emphasized the crossing of gender lines in a drawing of a woman with her hair coiled tightly on her head, dressed neatly in an officer's uniform that comes close to disguising her sex (fig. 11). The male and female figures sketched in behind her—men in similar uniforms (albeit not officers' uniforms) and a woman in a dress and shawl—point up the oddness of the *colonelle*. Her right arm and foot mimic those of the woman (although the *colonelle* has only her thumb tucked in her pocket, while the skirted woman has her full hand concealed), but her head and left side repeat the posture of a man who stands on the far right of the drawing. Neither male nor female, she stands alone, an unnatural figure who demonstrates the unnaturalness of the Commune.

Bertall's drawing "The Barricade," places the female warrior in action, capturing the passion and fury that Claretie and Mendès associated with these women (fig. 12). A disheveled amazon, brandishing the red flag of revolution and a burning firebrand (which instantly identifies her not just

FIGURE 11. Bertall, "La Colonelle." *The Communists of Paris, 1871: Types— Physiognomies—Characters with Explanatory Text Descriptive of Each Design Written Expressly for This Edition* (London: Buckingham, 1873).

FIGURE 12. Bertall, "La Barricade." *Les communeux, 1871: Types, caractères, costumes* (Paris: Gotschalk, 1871). Bibliothèque Nationale.

FIGURE 13. *The Taking of Paris (May 1871):* "The Barricade at the Place Blanche defended by women." Bibliothèque Nationale.

as a barricade fighter but as a pétroleuse), prepares to wreak havoc. Like his colonelle and Nérac's Jeanne d'Arc, Bertall's barricade fighter is isolated. Since far more men than women appear to have defended the barricades, and since this work was done collectively, Bertall's decision to represent the barricades with a female figure and to place her in isolation is deliberate. Bertall is not only fascinated by the female warrior. (His representation of her is compelling.) He also uses her feminine fury and isolation, to represent not just the street fighting of May but the unnaturalness of the Commune.

In contrast, a pro-Commune representation of the female defenders of the barricades places women and men within the same frame, working together to defend the Commune (fig. 13). In the foreground of this drawing, a guardsman on horseback leans down to shake hands (a male gesture of approval) with a woman. Behind them, two women help a wounded man away from the barricade while other women and men continue the fight. On the right, a woman reloads her rifle; on the left, a second mounted guardsman points toward the battle. A red flag flies over the scene, and a cloud of smoke rising from the battle obliterates much of the background and part of the barricade. (It also provides a frame within the frame for the figures.) Although the two guardsmen on horses look like figures of authority, the handshake is comradely, as though this woman were in charge of this defense. What distinguishes the women from the men is their clothing. The women wear skirts; the men, pants. Otherwise, gender distinctions would be impossible to make, as Bertall's *colonelle* demonstrates. All these barricade defenders are armed (including those helping the wounded guardsman) and all of them are active.

What seems historically odd about the scene, given its identification as the defense of the place Blanche, is the presence of men. In legend and history, the place Blanche was defended only by 120 women.[116] But the truth the drawing conveys is not historical literalness. Instead, the message lies in the reversals between this scene and those depicted by the anti-Commune caricaturists. Here the communards and communardes work together, caring for each other, respecting each other, and defending both the idea and the existence of the Commune. They will not win, as the viewer knows. They will be overwhelmed as the figures in the drawing are almost dwarfed by the buildings and smoke around them. But they and the cause they defend are portrayed as noble.

Female Orators

By 1871 nightly debates in churches, converted into political clubs, were a standard feature of French revolutions. Ordinary citizens and elected officials, women and men, the old and the young, the educated and uneducated thronged the naves and mounted the pulpits to proclaim their ideals, threaten their enemies, and engage in political theater. For politically minded women, these nightly debates were an important forum, since they were excluded from the electorate and from the governing body of the Commune. Some clubs were exclusively female; others attracted a mixed audience. Paul Fontoulieu, whose history of the churches of Paris under the Commune is the most extensive source of information about the political clubs, commented frequently (and critically) on the attendance and participation of women. We learn from him that there were "as many female as male orators at the Club de Saint-Eustache." At the club in Saint-Leu, "one always saw a large number of women. And at the club in Notre-Dame de la Croix at Ménilmontant, "women were numerous at the meetings and often there were only women." Indeed, "so many women wanted to speak that two or three times there were quarrels."[117]

Many who spoke at the clubs were simply women of the people who had something they wanted to say. Others already were or would become well-known radicals. Louise Michel frequently presided over the Club de la Révolution in the church of Saint-Bernard de la Chapelle. Beatrix Excoffons was the vice-president of the Club de la Boule Noire. André Léo spoke at the Club de la Délivrance at the Trinité. Paule Minck often spoke at the club in the church of Saint-Sulpice and presided over the club at Notre-Dame de la Croix at Ménilmontant.[118]

The women who mounted the pulpits in churches and the lecterns in meeting halls embraced a variety of political positions and espoused a variety of actions. Some focused their attention on priests, nuns, draft dodgers, and the idle rich—the "enemies of the revolution." Others wanted social reforms and political rights for women.

The strain of anticlericalism in the Commune was given voice in the political clubs. Women as well as men called for the investigation, arrest, and execution of priests and nuns. At Saint-Nicolas des Champs, a woman suggested that the bodies of the sixty thousand Parisian priests (her count) should be used instead of sandbags for constructing barricades.[119] At Saint-Eloi, another woman said all the nuns should be thrown in the Seine because they had poisoned the wounded guardsmen in the hospitals.[120] Fontoulieu, who recounted these stories, was particularly concerned about anticlericalism. "It was the rule in all the clubs to excite the worst passions against the Church and its ministers," he announced at the beginning of his book. "The same attacks were reproduced at each session in different forms."[121]

The Commune's anticlericalism alarmed the bourgeoisie in general. In some churches the communards and communardes took over completely. One (Saint-Pierre de Montmartre) was even converted into a workshop where fifty women made military uniforms. The workers turned the main altar into a buffet table for meals and sang, according to Fontoulieu, "the most obscene songs."[122] Such scenes were intolerable to the religious Fontoulieu, but the Commune's anticlericalism was not as strong as that of the Revolution of 1789 had been. In other churches priests and political radicals achieved accommodation; the priests conducted worship services during the day, and the radicals held meetings at night. Such an arrangement was unheard of in the first revolution.[123]

While some women voiced anticlerical sentiments, others devoted their attention to the war and the men who were supposed to be fighting it. Men who shirked service in the national guard by hiding or trying to escape the city were castigated. At Saint-Eloi in the rue de Reuilly, Catherine Rogissart threatened to "tear out the livers" of the "cowards and sluggards" who refused to fight against the "assassins of Versailles." Two days later, another communarde at the same club exhorted women to shoot their husbands if they refused to fight. Others were suspicious of the National Guard officers who, it was alleged, were resisting confrontation with Versailles. Others complained of the way the officers were treating the ambulancières.[124]

The rich were equally unpopular. At Saint-Jacques du Haut-Pas, a cantinière demanded the erection of four permanent guillotines in Paris to terrify the aristocrats. At Saint-Leu, a woman demanded that the rents the rich collected should be "uniformly reduced to 500 francs." At La Trinité a mattress maker wanted to remedy the shortage of linens and mattresses for the mobile hospitals by requisitioning them, or at least the money for them, from the homes of the wealthy. She knew, she said, "some houses where there are heaps of jewels." A woman at La Délivrance told an audience that the rich, along with priests and nuns, should be eliminated. "We will be happy," she declared, "only when we have no more bosses, no more rich people, no more landlords!"[125]

Others demanded the freeing of Auguste Blanqui from jail and proposed the daily execution of hostages until that happened. (Blanqui was a social theorist and veteran revolutionary whose leadership was sorely missed by the Communards. He had been imprisoned by the national government on the eve of the Commune for his role in the October 31, 1870, uprising against the Government of National Defense. The Communards had hoped to exchange him for the archbishop of Paris whom they held captive, but Thiers refused the exchange.) Some urged women to work on the barricades, to become ambulancières, or to take up arms. Women were ready to fight even if the men were not, they declared. On May 12 Nathalie Lemel told a large female audience at La Trinité, "The decisive moment is coming, when we must be prepared to die for our country. No more weakness, no more hesitation! To arms, all of you! Let every woman do her duty!"[126]

The most political women debated the tenets of socialism and republicanism. Others proposed that the houses of prostitution should be abolished and called for the legalization of divorce and the recognition of free unions. Some wanted an end to religious instruction. One woman wanted the flowers that were left in the churches to be given to schoolchildren as prizes. And everywhere women and men sang the "Marseillaise."[127]

What was a serious political activity for communardes and communards was a spectator sport for bourgeois men, who seem to have visited the clubs for the sheer pleasure of being scandalized. Among them were Paul Fontoulieu, Philibert Audebrand, Denis Arthur Bingham, Ernest Vizetelly, Catulle Mendès, Edmond de Goncourt, E. B. Washburne, John Russell Young, Jules Claretie, Maxime Du Camp, and the correspondents for the

Times, and the *Daily News.* As a source of information about the clubs and their female participants, these men were far from unbiased, but they provide most of the information we have, since the Communard press published very little about them.[128]

Several bourgeois observers commented on the decorum of the audience and speakers. Goncourt saw men "automatically raise their hands to their caps," although they left them on when they saw others had not removed them.[129] The *Daily News* correspondent found it odd that the women "dipped their fingers in the now empty basin for holy water, and devoutly crossed themselves," although "none of them appeared in the least degree shocked or even surprised at the desecration that the temple . . . was being subjected to."[130] Bingham, in contrast, thought the "sanctity of the building was not lost upon the scoffers."[131] Young found the audience "quite docile and polite" even when the speeches were boring.[132] Washburne saw "nothing calculated to offend the taste of any one."[133]

The women who frequented the political clubs were primarily from the working class. Those who played organizational or leadership roles wore red scarfs, as did the male leaders of the Commune. Some had pistols tucked into their sashes; most did not. Some smoked pipes; others nursed their babies. Those who did not give speeches "chatted away about every topic, and wandered in and out."[134] To the bourgeois observers, all this behavior, as well as the women's clothing and rhetoric, was shocking. If it had not been, they would have been disappointed. If they heard or saw nothing scandalous, they reported on the rumors that had drawn them to the clubs in the first place. Washburne, for instance, had been told "that they sometimes had there the most extraordinary discussions, in which women mingled, particularly on the interesting subject of divorce," even though when he went, he heard no such discussion.[135] Young believed that if he had stayed long enough, he "might have heard an address or two upon the division of property and the duty of general pillage."[136]

The *Times* correspondent attended a club on the boulevard d'Italie with a female companion whose role was to defend him "from rabid 'citizenesses' in case of danger." The club met in a "filthy room reeking with evil odours." The citizenesses, who seemed quite uninterested in him, were from "the lowest order of society." They wore "loose untidy jackets," surely signifying loose morals, despite the "white frilled caps upon their heads."[137] Fontoulieu, who visited many clubs, was obsessed with the presence of pipe-smoking and armed women.[138]

Catulle Mendès, with heavy sarcasm and insinuations of alcoholism, described the scene he "saw" in Saint-Eustache. Women in "the heroic rags of the ladies who sweep the streets in the morning" were gathered, several of whom "were proud to bear in the center of their faces a [rubicund] nose that could fly over the Hôtel de Ville."[139] The *Daily News* writer, who went to the same meeting at Saint-Eustache and who was more sympathetic to the Commune, saw "respectably dressed women with their grown-up daughters, little shopkeepers' wives with their young families, [and] jolly looking *dames de la halle, cocottes, ouvrières, femmes du peuple*" (market women, loose women, working women, and women of the people), but he also saw "those repulsive looking females of almost all degrees of age who form the typical furies of excited Paris mobs."[140] Washburne and Young, who could find nothing else to criticize, were mesmerized by women knitting,[141] a sure sign of revolutionary violence to come.

The speakers attracted particular attention, represented variously as repellent hags or compelling furies. Mendès saw "a tall gaunt woman with a nose like the beak of a hawk, who appeared to have jaundice."[142] The *Times* correspondent heard "a fine-looking young woman with streaming black hair and flashing eyes . . . [who] looked very handsome, and might have sat for the portrait of one of the heroines of the first Revolution," a "respectable"-looking woman "wearing a decent black gown and bonnet," and a woman who "looked like a laundress."[143] Fontoulieu dwelled less on physical description and more on the immoral and criminal background of prominent speakers. The details were lurid. One woman had committed infanticide; another had been a mistress; a third was a prostitute; a fourth had been condemned five times for theft. One had been nicknamed "the amazon of the insurrection" for her role in the revolution of 1848; another had spent four years in a harem in Constantinople. Some were tried as pétroleuses; two participated in the assassination of the hostages during the semaine sanglante; and another, he claimed, "prowled around the barricades in order to cut off the heads of the dead and perhaps of the living."[144]

The speeches that most interested bourgeois observers were about men, women, marriage, and divorce. (Fontoulieu was an exception; he was most concerned with the women's anticlericalism.) Orations on these topics confirmed the men's worst fears. The women were advocating not only equality between the sexes but an end to marriage, and they were asserting the superiority of women. Western civilization was in danger. Catulle Mendès quoted the woman with a beaklike nose at length: "To be married is to be a slave. . . . [It] cannot be tolerated any longer in a free city. It ought to be considered a crime, and suppressed by the most severe measures." Divorce alone was not a solution. It was only an "Orleanist expedient."[145] Marriage itself had to be abolished. Pausing a moment for "thunderous applause," she next declared that the pension benefits the Commune had

granted to the widows and long-term companions of fallen guardsmen
should be granted to the illegitimate companions only. "We, the illegitimate companions," she announced, "will no longer suffer the legitimate
wives to usurp rights they no longer possess, and which they ought never
to have had at all. Let the decree be modified. All for the free women, none
for the slaves!"[146]

Like bourgeois writers, anti-Commune caricaturists selected divorce as
the issue to convey the scandal of women orators, and to depict them as
anti-male. In "The Grrrreat Female Orator," the well-dressed but far-from-
pretty orator dominates the scene from the raised pulpit in an unnamed
church (fig. 14). She holds a paper with the words "Loi sur le divorce" (Divorce law) out to the crowd below her. To her left and slightly above her is
a small statue of Jesus who holds an olive branch or palm frond in his right
hand. His head is surrounded by a halo; hers by a strange-looking, but presumably stylish, hat. His patient and calm demeanor contrasts with her unhappy bid for attention. Who is at home here, and therefore who is in his
natural place, and who is not, is clear.

Other drawings carried the same theme and message, although they did
not necessarily refer explicitly to divorce. In September, *La Vie Parisienne*
carried a picture by Gillot which also depicted a woman speaking from the
pulpit in a church. Her message, according to the caption under the drawing, was that concubinage would take the place of marriage, which was now
recognized as immoral; women would become men and vice versa; and
children would be recognized as the offspring of everyone.[147] Léonce
Shérer placed a woman, holding a dog under her arm (rather than a child)
in the pulpit, and had her announce, "Citoyennes, death to the men. . . . I
offer mine in sacrifice to the country; you should all do likewise." The audience responds "Yes, yes."[148]

When the *Times* correspondent visited a club, he heard declarations of
women's strengths and men's weaknesses. Much as a "fine-looking young
woman with streaming black hair and flashing eyes" intrigued him, there
was something in her eye that made him think that he "should not like to
be her husband." No doubt he was repelled by her declaration that those
"who call themselves the masters of creation" are "a set of dolts" and her
announcement to the women that the men who "complain of being made
to fight, and are always grumbling over their woes," could go and join "the
craven band at Versailles." The women would defend the city without them.
"We have petroleum, and we have hatchets and strong hearts," she declared, "and are as capable of bearing fatigue as [men]. . . . Those who wish
to fight may do so side by side with us."[149]

The illustrator Frédéric Théodore Lix played with notions of the ama-

FIGURE 14. "The Grrrreat Female Orator of the Grrrrand Amazon Club of the Commune." *Paris sous la Commune.* Bibliothèque Nationale.

zon and betrayals of class and gender in his depiction of the female orator in *Le Monde Illustré.* (fig. 15). Placing an attractive, well-dressed bourgeoise in the pulpit, speaking to a predominantly working-class female audience, he raised questions about bourgeoises who took the Commune's side in the war with Versailles. The elegantly dressed orator seems more at home in the ornate church of Saint-Germain-l'Auxerrois, located beside the palace of the Louvre, than does her working-class audience, and yet the bourgeois readers of *Le Monde Illustré* would have known that she did not belong in the pulpit. Lix's literate audience would also have identified her as an amazon from nineteenth-century paintings. Her fashionable black bonnet is inconsistent with the standard representation of the elegant woman on horseback, but the blackness and elegance of her clothing and her slender physique placed her within the same amazon category.[150]

The audience is full of the same stereotypes that appear in the writings of the bourgeois voyeurs. Larger, because they are foregrounded, and more substantial in physique than the amazon, these representatives of working-class women range in age from young to old. They nurse their babies, relax, gesticulate, talk, and knit. All that is missing is a woman with a pipe in her mouth. By bourgeois standards, they are not very feminine, but they also are not threatening. Lix, like other contemporary bourgeois observers, was intrigued, not frightened, by these women.

Writing later in the decade when French feminists made small but important gains in civil rights and education,[151] Maxime Du Camp believed the goal of the "evil" women of the Commune had been to "elevate themselves above men while exaggerating their vices." "From the pulpit in the churches that were converted into clubs, [the women] revealed themselves," he declared. "In their yapping voices . . . they demanded 'their place in the sun, their civil rights, the equality that had been refused them' and other vague claims that hide perhaps the secret dream that they would gladly put into practice: the plurality of men."[152] "The plurality of men" (*la pluralité des hommes*) is an unusual phrase whose meaning is difficult to discern. Du Camp may have been insinuating any number of things: that women wanted to extend the rights of men (*les droits des hommes*) to women; that they wanted to become men; that they wanted to share men sexually; or even that they wanted to institute polyandry. Given the vitriolic tone of Du Camp's statement, it is clear that he found the women themselves as well as their ideas repellent. Unlike the many women who would claim political rights on the basis of their differences from men, the communardes, he believed, acted more like men than women. By speaking in public—an activity that was reserved for men—they were figuratively, if not literally, masculinized.

FIGURE 15. Frédéric Lix, "Scenes of Paris—A meeting of the women's club in the church of Saint-Germain-l'Auxerrois." *Le Monde Illustré,* May 20, 1871, p. 312. Bibliothèque Nationale.

Vizetelly, whose details about the speakers are not his own but are drawn from Fontoulieu's work, wrote in 1914 when the woman suffrage movement was a topic of considerable debate and turmoil in Britain. Departing from his sources, he associated the woman who was alleged to have decapitated corpses with his own particular nemesis, the suffragettes. "At the club," he reported, "this creature raved frantically, her face wearing the while much the same expression as that which may be observed on the countenances of militant suffragettes when they are hurling choice imprecations at police-magistrates and others. She was doubtless of much the same breed—the breed of the *possédées de Loudun* and the *convulsionnaires de Saint-Médard.*"[153]

Later historians sometimes adopted the same deprecating tone as their bourgeois sources in discussing the political clubs, but their focus was on sex, not politics. Alistair Horne, in his only reference to the "Red Clubs," reported that "at St.-Eustache Washburne listened to a *tricoteuse* ranting from the pulpit, in favour of the abolition of marriage."[154] In fact, this statement misreports Washburne. Richard Cobb opined that "most of the spokeswomen of the movement . . . probably . . . were as much concerned with clerical condemnation of free love and of the unmarried mother as with the Church as a pillar of Versaillais order."[155] To these twentieth-century men, the politically radicalized communardes seemed as irrational and threatening as they had to their nineteenth-century bourgeois critics, but the threat appeared moral rather than political. Having left their place beside the hearth and ventured into the pulpit, the communardes were the very antithesis of womanhood and a threat to morality and civilization. Their ideas, therefore, did not have to be taken seriously. Indeed, historians were so convinced that they knew what the women really wanted (free love), that they did not have to quote their sources correctly, and they could wander into the terrain of "probably" without trepidation.

As contemporaries and historians have told the story of the Commune, they have drawn upon what Marina Warner calls "a lexicon of female types" to explain and contain the actions of its female adherents.[156] The lexicon includes grieving mothers and widows, dedicated and heroic amazon warriors, horrific furies, scandalous orators, and angels of mercy. All these categories were culturally available in 1871. Some were very old; others had acquired new connotations in the preceding century of revolution; but all of them defined and limited understanding of the Commune by caricaturing the actions of its women and denying the complex and conflicting thoughts and feelings that motivated them.

The major appeal of these female types lay in their ability to convey moral and political judgments about women and the Commune. Both sides in the conflict could and did use female victims and grieving women to focus attention upon the evils of the opposition. Cantinières and ambulancières who accompanied the guardsmen into battle symbolized the nobility of the Commune's cause to its supporters, but they were objects of ridicule and hatred for the Versaillais. Supporters of Versailles similarly caricatured and villified the public orators and female warriors of the Commune. As the women were ennobled, ridiculed, and villified, so was the Commune. As had long been the case, the women made far better representations than did their male comrades.

For conservatives who opposed the Commune, the most troubling women were its orators and warriors, since they did not have even the facade of a traditional female role to cover their activities, as the cantinières and ambulancières did. They posed a threat to conceptualizations of gender which dichotomized male and female traits. Seen as aggressive rather than passive, self-sufficient rather than helpless, warriors rather than peacemakers, critical rather than supportive of men, self-confident rather than demure, independent rather than dependent, and definitely not fragile, they raised questions about normality and femininity in a culture that defined such traits as natural rather than cultural.

If these were "natural" women, they posed a threat to the organization of society and politics. If they were "unnatural" women, they posed no such threat and the current gender definitions and the cultural institutions based on them could be maintained. Representing them as amazons, furies, tricoteuses, and viragoes protected the boundaries between the sexes by calling their femininity or naturalness into question. The ease with which anti-Commune writers and caricaturists undertook to represent them in this light and the relative ineffectiveness of attempts to represent them more positively, demonstrate the power of cultural categories to mediate understanding and meaning. Women, as well as men, had access to these cultural categories and they saw their own actions, as well as those of other women, in terms of them, as the next chapter will demonstrate.

CHAPTER FOUR

The Femmes Fortes of Paris

M ost of the women, like most of the men, who lived through the Commune, whether they supported or opposed it, are lost to us by the passage of time and scarcity of sources. A few women, however, have left us their own accounts of the Commune. Some wrote anonymous appeals to other women and concealed their names as well as their personal experiences. Others wrote diaries, letters, memoirs, and newspaper articles. Three who left records occupied positions of public prominence: André Léo, the only female journalist of the Commune, who believed passionately in and argued forcefully for sweeping social change; Elizabeth Dmietrieff, who founded and led the Union des Femmes; and Louise Michel, who fought for the Commune from beginning to end, becoming in the process the famous "Red Virgin" of France. A fourth, Céline de Mazade, a young bourgeoise who remained in Paris to keep her family's business afloat, opposed the Commune. A fifth, Augustine-Melvine Blanchecotte, a pacifist dismayed by the conflict, tried to remain neutral.

A more complex view of the Commune's women emerges from these writings than from the general literature, especially the anti-Commune literature, but women's understanding and presentation of themselves (and other women) were influenced, nonetheless, by the same lexicon of female types and conceptualizations of femininity evident in men's representation of them.

The writings that form the basis for this chapter, can by no means be regarded as presenting the entire range of women's experiences and views. But they give us some access to the cultural images and values women used to organize, justify, and make sense out of their experiences. They also reveal some women's judgments of the Commune and its supporters and the gender conceptualizations that informed and limited their actions. The chapter's title comes from Céline de Mazade's identification of herself as a *femme forte* (a strong woman).[1] She claimed the identity lightly as a reassurance to her husband who was worried about her remaining in Paris when he could not. It expresses, however, the way many Parisian women saw themselves during this period. They endured and persevered and, to the surprise of some, thrived as they coped with the second siege of Paris.

Anonymous Appeals

Throughout the Commune, announcements and appeals placarded the city's walls and appeared in its newspapers. Most were directed toward men, but some urged women to take action of one sort or another. Some of the appeals to women were signed by representatives of organizations (usually the Union des Femmes; others were written anonymously. The authorship of the anonymous appeals is, of course, impossible to determine. Some or all of them might have been written by men rather than women. But men on both sides of this conflict demonstrated no reluctance to advise women openly on what they should and should not do. Nor is there any evidence that the anonymous appeals were written by men. I have assumed, therefore, that anonymous authors who exhorted women to act were women.

The first anonymous female-authored article appeared in the *Cri du Peuple* on April 4, the third day of fighting between Versailles and Paris. The writer, *une véritable citoyenne* (a real woman citizen), called upon women "of all classes" to go to Versailles to explain "what the Revolution of Paris is about" and to make "a final attempt at reconciliation" between the cities. The *véritable citoyenne* urged peace not because she was a political neutral. She was a communarde. For her, the guilt of Versailles and the innocence of Paris were beyond question. Versailles had "slandered," "betrayed," and "tried to disarm Paris by surprise." In response, the city had created the Commune because it wanted "to remain free." Far from being the aggressor in this conflict, Paris had acted only to "defend herself" against attack.[2]

Despite its crimes, Versailles, the *véritable citoyenne* believed, might be susceptible to persuasion. If it were presented with the truth about the Commune, surely it would abandon its attack on the city. Even if it now mended its ways, however, the writer believed the aggressor must be held responsible "for the blood of our brothers, . . . and for our breavement."[3] How Versailles was to be held responsible was unclear.

Two days later, when the first ceremonial funeral for fallen guardsmen was held, a longer article, signed by *une vraie citoyenne* (a true woman citizen), appeared in the same newspaper. Despite the change in the writer's nom de plume, the two pieces may have been written by the same person. At the very least, the writers seem to have been in communication with each other. The *vraie citoyenne* acknowledged that the military victories of Versailles had destroyed any hope of reconciliation between the Commune and the government of France. "We would have gone to Versailles," she wrote. "We would have stopped the shedding of blood. . . . We would have carried the grievances of our fathers, husbands, and children to Versailles." But "the government has attacked Paris, blood has flowed," and a mission of "conciliation and humanity" was no longer possible. So she issued a new appeal. Women should return to their families, organize aid stations, encourage the National Guard, and care for the wounded. They should not engage in further demonstrations, for these might "impede the movement of the troops and the orders of the Commune." But if the time for demonstrations and reconciliation had passed, the time for judgment had not. Like the *véritable citoyenne*, the *vraie citoyenne* held the government of Versailles responsible for the "spilling of blood" and praised the Commune for its "calm and serious" decisions and "humane" actions.[4]

The gender divisions and political judgments of the two statements are identical. Both writers appealed only to women; they made no attempt to speak to or for men. Peacemaking or "conciliation" was women's peculiar mission; war, in a sense, was men's. If peacemaking failed, as it had in this case, they believed men should fight and women should care for the wounded. There is no hint in either appeal that women should take up arms and join men in the city's defense. But if women could not stop the war or even participate in it, they could pass judgment on it and its instigators. (The very notion that peace was preferable to war involved moral judgment.) Both writers believed firmly in women's right to judge men's actions, and when they did so, they no longer saw themselves as speaking to and for women alone. In an interesting use and reversal of female allegory, they saw themselves, if not as the nation, at least as its moral conscience. "Before our hearts and before all of France," the *vraie citoyenne* declared, "we will hold the government of Versailles responsible for [its actions]."[5]

There were no shades of gray in these women's assignment of culpability. Versailles had signed the treaty that allowed the triumphal march of the Prussians through Paris, had authorized the secret attempt to remove the cannons on March 18, had slandered Paris for the deaths of the generals, and had attacked the city.[6] It was thus guilty of betrayal, slander, attack, and the killing of Frenchmen. The Commune, in contrast, had established "an honest and simple government . . . a government of freedom and work that will convey, as soon as possible, a little well-being to all indigents."[7] Guilty of nothing, Paris was the repository of honesty, self-defense, freedom, and work.

Five days later (April 11), angrier and more aggressive female voices were raised in the Commune newspapers. An anonymous *groupe des citoyennes* (group of female citizens), who would become the founders of the Union des Femmes and whose identities can therefore be guessed at but not precisely determined, issued an appeal to women that moved beyond reconciliation and care of the wounded to revenge and armed defense of the city. Like the *véritable* and *vraie citoyennes*, these women claimed the right to speak on the basis of their womanhood, identifying themselves as the "mothers, wives and sisters of the French people." They also spoke only to women and not to men (although they spoke at length about men), and they appealed to women's fears for their children, brothers, and husbands. Unlike the *véritable* and *vraie citoyennes*, however, they placed their appeal in a longer historical context than the current revolution, appealing to women as "the descendants of the women of the grand Revolution."[8]

Like the real and true citoyennes, these women believed that they had the right to judge the conflict between Paris and Versailles, but their judgments were harsher and more ideological than those expressed on the fourth and sixth. The Versailles government was not just the guilty party; it was the enemy of the people of Paris. It had exploited, oppressed, and executed the people and forced them to work without just compensation; it had initiated a fratricidal civil war; and it had executed its prisoners of war. The language of these citoyennes was harsh. The Versaillais were "assassins of the people, . . . oppressors, who want to annihilate Paris." The Commune, on the other hand, was the champion of liberty, equality, and fraternity (the ideals of the Revolution of 1789). It wanted "government of the people [and] by the people," the end of exploiters and masters, and "work and well-being for everyone." "All civilized people," they declared, are watching to see if freedom will finally triumph against oppression in Paris, so they can "free themselves in their turn."[9]

Central to the group's analysis of the war was its analysis of class conflict. Unlike the *véritable* and *vraie citoyennes* who appealed to "women of all classes," the *groupe des citoyennes* saw the civil war between Paris and Versailles as part of a long struggle between the rich and the poor. The Versaillais were not just guilty of betraying Paris; they were "the privileged . . . who have always lived on [the people's] sweat and grown fat on [the people's] misery." In their eyes, the war was "the final act of the eternal antagonism between right and might, between work and exploitation, between the people and its executioners!" Among the most important Parisian demands were the right to work and the workers' right to the product of their labor.[10] To the women who made this analysis, any appeal to the women of all classes would have seemed idiotic.

Appeals for conciliation seemed equally nonsensical. In sharp distinction to the *véritable* and *vraie citoyennes*, the *groupe des citoyennes* called on women not to care for the wounded but to prepare to fight and die. They wanted revenge, not reconciliation; victory, not peace. "Citoyennes, resolute, united, watching over the safety of our cause," they cried, "let us prepare to defend and to revenge our brothers! At the gates of Paris, on the barricades, in the faubourgs, no matter where, we must be prepared to join our efforts to theirs at the right moment." Defense of the Commune was the important thing, but if Versailles chose to turn its guns against innocent women, their deaths might serve a great symbolic good. "If the infamous ones who shoot the prisoners and assassinate our leaders turn their machine guns against a crowd of unarmed women, so much the better! The cry of horror and indignation from France and the world will achieve what we have wanted!" But such innocence and martyrdom were not what they advocated; they wanted women to fight with whatever weapons came to hand—guns, bayonets, or even paving stones.[11]

Although this call to arms was the direct opposite of the calls to conciliation, similar conceptions of gender underlay the exhortations. All the writers identified themselves as citizens, but they based their appeals not on citizenship but on their shared gender. Whether they urged women to take up arms, to care for the wounded, or to work for conciliation, the basis on which they urged them to act was the same: it was their duty as women to save as many men (their brothers, husbands, and sons) as possible. Because women cared about men (as adults and children), not because they were like men, they would have to act like them. The *groupe des citoyennes* put it this way: when mothers and wives realize that "the only way to save those who are dear to them—the husband who supports them, the child in which they place their hopes—is to take an active part in the battle," they will do so.[12]

All the writers saw the ideological uses and moral authority of the unarmed woman. The *véritable citoyenne* believed women (by definition unarmed) could engage in moral suasion; the *vraie citoyenne*, that they were the nation's conscience; the *groupe des citoyennes*, that the deaths of unarmed women would create an outcry of "horror and indignation."[13] All these proposals were based in the cultural designation of men as the defenders of women. Where the writers differed was on whether women should cross the gender line and take up arms themselves. The *groupe des citoyennes* thought, at the very least, that the survival of the Commune required women to cross this gender line. For them the choice was to "win or die," and winning would necessitate joining the men in combat. The *vraie citoyenne,* in contrast, stayed within gender conventions by calling on women to care for the wounded but not to fight.

Dmietrieff and the Union des Femmes

The appeal of the *groupe des citoyennes* was followed immediately by the announcement of a meeting, at which the Union des Femmes was created. The leading force behind this organization was Elizabeth Dmietrieff, a young Russian radical who was a friend of Karl Marx and a member of the International Working Men's Association. The Union des Femmes would function as the women's section of the French branch of the International and would win considerable attention from the national government once the Commune was defeated.[14]

The Union des Femmes always spoke with a collective voice, but Dmitrieff's ideas and influence can be seen in its public statements, which were more concrete in their demands, more feminist in their ideology, and more ideological in their view of the Commune than the earlier anonymous appeals to women. The union's first public statement appeared on April 14 in the *Journal Officiel.* For Dmietrieff and the Union des Femmes, the Commune represented "the extinction of all privilege and inequality," the "end of corruption," the "regeneration of society," and "the rule of labor and justice." By implication, the Versailles government represented the opposite values: privilege, inequality, corruption, the denigration of labor, and injustice. This struggle between good and evil could not be reconciled. In language that reverberated with religious imagery—the battle of Jericho ("danger is imminent and the enemy is at the gates of Paris"), sacred causes ("it is the duty and the right of everyone to fight for the sacred cause of the people") and apocalyptic struggle ("to put an end to corruption and ultimately to regenerate society")—the Union des Femmes urged women to prepare to "fight to the finish."[15]

In conceptualizing gender, the statement went well beyond the thinking of the *véritable* and *vraie citoyennes* and the *groupe des citoyennes.* From its opening sentence, the Union des Femmes moved away from justifying women's support of the Commune on the basis of their relationships with men; they justified it, indeed demanded it, on the basis of men's and women's common interest in the outcome of the struggle. Women, as individuals, not only had a right to join in the fighting but had as much at stake in the outcome of the struggle as men did. It was as much their "sacred cause" as it was men's. It was "the duty and the right of everyone" to defend the revolution.[16]

Elizabeth Dmietrieff and the other seven signers of the article did not speak *to* women, as previous writers had, but *for* women and *to* the leaders of the Commune, declaring women's interests in the Commune and their right to be heard. Women had grievances too, they asserted, departing from the *vraie citoyenne,* who urged women to carry men's grievances to Versailles, as though women had no grievances of their own. Versailles had discriminated against women "as a means of maintaining the privileges of the ruling classes." Later, in an undated letter to the Commune's Commission on Labor and Exchange, Elizabeth Dmietrieff, signing for the Executive Commission of the Union des Femmes Central Committee, clarified the nature of the discrimination women had suffered. "The work of women was the most exploited of all in the social order of the past," she wrote, and "its immediate reorganization is urgent." In addition to other reforms in the organization and duration of work, which she believed would benefit all workers, Dmietrieff called for "the end of all competition between male and female workers" and "equal pay for equal hours of work"—proposals that would have increased employment and wages for women.[17]

Dmietrieff was worried that the "increasing poverty" created by the "suppression of work for no apparent reason," would persuade "the feminine element of the Parisian population, revolutionary for the moment, to return to the passive and more or less reactionary state that the past social order had created for them."[18] Dmietrieff's fear may not have been unfounded, for in the late 1790s women's disaffection had undermined the Revolution and led to the reopening of churches.[19] But it reveals the considerable extent to which even the most active and articulate Communard women feared the hold of the past on women. Such a fear was never articulated with regard to working-class men, whose loyalty to the Commune was accepted largely without question by Commune leaders, the existence of draft dodgers notwithstanding.[20] To ensure women's loyalty, Dmietrieff argued, the Commune would have to ensure work and justice for everyone. To that end, she thought the Union des Femmes should reorganize the distribute work to the women of Paris, beginning with the manufacture of military supplies. The Commune's contribution to this plan would be to fund the reopening of abandoned factories and workshops that had primarily employed women.

A Public Disagreement

In April the differences in these calls to action might have been interpreted as the progressive radicalization and politicization of women's thoughts on the Commune and what their role in it should be. In May it became clear that they were evidence of conflicting female views, when a second anonymous *groupe de citoyennes* placarded the walls of Paris with a call for an armistice. They spoke, they said, "in the name of the country, in the name of honor, even in the name of humanity," and for women. "All women," they declared, "those who have small children whom the bombs can find in their cradles, those whose husbands fight out of conviction, those whose husbands or sons earn their daily bread on the ramparts, those who today guard their homes alone, . . . wish for Peace! Peace!" (Ambulancières, cantinières, and communardes who had taken up arms and might not have wanted peace at any cost are notably missing from this litany.) The request was a supplication, not a demand. This group claimed the right to speak on the basis of their "courageous resignation," not their activism. They were "weary of suffering" and "appalled at the misfortune" that threatened them again. They wanted to protect their children and their husbands. They wanted an end to the war, not a victory.[21]

This call for peace resembles that of the *véritable citoyenne* who wrote the call for reconciliation published on April 4. The *véritable citoyenne* appealed to "the women of all classes"; the group wrote on behalf of "the women of Paris." Both appeals presented women as united across class if not across geographical lines. Both conjured up images of dead men and grieving women. Both assumed and accepted a gender hierarchy, speaking out of their concern for men, not as their equals. Both sought an immediate end to the bloodshed and reconciliation between Paris and Versailles.

But there are significant differences between the statements as well. The *véritable citoyenne* who wrote in April was a communarde, and she blamed Versailles for the strife. She considered women capable of logical and persuasive reasoning, able to persuade the Versailles government that it was responsible for the bloodshed and should reconcile with Paris. The citoyennes who wrote on May 3 took no side and cast no blame. They appealed to both Versailles and Paris to lay down their arms. Although they argued a case for peace, they hoped to change the "hearts," not the minds, of the antagonists. Their appeal was to the "generosity," not the intelligence, of the two sides. Regardless of the issues and causes of the war, they asked the men to stop fighting, essentially as a gift to the women, who were frightened for their husbands and children.

The Union des Femmes was appalled. Two days later, it too placarded the city. The union was barely able to control its outrage at the "anonymous group of reactionary women" who had written such a "shocking proclamation." In contrast to the citoyennes who had spoken in the name of "country, honor, and humanity," the union spoke in the name of "the social revolution, the right to work, and equality and justice," socialist republican principles that immediately indicated their commitment to the Commune. Sliding into sarcasm, the Union des Femmes denounced the self-contradictions in the proposal. The generosity of Versailles was the "generosity of cowardly assassins"; conciliation between the two sides would be the "conciliation between freedom and despotism." There could be no compromise. A negotiated peace would be the equivalent of defeat. It would destroy the workers' hopes for "complete social transformation, . . . for the suppression of all privileges and exploitation, for the substitution of the reign of work for the reign of capital." In short, it would be "treason."[22]

As it had on April 14, the Union des Femmes spoke not to women but for women. It made no pretense, however, of speaking for all women. These women's identification was with "the working women of Paris." They were not pacifists; they wanted victory. "The torrents of blood shed for the cause of liberty," the union declared, entitled the people (by which it meant the workers) of Paris to "glory and vengeance." Refusing to accept the gender conceptualizations that made them the inferior supplicants of men, they urged women to prove that they knew how to "shed their blood and give their lives for the defense and triumph of the Commune," just as their brothers did. In their utopian vision of the "social and universal republic," working men and women would be "joined in solidarity."[23]

André Léo

The most prominent individual female voice in the Commune press was André Léo's. Unknown to some of her readers, perhaps, but well known to other journalists and the political leaders of the Commune, André Léo was not the man she appeared to be in print. She was Léodile Bréa Champseix, the only female journalist of the Commune. Born in 1832, married in 1851 to Grégoire Champseix, and widowed in 1863, Léodile Champseix was the mother of twin boys, André and Léo, the source of her pseudonym.[24] She married Benoît Malon, a member of the Commune, whose praise of her in his history indicated the difficulties even radical men had in categorizing the femmes fortes of the Commune. "This woman," Malon wrote, "whose name is among those of the greatest writers of our time, and whom Rossel, who knew what he was talking about, called *'citoyen'* André Léo, was equally devoted to the cause of the people and to serving it with her writings, her speeches, and her total support."[25]

Léo began her literary career writing novels, but by the later years of the Second Empire, she had turned to speaking and writing about politics and women's rights. In 1869 she published a long political essay, *La femme et les moeurs: Liberté ou monarchie*, in which she contrasted the realities of women's lives, which no one talked about, to the bourgeois view of women. The reality was grim. She cited "the frightful and growing number of abandoned children; the friendless young girls [*filles délaissées*]; the prostitutes and courtesans; the workers debilitated by excessive work and poverty; . . . the mothers of families, beaten, exploited, and raped by their husbands; the traffic in dowries, in marriage; the exploitation of poor girls in free unions." This was the actual treatment of the women whom bourgeois men imagined to be "delicate and charming, born for the pleasure of men." Among other things, such a fantasy allowed bourgeois men to see themselves as "strong and chivalrous."[26] Léo's outrage was palpable.

Léo was particularly angry at the advocates of democracy who "proclaimed that liberty was necessary for the dignity and morality of human beings" and yet believed that "to give women liberty would infallibly create a monster of egotism and indecency." What was at stake in this inconsistency, she knew, was the perpetuation of male-dominated marriage. Men who badly wanted to end political and social hierarchies wanted no such change in marriage. If husband and wife were equal, men worried, who would make decisions? In marriage there had to be "one head, one direction." Léo thought such arguments were self-serving. Nor could she accept the exclusion of women from the franchise and other forms of political and social equality. In her view, women were slaves, at work and in marriage, and the only way to end their enslavement (and hence the enslavement of their children) was to extend equal rights to them. Only then could a truly democratic society be achieved.[27]

The journal *La Sociale* was Léo's major forum during the Commune.[28] In it, she championed the Commune's cause, praised the men who defended it against Versailles, and criticized its leaders whenever she thought they had acted foolishly or injudiciously. In contrast to the anonymous citoyennes and the Union des Femmes, Léo spoke neither to nor for

women. She spoke to men and for herself. A socialist but a member of no
particular faction, she was one of the Commune's most intelligent critics.
She was deeply concerned about the failure of the Commune leaders to
seek the support of the provinces,[29] to control its most fanatical as well as
its most conservative members, and to accept and mobilize the support of
women. She was convinced that each of these failures weakened the Commune; together, they could lead to defeat.

Of all the Commune journalists, only André Léo addressed the subject
of women. For her, the Commune's rejection of women's offers of help was
a major problem both for women and for the success of the revolution. Between *La Sociale*'s first and last issues (March 31 and May 17), she wrote
four long articles, describing, analyzing, and criticizing the Commune
leaders' attitudes toward women. Like Elizabeth Dmietrieff, she feared
that the working women of Paris might abandon the revolution if the Commune leaders did not seek their help and if their vision of the future did
not include equal rights for women.

In an April 12 article titled "Toutes avec tous" (All women and all men
together), Léo introduced the themes that interested her: women's commitment to the revolution, men's narrow-minded refusal of women's offers of help, and the potential consequences of their obstinacy. First, she
declared, "we should recognize that all great causes excite the same sentiments in all human hearts, and that unless they are simple vegetative phenomena, women must feel the same strong passions as men do in such moments." Women, of course, were not "simple vegetative phenomena," and
their passion for the revolution was the same as men's. Like men, they had
"naturally" participated in the defense of Paris during the first siege, vol-
unteering for the Amazones de la Seine even when there were already am-
ple numbers of troops to defend the city. Now, women were defending the
barricades alongside men. Only fools would deny their commitment to the
Commune, and those who did so ran the risk of undermining it. Not only
did Paris face a shortage of soldiers and need the help of women but those
who were denying women the right to participate in the Commune's defense were risking the possibility that women would turn against the revolution. "Until now," she declared, "democracy has been defeated by
women, and democracy will triumph only with them."[30]

From Léo's perspective, women's detractors were not just shortsighted;
they were hypocrites. The very men who had celebrated the heroism of
women in the past were ridiculing and slandering the women who wanted
to defend the Commune. In response to such hypocrisy, Léo argued that
men and women were equal on the only level that mattered, or should matter, in the current circumstances: they were willing to sacrifice themselves

for a great cause. "Every human being has an instinct for [self-] preservation," she wrote, "and it is not a beard, but a superior passion, that [allows one to] overcome this instinct." Women had this passion, and they were "suffering from the inaction" that Commune leaders had imposed upon them. A "holy fever" was burning in their hearts. Like men, they were willing to sacrifice themselves for the cause.[31]

Léo did not say that all women should take up arms. Some, such as young mothers who needed to be by their children's cradles, clearly could not do so. But the women who were willing to fight should not be denied the right to defend the city. Moreover, the National Guard needed women's help, as a recent battle outside the walls of Paris had amply demonstrated. "The men, who endure great hardship in the face of death, are poorly nourished and poorly aided," she wrote. "The medical care for the wounded is neither prompt enough nor abundant enough." That women were not allowed to help the troops was disgraceful. "Is it not lamentable," she asked her readers, "that these brave men, whose heroism excites our admiration and who have the right to so much recognition from us, lacked the necessities of life at our very gates? Is this the way we honor those who serve us?"[32]

That the leaders of the Commune and the National Guard were responsible for the policies that excluded women was clear. To them she offered both practical advice—they should create registers of women who were willing to help defend the city and support the troops—and a victory scenario—the presence of women on the battlefield would tell the Versailles troops "that what they have in front of them is not a faction but a whole people, whose conscience . . . is raised up for vengeance." A whole people, men and women fighting together, could not be defeated, and "the little historian [Thiers] who attacks the great city" would be forced to add a new paragraph to his history, a paragraph that would say: "There was then in Paris such a frenzy for liberty, equality, and justice that the women fought alongside the men, and in this city of two million souls, there was enough moral force and energy to withstand all the rest of France and to defeat the material effort of two armies."[33]

By the end of April, Léo's commitment to the Commune and her respect for its soldiers remained undiminished, but her confidence in victory had been shaken by the death toll. "Each day and each night, the ranks are thinned, comrades fall; . . . the mouth that cries, 'Vive la République!' is closed and stiffened. We see the remains of friends and neighbors carried to the cemetery," she wrote, Like her male colleagues, she evoked "the cries of wives and children" to convey the tragedy of these deaths. But she lauded the "dear and noble heroes, soldiers of the idea, poor sublime artisans," for their bravery and their devotion to the revolution. "There is one race, better yet, one class," she declared, "that runs away from putrefaction . . . [which] will spread out over the world and found peace by justice and equality." This class, of course, was the working class.[34]

On May 6 Léo returned to upbraiding the male leaders of the Commune and the National Guard for their hypocrisy, ingratitude, and stupidity in rejecting women's help. The occasion for this critique was the guard's rejection of the services of nine ambulancières. No matter that the wounded needed the ambulancières. No matter that women like Louise Michel had helped defend the fort of Issy. No matter that the National Guard needed the services women could provide—"preparing warm nutritious food for our malnourished combattants," "bringing aid to the wounded and dying," and "work[ing] behind the barricades, to protect against the violation of the city." No matter that the men, the true soldiers of the republic, wanted women's help. Other men, "republican men," who found women's defense of the republic "in other epochs" to be "admirable," found their support of the Commune to be "inconvenient and ridiculous."[35]

Warming to the theme she had introduced three weeks earlier in "Toutes avec tous," Léo contrasted "the narrow and petty, . . . bourgeois and authoritarian" spirit of the revolution's "leaders" to the true revolutionary attitude of the laborers and artisans who understood that they were fighting for the rights of everyone and welcomed the women's efforts. For them, she wrote, "the presence of woman is a joy, a strength. She doubles his courage and his enthusiasm. . . . [She represents] the soul of the city saying to the soldier, 'I am with you. You are doing well.'" Only the Commune leaders and generals, who failed to understand the true nature of the struggle against Versailles, wanted women to stay away from the battlefields.[36]

Two days later, still angry about the National Guard's treatment of the ambulancières, Léo explicated the consequences of ignoring women in "La révolution sans la femme" (The revolution without woman). Having no fear of authority, indeed, being contemptuous of it, Léo lectured Jaroslav Dombrowski, the Polish revolutionary who was commander of the Commune forces, about the importance of women's support. Calling him General Dombrowski at first, Léo quickly switched to "*citoyen* Dombrowski," reminding him in true revolutionary style that he was the equal, not the superior, of the people he had dishonored. Women, she reminded him, were the major actors in the events of March 18. "Do you know, General Dombrowski," she lectured him, "how the Revolution of March 18 began? How it was won? *By the women!* On that great morning, the troops of the line were sent to Montmartre. . . . The national guard, without leaders, without orders, hesitated before an open attack. A few more turns of the [cannons'] wheels, *and you would never have been general of the Commune, citoyen Dombrowski.* But . . . the women, the citoyennes of Montmartre, in the crowd, seized the bridles of the horses, surrounded the soldiers, and said to them: 'What! Are you serving the enemies of the people, you, our children? . . . Are you not ashamed to serve these cowards?'" And the soldiers, hearing the women's "reproaches" and fearing that they might "wound the women and crush their children," "turned the butts of their rifles into the air."[37]

Léo recalled the Revolution of 1789. "Do you think you can make a revolution without the women?" she asked. "Eighty years ago, they tried it, and we are not going to stand for it again." The first French Revolution gave women the title of citoyenne but excluded them from the rights associated with citizenship. "Repulsed by the Revolution, the women returned to Catholicism and formed an immense reactionary force," and the revolution was lost. "When," she asked rhetorically, "will republican men discover that this has gone on long enough? When will [they learn] . . . that women do not want [to be] and cannot be neutral. It is necessary to choose between their hostility and their devotion." Warming to her subject, she suggested that "history since '89 could be written under the title: *The History of the Inconsistencies of the Revolutionary Party.* The subject of women would make the largest chapter, and the one in which one learns how this party found a way to cause half of its troops, who asked only to march and to fight with them, to pass over to the side of the enemy."[38]

Léo believed that men's refusal of women's assistance was based in their fundamental desire to control women rather than to treat them as equals. "They demand that women no longer be under the influence of the priests; but they do not want to see her think freely," she raged. "They do not want her to work against them, but they reject her help as soon as she offers it." Men act this way because they want to control women. "Many republicans (not true republicans) have dethroned the emperor and the good God with the intention of putting themselves in their places. . . . And naturally, in this intention, it is necessary to have subjects. . . . [So] women are to remain neutral and passive, under the direction of men; all they will have to change is their confessor." Such a plan would not work, she declared sarcastically, since God had an immense advantage over man. "He remains unknown which permits him to be the ideal."[39]

Léo's anger at the political and military leaders of the Commune made her a critic, but she did more than criticize. She articulated an egalitarian vision. "The Revolution," she wrote, "exists only by the exercise of reason and liberty, by searching for truth and justice in all things." No one had the right to draw a line and declare that some of the "marching spirits" could not cross it. The Revolution was the responsibility of "all human creatures . . . without any privilege of race or sex." Any lesser vision, any restrictions on the extension of liberty and justice, any hierarchy, any discrimination against those who believed in the revolution and were ready to defend it, was a betrayal of the Commune.[40]

Louis Rossel, the Commune's delegate of war, publicly denounced the orders of the Committee of Public Safety which had led to the rejection of women's help, and asked Léo for advice.[41] She responded at length with concrete suggestions and a further critique of the situation.[42] The problem, she declared, was that the women had both "masculine prejudice" and the "esprit de corps of the physicians" against them, and both of these impediments were "tenacious and multiple." To make matters worse, the ambulancières would not simply act on their own. They needed the direction of the physicians. Léo was not ready to give up the effort, however: "Should the republic, the Paris Commune, repulse and discourage the devotion of its citoyennes? Assuredly not. We ought, in spite of the current prejudice, the current customs, to bend all our efforts to arrive as soon as possible at the true fraternity of men and women, at the harmony of sentiments and ideas, which alone can establish honor, equality, peace, [and] the Commune of the future."[43]

In the meantime, there were concrete steps to take. A few physicians were ready to work with the ambulancières, and three or four young women who had passed their exams at the Ecole de Médecine de Paris could be put in charge of some of the aid stations. "I have no doubt of their ability," she wrote. "They had the audacity to force the doors of science; they will certainly not fail in the service of humanity and the Revolution." Next, "some of the most distinguished midwives" could be recruited to assist the troops. Finally, the commune could accept the assistance of the female arrondissement committees. (These committees had already taken responsibility for organizing women to cook and provide medical assistance for the troops.) The Commune's reluctance to accept such help was, of course, the point, but Léo was not ready to give up the struggle for acceptance. To do so would be to give up on the revolution.[44]

Léo's writings reveal the pervasiveness of gender dichotomies in nineteenth-century thought and the opposition women encountered from even the most politically radical men, who, like conservatives, believed there were fundamental (natural) differences between the sexes. Many Commune leaders who firmly believed in civil liberties and the right to work for all men extended no such beliefs to women. Their vision of the social republic did not include extension of the franchise, the right to work, equality in marriage, or equal pay to women. Much as they might praise women's heroic actions in the past, they wanted them to remain passive in the present. Such distinctions between men's and women's acceptable behavior and appropriate rights could be defended only if one believed, as these men apparently did, that the nature of man and the nature of woman were significantly different in ways that made it natural for men to dominate and direct women.

Léo's vision of human nature and human rights differed dramatically from those that she criticized. Hers was a strong female voice (albeit masked by a male pseudonym) for women's equality. She thought both women and men were motivated by a genuine love for the republic, that both were drawn to great causes, that both were ready to sacrifice themselves for the revolution. She praised women's bravery and hard work in preparing the city's defenses. She believed women had as much at stake in the revolution as men did, indeed, that women, especially single women who lived by themselves, were suffering more than men from the lack of work and the high cost of goods.[45] She believed in "the true fraternity" of men and women.[46] The revolution, if it hoped to win, should not, could not exclude women from full citizenship and rebuff their offers of help.

Léo did not maintain that men and women were alike in all ways. She seems to have seen them as equal and complementary. She emphasized, for instance, the importance of women's self-sacrificing, nurturing, and morale-building activities. "Devoted and courageous citoyennes" did everything from cooking for the combatants to aiding the wounded and dying to working behind the barricades. Insightful and hardheaded as she was about the revolution and its leaders, she was also a nineteenth-century romantic. She wrote repeatedly about women's passion for the revolution, the "fire in their eyes," and how they gave themselves "entirely to the grand cause," as men did.[47] When women worked with men, she believed, they inspired and strengthened them in a way that their male comrades could not. The courage of the women who worked behind the barricades, "double[d] the strength of the [male] combatants," because "arms are stronger when the heart is firm,"[48] and when women fought alongside, they "doubled the ardor" of the men.[49] For Léo, these contributions appear to have inhered in the nature of woman; they were not culturally imposed.

If Léo saw the sexes as complementary, she did not believe that women could not or should not take up arms. She saw not a rigid dichotomization of skills, intelligence, and will power but a range of these attributes in both sexes. Some women were smarter and stronger willed than others. Some

were capable of leading; some were not. Some women had "had the audacity to force the doors of science"; most had not. Some wished to fight;
others did not. The same was true of men. Some, especially ordinary
guardsmen, were models of self-sacrifice; others were not. Some were suited to lead; most were not. Some understood women's commitment to the
revolution; most did not. All these differences should be respected and
used to the commune's advantage. The problem the Commune faced, she
thought, was that its soldiers, whom she represented as the "poor sublime
artisans" who were sacrificing their lives for the social revolution, understood the Commune's principles better than its leaders did, including the
principle of political rights and equality for all people, female as well as
male.

Augustine-Melvine Blanchecotte

Augustine-Melvine Blanchecotte observed politics and women from a
different perspective. Her experiences and opinions are known to us
through the diary she published in 1872. The diary appears to be unedited, although it is impossible to be certain. If it was edited, it was in the early aftermath of the Commune, for the date on the introduction is December 15, 1871. Little would have occurred since the last entry in the diary
(June 23, 1871) to alter Blanchecotte's opinions about the revolution, the
war with Versailles, and the men and women she encountered during the
Commune.

Blanchecotte reveals little personal information in the diary. We learn
that she lived alone in an apartment near the boulevard Saint-Michel and
the Pantheon, that she worked as an ambulancière during the Prussian
siege, that she counted priests and perhaps some Commune officials
among her friends and acquaintances, and that she was a pacifist. She
seems to have been well known in her neighborhood, and she and her
neighbors helped and protected each other when they could. We know
nothing, however, about her family, her source of income, her age, or her
marital status. From documents she includes in her diary, we know that she
was called Mme Blanchecotte, which may indicate that she was married or
widowed, or may only indicate her age.[50]

Blanchecotte observed the revolution carefully. Like everyone else in
the city, she read the government's pronouncements on wall posters and
in the press, endured the army's shelling, watched the National Guard
marching through the streets, witnessed the building of barricades, and at-

tended funerals. While she claimed that she preferred to remain anonymous and out of the public eye, she engaged in public activity several times. Most notably, in April she wrote letters, visited officials of the Commune, and even braved the formidable Prefecture de Police to obtain the release of a priest, her friend and neighbor, who had been arrested with the archbishop of Paris. Her success in freeing him gave her great joy. It was, she said, "perhaps the only joy that I have had in my life! One, one poor day had not been absolutely useless!"[51]

In contrast to André Léo, Blanchecotte was a political outsider. She observed both sides in the conflict and passed her own judgment on them, lamenting the decisions that caused and perpetuated the war and finding more to criticize than to praise on both sides. At the beginning of the revolution, she thought "certain reforms that [the revolutionaries] are demanding are reasonable" but that France needed more time to recover from the war with Prussia before it could hear such demands.[52] In early April, she continued to believe that the assembly in Versailles had "favored the property owners too much and [had] not take[n] enough account of the public misery," but the Commune's laws "favor[ed] the renter too much." In short, the decrees of Versailles lacked "generosity"; those of the Commune, "justice."[53] Her criticism of Versailles seems harsher than her complaints about the Commune, however, and she seems less neutral about the outcome of the conflict. When she made a trip to Versailles in early May, for instance, she declared that "the atmosphere of Paris oppresses me, [but] the atmosphere of Versailles suffocates me."[54]

Blanchecotte's strongest criticisms were of the war and the two governments' failures to find a way to end it. As an avowed pacifist, she despaired at what she saw, particularly one terrible new invention. "People are talking about the *mitrailleuses blindées* [machine guns]," she wrote in early April, "each pierced with thirty-seven holes." Stunned by the killing capacity, she could only repeat the figure. "Thirty-seven holes! Thirty-seven times the number of bullets! Thirty-seven times the death!" Versailles's bombardment of the city was "the madness of barbarity."[55] Arising from the Parisian armaments at Trocadéro, she saw "the smoke of the murderous cannons, of the blind death that strikes at random."[56]

In Blanchecotte's view, war was a male activity. She felt none of the "holy fever" and "sublime passion" André Léo attributed to women. Men began wars, glorified them, fought and died in them; women could only suffer them. "There is, in all human causes, only unhappiness for us women," she declared on April 12.[57] This war, in particular, since it was a civil war, was a "frightful exhibition of ambitions, weaknesses, errors of judgment, and folly."[58] When it was over, this "unspeakable battle of civilized man against civilized man" would make all other tragedies ("even intimate ones") seem like "games."[59]

Blanchecotte was not inclined to give up the attempt to save men from their mistakes, however, nor did she believe other women should surrender their will to men's. "Real women" (*vraies femmes*) would try to save their husbands, sons, and brothers from themselves.[60] In a diary entry, written on the same day that André Léo's article "Toutes avec tous" called for women and men to stand and fight together, Blanchecotte echoed Léo's phrase more than once but called on men and women to join together in the cause of peace instead. "The horrible struggle can endure no longer; let us protest, *toutes et tous,*" she wrote. "Let us rise up, *toutes et tous,* with our hearts for banners; the whole country suffers and bleeds. Enough blood has been shed! Stop the killing!" Then, in words that themselves would be echoed in the appeal for peace with which the *groupe de citoyennes* placarded Paris on May 4, Blanchecotte continued her private appeal for peace, spoken only in her diary, emphasizing the relationships between women and men. "I appeal to mothers, to sisters, to daughters, to women without political distinction," she wrote, "I appeal to fathers, to brothers, to sons, to men of all flags and all armies. What are these geographical words: Paris, Versailles; Versailles, Paris? This is France, *la grande France,* that is killing itself! This is humanity, civilized humanity that is committing suicide!"[61]

These words make one wonder if Blanchecotte might not have been part of the *groupe de citoyennes* that called for an end to the war, but if she was, she made no mention of it in her diary. Indeed, her diary only summarizes the May 4 appeal, whereas it includes the entire text of the response by the Union des Femmes, with which she disagreed.[62] The Union's call to arms was not a surprise to Blanchecotte. She had read Léo's articles in *La Sociale.* She had observed a demonstration in early April and had seen "a pretty daughter of the people, admirably got up," contemplate the machine guns "with enthusiasm" and propose that women should march in front of the Commune's troops "so the army will not fire."[63] She had seen women, "armed with rifles, revolvers stuck in their belts, red scarves over their shoulders, accompany and urge on the combattants," and she knew about women orators in the churches.[64]

Blanchecotte disagreed with these women, but she understood them, at least in part. They had, she thought, been "excited by the men, and now, in their turn, were exciting the men."[65] They believed that they were engaged in a great social cause.[66] And many of them were young;[67] so their enthusiasm could be explained as lack of experience and the romanticization of war.

Another group of women was beyond her comprehension, those who sought revenge of one kind or another. They were not excited by a great cause or led astray by romanticism. They were driven by darker, appalling motives. Indeed, for Blanchecotte, they were hardly women, at all. And they existed on both sides.

When she made a trip to Versailles in early May, she was overwhelmed by the treatment of the prisoners who were being marched through the streets. She held her hands in front of her eyes, so she would not have to see either the vanquished or the victors. Her ears could not help but hear the "impassioned curses" heaped upon the prisoners, however, and amid the clamor, unbelievably, she had discerned "the voices of women" shouting, "Down with the prisoners! The firing squad is too good for them! Kill the bandits!" This was intolerable. "I understand exasperation at the leaders of the triumphant Commune," she wrote, "but I do not understand it vis-à-vis the vanquished prisoners, this troop of the unconscious, the misled, the sacrificial offerings of both sides, these outcasts of the struggle. Kill them in battle, enchain them, imprison them, judge them, condemn them in defeat, but do not insult them. They are not dirt!" Women's involvement, of course, made it worse. "After the madness of men killing men," she lamented, "the absence of pity in women is frightful!"[68]

Five days later, she witnessed a scene in Paris which was similarly intolerable. "An elegant citoyenne . . . I ought to say a creature," she wrote, "dressed in silk, with lace gloves," made "an act of patriotism . . . by denouncing and having arrested a *réfractaire* [a deserter from the army], her lover for the month." She believed "another woman—a real woman—would have killed herself in her shame," but "*she is going to kill him. It is hideous!*" she declared.[69]

During the semaine sanglante, Blanchecotte was incredulous when she heard about the pétroleuses. That women would help to burn the city was beyond belief, and she rhetorically asked in her diary, "Is it possible?"[70] To fight and kill and die in battle was one thing. To set fires or kill arbitrarily or vindictively was another. Such actions were morally indefensible no matter who did them, but when they were done by women, they violated not only society's moral code but also Blanchecotte's conceptualization of woman's nature. Real women were pacifists. They abhorred killing for any reason. They would not have engaged in vengeful attacks on people or property. Those who did, regardless of their politics, ceased to be fully human and became "creatures," acting out of animalistic intentions.[71]

Blanchecotte herself was adamant about not participating in the killing in any way. For two days during the Versailles invasion of the city, she refused to leave her apartment because anyone who ventured out onto the street was forced to help build the barricades. She believed even this defensive act would make her complicit in the killing. To add even one paving stone "could represent the death of men," she wrote in her diary, and she would not do it. "No one can make me put a stone on a barricade," she declared. "They will have to kill me before they will force me to do that."[72]

Just as she had hidden her eyes when the prisoners were marched through Versailles at the beginning of the month, she wanted to look away, to stop her ears from hearing and her eyes from seeing, as seemingly endless groups of prisoners were marched through the city to imprisonment or death: "I understand battle, the frightful fever of combat; I do not understand, at the hour of severe justice, the merriment of the gallery. At this moment I would like to live on the moon so I would not have to encounter another of these sad processions."[73]

And so she decided on the public act of publishing her diary, and to dedicate it "to the disarmament of the spirits, to peace, to unity, to harmony, to the healing of the opposing parties and, if it is possible, to public agreement, to common sense."[74] These desires, she believed, were those of every true woman, but her act in their behalf shows how contradictory her views of true womanhood were. She thought of herself and other women as politically neutral. Women lost, no matter what side they were on. Therefore, they were on no side. But to be a pacifist during wartime was a profoundly political act. Although she declared herself glad to be a woman, "to be able, like a child, to be treated as being without consequence, . . . to have nothing to dispute with the government of the country,"[75] she had a profound dispute with the government and she badly wanted to have her views taken seriously. She wanted her voice to be heard. It was an awkward and contradictory position for a "true woman" to be in.

Céline de Mazade

Céline de Mazade spent the first six weeks of the Commune in Paris, observing the revolution and running the Parisian end of her family's textile business. Her opinions and experiences are known to us through the letters she wrote to her husband Alexandre, which were published as part of the family correspondence in 1892.[76] In contrast to Augustine-Melvine Blanchecotte's diary, Mazade's published letters tell us a great deal about her personal life and little about her politics. There are ellipses in the letters, which may indicate omissions from the originals, some perhaps dealing with the Commune, but there is no way to retrieve any excised material, and the ellipses may be only Mazade's literary style.

In many ways, Mazade fits Blanchecotte's definition of a "true woman." She lived her life outside of politics, opposed the war between Paris and Versailles, and helped her husband evade the National Guard mobilization. She was religious and domestic, grieving over the arrests of priests, writing to Alexandre about friends and family, and even sending him news of the cat. "She meows also to have news of you," she told him. "In the morning, when she enters my room, she looks for you everywhere."[77] But there was more to Céline de Mazade's life than domesticity and religion, and she was not a pure pacifist.

Céline and Alexandre de Mazade were successful textile manufacturers with factories in Ronquerolles-Clermont in the Oise and a warehouse and shop in Paris. The Parisian shop purchased silk for the looms and other raw materials, shipped them to Ronquerolles, and arranged for the dyeing and finishing of the completed cotton and silk fabric. Céline was an active partner in this business. She coped with the business accounts, pressured suppliers for more silk, arranged for the transport of materials, and knew how to bribe the authorities when necessary.

In March both Céline and Alexandre de Mazade moved freely in and out of Paris, although even then their division of labor meant that Alexandre spent most of his time in Ronquerolles while Céline dealt with business in Paris. This arrangement ended on April 5, when Céline warned Alexandre not to return to Paris. The warning was prompted by a visit from a National Guard platoon that was searching for Alexandre. The bourgeois units of the National Guard had resisted mobilization since the end of the Prussian siege, since they, too, were disaffected from the national government. This resistance had aided the March 18 revolt of the working-class guardsmen when the bourgeois units refused to help the army. Now, however, the bourgeoisie's refusal to defend the Commune against Versailles both reduced the forces under the Commune's command and raised the possibility of a third column within the city's walls. To solve these problems, the Commune passed conscription laws and instituted citywide searches for draft dodgers.[78] Alexandre de Mazade was on their list.

Realizing the danger both to Alexandre, should he return, and to herself, should she be caught warning him, Céline nevertheless dispatched a letter, adjuring him to stay away.[79] Thus began her adventures alone in the Commune. She was not the only bourgeoise who remained in Paris while her husband resided safely outside the city. On April 6 she reported to Alexandre that she and Mme Auguste Thiébault were both feeling "very proud to have put our husbands in safety and to be guarding our houses," adding, with a touch of humor, "We are *des femmes fortes*."[80] Thus she played with the inverted gender roles in which the Mazades found themselves and evoked the cultural image of the amazon, but only temporarily, for herself. By April 18 Céline's mother-in-law could be counted among the femmes fortes, as could Mme Victor Pillon-Dufresnes, wife of another manufacturer, who also remained in Paris and reported to her husband in Ronquerolles that she "shared the calmness of the brave inhabitants of Paris," and had "not the least fear in the world."[81]

Céline and Alexandre corresponded almost daily. She sent him news from Paris: the successful attempt of the women of one quarter to free their *curé* (parish priest) from jail so he could say the Easter mass, the arrest of their own *curé*, the unending noise of the bombardment, the arrests of various members of the Central Committee, the suppression of opposition newspapers, and the National Guard's harassment of other women whose husbands had fled the city. What upset her the most was seeing priests and nuns marched through the streets surrounded by the National Guard.

That Céline was prepared to cope with the difficulties of life in Paris under the Commune was clear from the beginning. She got rid of the National Guard by telling them Alexandre was "usefully occupied at [his] factory." Told to "make him return," she replied, "Very well, gentlemen, I will alert him, but I doubt that my letter will reach him promptly." Then, instead of summoning him, she warned him to stay away, and continued to undertake hazardous trips out of Paris to meet him.[82] On April 18, however, she told Alexandre that her trips in and out of the city would have to end. Edouard (an employee) had advised her not to leave again, she wrote, though "there is no danger for the moment" in remaining in the city.[83]

In the beginning, Céline was cheerful about the constant bombardment of Paris. Even on April 18, when she perceived that it was no longer safe for her to come and go from the city, she wrote to Alexandre that she had heard no cannon or gunfire, "except two cannon shots" while she was entering the train station. These she wryly remarked were "probably to celebrate our arrival."[84] But the constant shelling of the city by the Versaillais eventually began to take its toll on her. On the twenty-fourth she wrote to Alexandre, now in Lille, that she was fine, "except for a small nervous tremor that I have had for two or three days, caused probably by the cannon fire of the night of Friday to Saturday that was frightful, but it is nothing." She signed her letter, "your poor love."[85]

At this point, Alexandre's concern about Céline turned to alarm. On April 26 he wrote to Victor Pillon-Dufresnes, whose wife was also in Paris, that he was "uneasy about the condition of the women" there. He thought it was "absolutely necessary that they leave that place, that they close the business."[86] But Céline had regained her equilibrium and sent Alexandre a reassuring note: "I assure you, dear love, that I see no danger in remaining in Paris; I am risking nothing."[87] Alexandre was not reassured. On the twenty-ninth, he wrote Céline, "You do not know how cruel it is to be separated from you, especially in such terrible circumstances. I am constantly in a state of anxiety; I feverishly open your letters which only reassure me a little, being written two or three days before I receive them." Alexandre was adamant. He asked Céline if she had done what he said and left Paris. "It is not necessary to push energy and courage to excess. . . . Let us be content at Ronquerolles for the moment; come what may in Paris."[88] Having confided on April 27 that she was "*very very* afraid,"[89] Céline acceded to Alexandre's wishes on May 1 and left the city.

What kept Céline de Mazade and other bourgeois women in Paris when it was no longer safe for the men to remain there was a twofold concern with the family's property and business. Rumors and Versailles press accounts of the pillaging of churches and houses provoked fear that their homes would not be safe if they were left unoccupied. This fear was exacerbated late in April when the Commune decided to house evacuees from Neuilly in abandoned apartments.[90] More central, however, at least in the correspondence of Céline and Alexandre, was a desire to keep the family's textile business operating. Alexandre repeatedly asked Céline to send him silk. "Press our silk throwers," he wrote on March 24. "About the silk, quickly, quickly... urgent," he wrote on April 18, and on the next day: "About the silk, send us the silk! Always as much as possible! It is absolutely necessary that you find, if not raw silk, at least weft yarn, send even partially prepared rovings, . . . Spur on our silk throwers also. Think how without silk all our factories will be stopped!"[91] On the twenty-fourth, he praised her for having begun to "buy so well" and encouraged her to buy as much as possible since they could "buy less later." Even in his letter of April 29 in which he demanded that she leave Paris, he went on to tell her about a trip he had just made to search out markets for the future.[92]

Céline was obviously a competent and resourceful businesswoman. She kept the Paris shop open, shipped silk whenever she could, and by April 20 was bribing officials with twenty-sous pieces, and arguing her case (this time unsuccessfully) with the "very decorated" National Guard commissioner of the train station.[93] On the twenty-fourth when she complained of a "small nervous tremor," she reported that business was fine, although the shop lacked merchandise.[94] On the twenty-sixth she reported that the other manufacturers could not find workers because they had all joined the National Guard, but she herself apparently still had workers.[95] Alexandre relied on Céline and was well aware of her competence, taking her role in the business, if not her safety, for granted. On May 12 he wrote to a friend in Etampes that Céline had spent an "infernal April in Paris, where her presence was a benefit because of the lively revival of business."[96]

The published versions of Céline's letters contain little reflection on the political and military struggles of the Commune. Her allegiance to Versailles is not in doubt, however. She opposed the Commune's arrests of priests and nuns, sympathized with those around her who opposed the National Guard, and considered herself the social and intellectual superior of the guardsmen and Commune officials whom she met. To her the men seemed more like recalcitrant children than serious opponents. Their "rage against religion" was "stupid,"[97] and she believed she could outwit them. Indeed, she did outwit them when they came in search of Alexandre, and she frequently succeeded in sending him silk despite the obstacles. When she could not convince the officials with logic, she tried bribing them with alcohol and money. Her tactics did not always work, but she felt no compunctions about trying them. She was a bourgeoise who knew what she wanted and how to get it. If the National Guard tried to arrest her, she had, she said, no intention of allowing herself to be "taken."[98]

The Mazade correspondence does not allow us to determine fully the gender conceptions of Céline and Alexandre and their friends. Nevertheless, it is clear that their views were complex and verged on the contradictory. For this young bourgeois couple, male and female spheres of activity were not sharply differentiated, although there was some division of responsibility between them. Alexandre appears to have been the one to travel in search of suppliers and customers, and Céline dealt with the Parisian end of the business. Alexandre clearly recognized and relied upon Céline's experience and competence. She knew how to run the family's textile business and did it ably. Indeed, the visit by the National Guard which precipitated Alexandre's permanent absence from Paris occurred while she was working in the shop. None of her family or friends thought her work peculiar. She was a resourceful businesswoman and in her rightful place.

Despite Céline de Mazade's competence and independence of spirit, she lived in a world that assigned character traits on the basis of sex. These assignments were not so rigid that they could not be manipulated in extraordinary circumstances such as the Commune, however. Courage is an interesting case in point. When Victor Pillon, another manufacturer, undertook to praise the women who had remained in Paris, he could only say that they had "demonstrated a *more than masculine* courage."[99] This praise was not unlike Malon's and Rossel's praise of *"citoyen"* André Léo.

The mutual decision for the women to remain in Paris allowed them to possess the masculine virtue of courage without becoming unfeminine.

But only temporarily. No one in this bourgeois group expected or wanted women to be more courageous than men on a daily basis. Nor did they want women to be exactly like men in other ways. Alexandre could and did express both his and Céline's sadness over the death of a friend's child and his concern for her safety, but he revealed no personal fears or fancies as Céline did when she wrote notes about the cat and revealed the toll the bombardment was taking on her. Femininity and masculinity were distinguishable, albeit occasionally overlapping, hierarchically related concepts.

Notably missing from Céline de Mazade's published letters are references to Communard women. She mentions only some who managed to free a priest. The April posters and newspaper articles alternately urging women to take up arms and to work for peace, the cantinières and ambulancières who marched through the city with the troops, the club orators—none of these women who attracted the attention of other bourgeois commentators, including Blanchecotte, appear in her correspondence. It is unlikely that she approved of any of these women (with the exception of those who called for peace), for she had no sympathy for the Commune and its supporters. The differences in class interests were too great for her to bridge. The Communards were her enemy, but she saw them as more inept than evil. She had no wish to treat them very harshly. Even when she had had a bad day, her most fervent desire was for their incarceration (a byproduct of victory), not execution. "I am coming to wish that all the national guardsmen were prisoners at Versailles," she wrote to Alexandre.[100]

But by the end of the Commune, Céline de Mazade had become vindictive, like many other bourgeois women and men. Bombarded with reports that pétroleuses were burning houses, fearful for their own homes, and removed from Paris with its columns of bedraggled prisoners and mass executions, women and men alike were drawn to vengeance in thought if not in deed. On May 30, a month after she had left the city, Céline had come to support the executions and mass arrests that were taking place, and she made no exception for women. She wrote to a friend in Paris: "I never believed that these abominable communards would be such vandals as to commit these atrocious deeds. I hope that [the government] will continue to give no mercy to these monsters, men and women, and that they are going to take their children and make them learn better sentiments."[101] Berthe Amiard-Fromentin, a friend of the Mazades, expressed even harsher sentiments. Writing to her father on April 29 from Etampes, she declared: "I have finally obtained a passport, and I intend to leave tomorrow morning for Paris, to see with my own eyes the irreparable disaster! How the blood flowed and still flows! One is without pity for these miserable incendiaries, and with reason. . . . On their part, it was a war to the death of those who are property owners."[102]

What bourgeois men thought of bourgeois women who expressed vindictive sentiments but remained inactive is not clear. Alexandre de Mazade's inclusion of vengeful letters among those he published suggests his approval, but on what level is unknown. Perhaps he (and other bourgeois men) regarded such feelings as human, shared by men and women alike. Perhaps he associated them with women, regarding vengeance as a peculiarly female trait. Perhaps he viewed them as another aspect of women's defense of their homes.

When bourgeois women moved from advocating "no mercy" to inflicting punishment, however, many bourgeois men found themselves as uncomfortable with this "unladylike" behavior as they were with that of the communardes. Journalists, essayists, and ordinary citizens described the "long caravans of prisoners [who] were to be seen wending their way to Versailles, innocent and guilty alike, to the great delight of substantial citizens . . . [who] revenged [them]selves indiscriminately."[103] Most of these observers singled out the behavior of the women among these "substantial citizens" for criticism. Gaston Cerfbeer, who was only twelve years old in 1871, recalled in 1903, "Above all, the women were without pity, screaming 'Kill them! To death!'"[104] Maxime Du Camp, one of the Commune's harshest critics, reported that "the women were, as always, the most agitated; they broke through military ranks and beat the prisoners with umbrellas, crying: Kill the assassins! Burn the incendiaries!"[105]

Whether the bourgeoises who taunted and abused the prisoners acted in any way differently from the men in the crowds is unclear. What is clear is that women's behavior was perceived differently. It may have been acceptable for women to protect their homes and families and to have fleeting hopes of vengeance, but it was not acceptable for them to attack men and women who, as prisoners, were defined as nonthreatening. To strike out at them was to move across the line from defense to offense. For bourgeois men, as for the National Guard commanders who tried to keep women away from the front lines, women who acted aggressively had crossed the boundary between female and male behavior. This boundary did not confine Parisian bourgeois women to domesticity in 1871, as Bonnie Smith has found it did in northern France.[106] Alexandre's reliance on Céline to run the Parisian business and protect their home demonstrates that it did not. But bourgeois culture certainly did restrict military and violent action to men. When women acted violently, their identity as women was called into question. So, correlatively, was men's identity. If women were not defenseless (as both the communardes and the vengeful bourgeoises seemed to demonstrate, then men could not be their "natural" protectors. Since the heroic part of male identity was already shaky for bourgeois men who had fled conscription and left their women behind, vengeful women posed a serious threat to their sense of how society should work.

Whereas Alexandre de Mazade may have understood and supported his wife's vindictive feelings, Augustine-Melvine Blanchecotte would not have. She believed that women and men were fundamentally different from each other in this regard. For her, vindictive sentiments and actions in women were incomprehensible and unacceptable. She disapproved of both the young communardes who spurred men on to battle and bourgeoises who taunted and attacked prisoners. She had seen such behavior on May 3 when she visited Versailles, and she saw it again in late May and early June. Both times, powerless to stop the taunting and attacking of prisoners, she tried not to see and hear what was going on. From her pacifist perspective, such action (and the thought that preceded it) was wrong whether done by men or women. But her bifurcated view of male and female nature led her to expect such behavior from men and not from women. Where women who encouraged or joined this male behavior fit in terms of gender was unclear, but they were no longer "true women." "Creatures" was the best word Blanchecotte could come up with to describe them and it seemed to deny their humanity altogether.

Louise Michel

The most famous femme forte of the Commune was the woman who stepped most firmly and willingly across the gender line, Louise Michel. In the grand tradition of female French revolutionaries, she was the illegitimate daughter of a nobleman.[107] Born out of wedlock in 1830 to Marianne Michel, a domestic servant, and Laurent Demahis, a young man of noble descent who left his parental home after Louise's birth, Louise Michel was raised by her mother and paternal grandparents in the Demahis's (formerly de Mahis) decaying château in the village of Vroncourt in the Haute-Marne. She was allowed considerable freedom by her mother and the republican Demahises, and her childhood appears to have been carefree and happy. Well-read and educated as a teacher, she ran a variety of small schools in the Haute-Marne and then moved to Paris.[108]

Michel's political activities began during the later years of the Second Empire. By 1870 she was traveling in radical political circles and enjoying the friendship of men like the mayor of Montmartre, Georges Clemenceau, and the poet and novelist Victor Hugo, to whom she sent her poetry. Deeply committed to republican government and social revolution, she opposed France's declaration of war against Prussia and participated in antigovernment demonstrations after the war had begun. In August she and André Léo led a demonstration of women to show support for the besieged city of Strasbourg. Well versed, as all Parisians seem to have been, in the power of symbolic acts, the women marched to the Strasbourg statue in the place de la Concorde, where they signed a book of names and placed it in the lap of the statue. Michel and Léo then proceeded to the Hôtel de Ville, where they demanded weapons so they and the other women could go to Strasbourg's defense. Thinking them quite mad, the authorities first arrested them and then let them go.[109]

The Government of National Defense, which replaced Napoleon III's government on September 4, did little to inspire the confidence or hope of radicals like Louise Michel, and so their political activities continued. During the Prussian siege, Michel, her mother, and Malvina Poulain ran the school she had founded in Paris, which now had two hundred students, having taken in the children of families that had sought refuge in Paris during the war. For these children and for all the people who came to her for help, Michel beseeched Clemenceau, Hugo, Malon, and anyone else who would listen for food.[110] She also presided over the Women's Vigilance Committee in Montmartre, attended the meetings of the Men's Vigilance Committee,[111] and was a member of the Association for the Rights of Women and the Society for the Victims of the War. She practiced marksmanship at the city fairgrounds, carried a gun, and joined the January 22 demonstration that ended in bloodshed at the Hôtel de Ville.[112]

The demonstration had been called to protest the slaughter of Parisian national guardsmen at Buzenval on January 19. When the Government of National Defense had decided to send the guard into battle, the Parisians had been elated. Edmond de Goncourt had thought it a "grand and glorious sight, that army marching toward the cannons that we could hear in the distance, an army with, in its midst, grey-bearded civilians who were fathers, beardless youths who were sons, and in its open ranks, women carrying their husbands' or their lovers' rifles slung across their backs."[113] What began so joyfully ended in slaughter. On the twenty-first, Goncourt noted elegantly that Paris had become silent. "I am struck most of all," he wrote, "by the silence, the silence of death, which a disaster creates in a great city. Today one can no longer hear Paris living."[114] The radicals were not content to mourn silently, however. Instead, they marched on the Hôtel de Ville demanding the installation of a communal government and provoked the fire of the Breton guards stationed there. In a foreshadowing of things to come, Louise Michel, dressed in a National Guard uniform, fired back.[115]

Michel's participation in the Commune began at the beginning. Sleeping at the National Guard post on the rue des Rosiers on the night of March 17–18, she was among the first to know that the army troops had invaded Montmartre. When Georges Clemenceau arrived to examine the wounded guardsman Turpin, he found her at his side. When he left to get a stretcher, Michel spread the alarm, running down the hill, her rifle under her coat, yelling, "Treason!" Then, having played Paul Revere for the fledgling Communards, she joined the throng as it climbed the hill to confront General Lecomte's troops.[116]

Had she been a man, Michel's activities during the Prussian siege, her commitment to revolution, and her prominence in radical circles might have resulted in her election to the Commune. She might even, given her commitment to the National Guard, have been one of its commanders. Since she was a woman, these formal political and military roles were closed to her. The barriers to governmental and national guard service did not stop Louise Michel, however, She was elated with the Commune and devoted herself to its survival. She debated policy with her friends, some of whom had been elected to the Commune; presided over the Montmartre Women's Vigilance Committee; and prepared a plan for the reorganization of education under the republic.[117]

Her commitment to the revolution was greater than it was to debating and governing, however, and after April 4 she devoted most of her time to the armed struggle against Versailles. She believed the Communards should send her to Versailles to assassinate Thiers. Théophile Ferré and Raoul Rigault, among the most violent of the Commune members, persuaded her not to carry out this plan, but she traveled to Versailles anyway, dressed as a respectable bourgeoise, just to prove that she could leave and reenter the city and that she actually might have been able to kill Thiers if they had wished her to.[118]

As her actions on January 22 had presaged, Louise Michel became the great female warrior of the Commune, alternately performing "men's work" and "women's work" on the battlefield, firing at the enemy and helping the wounded. From the moment the war between Versailles and Paris began, she was in the fray. The earliest battle accounts praised her "heroic conduct." "Citoyenne Louise Michel," the newspapers reported, "picked up the wounded under the royalist shells and, when necessary, returned fire."[119]

Michel fought with the 61st Battalion of Montmartre in major battles at Neuilly, Les Moulineaux, Clamart, and Issy. When she was not fighting, she found pianos and organs to play, rescued stray animals, cared for the wounded in the field, and helped organize ambulance stations in the city.[120] Despite her connections with the Commune's male leaders and her reputation as a tireless soldier, her services were not always welcomed by the men whose cause she shared. When the ambulancières of André Léo's article arrived in Neuilly, they discovered that Louise Michel was already there and that she, like them, had been denied the right to help in any way. When asked what was happening, she reportedly said, "Ah! If they would even permit me to care for the wounded! You would not believe the obstacles, the torments, the hostility."[121]

In her memoirs, Michel confessed that it was excitement that drew her to battle. "Was it sheer bravery that caused me to be so enchanted with the sight of the battered Issy fort gleaming faintly in the night, or the sight of our lines on night maneuvers, . . . with the red teeth of the machine guns flashing on the horizon?" she asked rhetorically. "It wasn't bravery; I just thought it a beautiful sight. My eyes and my heart responded, as did my ears to the sound of the cannon. Oh, I'm a savage all right, I love the smell of gunpowder, grapeshot flying through the air, but above all, I'm devoted to the Revolution."[122]

She defended the Commune to the end, patrolling and defending the Montmartre cemetery and fighting behind the street barricades. When the war was lost and she was still alive, she changed into a clean skirt without bullet holes and went in search of her mother. At Marianne Michel's house the concierge told her that soldiers had come looking for her, and "since you weren't here, they took your mother to shoot in your place."[123] Frantic to save her, Michel ran to the nearest army post and from there to another (accompanied by soldiers), where she successfully substituted herself for her mother. Now a prisoner, she was marched to Versailles and held for trial.

Much of Louise Michel's emotional and moral support came from women, her mother first and foremost among them. Before the Commune, she and Marianne worked and lived together in Montmartre. Like many a radical young woman, she tried to protect her mother from the most dangerous of her activities and wrote her cheerful letters that were meant to conceal her undertakings as a soldier and ambulancière. It seems unlikely that Marianne Michel was much deceived or much comforted by such ruses, but she supported her daughter no matter what, helping her with her school, searching for her in the crowds on March 18, visiting her in prison, and writing her letters in exile.[124] Her death in January 1885 plunged Louise into depression. Feeling responsible because she had not been there to take care of her for so many years, she invoked her "dear mother" and "poor mother" over and over again in her memoirs. Finally, in a statement that spoke at least as much to her own grief and loneliness as it did to her mother's past emotions, she lamented that "when [Marianne] came to Montmartre, all broken from the death of my grandmother, the Revolution came [and] I left her alone during the long evenings; then, these became days, then months, then years. Poor mother!"[125] One wants to add, poor daughter.

As the accepted, but illegitimate, granddaughter of the Demahis family and as the director of impoverished schools, Louise Michel was accustomed to crossing class lines and seeking support wherever she could find it. What concerned her were women's politics, not their class. "Heroic women," she declared in her memoirs, "were found in all social positions."[126] She was comfortable with all of them. During the siege, a group of women "from all social classes" formed the Society for the Victims of the War at Mme Poulain's *école professionnelle*. "All of them would have preferred death to surrender," she later wrote. "They dispensed all the aid they could procure, plundering those who could be plundered, saying: —Paris must resist, resist forever."[127] The Society for the Victims of the War was one of three organizations Michel created with bourgeois and working-class women. The other two were the Women's Vigilance Committee of Montmartre and the Association for the Rights of Women. Her continuing respect for the women who worked with her appears in her decision to name only those who remained public radicals or who later switched sides, in her memoirs. Thus, we learn that the founding group of the Association for the Rights of Women included Mme Jules Simon (the wife of Thiers's minister of education) and the radicals André Léo and Maria Deraismes, but those who might have been harmed by their association with her are identified only as Jeanne B and Madame F.[128]

Michel was equally supportive of working-class prostitutes who wanted to help the Commune. When men objected to their employment as ambulancières because they did not have "pure hands," she was incensed. "Who had more right to give their lives for the new [world]," she asked, "than those who were the most wretched victims of the old world?" In a show of solidarity she divided her own red sash into smaller sashes for the women, and found ambulance positions for them through the Women's Vigilance Committee.[129]

It is difficult to determine exactly what Michel thought about her society's conceptualizations of gender in 1871, since her reflections on the Commune were written well after the fact. But her reported response to the ambulancières in Léo's article and her friendship with feminists like Léo and Maria Desraimes (one of the founders of the Association for the

Rights of Women) indicate that she was well aware at the time of the norms she was breaking and of men's disapproval. By the mid-1880s when she wrote her memoirs, she based her call for an end to discrimination against women at least in part on her experiences during the Commune. She knew many of her male friends had not championed women's rights in 1871. "How many times, have I gone to meetings where women were excluded?" she asked. "How many times, during the Commune, did I go, with a national guardsman or a soldier, to some place where they hardly expected to have to contend with a woman?"[130]

By 1886 Michel believed deeply that a revolution in the position of women was needed. She foresaw a future in which "men and women will walk together through life, as good companions, hand in hand, no longer arguing . . . about who is superior to whom."[131] Challenging male radicals, she asked, "Are we not beside you fighting the great fight, [making] the supreme struggle? Will you be bold enough to play a part in the struggle for women's rights, after men and women have won the rights of all humanity?"[132] She knew the answer to this question had been "no" in 1871. Not only had she and other ambulancières faced opposition from the commanders of the National Guard but, she wrote in 1886, "at the [meetings] of the Rights of Women, as everywhere where the most advanced of men applauded the idea of equality, I noticed (I had noticed this before and I have noticed it since) that men, despite themselves, and because of the force of custom and old prejudices, gave the appearance of helping us, but they were always content with just the appearance."[133]

Despite their failings on the question of women's equality, Michel held her male comrades in high esteem. She was especially respectful of the men who belonged to the Montmartre Vigilance Committee. During the Prussian siege, she attended their meetings as well as the women's meetings, and spent long afternoons discussing issues with them. "Never have I seen minds so direct, so unpretentious, and so elevated," she wrote in her memoirs. "Never have I seen individuals so clearheaded. I don't know how this group did it. There were no weaknesses."[134]

She had generous praise for her female comrades, too, but whereas she complimented men for their intelligence, she lauded women for their courage. "I salute . . . all these brave women of the vanguard," she wrote in her memoirs. "Watch out for the old world on the day the women say, 'That's enough!' They will not slack off. Strength finds a refuge in them; they are not worn out. Watch out for the women. From Paule Minck who crosses Europe waving the flag of liberty, to the most peaceful daughters of Gaul, sleeping in the great resignation of the fields. Yes, watch out for the women, when they rise up, disgusted with everything that has happened. On that day, this [world] will end and the new will begin."[135]

The differences in her accolades for men and women reveal some of Michel's thinking about gender differences. The men of the Montmartre Vigilance Committee, the finest men she knew, were brilliant. They were theorists. Women, in contrast, were courageous, strong, and practical. They knew what needed to be done, and when the appropriate time came, they would do it, regardless of danger. In her history of the Commune, she declared: "Women do not ask if something is possible, but if it is useful, then they do it."[136]

Michel was more an intuitive than a systematic thinker. While she praised the women of the Montmartre Vigilance Committee for their courage, she also believed them to have had "remarkable intelligence." Unfortunately, most women did not have the same education as men. That they did not seemed nonsensical to her, for the world needed women's intelligence: "I have never understood why there was a sex whose intelligence people tried to cripple as if there were already too much intelligence in the world."[137]

Michel's emphasis on women's courage was both a reflection of her experiences during the Commune and a criticism of her male friends who had not believed in women's equality and had even opposed their efforts to defend the Commune. But in praising the intelligence of the communards and the courage of the communardes, she was also contradicting standard bourgeois conceptions and prejudices. One expression of the bourgeois notion of womanhood can be seen in Blanchecotte's writings. "Real women" shrank from war and tried to end it. They did not want to take up arms to support any cause.[138] Men like Victor Pillon might praise bourgeois women for their "more than masculine courage,"[139] but it was their endurance, not actions, that was being praised. To have gone farther would have been unfeminine and abnormal. Michel disagreed with these assumptions. She viewed all women as potentially strong and courageous. For her, femininity did not entail passivity, endurance, or pacifism. She also disagreed with the conservative assumptions that the leaders of the Commune had been fanatics driven by class prejudice and emotion. She "knew" them to have been rational political theorists motivated by humanitarian ideals.

Michel's statements about men and women are self-revelatory and self-protective. She regarded herself and other women as the men's equals in their willingness to defend the revolution. Her refusal to minimize her actions when she was tried in Versailles earned her the right to this opinion. But her defense of women's courage and activism can also be seen as a de-

claration that she was like other women and that she and they were not abnormal, not, to use the word of her day, "pathological."[140]

Where Michel succumbed to the culture of her day was in seeing her
male colleagues as her intellectual superiors. She respected the intelligence of other women, had the self-confidence to send her poetry to Victor Hugo, the most famous French poet of her era, voiced her opinions at
public meetings, championed female education, and believed the men
were wrong about women's rights. Still, she believed men, or at least these
men, were smarter—not better educated, more intelligent.

Louise Michel was, of course, an extraordinary femme forte as her life
and especially her unflinching defense of the Commune before her accusers in Versailles demonstrate. She was represented as extra- or non-or-
dinary, too. Conservatives questioned her femininity, thereby hoping to
discredit her. The political Left, in contrast, saw her as the embodiment of
the social revolution. When she returned from exile, the conservative press
called her "the angel of petrol," "the virago of the rabble," and "queen of
the scum," while Ferdinand Gambon, a former member of the Commune,
compared her with Jeanne d'Arc, and Edmond Lepelletier repeated the
identification in 1911.[141]

The most lasting representation of Michel was the *vierge rouge* or the Red
Virgin. So compelling was this image that liberal and conservative historians have used it in their histories of the Commune, even though the nick-
name was not created until long after.[142] The title appears to have dual origins. The journalist Félicien Champsaur represented Michel as *une nonne
rouge* (a red nun) when she returned to France in the general amnesty of
1880. Devoid of personal life aside from her love for her mother and her
cats, she was devoted to "the people."[143] The title was given visual sub-
stance by caricaturist Alfred Le Petit in his cover illustration for Champsaur's article in *Les Contemporains* (fig. 16). Clothing Michel in a red habit
and large white wimple, placing her right hand around a rifle and her left
around a wounded national guardsman, Petit captured the two sides of
Michel's activities during the Commune: she was both warrior and nur-
turer. In the contradiction lay what many saw as her essence and her de-
viance. Just as she was not a true nun (her cause was revolution, not religion), she was not a true or real woman (she fought like a man).

In a separate but perhaps related development, a terra-cotta statue of a
young girl was erected on the Ducos Peninsula where Michel and other
prisoners were held when they first arrived in New Caledonia. It was a
memorial to a young girl, Emma Piffault, who died there when her family
joined her deported Communard father. The color and subject matter of

FIGURE 16. Alfred Le Petit, "Louise Michel," *Les Contemporains*, no. 3, 1880. Bibliothèque Nationale.

the statue led first to its being called "Red Virgin" and then to its identification with Louise Michel.[144]

Maurice Agulhon has suggested that with the creation of the Red Virgin, "a new turning point had been reached in the fortunes of the allegory of the Revolution."[145] At the very least, it was a new addition to the pantheon of female allegorical figures, although the identification of the Red Virgin with a specific human woman sets it apart from such representational figures as Marianne (the Republic), Paris, the Commune, and France, which have no identification with specific women. The Red Virgin might represent revolution in general or the Commune in particular, but she also always represents Louise Michel.

Both the Left and the Right used the image of the Red Virgin. For the Left, the image was saintly and heroic, exemplifying unwavering devotion to the social (red) revolution. It was thus that Michel's friends and the crowds who came to hear her speak when she returned from exile used it.[146] Historians, as mentioned, have repeated it. Pictures of her are almost invariably identified as the Red Virgin.[147] Biographies often include the phrase in the title.[148] Even the English translation of her memoirs is titled *The Red Virgin.*[149] Other epithets—"the people's muse," "the virgin," "heroine," "saint," "druidess," and "priestess of the revolution"—have been less popular, but writers have used them, too, to convey what they have seen as her uniqueness.[150]

For the Commune's critics, the Red Virgin was not a saint but a virago. She was almost always described not as virginal but as lacking in femininity. Alistair Horne, for instance, tells us that "the redoubtable *vierge rouge*" was "a familiar, somewhat masculine figure, stalking into churches to demand money for the National Guard ambulances, wearing a wide red belt and seldom without a rifle (with bayonet fixed) slung from her shoulder." In this representation, Michel marches through his history of the Commune, "goading on the crowd" here, "escaping from her captors" there, and always "shooting to kill."[151]

Whether she was represented by Commune supporters or critics, Louise Michel was always the quintessential femme forte of the Commune. Only she was the Red Virgin. The image was uniquely appropriate since it represented her in terms of her political cause, simultaneously focusing attention on her and on the social revolution to which she had dedicated her life. When she returned from exile in New Caledonia to a tumultuous public reception, she presented herself as not wanting such attention. Refusing an interview with *L'Intransigeant,* she explained, "You know that even though I allowed myself to be the object of a reception, I want attention to be addressed not to my personality, but to the Social Revolution and the women of that Revolution."[152] She could not escape attention, however, nor, her biographer, Edith Thomas, has declared, did she really want to: "She needed to bathe in the crowd, to make direct contact with her enraptured or hostile, but always excited, listeners. She devoted herself to it entirely. She sought [attention] out everywhere."[153] To a considerable extent, she had become her representation. She was the Red Virgin, the living representation of the Commune, for conservatives and radicals alike.

The Femmes Fortes of Paris

Women's own writings present a more complex and contradictory picture of the experiences, ideas, goals, and personalities of the women who lived through the Commune than the representations of women in male-authored contemporary literature and histories. In their writings, we can see women responding to the events that touched their lives and challenged their sense of the world. Their responses involved attempts to order and alter those events. Sometimes they argued and proposed to act specifically as women; sometimes they acted with and virtually as men. Sometimes they were critical of men's treatment of women, which they defined as oppression; sometimes they proposed to help men. At all times, they were involved in a complex negotiation with their culture's expectations and idealizations of womanhood. Sometimes they conformed to those expectations and idealizations; sometimes they challenged and broke them.

Bourgeoise Céline de Mazade revealed a playful and nurturing side and a religious devotion that fit her class's definition of femininity, but she did not conform neatly to this role. She was also a skilled businesswoman who led a far from domestic life. There is, for instance, no mention of children in her correspondence with Alexandre. Nor was she reticent in her encounters with the National Guard. Most important, perhaps, she revealed a desire to wreak vengeance on the Communards which accorded neither with Christian morality nor with cultural definitions of bourgeois femininity.

Augustine-Melvine Blanchecotte came close to acting out the role of the bourgeoise, with her bifurcated notion of the nature of man and woman and her almost religious commitment to pacifism. But she, too, violated the norms of her gender. She chafed under the notion that women's ideas were of no account and she published her diary because she wanted to affect public policy.

Louise Michel, in contrast, willfully and gladly violated the norms of female behavior. The opposite of a pacifist, she was drawn to the excitement and danger of battle, carried a gun and used it to defend the Commune. She also thrived on intellectual debate and argued for women's rights to education and jobs. She tended, however, to regard men as more brilliant than women and readily adopted nurturing roles in relation to men, her mother, and her famous cats. However much conservatives denigrated her as masculine, her nurturing set her apart from the men who were her friends, as did her understanding of how badly women needed decent-paying jobs and good education.

André Léo's crossing of gender lines is revealed nowhere more clearly than in her pseudonym. While her writings show traces of some of the gender conceptualizations of her age (she suggested, for instance, that women could strengthen the morale of men and made no mention of the reverse), she believed that men's denials of women's passion for the revolution and civil rights were self-serving and hypocritical. She argued that women's passion for the revolution was the equal of men's and that only fools would deny them the right to participate fully in defending the great cause. She considered herself the intellectual equal of men, in fact, the intellectual superior of most of them, and she had no compunctions about criticizing them publicly.

The four women who spoke for themselves (rather than as the leader of an organization, as Elizabeth Dmietrieff did) are difficult to categorize. They shared characteristics and desires across class and political lines and combined what others thought were contradictory qualities. The most violent woman was the most nurturing. The pragmatic businesswoman was religious. The feminist journalist wrote under a man's name. The quiet pacifist wanted to save men from themselves, sharing this activist agenda with the journalist. The businesswoman and the revolutionary both supported the violent measures taken by their respective sides. The intellectual journalist was a mother. All four of them spoke their minds and thought the world would be better off if men would only listen to them. They were the strong women of Paris, and unlike the stereotyped fragile ladies and warrior amazons of Commune texts, they were complex human beings.

CHAPTER FIVE

Les Pétroleuses

During the final week of the Commune, when the Versailles and Communard troops fought in the streets of Paris and thousands of Parisians lost their lives, one of the most powerful political symbols of the nineteenth century was created—the pétroleuse. Virtually overnight, this representation of the dangerous, unruly female incendiary came to symbolize the evils of the Commune for its critics. She could not have been imagined without the fires that burned furiously in parts of the city, but she also was the heir of the female representations already circulating—the gun-wielding amazons, furies, viragoes, female orators, and cantinières. They preceded her on the Commune's stage and made it not only possible but easy for the bourgeoisie to believe in her existence.

For conservatives, the fires and the sinister pétroleuse were a godsend, since they distracted attention from the army's slaughter of the Parisians. For the Communards and their supporters, they were albatrosses they could not throw off. Long after it was apparent both that the fires had been set by men and that they had not been as devastating as was first believed, defenders of the Commune found themselves trapped into refuting charges that they had hired women to commit arson and destroy Paris. With the creation of the pétroleuse, the Communards lost control of symbolic imagery and propaganda. Despite repeated efforts, the Communards in exile were unable to shift public attention to the unwillingness of Versailles to negotiate or to the bombardment of Neuilly, the executions of prisoners, and the extraordinary death toll of the semaine sanglante. Instead, the pétroleuse lingered in people's minds, a powerful personifica-

tion of evil with which to condemn the Commune and to question the very
nature of woman. With the fires and the execution of its hostages, the Commune lost the struggle for Paris and for the hearts and minds of the world.

The Semaine Sanglante

The Versailles forces invaded Paris on the night of May 21–22. Well in-
doctrinated at Versailles to hate the insurgents of Paris and following orders to take no prisoners, they moved methodically through the city, killing
working-class Parisians.[1] Hardly better prepared to fight the army in Paris
in May than it had been to attack Versailles in March, the Commune abandoned all attempts at a unified response at the outset and called for the defense of the barricades. On the morning of the twenty-second, Charles Delescluze, the gray eminence of the Commune, a veteran of the Revolution
of 1848 and the Commune's last civil delegate of war, declared, "Enough
of militarism and staff officers with their gold-embroidered uniforms." It
was time for "the people" to take over. They "know nothing of clever maneuvers, but when they have rifles in their hands [and] cobblestones under their feet, they do not fear all the strategies of the monarchical school.
To arms, citizens! To arms!"[2] In the afternoon, the Committee of Public
Safety followed suit, placarding Paris with its own call to the barricades:
"Rise up, good citizens! To the barricades! The enemy is within our walls.
Do not hesitate! Forward! For the republic, for the commune and for lib-
erty! To arms!"[3]

The mystique of the barricades was great. With them, Parisians had defeated kings and won revolutions in 1830 and 1848.[4] As Mark Traugott has
observed, they had become "as much a representation of the revolutionary tradition as an instrument of combat pure and simple. . . . [they] mobilize[d] prospective combatants and reinforce[d] the bonds of solidarity
among them" by linking them with preceding generations of revolutionaries who had similarly built and defended barricades in Paris.[5] In the preceding weeks, all over the city, groups of national guardsmen had posed in
front of barricades for photographers.[6] So the decision to fight from the
barricades was popular, but it also would be deadly, for the Commune
could not win at the barricades against a well-trained and determined
army.

On May 22 women and men, adults and children rushed to strengthen
the barricades that remained from the March 18 confrontation and to
build new ones. Passersby (mainly journalists and bourgeois men who
could not resist the allure of battle) were pressed into service, but the Com-

munards did most of the building.[7] Men and women labored with enthusiasm and optimism. Edmond de Goncourt saw a woman near the Opéra pulling up paving stones, and Catulle Mendès watched a "tumultuous swarm of men, women, and children, coming and going, carrying paving stones" to construct a barricade on the Chaussée-d'Antin.[8] In another part of town, Augustine-Melvine Blanchecotte watched the building and defending of a barricade on her street, and she too commented on the fervor of its builders and defenders. "I have a barricade at my door," she wrote on the twenty-third. "Women and children built it to the tune of the *Marseillaise*. Four others are being built, beside it, opposite it, to the right and to the left of it. . . . The barricade guards, sentinels of the street, feverishly watched the street all night; some of them have fallen from fatigue."[9]

As the shelling and fighting continued and "the ambulances passed, red with blood," the building of the barricades intensified and the mood turned somber. On May 24 Blanchecotte reported, "Our barricade, judging from the expressions of the guardsmen, is becoming serious. . . . They have procured the murderous machines: a machine gun is already installed and a large cannon awaits its place."[10]

Similar scenes were repeated everywhere. The newspapers of May 24 extolled the courage and energy of the people as they prepared for battle. (For most of the Commune press, this would be their final edition.) In the *Tribun du Peuple* Lissagaray reported "along the entire line heroic courage, fierce resolution. Men, women, children, have risen up in all of the high *quartiers*. This is the battle front that we present to the royalists."[11] Félix Pyat's passionately pro-Commune newspaper, *Le Vengeur*, reported that "on the barricades, one sees women, children, and the elderly; everyone understands the grandeur of the battle and is united in a supreme effort."[12] The *Journal Officiel* reported that "the children construct the barricades that their fathers defend, and women, themselves mothers, guns in their hands, build up the courage of the citizens by their words and actions."[13]

In actuality, the battle had been lost by the time the newspapers appeared on the twenty-fourth, although the fighting would continue for several more days. There were to be no victories and little grandeur for the Communards, whose zeal was no match for the Versailles troops' indoctrination and training. Indeed, the desire of Versailles to send an unmistakable message to future generations who might contemplate revolution, combined with the Communards' knowledge that surrender meant not just the death of their ideals but literal death, kept the battle for Paris going long after it was lost.

Even if they misjudged the possibility of victory, the newspapers were right about the age and sex of the city's defenders. Women as well as men, children as well as the elderly defended the barricades.[14] On Blanche-cotte's barricade, "a hardy, strapping boy of twenty years, with a very sweet and fine figure," sat astride the cannon during the day, waiting for the Versaillais. At night, "old men who cannot fight as well as the young men," stood guard. This night, an old man, "who shivered under his thin jacket," had taken the watch. In the morning, "an old woman arrived, bringing him his soup." When the battle reached the barricade in the afternoon, women and national guardsmen defended it. "Women prepare the guns, the men fire them," Blanchecotte observed before she retreated to the basement of the building. When she emerged, "there was blood everywhere; by the doorways, by the sidewalks, a red rivulet ran," and the young artilleryman who had sat "so dreamily, on his cannon" the morning before, lay among the dead.[15]

Louise Michel was present at the end of the Commune as she had been at the beginning, carrying a message from General Dombrowski to the Montmartre Vigilance Committee, defending the Montmartre cemetery with a detachment of the National Guard, and fighting from one barricade to another with guardsmen and other women long after she knew the Commune had been defeated.[16] In the working-class sections of the city, the women who had worked together in the vigilance committees and the Union des Femmes built and defended several barricades.[17] The barricade at the place Blanche at the foot of the Montmartre cemetery was defended by women (see fig. 13). So, according to Lissagaray, were the intersections of the boulevard Saint-Michel and the rues Racine and de l'Ecole-de-Médecine.[18]

Those who fought, also died. On May 24 Lissagaray watched children fight alongside the men as they were pushed back from the Bourse to Saint-Eustache. There, he observed acerbically, "when the guardsmen were out-flanked and massacred, the children had the honor of not being excluded."[19] On the twenty-fifth, he reported that "a young girl of nineteen, Marie M...., dressed like a marine gunner, rosy and charming, with black curly hair, fought all day," at the Château-d'Eau barricade, only to be killed by a shell that landed in front of her.[20]

Sebastien Commissaire watched a company of young women, armed with chassepots, make their way toward one of the barricades in Mont-martre. "The little column did not go far," he reported. "Arriving at the place Pigalle, where there were the beginnings of a barricade, it was met by lively gunfire from the boulevard Clichy. Then it was turned and taken from the flank by a battalion coming from the rue des Abbesses and the rue Houdon. All of those who were part of this little troop were killed or taken prisoner. From my window, I saw several of the women, whom I had seen go down the street with their arms a few moments earlier, marched back up it, disarmed and surrounded by soldiers."[21]

Louis Jezierski, a writer on military affairs, reported that there were a "good many armed women" among the Communard troops, including "one small force composed entirely of women."[22] Archibald Forbes, the foreign correspondent for the *Daily News,* heard that the place Vendôme "had been held for hours by twenty-five Communists [*sic*] and a woman," and he saw the corpse of another "Hecate who fought on the Rue de la Paix barricade with a persistence and fury of which many spoke."[23] Elizabeth Dmietrieff was wounded but escaped capture at the barricade of the faubourg St. Antoine.[24]

As rank-and-file guardsmen and civilians fought and died and the Communal Council dithered, Raoul Rigault and Théophile Ferré, the angriest and most violent of the elected members of the Commune, determined to settle old scores and to avenge the massacre that was occurring all around them. Close to seventy prisoners held by the Commune would not survive this quest for vengeance.[25] First, Rigault engineered the execution of Gustave Chaudey, who had been in charge of the Hôtel de Ville on January 22 when the Breton troops had fired on and killed demonstrators. Chaudey had been imprisoned by the Commune because he had taken responsibility for the decision, although he had not given the order to fire. Ignoring his declarations of his republican credentials and his pleas for mercy, Rigault ordered his death.[26]

Next, Ferré decided to execute some of the Commune's hostages who were being held at La Roquette prison.[27] Six of them, including Monsignor Darboy, the archbishop of Paris, and Judge Bonjean, the president of the Parisian courts, met their deaths on the twenty-fourth.[28] Two days later, about fifty more La Roquette prisoners were marched through the streets to the *mairie* of the twentieth arrondissement and then to the rue Haxo, where they were executed by a crowd of men and women seeking their own revenge for the deaths of friends and kin. Jules Vallès, editor of the *Cri du Peuple,* and two other members of the Commune tried to prevent what was soon known as the massacre of the rue Haxo. They knew full well that this vengeance was immoral (even though Versailles was executing prisoners wholesale) and would be used as proof of the "evils" of the Commune.[29] Among the thousands killed by the Versailles forces were forty-two men, three women, and four children who were dragged to the garden on the rue des Rosiers where Generals Lecomte and Clément Thomas died. There, they were forced to kneel before being shot. Deaths like these, however senseless, had no similar impact on public opinion, however, since the victims were not public figures.[30]

While the hostages died, the killing of the Communards continued. Those who fought on were hungry, tired, dirty, wounded, scorched by the sun and then soaked by the rain that began to fall on the twenty-sixth, forced to retreat from barricade to barricade, and surrounded by corpses. The best that might be said for the Communards, as Lissagaray noted, was that they died well.[31] Those who fought were shot; those who surrendered were shot; those who hid in houses were dragged into the streets and shot,[32] until the last barricade fell on Monday, May 29, at eleven o'clock in the morning. Even then, the killing did not stop; prisoners continued to be taken, lined up in parks and cemeteries, and mowed down by machine guns.[33] Not everyone died immediately, of course, and at night, screams of agony could be heard from the piles of bodies.[34]

The Communard newspapers were no longer publishing and the conservative French papers had no journalists in Paris, but British journalists roamed the city along with displaced Communards and bourgeois observers. On Tuesday, May 23, Archibald Forbes reported on the sounds of the battle:

> About 10 the din began again. Shell after shell burst close to us in the Boulevard Haussmann, and there came the loud noise of a more distant fire, which seemed to be sweeping the barricade. In the intervals of the shell fire was audible the steady grunt of the mitrailleuses, and I could distinctly hear the adjacent Boulevard Haussmann. This dismal din, so perplexing and bewildering, continued all night.[35]

Lissagaray's account of the semaine sanglante often lapses into the first person. As a Communard supporter, he emphasized the killing, along with the noise and the fires. Writing about the night of the twenty-second (the end of the first day of fighting), he reported, for instance, "with nightfall, the fusillade slackens but the cannonade continues. A red glow rises from the rue de Rivoli. The Ministry of Finance burns. Throughout the day, it has received part of the Versaillais shells aimed at the Tuileries terrace, and the papers piled up in its upper stories have caught fire. . . . Then begin the seven tragic nights. . . . There were nights more noisy, more glaring, more grandiose, when the fires and the cannonade enveloped all of Paris, but none penetrated the soul more mournfully. . . . We seek each other in the gloom, speak in low voices, giving and taking hope. . . . Henceforth there will be no more rest."[36]

Blanchecotte spent the night of the twenty-third hiding with her neighbors. Her report indicated no lull in the fighting during the long hours of the night. "The raking sound of the machine guns, the cannon fire from the Panthéon which shook the house, the screams of the shells, the furious fusillade that seemed as if it would break down the door and let in the bullets, the racket of the paving stones, the yells of the combattants, the falling of bodies, the certainty of a nearby explosion, all this seemed to last an eternity,"[37] she wrote in her diary.

Conservatives and foreigners emphasized the damage to the city that became visible with daylight. "Looking out, and cautiously, up the Boulevard Haussmann," Forbes continued, "I saw before me a strange spectacle of desolation. Lamp-posts, kiosks, and trees were shattered and torn down. The road was strewn with the green boughs of trees which had been cut by the storm of shot and shell."[38] Goncourt wrote a similar account of the ruins of Auteuil.

> There is confusion and destruction such as a cyclone might make.
>
> You see enormous broken trees whose shattered trunks look like a bundle of kindling; pieces of rail weighing a hundred pounds that have been thrown on the boulevard; manhole covers, lead plaques four inches thick, reduced to fragments the size of a cube of sugar; bars of grillework twisted and knotted around each other like the handle of a wicker basket. . . .
>
> Underfoot there are unexploded shells, pieces of gun carriages, pieces of cannons, broken boxes with 4 de M written on them, debris and slag of every kind; in the middle of all this, water from the broken water mains gurgles like springs.[39]

The number of Parisians killed by the soldiers during the semaine sanglante and its aftermath is unknown, for thousands were buried in mass graves without being counted or identified. Estimates range from a low of seventeen thousand by General Appert, who headed the National Assembly investigation of the Commune, to a high of fifty thousand by various newspapers. Most historians subscribe to a figure of twenty thousand to thirty thousand, frequently settling on twenty-five thousand. This count does not include the fifteen thousand national guardsmen who were killed by the Versailles troops before the invasion of Paris began. Whatever the precise figure, the death toll was enormous compared to Versailles' losses—877 dead and 6,454 wounded.[40] It was also enormous for the nineteenth century. In the Revolution of 1830, the army killed two thousand Parisians; in the June Days of 1848, between fifteen hundred and three thousand, with hundreds more executed without trial.[41]

As the mass executions continued, some journalists rebelled and filed horror stories with their editors. On June 1 the *New York Tribune* carried a lengthy story about the execution of a group of thirty-three "Communists," including seven women. The prisoners were "made to kneel close togeth-er," and a large firing squad took aim. Then "a volley was fired, and when the smoke cleared away a horrible sight was presented. Three of the women, who were in the middle of the row, between the men, were still liv-ing, and writhing in agony. A second volley was fired and a third, and not until the sixth did all the prisoners cease to live. The dead bodies were then flung onto the three scavenger carts and carried away to be buried." On June 10, it was still publishing accounts of the "vindictive" government troops under the headline, "Paris after the Capture... Brutality of the Ver-saillists."[42]

Shorter reports, reflecting the journalists' growing dismay appeared in other newspapers. On May 25 a *New York Herald* correspondent reported, "The slaughter is awful."[43] On the twenty-sixth the *Daily News* correspon-dent revealed that some of the Commune's leaders had approached him for help, and he found it "heartrending to see the misery which has now overtaken them . . . and to be unable to do anything for any one."[44] The *New York Times* reported on May 27 that "the slaughter of the Nationals [Communards] is frightful and the Versaillists . . . are killing all prisoners," and continued on the twenty-ninth that "there are rumors of awful cruel-ties perpetrated by the Versaillists."[45] On June 1 the *Standard* published its correspondent's opinion that "it is high time that these wholesale and in-discriminate butcheries should cease." On the fifth he added that "the re-membrance of the scenes of horror I have myself witnessed in the way of reprisals makes me shudder as I write." On the seventh he chastised the Versailles troops for having shot people "down like dogs" and focused on the treatment of women: "It is not too much to say that a large proportion of these victims, especially as regards women, had no offence proved against them."[46]

The Female Barricade Fighters

The female barricade fighters had symbolic as well as practical impor-tance. The last news items in the last issues of two of the Commune's ma-jor publications emphasized the participation of women and children in the building and defense of the barricades.[47]

Although the fighting went on for several more days, it was appropriate that these newspapers' final words were about women and children. With these reports, the Commune returned symbolically to its origins. Like the women who had created the Commune by defending the city's cannons with their bodies, women were preparing to defend it on the barricades.

Like the women of March 18 *and* like those who grieved for the dead and wounded in the ensuing weeks, the barricade fighters were represented as mothers. That they were armed demonstrated their seriousness of purpose, not their kinship with the Commune's more controversial warriors and female orators, whom even radical men found troubling allies. The women wanted, Pyat said, "to make their children free." They were willing to sacrifice themselves (and, if need be, their children and husbands) for the sake of the revolution. They did not relish the struggle or their own participation in it. Their actions were not aggressive but defensive, not self-serving but self-sacrificing, not self-centered but altruistic. Their nobility and heroism symbolized the Commune.

Others would interpret women's presence on the barricades as a violation of their feminine nature, especially since they were armed with guns and bayonets. For these observers female combatants represented all that was dangerous about women and all that was evil about the Commune. The women's dangerousness was often represented in sexual terms. Catulle Mendès was delighted to mention that a group of women "tucked their skirts up and passed them through their belts," so they could pull a machine gun down the street to a barricade; he described them as "livid, horrible and superb."[48] Jezierski (and Vizetelly, who quoted him) mentioned the short skirts worn by a "small force composed entirely of women."[49] Forbes wrote of the zeal and tenacity of one female fighter,[50] but not everyone was convinced of the women's fighting ability. Jezierski and Vizetelly, for instance, reported that "these Amazons" were "hardy and daring, but at the last moment they shrank from death."[51]

In addition to the mothers of the barricades, Commune supporters presented other positive images of the revolution's female defenders. Lissagaray described a cantinière with a bloody handkerchief tied round her head as a "wounded lioness" and wrote of "a young girl of nineteen, rosy and charming, with black, curling hair, dressed as a marine fusilier," who fought "desperately" on the barricades for a whole day.[52] Commissaire reported on a "company of young women, armed with chassepots, . . . bareheaded and dressed in black," which made its way pluckily toward battle, and he felt "pity and compassion" when he heard one young woman confess to another that the fusillade scared her.[53]

Observers of all political positions shared one thing in common, however, and that was an inability to ignore the female barricade fighter. Had the Commune won the battle against Versailles, some image of her—a "lionness," a "rosy and charming" young woman, or a self-sacrificing mother—might have taken its place alongside Delacroix's Liberty in the pantheon of revolutionary iconography. Had the fighting not been accompanied by fires, a "livid, horrible, and superb" amazon of the barricades might have become the Commune's negative representation. But the barricade fighters were eclipsed by another female figure who arose from the ashes of Paris to become the personification of the Commune.

The Fires

The Versailles sweep through Paris began late on Sunday night, May 21. At no point did the battle go well for the Communards, although they did manage to halt the troops' advance at various points. By noon of the twenty-second, the army had captured the entire western side of Paris. Already, Versailles's incendiary shells had started a fire at the Ministry of Finance, and attempts to put it out had failed. As the army's shells continued to ignite buildings, the Communards added to the conflagration by setting fires to cover their retreat. By nightfall of the twenty-third, fires burned from the Madeleine to the rue de Rennes. The Palais Royal and the Louvre library had been set ablaze to halt the advance of the Versaillais, and the Tuileries Palace, out of revenge against the monarchy whose restoration the Communards feared would now occur. On Wednesday the twenty-fourth, the Hôtel de Ville was ignited as the Communal Council, Committee of Public Safety, and War Delegation abandoned it, partly to conceal their retreat and partly to deny its conquest to Thiers.[54]

Charred paper from the Ministry of Finance and Louvre library floated on the wind. The press reported that the museum itself was on fire. Like a reflection of the blood that ran in the streets, at night the city glowed red; smoke, sparks, and ashes rained down on the earth. For everyone who saw them, the fires were, as Gibson recorded, "a sight such as we shall never forget."[55] Journalists reported that it was "hard to breathe in an atmosphere mainly of petroleum smoke" and that "the sun's heat is dominated by the heat of the conflagration, and its rays by the smoke."[56]

An American woman who had spent part of her childhood in Paris, including the weeks of the Commune, later voiced a common sentiment: "I was often frightened during the Commune, but I do not remember anything more terrifying than the fires."[57] Gaston Cerfbeer, also a child at the time, remembered later that a friend of his had pointed out "a stirring of black things in the street moving rapidly. 'They are,' she told me, 'the rats from the ministry. Thousands of them, chased out by the fire.'"[58] Goncourt's servant told him that she "slept with her clothes on the whole time, . . . and provided herself with a mattress to put on her back to protect herself from all that was falling outside from overhead, in case the house was set on fire."[59]

Observers who watched from outside Paris were perhaps even more susceptible to rumor and alarm than those in the city. As they watched from the hills outside Paris and snatched at bits of charred paper, they were convinced that the entire city was burning to the ground. The *Standard*'s correspondent reported on the twenty-fourth that Versailles had "been in a state of indescribable agitation" since an early hour.[60]

When the fighting ended, it became apparent that the fire damage was not as great as had been imagined by either the journalists in the city or those who had watched from a distance. The Louvre museum, for instance, had not burned. The special correspondent for the *Standard* of London wrote from Paris on May 30 that he was "convinced that the first exclamation of the vast majority of those who may come over to see for themselves the destruction wrought in Paris will be, 'How grossly these newspaper correspondents have exaggerated.' Had I not been in Paris myself on Wednesday and Thursday, witnessed the tremendous conflagrations, and heard the unceasing crack of artillery, mitrailleuses, and musketry, I should certainly have myself been of the opinion that the accounts of what had taken place had been, to say the least of it, highly coloured. . . . the damage is exceedingly partial."[61]

The damage to the Commune's reputation was another matter. Bourgeois journalists, editorial writers, letter writers, and memoirists ignored the killings and focused on the fires. They could not find enough terrible things to say about the Communards. The *Times* opined that "the Red Republicans of 1871 . . . have revealed a spirit too inhuman to have been credited beforehand, and by their last act they will be 'damned to everlasting fame.'"[62] The *Standard* declared that "the recent news from Paris has inspired the civilised world with disgust and horror. The destruction of the beauty and splendour created by the art and taste of the most artistic and tasteful people in the world . . . the wanton annihilation of the treasures accumulated in the Tuileries . . . the yet more atrocious attempt to destroy the Louvre . . . these are crimes unprecedented in modern history, and only to be paralleled, and feebly paralleled, by some of the worst atrocities of the barbarians who ravaged the various provinces of the decaying Empire of Rome."[63] The *New York Herald* called for more executions: "Our advice is no cessation of summary judgment and summary execution. Devils let loose from their own place cannot be too soon sent home. . . . Root them out, destroy them utterly, M. Thiers, if you would save France. No mistaken humanity."[64] Céline de Mazade and her friend Berthe

Amiard-Fromentin voiced similar sentiments in letters. Mazade hoped that
the government would "continue to give no mercy to these monsters," and
Amiard-Fromentin exclaimed, "How the blood flowed and still flows! One
is without pity for these miserable incendiaries."[65] These vindictive sentiments would linger for a long time.

The Pétroleuses

How women came to be held responsible for the fires is the intriguing
question, since there is clear evidence that, while women may have participated in the burning of the Tuileries Palace, the vast majority of the fires
were set by men.[66] Indeed, women were not the first to be blamed. On
Wednesday, May 24, Adolphe Thiers condemned the setting of the fires in
a speech to the National Assembly at Versailles. Ignoring the army's use of
incendiary shells as well as the inevitability of fires in a city under attack,
he blamed the Communal Council and the National Guard: "These miserable wretches have for a long time had a scheme to make Paris an immense ruin in case their own plans did not succeed. They have set fires. . . .
The insurgents have made use of petroleum. . . . These attrocious villains
. . . have tried to deliver the entire city up to the flames. . . . They have done
more: they have used petroleum bombs against our soldiers, and several of
them have been wounded."[67] By Thursday, May 25, when the destruction
was thought to be far greater than it actually was, the press began to focus
on vengeance rather than strategy and accident as the source of the fires.
The *Times* (whose political conservatism is revealed in its persistent use of
the term "Communist" rather than "Communard") declared that the fires
were "wrought without a shadow of provocation; . . . it is an act of deliberate and demoniacal malice . . . a mere act of revenge, when the Communists saw their cause was ruined."[68] The editors of *Le Figaro* also subscribed
to the revenge theory when they began to publish again on May 30. On
the thirty-first, the paper reported that the fire at the Ministry of Finance
(set by the incendiary shells of Versailles, *not* by the Commune) "was carefully and diabolically prepared, kerosene bombs [*bombes à pétrole*] [and]
cartridges strewn everywhere, constantly rekindled the flames."[69] The *New
York Herald* had a different theory—hereditary depravity. "Paris was always
peculiarly susceptible to communistic tendencies," it announced on June
4. "If the theory of hereditary depravity be correct, then we have an explanation for the horrible ferocity and absurd idealism of the Paris mob.
The city was largely settled by desperadoes, to whom morals and religion
were idle, meaningless words, and their descendants have for centuries
made the French capital the most disorderly metropolis in Europe."[70]

Rumors escalated and suspicion began to fall on noncombatants, including male fire fighters, women, and children. The *Times* on May 26 and *Le Gaulois* (a Versailles newspaper) on May 29 reported that firemen had been shot when it was discovered that they were pumping petroleum rather than water into the flames, and both announced that windows were being barricaded to prevent the fire bombing of houses by women and children. Walking through the city, the *Times* correspondent had discovered that "the fears of petroleum and explosions are universal. The inhabitants had either stopped up, or were engaged in stopping up, every chink through which petroleum might be thrown into their houses. . . . The precaution was taken because *women and children,* partisans of the Commune, have in numerous instances been detected throwing petroleum into houses."[71]

Most suspicion fell on women. On June 3 *Le Monde Illustré* published both a verbal and a visual representation of them (see frontispiece.) "The women show particular venom," it announced. "These furies glide through the rich quarters, profiting from the darkness or the desertion of the streets that the civil war has caused; and fling their little vials of petrol, their devil's matches, their burning rags [into cellar windows]."[72] E. B. Washburne, the American minister to France, quoting an unnamed source, gave even more detail:

Here is a description of a *Pétroleuse:* "She walks with rapid step near the shadow of the wall. She is poorly dressed; her age is between forty and fifty; her forehead is bound up with a red checkered handkerchief, from which hang meshes of uncombed hair. Her face is red, her eyes blurred, and she moves with her eyes bent down. Her right hand is in her pocket, or in the bosom of her half-buttoned dress; in the other hand she holds one of the high, narrow tin cans in which milk is carried in Paris, but which now contains the petroleum. If the street is deserted she stops, consults a bit of dirty paper that she holds in her hand, pauses a moment, then continues her way, steadily, without haste. An hour afterward, a house is on fire in the street she has passed. Such is the *pétroleuse.*"[73]

The fear of such treachery would keep the cellar windows of Paris closed throughout the long hot summer that followed the Commune. Yet, it was absurd to be so fearful, as Colonel Wickham Hoffman of the U.S. Legation pointed out: "The windows were barred, and the cellars in Paris are universally built in stone and concrete. How [the pétroleuses] effected their purpose under these circumstances is not readily seen. If this was their *modus operandi,* they were the most inexpert incendiaries ever known."[74]

Rumors about the number of women involved grew rapidly. At first only the isolated woman was suspected, but soon reports were claiming that "many" of the arrested women were pétroleuses.[75] On May 28 and 29 *Le Gaulois* reported that men, women, and children had been paid ten francs per building to start fires. Washburne repeated this story in his memoirs, embellishing it with the "information" that eight thousand men, women, and children had been employed to distribute incendiary devices.[76] It quickly became commonplace for newspaper stories and the titles of illustrations to refer to all of the arrested communardes as pétroleuses, regardless of whether they were charged with the specific crime of incendiarism.

The credibility of the "reports" was enhanced by their specificity. *Le Gaulois* was especially inclined toward detail. On May 28 it reported that the pétroleuses were "armed with tin boxes, about the size of a large sardine can and containing a mixture of kerosene [*pétrole*], tallow, and sulfur," which they lit with a match. (Most people actually believed that the women carried bottles, not boxes.) On the twenty-ninth it reported that during the month of April the Commune had infiltrated "its most fanatical partisans" into the ranks of the firemen "whose mission was to stir up the fires when they were beginning to die out."[77]

Although men were also thought to be setting fires, women were widely regarded as more active than men and as the greater villains. M. Chastel, a librarian, reported in a letter on Wednesday, May 24, that it was "especially the women who are setting fires to the houses. Many have been taken in the act and shot at once."[78] Washburne declared in his memoir, "Of all this army of burners, the women were the worst."[79]

Children were commonly regarded as women's accomplices. Washburne, for instance, announced: "Whenever it was possible, the *pétroleuse*, who was to receive ten francs for every ten houses burnt, would find some little boy or girl whom she would take by the hand and to whom she would give a bottle of the incendiary liquid, with instructions to scatter it in certain places."[80] Children as well as women, if they were deemed suspicious looking, were arrested and executed. Residents and journalists reported seeing the bodies of dead children as well as child prisoners. Washburne and Hoffman reported the deaths of six or eight children (their accounts vary), the eldest "apparently not over fourteen," who were "caught" carrying petroleum in the avenue d'Autin.[81] Georges Renard remembered seeing a row of dead women and children lined up along the wall of the Collège de France.[82] Goncourt recorded in his diary on May 26, that he had seen "a band of frightful street urchins and incendiary hooligans" who were being held in the train station at Passy.[83] On May 28 Chastel reported that he had seen a large number of prisoners including "women and children, who sometimes were obliged to run to keep up with the rest, or they would have been trampled on by the horses."[84] And on the thirtieth the *Journal des Débats* announced that groups of "fifteen to twenty national guardsmen, civilians, women and children" were being systematically executed at the Place Lobau.[85]

Women were accused of other crimes as well, most notably the poisoning of the Versailles troops. These stories harked back to Jules Allix's 1870 plan to arm female warriors with *doigts prussiques*. On May 27 the *Times* reported that ten soldiers had been poisoned by a cantinière; on May 28 Edwin Child wrote to his father that forty men had been poisoned.[86] Eventually the story of the poisoners appeared in all the newspapers covering the fighting. Again the number of women assumed to be involved in this crime and the number of their victims escalated rapidly. The accusations lacked the staying power of the accusations of incendiarism in a city that had seen huge fires, however, and the press and public devoted far more attention to the pétroleuses.

The Prisoners

The horror of the semaine sanglante did not end with the street fighting and executions in Paris. Thousands were taken to Versailles to be interrogated and tried. Young and old, male and female, somewhere between thirty-five thousand and fifty thousand were marched out of the city, guarded by soldiers, some tied together in groups with cords, others manacled in pairs.[87] After a week of steady fighting, the prisoners were exhausted and bedraggled even before the long trek to Versailles began. Journalists and memoirists recorded their impressions of the prisoners' weary countenances, torn clothing, dirty faces, and dragging bodies.[88]

Male and female prisoners alike were treated inhumanely and humiliated. They were forced to walk bareheaded and without food and water under the hot May sun and through drenching rain. Those who could not keep up with the pace of the march and others for no discernible reason were executed along the roadside. All were subjected to the taunts and abuse of Parisians and Versaillais who had opposed the Commune.

As early as the twenty-fourth the *Daily News* correspondent reported that "the behavior of the crowd was far more horrible [than the horrible condition of the prisoners]. 'Shoot the wretches!' they cried. 'Show them no mercy!'"[89] The librarian Chastel similarly reported that the crowd "hooted" the prisoners as they passed along.[90] Bingham, the *Pall Mall Gazette* correspondent, recounted in his published diary: "For many a long day after the insurrection was quelled long caravans of prisoners were to be seen

wending their way to Versailles, innocent and guilty alike, to the great delight of substantial citizens . . . [who] revenged [them]selves indiscriminately."[91] The *Times* reported that "escorts with prisoners are continually
passing through the streets followed by a jeering job."[92] The *New York Tribune* repeated the story on June 7 for American readers.[93] Even *Le Gaulois*
reported that "the crowd, exasperated by the preceding days, accosted [the
prisoners] with invectives and cries of 'Kill them!'" and "even some stones
were thrown at the prisoners."[94]

Many found it painful to watch the exhausted and taunted prisoners
trudging through the streets, often to be shot without trial. The *Times* correspondent in Versailles called it a "harrowing" experience; Goncourt said
he felt "horror"; and Blanchecotte wished that she lived on the moon, so
she "would not have to encounter another of these sad processions.[95] Still,
people could not shake off their fascination with the prisoners and especially with the pétroleuses.

Accounts likened them to the Furies of Greek myth, wild animals, witches, and madwomen, and dwelled on the ugly and the beautiful. Goncourt
described a group of 66 women and 341 men:

> Among the women there is the same variety [as among the men]. Some
> women in silk dresses are next to a woman with a kerchief on her head. You
> see middle-class women, working women, streetwalkers, one of whom wears
> a National Guard uniform. Among all these faces there stands out the bes-
> tial head of a creature, half of whose face is one big bruise. . . . Many of them
> have the eyes of madwomen.[96]

Edwin Child wrote to his father on May 28:

> The women behaved like tigresses, throwing petroleum everywhere & dis-
> tinguishing themselves by the fury with which they fought, a convoi [*sic*] of
> nearly four thousand passed the Boulevards this afternoon, such figures you
> never saw, blackened with powder, all in tatters and filthy dirty, a few with
> chests exposed to show their sex, the women with their hair dishevelled & of
> a most ferocious appearance.[97]

The conservative *Paris-Journal* reported on May 31:

> In the midst of the atrocious scenes that shock Paris, the women are partic-
> ularly distinguished by their cruelty and rage; most of them are widows of
> Communards. Madness seems to possess them; one sees them, their hair
> down like furies, throwing boiling oil, furniture, paving stones, on the sol-

diers, and when they are taken, they throw themselves desperately on the bayonets and die still trying to fight.[98]

Gibson, who was not in Paris during the week of fighting and did not see
the prisoners himself, nevertheless recorded in his diary on May 27, "We
learn that women, more like furies than human beings, have taken a
fiendish part in the work of destruction."[99] Bingham called the female prisoners "hideous viragoes, . . . furies intoxicated with the fumes of wine and
blood."[100] The Reverend Mr. Ussher of Westbury, who was more sympathetic than Bingham, nevertheless told Ernest Vizetelly that he was "particularly struck by the awful expressions which he noticed on the
[women's] faces. . . . It was, indeed, for the most part something unnatural, a compound of savagery, revengefulness, despair and ecstatic fer-
vour. . . . Many of them were now sheer furies."[101]

The *New York Tribune* correspondent similarly singled out women when
he reported briefly on May 26 that he saw "a long file of prisoners pass,
many fierce women and soft girls, all bare-headed and begrimed, linking
arms with [one another] proudly as they marched."[102] *Le Figaro* in an article about the last group of prisoners to be marched from Paris to Versailles,
on June 2, declared that the journalists were not alone in their fascination
with the female prisoners. The crowd had the greatest interest in the
women, who came after the men, it reported. It was looking for the
pétroleuses. When people saw them, they "devoured them with their eyes,"
and "they tried to discern the leaders who had inspired this terrible battle
in the sinister heads of these witches; they stared at the hands that had
poured the incendiary petroleum on the monuments of Paris."[103]

Many contrasted the women's demeanor and behavior, both before and
after capture, to that of their male comrades. Goncourt found that none
of the arrested women had the same "apathetic resignation" as the men.
"There is anger and irony on their faces."[104] *Le Figaro* reported that the
women and children in the convoys of prisoners "marched with a hardier
step than the men. . . . The men are more solemn and seem to be asking
themselves if it would not have been better to think before serving against
their brothers in the army." The older women, in particular, were presented as unbowed. "Their mouths have a kind of sardonic smile; their
feverish eyes glow like hot coals. One of them regards the crowd with the
glazed eyes of a dead person and seems placed there to personify the sinister *tricoteuse* of the revolutionary tribunals."[105] The *Times* correspondent
reflected on the fighting, "More courageous than the men, the women
show fight to the last moment, and meet their death, according to the accounts of those who have witnessed their executions, with an undaunted

courage."[106] In contrast to the women, the male prisoners who march through the pages of the *Times* "are depressed, walk with bowed head, and shedding tears, which trace muddy streaks down their blackened cheeks."[107]

Goncourt even managed to see the women's demeanor as sexually provocative; certainly he attributed no such attitude to any of the men:

> The rain increases. Some of the women pull up their skirts to cover their heads. A line of horsemen in white coats has reinforced the line of foot soldiers. The colonel . . . shouts: "Attention!" and the African infantrymen load their guns. At this moment the women think they are going to be shot and one of them collapses with an attack of nerves. But the terror lasts only a moment; they quickly renew their irony, and some their coquetry with the soldiers.[108]

Gender and Judgment

The heroic mothers and splendid tigresses of Pyat, Lissagaray, and the editors of the *Journal Officiel* were no match for the furies, madwomen, witches, harpies, seductresses, and pétroleuses of the conservatives. Forgetting, or perhaps never understanding in the first place, the political grievances that had triggered the revolt, the lack of violence with which the Communal Council had governed the city, and the no-prisoners policy of the national government which had prolonged the semaine sanglante, bourgeois men and women were obsessed with representations of the women on the barricades as immoral and unnatural. Children and men had committed crimes, too, but their actions (and, hence, they themselves) were rarely seen as quite so evil.

Undistracted by the misery and humanity of the prisoners, editorial writers and columnists far from the scene voiced opinions about the women. Francisque Sarcey, an ultraconservative columnist for *Le Gaulois,* offered his readers the analysis of a physician on May 28, while the killing of Communards was far from over. In his view, the women, or at least most of them, had not set fires for money. On the contrary, they had been "under the epidemic influence of the incendiary mania," which the doctor suggested, resulted not from willfulness but from the misery of the Prussian siege. "The revolt of March 18 struck the last blow to those already disturbed brains; and the mental derangement ended in a violent explosion, seizing at the time the largest part of the population. It is one of the most astonishing cases that physiologists have observed, this epidemic of madness, which is well known to *médecins aliénistes* [psychiatrists]." Having laid out this "medical" theory of *folie contagieuse* (contagious insanity), the doctor (and Sarcey) then explained women's involvement in the setting of fires: "The women carry in this attack of madness an exaltation more ferocious than the men; it is because they have a more developed nervous system; it is that their brain is weaker and their sensibility more lively. They also are one hundred times more dangerous, and they have caused without any doubt much more evil."[109] Sarcey had reservations about the implications of this theory for retribution (if the women were mad, punishment might not be appropriate), but he was absolutely convinced that the women were more dangerous and had caused more evil than the men.

Two weeks later, he returned to the question again. This time his experts were men "whose judgment and word" he could not doubt and who had "spoken with him with an astonishment mingled with horror of the scenes they had seen, seen with their own eyes." These unimpeachable eyewitnesses had told him of "young women, with pretty faces and dressed in silk," who had come down the street armed with revolvers, "firing at random" and asking, "with proud mien, loud voices, and hate-filled eyes," to be shot. When the soldiers accommodated them, they died, with "insults on their lips [and] contemptuous laughs, like martyrs who, in sacrificing themselves, accomplish a great duty." Sarcey found much to contemplate in this report.[110]

Whether the silk dresses of the women meant they were bourgeoises acting against their class interests or prostitutes acting in theirs, is unclear. Other accounts are not so ambiguous. Many ascribed the fires to prostitutes. The *New York Herald* wrote floridly on the twenty-eighth about the "loose women of Paris, those debased and debauched creatures, the very outcasts of society, . . . knowing no shame, dead to all feeling, without homes, without friends, no little ones to claim their attention," who had set the fires.[111] The government reiterated this theory later, when it tried the female prisoners, and in the official National Assembly report on the Commune, General Appert declared that the 850 women who were taken to Versailles were "almost all nomads, given up to disorder and prostitution." Well over half of them were married, he was forced to admit. Nevertheless, even they "did not give the appearance of having a regular life and, like the others, had for the most part long since forgotten all the sentiments of family and morality."[112]

The *New York Tribune* correspondent did not agree. He noted the variety of female prisoners: Some "were dressed as vivandières. . . . One had a child strung on her back. The arm of another was in a sling. The habit-skirt on another pretty brunette was covered with fresh blood. Another Amazon was wounded." Whereas "they all showed symptoms of fatigue," he declared, they "still wore a defiant air, and did not seem to belong to the class with which the Magdalen asylums are peopled."[113] *Le Gaulois* had an entire catalog of guilty female types which included prostitutes but was not limited to them "the amazons of the Commune, the incendiaries of the monuments and of Paris, the poisoners of the French soldiers, the pimps and prostitutes of the Satraps of the Hôtel de Ville, the promulgatrices of the code of free union in free debauchery, the female dethroners of God . . . and priestesses of Marat, . . . the heinous shrews who invented the motto 'Murder and kerosene [*pétrole*].'"[114]

Others cataloged crimes according to sex and age. The *Times* suggested that it was a case of "women forgetting their sex and their gentleness to commit assassination, to poison soldiers, to burn and to slay; little children converted into demons of destruction, and dropping petroleum into the areas of houses; soldiers in turn forgetting all distinctions of sex and age, and shooting down prisoners like vermin, now by scores and now by hundreds."[115] The catalog in the *Standard* was pithier, but it, too, believed women had forgotten their sex. "Men have forgotten their chivalry, women their sex, children their innocence," it wrote on the thirtieth.[116] The anti-Commune *New York Herald* declared in the same vein, "Knowing no shame," the women had "unsexed themselves."[117]

Exactly what women became when they forgot their sex and acted violently was not entirely agreed. Some saw them as inhuman (e.g., creatures); some as immoral (e.g., furies, harpies, and witches); some as debased and debauched (e.g., prostitutes); and some as madwomen. It is difficult to know exactly what the *Standard,* the *Times,* and other critics meant by the phrase, but the *Times,* by linking their sex with gentleness, and the *New York Herald,* by referring to "lack of shame," give us some clue. For many, the gentleness and purity these women seemed to have forgotten or lost were essential parts of their nature, synonymous with femininity.

No comparable loss of essence was implied by men's actions. They might have committed crimes. They might have forgotten to be chivalrous, might have shot prisoners like vermin. But they had not ceased to be masculine, had not forgotten their sex or violated their essential nature (although they might have forgotten their humanity). Although it is perhaps an oversimplification, it is relatively accurate to say that for many nineteenth-century observers, women's crimes were crimes *against* femininity, not *of* femininity, whereas men's crimes were crimes *of* masculinity.

Bourgeois culture conceived of woman's nature as bifurcated or dual. Man's nature was more unified. This difference made it possible for women to seem more duplicitous than men. A virtuous woman could become wicked. Exactly how this happened was not clear, but if a woman shook off the restraints of civilization, the church, and the family, she could go from being Mary to being Mary Magdalene, from being pure and moral to being impure and immoral, from virginity to prostitution, from feminine reticence to promiscuity. Only one-half of these dichotomies was truly feminine. The other half was still female (i.e., not male) but also somehow antifeminine. If woman's nature was fundamentally fissured, if the moral mother could become the seductive fury, then the communardes had not so much violated their sex as they had become another part of it, not willfully but inevitably. They had moved from the good to the bad side of their nature. No longer virtuous and maternal, no longer staying in their homes to care for their children, they had become the incarnation of evil, tempting men, corrupting their children, and burning the homes in which they "naturally" belonged. Indeed, one of the "crimes" ascribed to the pétroleuse was that she had corrupted her children and turned them into little incendiaries. Such women had lost or forgotten or violated their femininity.

Some analysts worked with other dichotomies having to do with particular aspects of nineteenth-century notions of gender. For them, women's weakness (versus men's strength) was the explanation for the pétroleuses and other wicked women of the Commune. Sarcey's physician offered a version of this theory in his view of women's weaker brains and livelier sensibilities. Jules Bergeret, an elected member of the commune, voiced another. "The woman is destined, by her physical and moral nature, to remain within the narrow circle of the domestic hearth," he wrote. But if the sanctity of the home were violated, as Bergeret believed it had been by the Versailles invasion of Paris, "then, and only then, do women rise up enraged." "You may call them furies," he declared, "but it is society that has driven these passive creatures into madness."[118]

The inevitable conclusion of such theories, as both Bergeret and Sarcey could see, was a radical alteration in the question of guilt and innocence. For Bergeret, this was part of the theory's appeal. If society had driven the women to fight, then "he who would strike them without pity was himself condemned."[119] For Sarcey, on the other hand, the idea that women were not responsible for their actions and should not be punished was unthinkable and he backed away form it immediately. Having already suggested that there were "horrible shrews" among the demented women, "who know what they are doing and act cold-bloodedly," he demanded that they, at least, be punished. "Those who have schemingly contributed to spread this madness, who have excited and carried it to this state," he wrote, "let us hope that at least they will not escape the severe punishment that they merit."[120] How the wicked were to be distinguished from the merely mad was unclear. What was clear was that it was one thing to draw a distinction between the nature of man and the nature of woman which would define the pétroleuses as evil and another to draw a distinction that would absolve women of responsibility for their actions.

Punishment

The Versailles soldiers wreaked great vengeance against the National Guard and the Commune leaders when they invaded the city, killing men by the hundreds and thousands. Even republicans who had not supported the Commune were executed.[121] In addition to simple execution, the soldiers used various forms of humiliation against their victims. This was true for both men and women, but the punishment meted out to women often had a sexual dimension that was absent in the treatment of the men.

Several men reported that women's clothing was torn or stripped off before they were executed. Recall Child's report that some of the prisoners who were marched through the streets had their "chests exposed to show their sex."[122] On May 26 the *Times* correspondent reported that thirteen women, "caught in the act of spreading petroleum" had been executed "after being publicly disgraced in the Place Vendôme."[123] The ripping of the women's bodices to reveal their breasts may have been the least of this humiliation, judging from other reports. Bergeret, citing the journals of Versailles as his source, reported that the women who were arrested in the first, eighth, and ninth arrondissements were taken to the place Vendôme, "stripped, raped, and massacred."[124]

Sometimes the humiliation followed execution (more or less). Georges Jenneret, quoted from the *Droits de l'Homme* of Montpellier, "As for the women who were shot, they treated them almost like the poor Arabs of an insurgent tribe: after they had killed them, they stripped them, while they were still in their death throes, of part of their clothing. Sometimes they went even further, as at the foot of the faubourg Montmartre and in the place Vendôme, where some women were left naked and defiled on the sidewalks."[125] Lissagaray reported a similar scene in the eleventh arrondissement. Risking arrest for his support of the Commune, he walked cautiously toward the *mairie* on the twenty-eighth. There, he saw a dead woman and "a marine fusilier [who] was dividing the entrails that protruded from her with his bayonet."[126]

Symbolic undressing also occurred. Goncourt reported that some of the women he saw being marched through the city were concealed behind

veils until a "noncommissioned officer touched one of the veils with a cruel and brutal flick of his whip" and demanded, "'Come on, off with your
veils. Let's see your slutty faces!' "[127] Unveiling a woman's face, like tearing
her clothing, accomplished several objectives. On the simplest level, it revealed her sex. Since some of the women were dressed in National Guard
uniforms, tearing their bodices to show their breasts confirmed that they
were women. But more than simple identification was going on here. Soldiers undressed and unveiled women to humiliate them.

For men, simply being captured and thus rendered powerless was hu-
miliating, as their reportedly passive behavior in the convoys demonstrated to the crowds along the way. Since women were supposed to be powerless anyway, capture alone would not humiliate them, as their reported
defiance and coquetry "indicated." Merely imprisoning them was not sufficient punishment; more was needed. Stripping a woman (not to mention
raping her and thus violently reminding her of woman's powerlessness)
was intended to accomplish the desired humiliation. It would reveal to the
world, or at least to the spectators and firing squads, that she was only a
weak woman after all, not a fury with the power to burn houses and kill
men.

In addition to capture, men were subjected to other forms of humiliation. Some were shot in the back; others were forced to kneel before their
executioners. Prisoners in convoys had to remove their kepis and turn
their uniform jackets (if they wore one) inside out. Goncourt found that
the turning of men's jackets made them seem "half undressed," even
though they remained fully clothed.[128] Here, the ritual degrading of men
stopped, presumably because even mild forms of humiliation (compared
with rape) put men in the passive position of women and thereby emas-
culated them, and because the punishers were themselves men.

For women, undressing went further. But no matter what men did to the
women, the pétroleuse remained a frightening but compelling figure, a
fury with unbound, flying hair; a defiant madwoman, captured but wild;
sometimes ugly and sometimes beautiful, often seductive, and always more
powerful and more fascinating than her cowed male counterpart, who,
once arrested, became serious and unnaturally passive, while she continued to appear unnaturally aggressive. To make matters worse, the sexual
humiliation, rape, and killing of women had some potential to produce re-
pulsion not against the women but against the soldiers. After all, in the
proper bourgeois order of things, women would be protected by men. To
degrade and kill them, even if they had gotten out of their proper place,
was problematic. As the *Standard* pointed out, it could happen only if men
forgot their chivalry.

The Bourgeoises

Just as men repeatedly "described" the female prisoners, they also commented over and over on the bourgeoises who taunted and tortured the prisoners as they marched through the streets. The *Times* reported on May 27 that the jeering mob following the prisoners contained "more women than men among its ranks—women who hoot and clap their hands and insult their victims to their hearts' content"; and reiterated Voltaire's misogynist declaration that a Parisian woman was "half tiger and half monkey!"[129] Forbes reported the lynching of a communard by a mob and Versailles soldiers on May 24 in similarly misogynist language: "Very eager in their patriotic duty were the dear creatures of women. They knew the rat-holes into which the poor devils had squeezed themselves, and they guided the Versaillist soldiers to the spot with a fiendish glee.... They yell, ... `Shoot him! Shoot him!'—the demon-women most clamorous of course."[130]

Cerfbeer long remembered the columns of prisoners and how the spectators had treated them. As the prisoners made their weary way through the city, he recalled in 1903, "one heard no cry of pity; horrible epithets, insults, *injuries,* rained down upon them along with pieces of charred wood and stones.... Above all, the women were without pity, screaming 'Kill them! To death!'"[131] Even Maxime Du Camp, one of the Commune's severest critics, was distressed by the women's behavior: "When a band of prisoners appeared, people rushed toward them and tried to break through the cordon of soldiers who escorted them and protected them; the women were, as always, the most agitated; they broke through the military ranks and beat the prisoners with umbrellas, crying: Kill the assassins! Burn the incendiaries!"[132]

Whether the women in fact behaved substantially differently from the men is unclear. What is clear is that many male and some female observers perceived and judged that behavior differently.[133] The perception was born of bourgeois notions of class and gender which made the behavior of the bourgeoises as appalling and even more surprising than that of the working-class communardes. Unlike the communardes, the bourgeoises could not be dismissed as loose women, living in disorder and prostitution, or as suffering from *folie contagieuse.* Indeed, it was precisely because they were perceived as having middle-class homes, husbands, and children, and hence as having been relatively protected during the ordeals of the two sieges, that their vengeful public behavior was so troubling.

Perhaps even more than the communardes, the bourgeoises confirmed men's fears about the nature of women. If bourgeois women could lose control, "forget their sex," and become furies, then all women were potential viragoes, and no woman could be completely trusted to remain loyal, submissive, and nurturing. To make matters even more complicated, the bourgeoises also violated the code of middle-class behavior toward defeated enemies. The *New York Tribune* reported on Wednesday, May 31, "The women of Versailles display a *cowardly violence* against the helpless prisoners."[134] The journalists expected bourgeois women, like their men, to be brave under duress and gracious in victory, not cowardly and vengeful. Coming on top of the unexpected and frightening behavior of the communardes and violating gender and class codes at the same time, the behavior of the bourgeoises seemed to provide proof both that French society was in a state of collapse and that every woman was a potential fury.

The bourgeoises could not be punished by arrest and imprisonment as the communardes could. They had broken only the laws of propriety, not the laws of the state. But their unladylike behavior could be thoroughly condemned in the press, and it would not soon be forgotten by bourgeois men.

The Pétroleuse and the Artist

Artists and caricaturists produced visual representations of the pétroleuses, sometimes to accompany the descriptions of journalists and sometimes to stand alone. These images, perhaps more than the written descriptions, gave staying power to the myth. In the artists' hands, however, the variety of pétroleuses described by reporters and other eyewitnesses— the implacable fury, her hair disheveled and unrestrained, her eyes wild with insanity; the madwoman, her face distorted by rage; the stunning beauty; the coquettish and seductive young woman—was lost. Replacing them were two major images—the hag and the victim.

In unsympathetic representations, artists emphasized the hideous, stripping the women of the compelling fury and sexuality of the written descriptions. They became banshees racing around Paris with their cans of petrol (fig. 17); hags pouring petrol through windows, sometimes assisted by their corrupted children (fig. 18); or in one of the most vicious anti-communarde cartoons of the period, a pig (fig. 19), a reversal of the myth of Circe, who seduced the companions of Ulysses with her beautiful voice and hair and turned them into swine.

The horror and rage conservatives felt toward the pétroleuses is obvious in the caricatures, as is their sense that these were unnatural women. Natural women do not have pigs' snouts, crouch around cellar windows like Macbeth's witches around a cauldron (see frontispiece), or race through

FIGURE 17. Eugène Girard, *The Emancipated Woman Shedding Light on the World.* Bibliothèque Nationale.

FIGURE 18. [Nevel] Untitled—pétroleuse and child. Bibliothèque Nationale.

FIGURE 19. Dubois, "A Pétroleuse. Ah! If her man could see her." *Paris sous la Commune*. Bibliothèque Nationale.

the streets with burning faggots and cans of petrol. By emphasizing the hideous in their drawings of the pétroleuse, the anti-Commune cartoonists went one step farther than the verbal descriptions in their hatred of women. But they also missed one of the things that made the journalists' pétroleuse so horrifying, and hence so hated—her sexuality.

For the conservative artist, the pétroleuse was to be the embodiment of evil, not a sexually attractive woman who could command the attention of men or a victim for whom the viewer might feel sympathy. To draw Goncourt's beautiful young fury with wild curly hair, steely eyes, and reddened cheeks would have been counterproductive. Attraction or sympathy on the part of the viewer would interfere with the message of the caricaturists. Baring the breasts of the pétroleuses, as the written accounts indicate occurred, was also impossible. It might have confused the message by reminding viewers of the powerful and virtuous bare-breasted goddesses of contemporary and classical art and caricature, or by turning the pétroleuses into victims.[135]

Frédéric Lix, in his representation of the pétroleuses for *Le Monde Illustré* (see the frontispiece) emphasized the evil of the female incendiaries by foregrounding them and juxtaposing them to ideal bourgeois women—a well-dressed, nurturing mother with a child in her arms and a well-coiffed, well-dressed young woman. They, along with a defenseless old man, are fleeing (or in the case of the woman at the upper window, trying to flee) a burning building. Lix's subjects illustrate what he saw as the horror of the pétroleuses and the Commune. Evil had triumphed. Working-class women, who had "forgotten their sex," had taken control and were destroying the city. Men, in the form of two national guardsmen, who should have been in charge at least of the women of their class, had turned their backs and stood passively by. Defenseless (and good) bourgeois women, children, and old people were no longer safe in their homes. The world had been turned upside down in more ways than one.

In sympathetic representations, artists stripped the pétroleuses of both their sexuality and their fearsomeness and hence of their power. Their pétroleuses were young, attractive women (fig. 20), captured and afraid, who shrank back in fear against the walls where they were about to be executed. Powerless and helpless, these pétroleuses were not the furies of the bourgeois imagination but innocent victims of the Versailles soldiers. They could not be sexually seductive or coquettish or strong, or they might appear to be in some way responsible for their fate. Nowhere to be seen in these drawings is the woman whose beauty and defiance attracted Goncourt: "Among these women there is one who is especially beautiful, beautiful with the implacable fury of a young Fate. She is a brunette with

FIGURE 20. "The End of the Commune: Execution of a Pétroleuse," *The Graphic*, June 10, 1871. Bibliothèque Nationale.

wild curly hair, with eyes of steel, with cheeks reddened by dried tears. She is *planted* in an attitude of defiance."[136]

Although the artists eliminated sexuality from their drawings, the pétroleuse had to be immediately recognizable as female. For sympathetic artists, her femininity (as distinct from her sexuality) was integral to her victimhood. For unsympathetic artists, femaleness rather than femininity was the issue. If the figure could be misconstrued as male, the power of the message would be lost. Some caricaturists did draw an occasional *pétroleur,* but this figure soon disappeared from the histories and memoirs of the Commune. For men, the horror of the fires could be represented adequately only in the figure of the unnatural woman, the female incendiary. As a result, the drawings always depicted the pétroleuse in a dress, even though the written accounts indicate that *communardes* often wore men's clothing.[137]

In the pétroleuse, the Commune acquired its own particular and powerful representation of the unruly woman. Beside her, the amazons, furies, viragoes, harpies, and *vivandières* of history (and of the earlier days of the Commune) paled into insignificance. Her image would illustrate memoirs, histories, and textbooks for more than a century. What made her so frightening was the perversion of nineteenth-century femininity that she embodied. Unlike unruly women from the Amazons of ancient Greece to Jeanne d'Arc, she did not fight men on their own terrain, where they might be expected to win, inasmuch as even the strongest, fiercest woman was after all still a woman, and would, they believed, flinch from death. Instead, she turned the cunning and deviousness that was thought to be charming in the most feminine women[138] to evil purpose; she crept through the night to burn and destroy.

How could men fight this unruly woman who perverted femininity? How could men know which women were likely to succumb to this evil? How, indeed, were men to avoid the seductive power of such women? The answer, they hoped, lay in the punishment of any woman—pétroleuse or poisoner—who had perverted her femininity. And so, women who were thought to be pétroleuses were executed by the soldiers, taunted by the good bourgeoises of Paris and Versailles, and brought to trial for their "crimes." And in good symbolic fashion, a woman who was accused of poisoning forty soldiers was "taken to her home to be shot at the door of her house as an example."[139] William Gibson, who made this statement, saw no need to elaborate on what kind of an example the soldiers had in mind (assuming, no doubt, that no elaboration was necessary), but there can be little doubt about the meaning he read into this act. A woman's place was in her home. If she left it to behave unnaturally, she was no longer truly a "woman," no longer deserving of a "man's," protection, and she would be killed. Shooting a woman on her doorstep symbolically reinforced the message. Indeed, the entire semaine sanglante might be seen as a warning to the men and women of Paris of the kind of retribution they could expect if they rebelled again. Other warnings would sound from the courts in Versailles.

Women on Trial

While the killings continued in Paris and on the roads to Versailles, prisoners streamed into Louis XIV's city, sometimes for immediate execution but mostly for imprisonment, interrogation, and trial. For many writers, this part of the Commune's history has seemed an unnecessary appendage or epilog to the rise-and-fall narrative of its seventy-three days, and they have paid it little or no attention.[1] For the government and the surviving Communards, however, the Versailles trials were an integral part of the conflict that had begun on March 18. The government, embodied in military prosecutors and judges, set forth its case against the Communards and their government. The trials had three goals: to punish the Communards, to discredit the Commune and its principles, and to demonstrate the price of social revolution to those who might contemplate it in the future. The Communards defended themselves as well as they could, but for them, it was the national government and not the Commune which was on trial. The harsher the sentences the government meted out, the more it proved its own moral bankruptcy and guilt.

In the women's trials, a fourth issue was at stake for the government and its conservative supporters: the nature of woman. They wanted to know what kind of women these furies of the Commune were and what had provoked them to the crimes everyone was certain they had committed. Why hadn't they left this conflict to the men? Why hadn't they stayed at home with their children? Why had they joined in the fighting? Were they an aberration, or were all women potential pétroleuses and gun-wielding furies?

The questions went to the core of human nature and human relations. If women were not what men (and women like Augustine-Melvine Blanchecotte) believed them to be, what were they? If they were not pacifists by nature, then how did they differ from men? And if all women were potential furies, what was to prevent them from attempting to seize political power from men, from turning into "the monstrous regiment of women"?[2] The ramifications of these questions were enormous, for constructions of femininity and masculinity were diametrically defined, and changes in the definition or construction of femaleness automatically challenged the definition or construction of maleness. The men's trials raised no comparable questions; explanations of their actions lay readily to hand. Men were expected to have political convictions, class interests, and self-interests, as well as the capacity for violence. For them, revolution was reprehensible, and they would be punished for it, but it was also explicable; for women, it was both reprehensible *and* inexplicable.

Prisons and Prisoners

The number of men, women, and children who left Paris under arrest, as well as the number who arrived in Versailles, is unclear. So many people were executed en route, so many arrived, and so many were sent on to other prisons to be held for trial that no one could keep track of them. Even the figures used in the National Assembly's official report on the Commune are not entirely consistent. The most frequently cited figures for prisoners who arrived in Versailles are 1,051 women, 32,614 men (categorized as civilians, although most of them were members of the National Guard), 651 children and 5,000 members of the military who were in Paris when the conflict ended (the vast majority of whom were freed without trial). Versailles could not possibly house forty thousand prisoners; so twenty thousand were packed off to be incarcerated in the holds of ships, and eight thousand were transferred to coastal fortresses, where they were held in dreadful conditions for months.[3]

For those who remained in Versailles, there were, as Frank Jellinek succinctly observed, "four hells called prisons," where men and women, children and adults, were incarcerated.[4] People were crammed into the cellars of the Grandes Ecuries and the Orangerie at the Château de Versailles, the stables of the Saint-Cyr military school, and the buildings, stables, and open fields at the Satory docks. Lissagaray's description of the conditions at the château and the riding school, based not on his own observations, since he had escaped arrest, but on those of this friends, convey some of the horror that awaited the prisoners after their march from Paris.

> Into these damp, loathsome cellars, where light and air penetrated only through a few narrow openings, the captives were crowded, without straw during the first days. When they did get straw, it was soon reduced to mere dung. [There was] no water to wash with, no means of changing their rags. Relatives who brought linen were brutally repulsed. Twice a day, in a trough, they got a yellowish liquid, a slop. . . . There were no doctors. Gangrene attacked the wounded; ophthalmia broke out; deliriousness became chronic. In the night, cries, groans of the fever stricken, and howls of the mad mingled together. The gendarmes [watched], their guns loaded, more merciless than ever.[5]

The "worst" male prisoners were held in even grimmer circumstances, in the so-called Lion's Den under the red marble staircase to the château's terrace. The prisoners incarcerated there endured utter darkness, stiffling heat, and virtual starvation.[6]

Satory, in contrast, was "hell in the open air."[7] The large clay plateau surrounded by high walls "housed" both male and female prisoners. Thirteen hundred huddled inside the buildings; hundreds more lived out of doors, subjected in turn to sun and rain, heat and cold.[8] One woman prisoner who arrived at Satory on Thursday evening, May 25, described the scene to Lissagaray.

> Many of us had died on the way; we had [eaten] nothing since morning. It was still daylight. We saw a great crowd of prisoners. The women were apart in a shed by the entrance. We joined them.
>
> They told us there was a pond. Dying of thirst, we rushed to it. The first who drank uttered a loud cry and vomited. "Oh, the wretches! they make us drink the blood of our own people." For since evening the wounded had gone there to bathe their wounds. Thirst tormented us so cruelly, that some had the courage to rinse out their mouths with this bloody water.
>
> The shed was already full, and we were forced to lie on the earth in groups of about 200. An officer came and said to us, "Vile creatures! Listen to the order I give: 'Gendarmes, at the first who moves, fire on these whores!'"
>
> At ten o'clock we heard gun shots quite near us. We jumped up. "Lie down, wretches!" cried the gendarmes, taking aim at us. They had shot some prisoners a few steps from us. We thought the bullets would pass through our

heads. . . . The gendarmes . . . grumbled at those who writhed with terror and cold, "Don't be impatient. Your turn is coming." At daybreak we saw the dead.[9]

Thursday night had been merely a prelude to the horrors that would follow. On Friday the rain began, and the guards continued to force the prisoners to lie on the ground, now mud, at night. The wounded and sick did not survive the experience. The night killings continued; prisoners were given picks and shovels to dig their own graves before they were shot. Holes were hacked in the walls of the shelters and the muzzles of machine guns inserted and sometimes used.[10] The only source of water was the pond, and the prisoners drank from it when, as Louise Michel later wrote, they "were too thirsty and when the heavy rain which was falling on them had swept away the pink foam."[11] This particular horror, being forced into a form of cannibalism, into drinking water tainted with their comrades' blood, which symbolized the inhumanity of the Versailles government in Communard memoirs, escaped notice, or at least comment, by the bourgeois visitors to the camp.

Other horrors did not, however. The correspondent for the *Standard,* one of the first journalists to visit Satory, was appalled at what he found. When he arrived on the twenty-eighth, it had been raining for forty-eight hours. As his carriage approached the prison, it sank in the mud halfway up to its axles. The prison yard and surrounding area was an ankle-deep "sea of mud." Three to four thousand male prisoners who had spent the night out of doors, were "drenched through, blue with cold and misery, hopeless and disheartened." Their only shelter from the rain had been some straw, which a few still held over their heads. Indoors, the prisoners were dry, but the "stench" in the men's barracks and the "close, noisome smell" of the women's were overwhelming.[12]

The most painful sight of all, for the correspondent, was the incarcerated women. Bad as he believed many of them were, he felt his presence was "an intrusion upon their misery." He comforted himself and his readers with the thought that "with them the worst was probably over. The busy horrors of the fight, the fear of instant execution, the long, weary tramp to Versailles, the jeers of the brutal crowd of Versailles, these had been suffered and were past. There remained only a term of imprisonment of more or less duration."[13]

Other newspapers that were sympathetic to the Commune reported more briefly, but nevertheless critically, on the conditions at Satory. On the thirty-first, the *New York Times,* citing *Le Soir* as its source, reported that "the prisoners at Satory are in a dreadful state. . . . thousands sleep without shelter in the mud. There is no food but black bread and the water is insufficient. The women are huddled with the men. The people cease to count the executions, there have been so many."[14] The pro-Versailles press, in contrast, ignored the conditions of the prisons and continued to report on the character and actions of the Communards, especially the women, to titillate their readers. The *New York Tribune,* for instance, strung together paragraph-long excerpts from British and American newspapers under headlines including "The Horror of Victory: Desperate Acts of the Female Insurgents," "Young Women Buried in the Ruins," "A Woman Who Had Killed Four Men Is Captured and Shot," and "The Captured Men and Women at Satory." Despite its headline, the last excerpt included only what the *Standard* correspondent had written about the female prisoners.[15]

An additional prison for women was created on the rue des Chantiers. Here, the women sat and slept on the floor, at first on the wood itself, eventually on bundles of straw. Their clothing was dirty and torn. For weeks, they were forbidden to see their families who tried to bring them clothing and food. Lice swarmed on the floors. Some of the women had had no involvement with the Commune; others, like Louise Michel, who was transferred there, had been devoted communardes. Some went insane; some survived. Constantly guarded, the women had no privacy, and they felt the lack of it more than did the male prisoners since the guards were men.[16]

The physical characteristics of the prisoners interested the visitors as much as their physical surroundings did, since "physiology" was thought to reveal character. The same would be true during the trials. Physiologists regarded the mind or "mental life" as a manifestation or product of "the intricately organized physical stuff composing the human body." Healthy and pathological anatomies, identifiable by sight, revealed a person's mental and moral condition. Facial features or physiognomy were not the only indicators of mental health and illness, but they were particularly important signs.[17]

The popular version of physiology to which the prison visitors subscribed was particularly appealing to the bourgeoisie because it considered class-based behavior as well as innate physical characteristics as indicators of mental life, values, character, and personality. This adaptation of physiological theory was particularly useful for conservatives who believed that the Commune was a proletarian revolution. Visual inspection could determine a prisoner's class and guilt or innocence, simultaneously. Bourgeois-looking men and feminine (i.e., bourgeois-looking) women looked innocent and were presumed to be innocent; proletarian-looking men and unfeminine (proletarian-looking) women looked guilty and were presumed to be guilty.

The foreign correspondent for the *Standard* subscribed to this popular-

ized theory of physiology as thoroughly as anyone. Searching the faces of
the male prisoners, he told his readers that "such a collection of villainous
faces, low, scowling foreheads, broad animal chins and mouths, and heads
of the convict type, were probably never seen together before."[18] He felt
no doubt about these men. Their features revealed them to be dangerous
and deserving of punishment (and to be proletarians). Among these obvious villains were some who "lacked the ferocity, the vigour, and the dogged
sullenness or defiant boldness of their fellows." These men looked "miserable and downhearted"; they bore "on their faces the bourgeoise [*sic*]
type." The correspondent was convinced that they had been pressed into
service against their will or had even been falsely arrested. He wanted to
free them instantly, especially a "bright, bold-faced lad of 14 or 15 [who
was] respectably dressed." He was hopeful for the lad, however, believing
that "his face" would be a "sufficient passport" when he was questioned by
the authorities.[19]

A second observer, quoted at length in W. P. Fetridge's 1871 history of
the Commune, echoed these opinions. Having commented on the number of "ignoble faces, and with such a vile expression," which he saw among
the prisoners, he opined that "it was almost in vain to seek a countenance
that would not have condemned its owner in the eyes of the most lenient
physiognomist."[20]

Women were subjected to the same judgment, but with an extra twist. In
addition to the physical features and demeanor by which the character and
class of both men and women were determined and judged, clothing and
hygiene served as indicators of femininity for the women. Women who
were truly feminine (i.e., innocent) cared about their appearance even in
settings of extreme deprivation. That cleanliness and a concern with hair
and clothing were class-differentiated behaviors was irrelevant, since class
was essentially what the voyeurs were judging. The women who retained
bourgeois female habits of cleanliness and neatness looked innocent and
were presumed innocent; those who appeared not to care about hygiene
and personal appearance, especially their hair and clothing, looked guilty
and were presumed guilty.

The *Standard* correspondent understood the criteria for judging
women's guilt and innocence as well as anyone did. One group "stared
boldly and defiantly" at him, "with faces from which all show of modesty
had disappeared years ago." These women were "ferocious-looking viragoes, the *tricoteuses* of the last revolution, the furies who poured blazing petroleum upon the heads of the troops as they advanced in this insurrection." A second group "looked down, abashed at the position and company
in which they had found themselves." These were "mild, frightened-look-
ing creatures, who had probably stood by some husband they loved on the

barricades, their love overcoming their fear." The first were dressed "in rags with wild hair, unkempt and matted, falling on their shoulders"; the second, "in decent clothing, and [they] had made some efforts to tidy their hair, and to preserve the look of women."[21] Who was guilty and who was innocent (or, at least, less guilty) needed no further explication.

Where the *Standard* correspondent saw strong female revolutionaries and viragoes and misled but devoted and moral wives, others saw immoral and "fallen" women. The female prisoners, one anonymous journalist reported, were "for the most part such as are commonly found in the neighborhood of soldiers' barracks, or in the lowest outskirts of Paris, squalid and dangerous localities, of which sketches are to be read in the pages of Suë and other romance writers, whose taste it is to dive into the lowest depths of human depravity and degradation."[22] In the trials, evidence of immorality would be taken as proof of other crimes. Only women who were sexually monogamous, that is, married, living with their husbands, and free of accusations of promiscuity, would have a chance of proving their innocence.[23]

The confusing and mesmerizing women were those whose appearance mixed bourgeois and unbourgeois elements. Fetridge's journalist was fascinated, for instance, by a girl, "slender and well formed, with a profusion of fair hair . . . [and] blue eyes." Such features would generally signal innocence to bourgeois observers. Yet her hair was "terribly dirty and tangled," her eyes were "shifting," and she had "the expression of a wild animal . . . as she roved restlessly up and down one end of a room, keeping close to the wall, brushing against it as a hyena does against the bars in its monotonous, weary pacing of its narrow prison."[24] Such signs of guilt (and madness) overwhelmed the signs of innocence, as the analogy of the prisoner to the hyena, rather than to a lioness or other revered female animal, reveals.

A third bourgeois observer, Edouard Dangin, visited the prison for women on the rue des Chantiers nearly a month later, primarily to disarm the continuing criticism of the government's treatment of the women.[25] Conditions had changed somewhat since the first days, but bourgeois theories and perceptions had not. Dangin reported that some of the women had fixed their hair and had "an honest and proper appearance"; others had unkempt hair and clothing that revealed "their moral state and social position." Some had retained the "instincts of propriety which the woman should never lose" and had washed their linen and hung it up to dry; others had not. As before, the outward appearance of what the bourgeoisie defined as femininity was read as a sign of innocence. Conversely, neglect of appearance—uncombed hair, disorderly clothing, and unwashed linen—was read as a sign of inferior social class, immorality, and guilt.

The condition of the prisons and the female prisoners presented a dilemma for the men who visited them which the journalists among them implicitly passed on to their readers. If the women were guilty, especially of incendiarism, they needed to be punished. But they had not been proved guilty yet, *and* they were still women. If they were not guilty of great crimes, and journalists doubted they were in many cases (a judgment that perhaps was supported by the government's eventual release of 643 women without trial), then the dreadful conditions to which they were subjected were wrong as were those who officially or tacitly approved of them.

Even if the women were guilty of crimes, subjecting them to inhumane conditions made men who were socialized to protect women (a standard rallying cry for male soldiers was the protection of women and children) uneasy. Lieutenant Guinez, appointed to defend one of the five defendants in the first female trial, expressed the dilemma. Asking for leniency for his client, he recounted a personal experience from the end of the Commune. "I was at Versailles," he told the court. "I was watching a convoy of prisoners among which there were several women who had covered their faces. Amid the screams that were directed at them, a *femme du monde,* an old woman, thinking I had some power to protect these unfortunate women, approached me and said, 'Have pity, Monsieur, these are women!'" "These few words, spoken with simplicity and a very military passion," the press reported, "provoked a murmur of approval in the audience."[26]

Uneasiness did not lead everyone to press for leniency, however. The government and military officials who tried the prisoners reacted in anger to the challenge the communardes had posed to their gender conceptualizations and asked for and gave harsh sentences to the women, sentences that justified (in their eyes at least) the conditions under which the women had been held. The sentences did not ultimately resolve the anxiety of bourgeois men, however, although that was the intention. The more violent the women were thought to have been and the greater the crimes for which they were convicted, the more they threatened to undermine the gender beliefs and values of their captors. Punishment would not remove the threat that the unruly women of the Commune had posed to the bourgeois understanding of women and the society it had created.

The Debate

Reports on the female prisoners were part of a debate about the communardes and the nature of woman that took place while people waited for the trials to begin. In the beginning, this discussion included criticism of the bourgeoises who had attacked the convoys of prisoners throughout April and May and especially at the end of May. But once the prisoners were out of sight and the bourgeoises had returned, figuratively if not literally, to their proper places, concern focused on the communardes and not their female attackers. The knowledge that female violence had crossed class and political lines did not disappear, however, and the memory of the conservative burgeoises who had become unruly women hovered silently over the ensuing debate about woman's nature, even though they were not on trial. Exacerbating the ambiguity were the bourgeois origins of leading communardes (women like Louise Michel, André Léo, and Elizabeth Dmietrieff), together with their bourgeois clothing and their good educations. Working-class communardes were not the only women who had broken the bonds of womanhood.

Francisque Sarcey's article "Les aliénistes" inaugurated the post-Commune debate about the nature of women even though it appeared before the fighting had ended.[27] Sarcey and his physician informant gave a "psychological" explanation for the "savage fury" of the Communards and pétroleuses, which attributed women's actions to their nature. The Communards were suffering from a "mental derangement" caused by the breaking of their spirit during the Prussian siege. The women were more dangerous and had done more evil than the men, however, because their "brains were weaker and their sensibilities livelier." In short, it was women's nature, not an aberration of it, that accounted for their behavior.[28]

Sarcey did not believe this contagion of madness accounted for all the communardes, however. In particular it did not account for their leaders who, Sarcey believed, had not been affected by the madness and instead had "schemingly contributed to spread [it]." Sarcey left them unnamed, but those who knew what they were doing and "cold-bloodedly" incited others to crime included, if they were not limited to, the female orators. These were often identified as bourgeoises, as they had been just two weeks earlier in Lix's illustration of a female club for *Le Monde Illustré*.[29]

Five days after Sarcey's article, *Le Gaulois* and *Le Figaro* broached the issue of woman's nature again. While the fires still burned, the executions still raged, and the prisoners flowed into Versailles, both newspapers devoted part of their front pages to an article, "La femme libre," by Francis Marnard, who was drawn to the figure in Lix's pulpit. Ostensibly, "La femme libre" was about the Commune. It began with a description of a dead communarde. Unlike most of the women who supported the Commune, she was not of the working class, as the description made clear: "Her head, which had been pretty, almost distinguished, in death wore an expression of fierce hatred." Even "at the last hour, [she] had not clasped her hands together to ask God for the forgiveness that men could not give her" but had died with "her right arm extended." Marnard shuddered with horror and pity as he contemplated the body of this young *malheureuse* (unfortunate one), who should have lived a long life "full of the sacred pain of maternity" but instead had become an assassin.[30]

Marnard's representation of the communarde used common images of bourgeois women. Her pretty, almost distinguished visage told him and his readers that she was not an ordinary communarde or pétroleuse. To reinforce the point, he identified her as a *malheureuse,* an appellation not usually given to working-class women. Even her crime—attempted assassination—removed her from the ranks of ordinary defenders of barricades and burners of buildings (in the popular fiction) and associated her with Charlotte Corday, the upper-class assassin of the journalist Jean-Paul Marat during the French Revolution. Neither poverty nor the hardships of the Prussian siege nor the contagion of folly could explain the actions of this young woman, who had taken to the streets, leaving behind, at least figuratively, a life of domesticity and maternity.

Turning from the dead communarde, Marnard moved on to his real topic, the liberated woman.[31] The *malheureuse* may have looked like the female orator in Lix's drawing, but Marnard also saw in her what Eugène Girard saw in the pétroleuse. She was "an emancipated woman," a feminist, and she was dangerous. She had tried to kill someone (see fig. 17). "Do you remember with what élan these hybrid creatures, half bluestockings, half tricoteuses, rose to attack our masculine privileges," he asked his readers. "They wanted to share everything with us, academies, courts, clinics; they demanded their place in the universal suffrage; they were no longer content with their homes, with the dear little intimate kingdom where their mothers lived, and loved their husbands, and raised their children. The grand universe, the entire world, was necessary for them to develop their talents and furnished a field for their reforms."[32]

These hybrid women, these "literary females, freethinking novelists, unclassed schoolteachers," were the real threat to civilization. Working-class women, in Marnard's bourgeois representation of them, understood nothing of politics and had no desire to be like men, except when they were led astray by the likes of Paule Minck, André Léo, and George Sand.[33] Left alone, they aspired simply "to buy linens—linens are the fortune of housewives—, to make economies, to send their children to a good school." They were content to stay in their "intimate kingdom" and to leave politics to men.[34] They might occasionally succumb to the "folly of contagion," but even then they were led by women like the dead communarde, who knew what they were doing and chose to do it.

Embedded in Marnard's logic is a bourgeois conceptualization of gender, space, and woman's nature, and a historiography of women's revolutionary activity which condemned feminists (especially those with careers in journalism and literature—the male writer's preserve). He placed them in a continuum between the tricoteuses of 1793 and the communardes/pétroleuses of 1871, and he contrasted them to women who realized that their calling was to remain within the "intimate kingdom" of the home, where lay piety and morality. In the public arena women could become "the equal of man [only] in his lowest vices, in his darkest passions."

Like Sarcey, Marnard was obsessed with woman's nature and not man's.[35] The effects of careers and politics on men were of no concern to him, for they were men's natural activities. What was improper and unnatural was for women to become like men, not for men to be men. In a final, complicated, logically inconsistent, and widely accepted statement of bourgeois gender theory, Marnard declared that women should prevent, or at least should try to prevent, men from acting in accordance with their nature. Had they done so, the war between Paris and Versailles would not have happened. "When the man takes up arms, the woman ought to take his gun away from him," Marnard suggested (a sentiment Blanchecotte would have applauded), "unless the country demands the blood of all its children."[36] Women, thus, could be held responsible for the terrible bloodshed of the semaine sanglante and, indeed, for the entire conflict between Paris and Versailles. They had failed in their female duty.

The government shared the general bourgeois concern with the women it had arrested, and although its general report would not be released until after the trials, its judgment of them took place long before the trials began. Its focus was not on the women's leaders, but on the women who, it believed, had constituted the bulk of the Commune's female supporters. Deeply convinced that the communardes were sexually promiscuous, if not actual prostitutes, the government agents who sought out witnesses and compiled dossiers repeatedly asked about women's sexual behavior.[37] Any sexual liaison outside of marriage was interpreted as a sign of corruption.

The Trials

On August 7, 1871, the first of the great show trials of the Paris Commune began. Ten weeks had passed since the Versailles troops had filed into Paris on the night of May 21 and the bloodletting had begun. Now the survivors who had not escaped arrest were to meet their accusers and judges. The trial was held in a hall that seated two thousand spectators. On the wall hung a large crucifix, a sign with multiple meanings for the accused. For almost a month (August 7 to September 3), fifteen members of the Commune and two of the National Guard Central Committee sat together in its shadow.

The arrested leaders, like all the prisoners, were tried before military tribunals or courts martial (*conseils de guerre*), ostensibly because the departments of the Seine and Seine-et-Oise were under martial law. (The Versailles government established martial law on April 6 when the fighting between Paris and the national government began.) The government could easily have returned the area to civilian law and tried the men in civilian courts. It chose not to do so because the military courts were likely to be more severe. While it was inevitable that the losers in this conflict would be tried by the winners, the use of courts martial meant that the prisoners would be judged by the men against whom they had fought, or at least were believed to have fought, rather than by civilians. It also meant that everyone was tried for criminal rather than political offenses. For the leaders of the Commune as well as its journalists, such charges meant not only that the crimes with which they were charged bore little or no relation to what they had actually done during the Commune but also that they could be sentenced to death, a punishment that had been abolished for political crimes in 1848.

Although the vast majority of arrests, interrogations, trials, and convictions took place within a short period of time, thousands more were made over a period of months and years. As a result the government's own figures changed constantly. By January 1872 the government had arrested 38,499 people. Twenty-two courts martial were sitting; 10,448 had been tried; and 8,535 had been convicted.[38] By the beginning of 1875, the government had processed 50,559 prisoners. Of that number 13,230 men, 158 women, and 62 children under the age of sixteen had been convicted and sentenced.[39]

The government was convinced that far more women had defended the Commune, or to use the government's language, had committed crimes in the name of the Commune, than it was able to arrest, and that far more of the arrested women were guilty than it was able to prove. The problem of proof was twofold, Appert explained in his final report to the National Assembly. First, many women had escaped arrest even though they had "been seen fighting in the ranks of the National Guard, lighting fires, slaughtering hostages, and killing officers and soldiers in cold blood in the streets of Paris." The soldiers had found it hard to believe that women were capable of such violence, he explained, and had been reluctant to arrest them unless they had weapons in their hands or had been singled out by public indignation. Otherwise they had allowed "the immunity that ought to cover their sex" to influence their decisions and had not arrested them.[40]

Second, to make matters worse, the government had had to free the majority of the female prisoners because witnesses had not been able to identify them. (Of the 1,051 women who were taken to Versailles, only 168 were brought before the conseils de guerre. Thirty-three women died in prison or were remanded to the civil court system; 202 were released for lack of evidence; 816 were interrogated, and of these an additional 648 were freed before trial.) Because the women had no "fixed abode, following the battalions of guardsmen who moved every day," Appert maintained, "they had left in their wake the memory of their exaltation [and] their crimes, but the witnesses had not been able to identify in the prisoners, the madwomen whom they had seen earlier with guns in their hands and dressed in the costumes of the National Guard and the marines."[41]

Certainly cantinières and ambulancières had moved around the city with the National Guard, but Appert's assumption that most of the communardes had been camp followers is not supported by other texts, which present the building and defending of the barricades as neighborhood activities.[42] The literal truth of Appert's statement is less important, however, than his certainty that the women who were released were guilty and his construction of their activities and character, for these had existed before the women were arrested, and they would help to convict the female prisoners who went to trial.

Viewed as an inquiry into guilt or innocence, the trials are deeply troubling. Lawyers assigned to the prisoners did not meet with them and often failed to appear in court. Spectators hissed at the prisoners and their lawyers. Witnesses who had made statements to prosecutors before the trials changed their testimony or failed to appear. Judges expressed their opinions on the guilt of the defendants during the trials. Impartiality was not the primary issue, however. These were show trials, or at least the first prosecutions were. They were designed to assuage the bourgeois desire for vengeance and to stand as a warning for anyone contemplating revolutionary activity in the future, not to determine the justness of the Commune's cause or its defenders' actions. Evidence was of little importance, as was the testimony of the defendants themselves. The judges, prosecutors, spectators, and press had determined in advance that the prisoners were guilty. In most cases, all that remained to be determined at the trial were the sentences of the accused, although the judges found a quarter of the women and 15 percent of the men to be innocent of the charges and set them free.

The trials of women and men were similar in many regards. Justice was summary, trials were short, and sentences bore little relation to the crimes with which the defendants were charged. Both women and men were sentenced to death, deportation, and various forms of imprisonment. Both were frequently unrepresented by lawyers. Both were taunted by the spectators. Both were tried before partial judges. Both were subjected to the courts' class biases and desire to wreak vengeance and create examples. And both confronted inconsistency among the courts martial. Those who were accused of the same crime and appeared before different courts could receive very different sentences.

Gender did matter, however. The major crime with which women were charged—incendiarism—had been particularly horrifying to the bourgeois who believed that their homes were the primary target of the working-class pétroleuses.[43] The bourgeois wanted them punished, as the attacks on the women prisoners en route to Versailles had already demonstrated, and the government was prepared to treat them harshly. Even more important, the women's trials became a final occasion for the government and conservative press to assess the causes of the women's actions and to condemn the ideas and individuals it believed had led them into their unnatural acts. The theories that had been aired in June would reemerge.

All the trials began with the reading of the defendants' alleged crimes. For the Commune leaders, these took the form of a standard catalog of the Commune's crimes as viewed from Versailles: participation in or support of the assassination of the hostages; the setting of fires; pillaging; raising or leading insurrectional troops; and contributing to the criminal intention to change the form of the government. Most of the leaders who were tried were guilty only of the last charge and even that could be debated, since the national government had precipitated the conflict on March 18, abandoned the city, refused to negotiate, and then attacked. Indeed, as republicans, the Communards' goal had been to preserve the existing form of government, not to change it.

The message of the accusations and the trial of the Commune's political leaders was clear: if you engage in revolution, you will be tried as a common criminal and punished. As an outlet for bourgeois anger, the trial was probably salutary, judging by the hissing and shouting at the prisoners and the vituperative press coverage in Paris. But as a model for future trials and sentencing, its outcome was confusing. Many of the sentences were indeed harsh. Théophile Ferré and Charles Lullier were sentenced to death. (Lullier's sentence was reduced to transportation by the Board of Pardons; Ferré's was not.) Seven men (Adolph Assi, Alfred Billioray, Louis Henri Champy, Dominique Régère, Paschal Grousset, Paul

Férrat, and Augustin Joseph Verdure) were sentenced to transportation to a fortified place; two (Francis Jourde and Dr. P. Rastoul) to simple transportation; two (Raoul Urbain and Alexis-Louis Trinquet) to hard labor for life. But two men (Victor Clément and Gustave Courbet) received short jail sentences, and two (Descamps and Parent) were acquitted.[44]

The Pétroleuses

The trial of the male leaders was followed immediately by a two-day trial of five women for incendiarism, the crime that was most associated with women. The five were accused of setting fires in the rue de Lille and burning the Légion d'Honneur. The debate about women flowed from the press to the courtroom and back again as this and the other trials of women commenced, influencing both their outcomes and the public reaction to them.

Journalists' "descriptions" and caricaturists' drawings in the conservative press had already turned the pétroleuses into the personification of evil. The *Figaro* reporter laid out two versions of the popular myth in his first paragraph on the trial, the first representing them as uncivilized and evil; the second, as unhuman creatures from the netherworld—a representation that went well beyond the usual portrayal of the pétroleuses: "The word 'pétrole' has taken on a special meaning which arouses sinister ideas since these recent events. The name of 'pétroleuse' recalls the savage hords of *mégères* [she-devils] enrolled under the orders of the Commune who accepted the odious mission of burning Paris while the organizers of the civil war and the builders of the barricades fled."[45]

The crowd in the courtroom, he reported, had an air of "lively curiosity" about these women. People expected to see "ruined women, grown pale from their nightly labors or darkened by the sun, their voices hoarse, their eyes dull, no longer feminine or masculine, creatures without a sex, without morality, without conscience, without even cynicism, recounting the most horrible things as though they were scenes of a regular and normal life."[46] When "five pitiful, odd women" entered the room, anticipation turned to uneasiness and aversion.[47] These women met no one's standards of evil, and they certainly were not creatures without a sex. The worst that could be said about their appearance was that they were ugly (a cultural judgment), and Léonce Dupont, a Bonapartist, said it. The first one had a large nose; the second, "a mouth that had drunk violent liquids"; the third, a "ferocious" expression; the fourth, "an enormous chin"; the fifth, a small nose and a large mouth. Like the *Standard* reporter who visited Satory,

Dupont deduced immorality and guilt from these physical defects. These women, he declared, had "the ugliness [*laideur*] of vice, the ugliness that creeps around in dark alleys, the ugliness of the workhouses."[48]

Similar judgments were made about the men's appearance and character at their trials. *Le Figaro* reporter described Ferré, for instance, as "a small man of 25 to 30 [he was 24], with a curved nose, an eagle's beak; glittering eyes behind his eyeglasses, which constantly shaded them; white teeth like those of a wild beast."[49] Clearly, the reporter had no question about his guilt. The same was true for Jules Claretie, who suggested that Ferré's "physiology itself explained the intrepidly ferocious temperament of this fierce and bitter little man."[50]

Communards and Commune supporters also believed in physiology, but they "saw" their colleagues differently. Communard Gaston Da Costa, for instance, described Trinquet who, like Ferré, declared his commitment to the Commune at the trial of the leaders, as having "an intelligent and sympathetic physiognomy."[51] The theory had difficulty with the five pétroleuses, however. The women had worn their best clothes (which weren't very good), and two of them had tied ribbons around their hair, one green and the other violet with black lace,[52] and many men found it difficult to see in them the malevolent and savage pétroleuses.

Ignoring the disparity between the mythical pétroleuses and the women on trial, the prosecutor Jouenne recalled "the horrible campaign against civilization" that had begun on March 18. It was bad enough that "men who believe neither in God nor in the country" had taken control of Paris, but worse yet that women had "deserted their sacred mission [and] their influence [over their families] . . . and had become moral monstrosities." Echoing Sarcey's views, the prosecutor declared that these women were "more dangerous than the most dangerous man." Figuratively, if not literally, they were the "daughters of the she-wolves of 1793."[53]

Despite the presence of the defendants, who clearly were members of the working class, Jouenne, like Sarcey and Marnard, was distracted by the women of his own class. Guilty as he was convinced the pétroleuses were, he did not hold them solely responsible for their actions. They had been led astray by doctors who favored "the emancipation of women," and *institutrices* like Louise Michel who preached revolution from the pulpits of churches during the Commune and taught immoral doctrines to children in their schools.[54] It was the same connection between feminism and the pétroleuses made by Eugène Girard when he identified the pétroleuse in his caricature as "The emancipated woman shedding light on the world" (see fig. 17).

Feminists were not literally on trial, however. Instead, five working-class women were. They ranged in age from twenty-four to thirty-nine. Elisabeth Rétiffe was a cardboard maker and cantinière; Léontine Suétens, a laundress; Joséphine-Marguerite Marchais and Lucie Bocquin, day workers; and Eulalie Papavoine, a seamstress. Only Lucie Bocquin was married. Dossiers had been compiled for each of the women, as for most, if not all, prisoners who were brought to trial.[55] In court witnesses who had given information to the prosecutors before the trials, testified about what the women had done, or what they thought they had done, and about what they had worn during the Commune. In this trial, witnesses testified that they had seen all the women on or near the barricades, but no one had seen them light fires.[56]

Three witnesses provided evidence that Elisabeth Rétiffe had been an open supporter of the Commune. One man identified her as the cantinière who had given him ammunition for his gun during the fighting, and another as having carried food and drink to the barricades. A woman testified that Rétiffe had worn a white blouse and a red scarf and a gun slung across her shoulder—all signs of allegiance to the Commune. But Léontine Suétens, one of the defendants, provided her with an alibi when she testified that Rétiffe had been "completely drunk" and had spent the night in question sleeping with her lover on a mattress at the barricade.

Suétens was similarly accused of having worn a red scarf and a National Guard uniform and of carrying a shotgun over her shoulder. Eulalie Papavoine and Lucie Bocquin testified that Suétens had carried eau-de-vie and wine to the insurgents and had help build the barricades, and worse yet, another witness testified that she had engaged in pillaging and had been paid ten francs for her help.

Joséphine Marchais's concierge testified that she had worn a tyrolean, or cantinière's, hat (see fig. 9), carried a gun, urged on the Communard troops, and engaged in pillaging. The witness did not know if Marchais had set the fires, but she was "more dangerous, in his opinion, than the Enfants-Perdus," a military group.

Eulalie Papavoine had been seen wearing a red scarf and carrying a gun over her shoulder at the Légion d'Honneur. A witness also testified that she had helped build the barricades, pillaged, and "participated in orgies involving stolen wine." Lucie Bocquin had been seen at the Légion d'Honneur and had carried wine and eau-de-vie to the barricades. She had also, according to testimony, pillaged wine cellars.

Testimony about the women's revolutionary dress, gun toting, pillaging, and support for the National Guard identified them as active Commune supporters, but it did not mean they had set fires. As the *Standard* correspondent reported, "The act was not brought home to them."[57] Worst of all for the prosecution, one might have thought, the government had not been able to find (and arrest) "a certain *femme* Masson," reportedly of Prussian origin, who they believed was "the most guilty" of them all.[58]

The five women acknowledged that they had supported the Commune and had taken care of the wounded and that they had been in the rue des Lilles and at the Légion d'Honneur on the night in question or on other nights, but they denied that they had set fires. Their lawyers (one of them appointed at the trial when another did not show up) argued that the women had been ambulancières and cantinières, not pétroleuses; that they were poor women who needed the money they were paid by the National Guard, but that they would have supported the other side if circumstances had been different; that the charges had not been proven; and that the court should have a soldierly consideration for them as women. The pleas fell on deaf ears. Elisabeth Rétiffe, Eugénie Suétens, and Joséphine Marchais were condemned to death; Eulalie Papavoine, to deportation; and Lucie Bocquin, to ten years' solitary confinement. (The appeals board reduced the death sentences to deportation and hard labor for life.)[59]

The sentences immediately provoked consternation, especially since only two of the seventeen male leaders of the Commune, whose trial had ended two days earlier, had been sentenced to death (compared with three of the five women), and two of the seventeen had been acquitted altogether.[60] Government supporters like Jules Claretie agreed with the guilty verdicts, seeing the women as "spirits of darkness, of brutality, of envy, consumed by wretchedness," but even he believed the sentences should not be carried out.[61] Part of the difference in sentencing may be accounted for by the different courts martial before which the men and women were tried (the third and fourth, respectively), but differences of class, education, and gender were also at play.

Men were thought to be naturally interested in politics. Those who led and participated in the Commune were seen as having made the wrong political choice; they had to be punished for it, but everyone agreed that they had a fundamental right to act in the public arena. Woman's proper place, on the other hand, was at home with her children. As Prosecutor Jouenne declared, "The legitimate woman [is] the object of our affections, of our respect, when, completely dedicated to the care of the family, she is its guide and protector."[62] A woman was what she did. Her actions defined her essence. Any woman who left her hearth was already acting illegitimately, and she herself ceased to be a legitimate (or feminine) woman. This notion was a bourgeois fantasy that ignored the fact that economic survival for working-class families required most women to spend their days in the paid labor force, not in nurturing children and creating moral havens for their husbands.[63] For most Parisians, the notion that a woman's legitimacy depended on her dedicating all her time to the care of her family would have seemed nonsensical.

In terms of the trials, Jouenne's statement about women's "legitimate" roles and the "moral monstrosities" they became when they entered the public sphere had considerable importance. If political activity turned women into immoral creatures, then other immoral or illegal activity, especially sexual activity outside of marriage, could be interpreted as proof of political activity. Following this logic, the men who sought out witnesses and compiled dossiers repeatedly asked about sexual behavior.[64] Lacking other proof of a woman's participation in the Commune or, in the case of the women in this trial, of incendiarism, Jouenne turned to this information and to previous criminal convictions to make his case. The more the women's behavior deviated from bourgeois morality, the more guilty they became.

Thirty-nine-year-old Elisabeth Rétiffe had lived with a man for seven years and then left him because he beat her. She had been arrested twice, once for fighting with another woman and once for insulting a policeman. Twenty-five-year-old Eugénie Suétens had lived with a man for six years. She had previously spent a year in jail for theft. Joséphine Marchais did not come from a "good" family. Her mother and sister had spent years in jail and she herself had spent six months in prison for theft. She had been a cantinière for the battalion of her lover, and was said to have forced him to continue fighting when he wanted to desert. These women received death sentences.[65]

Twenty-five-year-old Eulalie Papavoine lived with a *fédéré*, bore him a child, and followed him as an ambulancière. Twenty-eight-year-old Lucie Marie Bocquin was an adulteress. When her husband left to join the army, she fell in love with and moved in with a *fédéré* and "abandoned her poor little child to follow a bandit." This kind of sexual activity was enough to win Papavoine and Bocquin harsh sentences, but they did not have the criminal records of the first three women and were not condemned to death.[66]

Louise Michel

Louise Michel, the most famous of the communardes, was tried alone on December 17, 1871, before the sixth Conseil de Guerre. She had refused counsel and spoke for herself. Other female leaders, including André Léo, Elizabeth Dmietrieff, and Paule Minck, had escaped arrest, and Michel was arrested only when she turned herself in to win freedom for her mother. Michel was not as well known in 1871 as she would be later, even though her name had been invoked at the trial of the five pétroleuses.[67] Indeed, some of her fame as a revolutionary would come from her lack of repentance at her trial. But she was well enough known to attract the press.

Dressed in black, she stood alone before her accusers. No violet or green ribbons relieved the severity of her appearance. She would make no request, either implicitly or explicitly, for leniency or forgiveness, no claim that she had been falsely arrested or falsely accused. She was a revolutionary and would present herself as one. She accepted responsibility for her actions and, indeed, even for things she had not done, including incendiarism.[68] She declared that she had had no accomplices. Alone, she had wanted to "fight the Versaillais with a barrier of flames," but it is unlikely that she had set fires. She made no such claims in her memoirs, and she was not identified as a pétroleuse.

Judging by her later statements, other confessions were true. She acknowledged both in court and in her history of the Commune that she had wanted to assassinate President Thiers and had been stopped by Théophile Ferré.[69] Still other confessions were complicated. She agreed that she had participated in the assassination of the generals on March 18, although she was not present when they were killed. If she had been at Montmartre when the generals wanted to fire on the people, she said, she "would have had no hesitation about shooting people who gave orders like those," but still, she believed they should not have been shot after they were prisoners. To shoot prisoners was a "villainous act." Unlike virtually everyone else, male and female alike, she did not plead innocence to any charge or claim extenuating circumstances.

In pleading guilty and claiming responsibility for her actions (whether they were literally hers or not), Michel defended the Commune. Her actions had been hers alone, she declared. The Commune "had had absolutely nothing to do with assassinations or burning." It had wanted to bring about the social revolution, and the social revolution was her "dearest wish." She was, and no one doubted it, "honored to be singled out as one of the promoters of the Commune."

But claiming responsibility was more than a way of defending the Commune for Michel. It was also an attempt to control her own destiny. She wanted to die. She had had enough, especially after the government had executed Ferré. "What I demand from you," she told her judges, "is the field of Satory, where our revolutionary brothers have already fallen. I must be cut off from society. You have been told that, and the prosecutor is right. . . . If you let me live, I will not stop crying for vengeance, and I will denounce the assassins on the Board of Pardons [who had not commuted the sentences of Ferré and twenty-two others] to the vengeance of my brothers. . . . If you are not cowards, kill me."

What Michel's relationship was with Théophile Ferré is an often asked and largely unanswerable question. He was one of the leaders of the Montmartre Vigilance Committee whom she praised so highly for his intelligence and a member of the Commune. While they were imprisoned and awaiting trial in Versailles, they wrote to each other, and her letters have often been interpreted as love letters. Her desire to die after Ferré was executed lends support to the theory that she was in love with him, as does her visit to his grave when she returned from New Caledonia. Edith Thomas, Michel's sympathetic biographer, thought that Michel was indeed in love with the younger Ferré but that her attachment was unrequited.[70] Marie Mullaney regards Thomas's position as an implicit defense of Michel against conservative accusations that she was a lesbian.[71] Whatever Michel and Ferré felt for each other, speculation about their relationship is simply an extension of the battle of representations that has surrounded Michel since she entered the docket in 1871.

The court would not grant Michel's death wish, perhaps precisely because she had asked for it. By the time she was tried it had decided to create no more martyrs by execution, especially of women who, instead of pleading for mercy as women should and men did, looked her judges defiantly in the eye, duplicitously announced "You are men, and I, I am only a woman," and then asked for death. And so it sentenced the most famous of the Commune's unruly women to deportation to a fortified place. When the sentence was read, Michel declared that she "would have preferred death."

Like the amazon in Lix's pulpit, Louise Michel dominated the scene in the courtroom (see fig. 15). She was uncowed and unrepentant. From the beginning to the end of her trial, she challenged and defied the generals and spectators who had come to judge her. The *Standard* correspondent was in awe: "If the men of the Commune had had in them the spirit of this fanatical woman, the troops would have had harder work than they had to re-occupy Paris."[72]

Louise Michel's tightly controlled, death-defying self-representation was not the only portrait of her that would emerge from the trial. The government prosecutor and journalists presented other Louise Michels in an effort to categorize her unnaturalness and to account for it. Because she was a bourgeoise, it was even more important to explain her behavior than it was to explain that of the working-class pétroleuses. She was an intelligent, well-educated woman. She had pursued the only acceptable profession for an unmarried woman—teaching. She dressed conservatively, spoke well, and wrote poetry. And yet, she had fought like a man, defied her accusers, and demanded death. This was a troubling combination of attributes, and it was essential that her "descent" into politics and revolution be explained. If she or her experiences were unique (or at least limited), she posed no serious threat to contemporary gender conventions. The wives and daughters of the bourgeoisie would not follow in her footsteps. If she was not unique (and therefore, abnormal), then the threat was serious, and resistance to those who believed women should participate in the political sphere would have to be increased. The enigma of Louise Michel lay at the heart of the bourgeois dilemma.

Male writers tried all the usual gambits to discredit her. The *Gazette des Tribunaux* identified her as an amazon, at least by association.[73] The prosecutor linked her to the tradition of witchcraft and the revolutionary tricoteuses by calling her a "devil-ridden fanatic," and a "she-wolf eager for blood."[74] But these references to other unruly women satisfied no one. Louise Michel stood both figuratively and literally alone. She fit poorly into historical categories, and many of the usual terms for unruly women were absent from the press accounts of her trial. No one called her a vivandière, harpy, virago, madwoman, or fury. She was not an ordinary unnatural woman, as the appellation Red Virgin would later verify.

The prosecutor and the press discussed Michel's appearance and family origins to demonstrate that she was not truly bourgeois and not truly feminine. She had been an illegitimate child, raised by charity; "her features reveal[ed] an extreme severity"; she had "a hard physionomy, with haggard eyes, a dry and mordant voice"; she was "indifferent as to her personal appearance" and lacked any feeling for coquetry;" she had "given up the dress of her sex" and had worn a National Guard uniform.[75] "Facts" like these had been used to good effect to judge other female prisoners, but like the traditional categories of unruly women, they were inadequate to explain Louise Michel's behavior.

The personal accusations had some effect on Michel herself, however. While she embraced every accusation of revolutionary activity, whether accurate or not, she chafed under false accusations about her personal life and morality. She declared that she had not worn men's clothing, except on March 18 when she had worn a National Guard uniform so she would not stand out. Otherwise, she had worn a red sash over her regular clothing.[76] In this regard, at least, Michel differed from Jeanne d'Arc, the great heroine of France, who wore men's clothing (and with whom sympathetic men identified her), and from other nineteenth-century female radicals.[77] She had no desire to be mistaken for a man.

Michel also denied that she had ridden in a carriage, except when she was recovering from a sprained ankle. The accusation impugned her so-cial and political principles, and she corrected it in court.[78] Later, she cor-rected two other errors made by the prosecutor. She had been reared by her paternal grandparents, not on charity; and she was tall, not short.[79] She wanted the personal record to be accurate.

While the court, and later the press, spent time on these topics, the im-portant undertaking for the prosecutor and journalists was to offer a com-prehensive theory to explain Michel's behavior. The prosecutor saw her as driven by pride, an unfeminine attribute in a gender system that believed women were naturally altruistic and self-effacing. Desiring "public atten-tion," he said, she had left her benefactors in the countryside, and had "run away to Paris for adventure." Once she was there, "an anonymous role was repugnant to her." She wanted "to draw public attention and to be in the headlines of false proclamations and wall posters." She taught false doctrines to her students, presided over the Club de la Révolution, rode in a carriage "like a queen,"[80] and supported such heinous acts as the exe-cution of hostages—all in the search for fame. Natural women desired anonymity, stayed at home, resisted adventure, and were humble. By this logic, Louise Michel clearly was not a natural woman.

The correspondent for *Le Figaro* had a different theory. Harking back to Sarcey's "medical" analysis of the pétroleuses, he declared that Louise Michel had been "prey to one of the crises of revolutionary hysteria." She had held an honorable position as a teacher and was normally calm and honest, but the contagion of hysteria had "plunged her into the disorders and crimes of the Commune," as it had other women.[81]

The British correspondent for the *Standard* offered a "biology is destiny" theory that included an attack on feminists. To begin with, he argued, Louise Michel had been led astray, not by illicit sexual activity, as the five pétroleuses and many other women who were tried had been, but by sex-ual inactivity.[82] All women, according to the *Standard,* were destined by na-ture "to nurse and bring up babies." They ignored this destiny at peril to themselves and society. Louise Michel was a case in point. When she should have been getting married and having children of her own, she had been "teaching urchin Democrats their pothooks and hangers." Not having mar-ried and borne children when she should have and having reached "that peculiar time of life" (over thirty), she had become "sour and disappoint-ed" and was "roused . . . to such a pitch of excitement" by the siege and rev-olution that she "joined the insurrection body and soul."[83]

To make matters worse, her "half-education" had "raised [her] above her class without placing her in a class above" (another version of the bi-ology-is-destiny theory: she had tried to become something she was not), and she had "read herself into a kind of frenzy about the 'emancipation of woman.'" These ideas, combined with her unfulfilled nature, put her "precisely in the frame of mind which dupes, martyrs, and fanatics are generally made of."[84]

The number and variety of these theories—pride, contagious hysteria, biological destiny, half education, and "the rant and rubbish concerning women's rights"[85]—demonstrate how difficult it was for the dominant bourgeois conceptualization of gender to account for nonconformity. No one theory could explain all the communardes' activities. If Louise Michel had acted out of pride, the five pétroleuses presumably had not. If lack of sexual activity explained Michel's actions, the obverse was suggested for the pétroleuses. If half education or exposure to women's rights explained the activities of Michel, Léo, Dmitrieff, and other bourgeois supporters of the Commune, they did not explain those of working-class women. Only contagious hysteria had the potential to apply to all the women, and even so, Sarcey, who had first offered it to his reachers, did not believe it applied to such women as Louise Michel, who had had exhorted other women to revolutionary acts. In the end, it would be easier for the government to silence and punish the women by deporting and incarcerating them than it would be for men to explain them.

Gaston Da Costa

The question of sexual activity, which played such a central role in the trials of women, either by its presence or its absence, was missing from virtually all the men's trials, partly because the activities for which men were being tried were more public—they had been either government leaders or members of the National Guard—and partly because the government thought their activities had been merely wrong, not abnormal. The exception to this rule came in the trial of Gaston Da Costa, who, unlike most of the male defendants but like the women, was an enigma to the government. In addition, Da Costa was accused of a crime for which the government dearly wished to convict someone.

Da Costa was a twenty-one-year-old, well-educated disciple of Raoul Rigault, one of the Communards most hated by Versailles. Rigault, himself only twenty-five, was an elected member of the Commune and the delegate to the Prefecture of Police. In that position he had been able to arrest anyone whom he considered an enemy of the revolution, including bourgeois citizens, priests, and former police spies and gendarmes. Among Rigault's charges were the Commune's prominent hostages, for whose execution Rigault regularly called during the Commune. During the semaine sanglante, he personally authorized the killing of several prisoners and arranged for the transfer of the hostages from the jail at Mazas to one at La Roquette, where many of them were subsequently executed. Rigault was killed during the semaine sanglante, disappointing the conservatives, who wanted to try and execute him. (They condemned him to death anyway on June 29, 1871.)[86] On the other hand, Da Costa, who had been Rigault's friend and assistant and who had overseen the transfer of the prisoners to La Roquette, was alive and available for trial.

On July 27 and 28, 1872, more than a year after the defeat of the Commune, Gaston Da Costa was brought to trial on typical charges for the leaders of the Commune—having tried to change the form of the government and complicity in illegal arrests and assassinations.[87] Wanting to punish someone for the deaths of the hostages and annoyed perhaps by an educated young man whom he believed had betrayed his class, Dulac, the presiding officer, was openly hostile. He informed Da Costa that his ideas were not those of "a well-brought-up man." Then, instead of pursuing his political ideas and activities, as one might have expected, given the charges against him, the judge turned to his personal life, questioning his morality and introducing an insinuation of homosexuality into the trial.[88]

First, Dulac questioned how Da Costa could have lived with a *grisette* in the Latin Quarter "as though he were married." A *grisette* was a young working girl; the term, from the gray color of their uniforms, implied questionable morals to the bourgeoisie. For a young bourgeois to have a *grisette* as a mistress was one thing; to live with her as though they were married was another. This, Dulac claimed he could not understand. In actuality, as the judge undoubtedly knew, bourgeois men more and more often frequented glorified beer halls known as *cafés-concerts* or *cafés-chantants*, where they mingled with the lower classes. But he also knew that it was fashionable to pretend to stand above such mingling.[89]

The judge then moved to a far more deadly accusation, hinting darkly that Da Costa's relationship with Rigault had been "shameful."

> After 1867 you threw yourself into the Latin Quarter, and bound yourself to an individual named Raoul Rigault, who became your intimate friend. . . . Here is the information the police have given us about your affairs: Da Costa and Rigault were inseparable; Da Costa was completely faithful to Rigault. When Rigault got out of bed, Da Costa got out of bed; when Rigault ate, Da Costa ate; when Rigault went to bed, Da Costa went to bed.[90]

Da Costa and his lawyer Gatineau were alarmed and demanded a physical examination, which eventually led to a medical declaration that Da Costa was not a homosexual. It is impossible to know what kind of physical evidence led to this conclusion since Da Costa is silent about the exact nature of the physical examination to which he submitted. It is also impossible to know anything other than what he himself tells us about his sexuality.[91] The medical opinion, as well as Gatineau's reasoned defense and the appearance of respectable witnesses who testified to his kindnesses during the Commune, would be to no avail. The prosecutor, Captain Jolly, argued in summation that he would be the first to ask pity for men who served the Commune because they were illiterate and knew no better or were hungry and needed employment. But "for those like Da Costa, who were well educated and enlightened" (i.e., bourgeois), he was for "inexorable severity, because they had violated all of the laws of God and humanity." The court found Da Costa guilty and sentenced him to death. His sentence was reduced to forced labor in New Caledonia by the appeals court seven months later.[92]

The Immoral and the Unnatural

Despite their very different social backgrounds, Da Costa's position at his trial was remarkably similar to that of the five pétroleuses. Neither his nor their participation in the Commune was in question, but the specific accusations against all of them were. The women acknowledged that they had worked as cantinières and ambulancières, carrying food and drink to the guardsmen, but denied having set fires. Da Costa acknowledged that he had transferred the prisoners from one prison to another during the semaine sanglante, but he claimed that he had believed he was transferring them to ensure their safety. The same was true of his order to transfer Gustave Chaudey from Mazas to Sainte-Pélagie, where Rigault ordered his execution. Da Costa said he had transferred Chaudey because his wife had asked him to.[93] He agreed that his research into the prefecture's records had resulted in the arrest of at least one alleged police spy but contended that the arrest itself had been carried out by Rigault. Had the judges taken the defense seriously, they might have found Da Costa, and the pétroleuses, guilty of participating in the Commune, but they might *not* have sentenced any of them to death.

The fires and the executions of the hostages were the Commune's two greatest crimes, however, and the judges wanted convictions and death sentences in both cases. Earlier criminal records, sexual activity outside of marriage, and the implication of homosexuality were introduced as signs of depravity and hence as indicators of unnatural inclinations. In the women's cases, sexual affairs alone indicated immorality. In Da Costa's case, more was necessary. The bourgeois double standard for sexual activity by men and women meant the accusation that he had lived with a *grisette* raised bourgeois eyebrows, but it was hardly proof of great immorality. The serious charge was homosexuality. If Rigault and Da Costa had been lovers, then Da Costa's participation in "unnatural" sexual activity was proven and his guilt on other counts could be assumed.

The accusation of homosexuality was unusual, if not unique, in the trials of the Communards, and is a sign of how disturbing his crossing of the class line between respectable and revolutionary activity was, at least for his chief accuser, the presiding judge, Dulac.[94] For the most part, accusations of immoral and at least vaguely unnatural sexual activity or inactivity were used only in the women's cases, because only their participation in the Commune was seen as unnatural.

Sexual activity or inactivity was an attractive explanation of women's participation in violent revolution because it contained a prescription that supported bourgeois values and the bourgeois organization of society and the family. Woman was born to be nurturing and maternal, but her nature was corruptible. She could fall into immorality and then violence if she were seduced away from her natural roles at home by the lure of sex or the proponents of women's rights. To prevent this danger, free sex, celibacy, and political rights should be discouraged for women. Domesticity was both the goal and the solution to the problem of the unruly woman. Or at least, so the bourgeois chose to believe.

CHAPTER SEVEN

The Unruly Woman and
the Revolutionary City

In prose and caricature, unruly women parade through the pages of the Commune. On March 18 they confront the French army over the cannons on Montmartre, daring them to fire on their unarmed bodies, then carve up a dead horse, and then encourage the killing of Generals Lecomte and Clément Thomas. From April 3 to May 21 they mourn the dead of Paris, pound the pulpits in churches, care for wounded soldiers, and prepare to fight the Versailles troops. From May 22 to May 28 they defend the barricades, burn the city, and abuse the Communard prisoners. In their various guises, from pétroleuse to sainted mother, communarde to bourgeoise, these female figures play central roles in creating and communicating the significance of this tumultuous revolution. They reach out from the past to control our understanding of it and to guide us to judgment.

Woman as Symbol

In the last week of May 1871 the Commune lost more than military battles; it also lost the war of representation. Its enemies would successfully portray its adherents as the immoral killers of the archbishop, and the destroyers of Paris by fire. No Delacroix would emerge to represent the nobility of its struggle. Even those who tried to represent the Commune positively presented rather silly and saccarine communardes, worse than pale imitations of Delacroix's *Liberty Leading the People* (see fig. 2). A drawing dedicated to the National Guard reveals how static was much pro-Commune art. While Delacroix's masterpiece is clearly the model for *Souvenir of 1871* (fig. 21), the contrasts are greater than the similarities. In the allegory, a communarde takes the place of Liberty. Dressed demurely in a bodice with a high neckline and short sleeves, her breasts covered with a double layer of material, and her skirt covering even her feet, she has none of the power or movement of Delacroix's barefoot Liberty in a slipped chiton. With both feet planted on the ground, the communarde seems to preside over rather than to lead the guardsmen who struggle with the enemy. Armed with a sword instead of a rifle, she seems ill equipped to lead this battle, although one of the guardsmen is similarly ill armed. Indeed, the guardsmen appear to be fighting for the communarde/Commune (literally around her) rather than being led by her, as was the case in the final battles between the National Guard and the Versaillais.

Artists who represented the Commune powerfully dwelled on two subjects. Like Edouard Manet, they represented the horrors of the semaine sanglante in the figures of the dead (fig. 22), or like the caricaturists, they represented the horrors of the Commune in the figure of the pétroleuse, the symbolic inversion of Delacroix's Liberty. In her most powerful incarnations, the pétroleuse might carry a flag, but she led no troops. She might stride powerfully forward, but she strode alone (fig. 23). No one else was within the picture's frame. In place of a flintlock, she carried a burning firebrand. Revenge and destruction, not victory and the creation of a new state, were her goals (see fig. 12).

Although the pétroleuse became the most famous representation of the Commune, she was not the only female figure used in this regard. A whole panoply of female representations appeared in texts and drawings. As a lioness protecting her cubs, the communarde personified the glory of the revolutionary struggle; as grieving mother and widow, the sins of Versailles. As female orator, she represented the unnaturalness and folly of the Commune's cause; as naive cantinière, its stupidity; as pétroleuse, its evil. Her symbolic content was maleable and various.

The symbolic content of the communarde's male counterpart was more limited. The communard was portrayed either sympathetically or villainously, depending on the politics of the writer or artist who presented him to view, but he did not personify the Commune. Whether noble or ignoble, he always represented politically and socially radical working-class men. The greater variability and symbolic usefulness of female figures like the communarde and the pétroleuse were the product of two cultural phenomena: a long-standing Western iconographic tradition that made most allegorical figures female, and dichotomous cultural conceptualizations

FIGURE 21. *Souvenir of 1871:* "Dedicated to the National Guard." Bibliothèque Nationale.

FIGURE 22. Edouard Manet, *Civil War* (1871). Rosenwald Collection, © 1995 Board of Trustees, National Gallery of Art, Washington, D.C.

of female nature which made it possible for them to represent both good and evil, the natural and the unnatural. Rebellious men might be wrong and bad, but they were not unnatural; rebellious women were all three, and therefore, their symbolic usefulness was far greater.

One set of female representations reflected perceptions of woman's nature as dichotomous and, to a certain extent, were variations on the Mary/Eve and Mary/Mary Magdalene oppositions. Grieving mothers, widows, and orphaned girls embodied what were perceived as the natural and saintly virtues of women. Sexually innocent and politically passive, they were coded positively and in their essence condemned anyone who harmed them or, by extension, the government they represented. Amazons, hecates, furies, and viragoes, on the contrary, personified what was perceived as women's frightening, unnatural (although the extent to which their actions were natural or unnatural was always in question, given the perception of woman's nature as dichotomous), and by implication, evil side. Sexually and politically active, these figures were usually coded

IMP. TALONS.

UNE PÉTROLEUSE.

FIGURE 23. Paul Klenck, *Une Pétroleuse*. Bibliothèque Nationale.

negatively in the nineteenth and early twentieth centuries, and they and the government they represented posed serious threats to civil order and to society generally.

A second set of female representations was built on a culturally constructed opposition between the feminine and the masculine which identified nature with woman and civilization with man. Presented as lionnesses, creatures, and to a certain extent, amazons, these images linked women to the wild (nature) and separated them from the civilized (male) world. A third image, the tricoteuse, depended on myth and memory of the Terror of 1793 and 1794 for its power. Its unnatural, evil, and bloodthirsty representation of women colored male reaction to the Commune and the communardes throughout the Commune.

The tricoteuse and the other representations of women that emerged during the Commune were overshadowed in May by the pétroleuse. To a considerable extent, in fact, the communarde became the pétroleuse. Part of this identification is explained simply by the fires and bloodshed of the semaine sanglante. The pétroleuse simultaneously focused attention on the crimes of the Commune and distracted attention from those of the Versailles government and the army. But belief in the actual existence of the pétroleuse grew too rapidly and was too long lasting for her acceptance into the pantheon of female representations to be explained simply by bourgeois propaganda. This particular personification of the unruly woman represented nineteenth-century men's worst fears about women.

The pétroleuse had threatened to overturn the entire social order. She had not only challenged male authority by leaving her home and acting in the public sphere; she had also attacked property, the source of the bourgeois male's wealth and the physical manifestation of his importance; she had burned down the home in which she was supposed to take care of her children; and she had corrupted her children by encouraging them to aid her in this deed. She was the evil mother, capable of killing her children, controlling men, and destroying the source of their wealth and power. She embodied the message that men could expect anarchy and destruction if women escaped the home and the bonds of civilization and were allowed to give rein to their very worst instincts. Freed women, they revealed, would forget their femininity, devour their (male) children, and destroy civilization.

In this sense, the communarde as pétroleuse returns us to the Goncourt brothers' reaction to their maid Rose's behavior, with which we began. For the Goncourts, Rose's secret life revealed "the duplicity of woman's nature, the powerful faculty, the science, the consummate genius, for lying that informs all of a woman's being."[1] The same was true of the communardes.

They, or at least the worst among them in male imagination (the prostitutes of March 18 who cheered on the troops to kill the generals and the
incendiaries who burned Paris in the semaine sanglante and who the government believed were also prostitutes), revealed the dichotomous or duplicitous nature of women. The virginal mother (Mary) who nurtured men
could turn into the unfaithful Eve who would deceive and steal from them.
Burning property was only an extreme form of theft.

The communarde-pétroleuse represented more than the untrustwor-
thiness of generic woman, however. She also represented feminists. It is no
accident that the caption for figure 17 identifies the pétroleuse as "the
emancipated woman shedding light on the world," and that the "Grrrrand
Female Orator" (see fig. 14) holds a paper on which we can read the words
"Loi sur le divorce" (Divorce law). Feminists, who were called emancipated women in the nineteenth century, were women who had left the domestic sphere for the political arena. A small, but increasingly well-orga-
nized movement in the later years of the Second Empire, feminism, indeed
the very existence of feminists, challenged bourgeois men's sense of order,
power, and well-being.[2] Conservatives feared for the family, among other
things, and this fear was represented twice over by linking the female orator (feminist) with a demand for the legalization of divorce. For political
and social conservatives, the conflation of the image of the feminist with
that of the pétroleuse is hardly surprising. The figure represented the unruly woman who challenged male authority and who, if she were not restrained, would destroy (male) civilization.

The pétroleuse worked symbolically not just because she embodied
men's fears but because women were just as much outsiders in 1871 as they
had been eighty years earlier, during the French Revolution. Just as Marianne could represent the republic in which she had no political identity,
the pétroleuse could represent the Commune that excluded individual
women from its ruling bodies and even, for the most part, from the ranks
of its defenders. She functions not as an individual but as a metaphor for
what she is not—a citizen of the Commune. In this regard, other female
images (like Delacroix's Liberty) could have represented the Commune
and might have, had the revolution been successful.

After the defeat of the Commune, and its demonization in the press, positive and even ambiguous female representations could not be used. Noteworthy in this regard is the figure of the amazon warrior who strides so frequently across the landscape of the Commune. Whereas the amazon was
hardly a positive image for conservatives, her major characteristics—virginity, independence, wildness, and power—were intertwined with those
of the heroine Jeanne d'Arc for nineteenth-century Frenchmen, making

her far too ambiguous an image to be used to represent the Commune negatively (see fig. 7).[3]

The pétroleuse inverted the amazon's characteristics. She was more often depicted as a hag than as a young virgin and was identified with insanity rather than pure wildness. Iconographically, she was always fully clothed, never revealing the bare breast that symbolized heroism, devotion, and sacrifice (see frontispiece and figs. 12, 17, 18, 19, and 23).[4] The pétroleuse was not desexed, however. (Indeed, one reason the positive caricatures of communardes on the barricades were so insipid was because they did desexualize women, presenting them as naive and childlike.)

The pétroleuse was a compelling figure not because she had acted like a man but precisely because she was a woman. Her appeal was her threat, and vice versa. She might be able to lure men to their destruction and to the destruction of their civilization in a way that a man never could. She had the power to seduce, as the men who were mesmerized by the beautiful and the hideous (both culturally defined) women among the prisoners reveal. And so, she had to be tamed, turned into the hideous, nonalluring pétroleuse of the anti-Commune cartoonists and the conservative editorial writers. The terrible dilemma was that, like the Goncourts' "ugly and ungainly" Rose, this hideous woman could attract men. She could lure them into the "nocturnal orgies," of which one of Rose's lovers declared, "It's going to kill one of us—her or me."[5] Men feared it would not be the woman who would die.

For men, revolution was the unruly woman. It threatened to turn on its head the social order that was supposed to make women subservient to men and workers subservient to the bourgeoisie, an order that was supposed to be natural but which, it was frightening to imagine, might not be, if it could be overturned. In the political arena, working-class revolution was the ultimate threat; in the personal arena, women's sexuality was. And so, in discourses and iconography that were controlled by men, the image that emerged to represent the political threat of revolution in 1871 was the pétroleuse.[6] One fear triggered and represented the other.

The Consequences of Representation

The lionesses, amazon warriors, mothers, hecates, tricoteuses, furies, and pétroleuses that inhabit the pages of the Commune both simplify and complicate our ability to see this decisive moment in history. Through them, writers have made and have wished us to make moral judgments about the Commune. As they move us to judgment, the female images conceal the complexities of the Commune, leaving us with a dichotomous good-and-evil picture of it. As a result, the Commune texts give us a clearer picture of their writers' ideologies than they do of their ostensible subject matter. We are meant to praise or condemn the Commune, not to see its complexities.

Our making these judgments "properly" depends upon our understanding the figures' symbolic content. Since we continue to share many of the cultural values and gender conceptualizations from which they derive their meaning, this is not as difficult today as it might become some time in the future. Two cautions are in order, however. First, it would be unwise to assume that these symbols have retained exactly the same content across time. Indeed, viewing these images outside their historical context could lead to complete confusion. If, for instance, we were to interpret the amazon as a positive rather than as a negative symbol, as late twentieth-century feminists are wont to do, we would reverse the message that she is meant to carry in conservative texts.

Second, women "see" female allegorical figures differently from the way men "see" them. Women participate in the representations in ways that men do not. For women, sameness rather than alterity is at issue, and the cautionary as well as the celebratory messages can be, and frequently are, personalized.[7] It is not clear, therefore, that all women have seen the depictions of the amazon warriors, furies, and pétroleuses in such negative terms as their male creators and viewers. Nor have they all regarded individual women like "the fire-eating Louise Michel"[8] as such villains.

In addition to carrying writers' and artists' judgments of the Commune, female images reveal their creators' attitudes toward women and gender. On the one hand, we have negative images of amazons, furies, viragoes, harpies, and pétroleuses, who exist outside the human community. On the other hand, we have positive, but essentialized, female images of widows, mothers, and female victims, who exist within the human community but are marginalized by their passivity. These binarily opposed images—good/bad, passive/active, dependent/independent, sexually passive/sexually aggressive—structure our understanding of the women of the Commune, just as they do our understanding of the Commune itself. They move us to judgment of the Commune's women rather than to an understanding of the complexities of their lives, personalities, and actions.

Women's lives, as well as their self-presentations, were constrained by the gender conventions that produced these representations. Even so, their representations of themselves and their ideas are more complex and less dichotomous than those that inhabit the pages written by most men, as revealed in the letters and memoirs of the hardworking Céline de Mazade, who could playfully declare herself a femme forte when she decided to stay in Paris, or of the dedicated revolutionary Louise Michel, who when not fighting with the National Guard was teaching young children and rescuing old cats.

The equation of the unruly woman with the revolution in the figure of the pétroleuse did more than obscure women, however. It actively harmed the communardes who were arrested. In order for the conservative bourgeoisie to establish its hegemony over Paris, it had to establish it over women. In essence, the bourgeoisie undertook to demonstrate its mastery of the revolution by mastering its representation, that is, by punishing and repressing women.

The identification of revolution with the unruly woman was not peculiar to nineteenth-century France. It lies behind the repression of women that has occurred in other times and places when governments have changed hands, regardless of whether women have participated in or made demands upon the revolution or the government.[9] Repression of the communardes was particularly inevitable, however, since women actually had participated in the revolt and had defended the city at the barricades. Whether they had burned the city or not (and the evidence is that they had not), they were fully implicated by their other "unladylike," "feminist," or "unnatural" activities, and they would be severely punished for them.

In an ironic reversal, the marginalized women of the nineteenth century gave birth to female figures that dominated the texts and hence the history of this period. While these figures conceal the complexities of the Commune and its struggle with Versailles, and reduce the women of the Commune largely to stereotypes and caricatures, they tell us a great deal about the conceptualizations and fears of their creators. If we focus upon them, three things become clear, or at least clearer. First, the women and men of 1871 lived their lives and developed their perceptions of themselves and each other in a conceptually and politically gendered universe. Second, our understanding and judgment of the Commune is mediated by female figures who convey and create moral judgments in their very essence. If readers share the general (if not the precise) gender conceptualizations and judgments of the eyewitness and historical accounts of the Commune and remain unconscious of the roles these figures play in the texts they read, the political agenda of the authors is easily conveyed to them. Third, in 1871 men's fear of the unruly woman led them to see social threats as sexual threats and vice versa.[10]

Whereas fear of the unruly woman cut across class lines, the fears of the bourgeoisie were more important than those of the proletariat and its allies, for the victors would control the symbolic representation of the Commune. In texts and pictures, the equation of social threats with sexual threats resulted in the foregrounding of the pétroleuse as unruly woman and as allegory for over a century. The Goncourts and other bourgeois men should have been worrying not about the duplicity of women they knew but about the power of the readily accessible female figures, which they mistakenly believed they controlled. Their stunning contribution to the pantheon of such women, the pétroleuse, was able to dominate their texts and hence the past. The female representations were as unruly as the women and the revolution they represented.

Notes

Introduction

1. Edmond de Goncourt and Jules de Goncourt, *Journal: Mémoires de la vie littéraire*, ed. and annotated by Robert Ricatte (Paris: Fasquelle and Flammarion, 1956), August 21, 1862, 1:1119–121. The Goncourts' novel *Germinie Lacerteux* is based on their discovery of Rose's deception.

2. See, for instance, Claire Goldberg Moses, *French Feminism in the Nineteenth Century* (Albany: State University of New York Press, 1984), pp. 151–72; Susan Groag Bell and Karen Offen, eds., *Women, the Family, and Freedom: The Debate in Documents*, vol. 1, *1750–1880* (Stanford: Stanford University Press, 1983).

3. Stewart Edwards, *The Paris Commune, 1871* (Chicago: Quadrangle Books, 1971), p. xiii.

4. Frank Jellinek, *The Paris Commune of 1871* (1937; rpt. New York: Grosset and Dunlap, 1965), pp. 325, 329, 365, 366, 368.

5. Paul MacKendrick, Deno Geanakoplos, J. H. Hexter, and Richard Pipes, *Western Civilization: The Struggle for Empire to Europe in the Modern World* (New York: Harper and Row, 1968), p. 521. The chronology of events in the *semaine sanglante* is not in doubt.

6. The Impressionists developed the style for which they are known in the Commune's aftermath. Moderate republicans, they reclaimed the city for the bourgeoisie by erasing the physical destruction of the city in their paintings. This symbolic erasure and reclamation was a deeply political enterprise. The second generation, children when the revolt occurred, reacted differently. In their controlled and orderly paintings, they sought to create a new, tolerant, noncompetitive, egalitarian world, not to reclaim power and control for the bourgeoisie. See Albert Boime, *Art and the French Commune: Imagining Paris after War and Revolution* (Princeton: Princeton University Press, 1995).

7. P.-O. Lissagaray, *Histoire de la Commune de 1871* (1896; rpt. Paris: Maspero, 1983), pp. 368, 353.

8. Sébastien Commissaire, *Mémoires et souvenirs* (Paris: Garcet et Nisius, 1888), 2:373; Félix Pyat, *Vengeur*, May 24, 1871, p. 2; Benoît Malon, *La troisième défaite du prolétaire français* (Neuchâtel: G. Guillaume fils, 1871), p. 504.

9. Francisque Sarcey, "Les aliénistes," *Gaulois,* May 28, 1871, p. 1.
10. Maxime Du Camp, *Les convulsions de Paris* (Paris: Librairie Hachette, 1881), 2:60, 62, 1:314.
11. Captain Beugnot, quoted in Edmond Lepelletier, *Histoire de la Commune de 1871* (Paris: Mercure de France, 1911), 1:448.
12. Lepelletier, *Histoire de la Commune* 1:459.
13. Jules Claretie, *Histoire de la révolution de 1870–71* (Paris: Bureaux du Journal L'Eclipse,* 1872), p. 651.
14. Alexandre Dumas, fils, *Une lettre sur les choses du jour* (Paris: Michel Lévy Frères, 1871), pp. 16–17.
15. Gaston Da Costa, *La Commune vécue* (Paris: Ancienne Maison Quantin, 1903–5), 1:20–22.
16. Jules Bergeret, *Le 18 mars: Journal hebdomadaire* (London: n.p., August 21–September 6 [1871]), p. 25.
17. Denise Riley, *"Am I That Name?" Feminism and the Category of "Women" in History* (Minneapolis: University of Minnesota Press, 1988).
18. There is a large and growing literature on the lives of nineteenth-century bourgeois women. Among the most important are Bonnie G. Smith, *Ladies of the Leisure Class: The Bourgeoises of Northern France in the Nineteenth Century* (Princeton: Princeton University Press, 1981); Mary S. Hartman, *Victorian Murderesses: A True History of Thirteen Respectable French and English Women Accused of Unspeakable Crimes* (New York: Schocken, 1977); Erna Hellerstein, Leslie Hume, and Karen Offen, *Victorian Women: A Documentary Account of Women's Lives in Nineteenth-Century England, France, and the United States* (Stanford: Stanford University Press, 1981); Riley, *"Am I That Name?";* Mary Poovey, *Uneven Developments: The Ideological Work of Gender in Mid-Victorian England* (Chicago: University of Chicago Press, 1988); Martha Vicinus, ed., *Suffer and Be Still: Women in the Victorian Age* (Bloomington: Indiana University Press, 1973); Leonore Davidoff and Catherine Hall, *Family Fortunes: Men and Women of the English Middle Class, 1780–1850* (Chicago: University of Chicago Press, 1987); Barbara Welter, "The Cult of True Womanhood, 1820–1860," *American Quarterly* 18 (Summer 1966):151–74; Carroll Smith-Rosenberg, "The Female World of Love and Ritual: Relations between Women in Nineteenth-Century America," *Signs* 1 (Autumn 1975):1–29; Kathryn Kish Sklar, *Catherine Beecher: A Study in American Domesticity* (New Haven: Yale University Press, 1973); Linda K. Kerber, "Separate Spheres, Female Worlds, Woman's Place: The Rhetoric of Women's History," *Journal of American History* 75 (July 1988):9–39.
19. Bell and Offen, eds., *Women, the Family, and Freedom,* 1:42–179; Moses, *French Feminism,* pp. 17–20, 31–39; Smith, *Ladies of the Leisure Class,* pp. 34–49; Cynthia Eagle Russett, *The Victorian Construction of Womanhood* (Cambridge: Harvard University Press, 1989), pp. 1–154.
20. Marina Warner, *Alone of All Her Sex: The Myth and the Cult of the Virgin Mary* (New York: Random House, 1983); Warner, *Monuments and Maidens: The Allegory of the Female Form* (New York: Atheneum, 1985), pp. 63–87; Margaret R. Miles, *Carnal Knowing: Female Nakedness and Religious Meaning in the Christian West* (Boston: Beacon, 1989); Elaine Pagels, *Adam, Eve, and the Serpent* (New York: Random House, 1988).
21. Warner, *Monuments and Maidens,* pp. xxi, 63–87; Madelyn Gutwirth, *The Twilight of the Goddesses: Women and Representation in the French Revolutionary Era* (New Brunswick, N.J.: Rutgers University Press, 1992), pp. 257–58; Sarah B. Pomeroy, *Goddesses, Whores, Wives, and Slaves: Women in Classical Antiquity* (New York: Schocken, 1975), pp. 4–9; Lynn Hunt, "Hercules and the Radical Image in the French Revolution," *Representations* 1 (1983):95–117.
22. The cultural tradition of female personification is so strong that even when the

grammatical gender of a concept is not female, its representation sometimes is. Warner, *Monuments and Maidens,* p. 68.

23. Gutwirth, *Twilight of the Goddesses,* pp. 255–59; Warner, *Monuments and Maidens,* pp. xx, 39.

24. Gutwirth, *Twilight of the Goddesses,* pp. 255–59; Warner, *Monuments and Maidens,* p. 37; Teresa De Lauretis, *Alice Doesn't: Feminism, Semiotics, Cinema* (Bloomington: Indiana University Press, 1984).

25. Warner, *Monuments and Maidens,* p. 37.

26. Maurice Agulhon, *Marianne into Battle: Republican Imagery and Symbolism in France, 1789–1880,* trans. Janet Lloyd (Cambridge: Cambridge University Press, 1981), pp. 11–34, 129; Warner, *Monuments and Maidens,* pp. 277, 292.

27. Anne Hollander, *Seeing through Clothes* (New York: Viking, 1978), pp. 202, 186–202; Warner, *Monuments and Maidens,* pp. 267–68, 270–78, 289, 292.

28. Several bibliographies on the Commune are available in print, in addition to the extensive bibliographies in many histories, such as Edwards, *The Paris Commune.* For a breakdown of the political alignments of twentieth-century historians, see Jellinek, *The Paris Commune,* pp. 423–29, 433–35; and Jean Bruhat, Jean Dautry, and Emile Tersen, *La Commune de 1871* (Paris: Sociales, 1960), pp. 391–420. For an example of misogynist history, see Richard Cobb's review of the English edition of Edith Thomas's book, "The Women of the Commune," in his *Second Identity: Essays of France and French History* (London: Oxford University Press, 1969), pp. 221–36.

29. Bruhat, Dautry, and Teresen, *La Commune de 1871,* pp. 179–94; William Serman, *La Commune de Paris (1871)* (Paris: Fayard, 1986), pp. 287–92; Georges Soria, *Grande histoire de la Commune,* 5 vols. (Paris: Livre Club Diderot, 1970), 3:124–42; Stéphane Rials, *Nouvelle Histoire de Paris: De Trochu à Thiers, 1870–1873* (Paris: Hachette, 1985), pp. 432–35. In a later section, Rials addresses the question of whether the fires of the semaine sanglante were set by women (pp. 495–509).

30. Edith Thomas, *Les "pétroleuses"* (Paris: Gallimard, 1963). Articles that focus on women include Eugene Schulkind, "Le rôle des femmes dans la Commune de 1871," *1848: Revue des révolutions contemporaines* 42 (February 1950): n.p.; Schulkind, "Socialist Women during the 1871 Paris Commune," *Past and Present,* no. 106 (February 1985):124–63; Vasili Soukhomline, "Deux femmes russes combattantes de la Commune," *Cahiers Internationaux* 16 (May 1950):53–62; Hélène Parmelin, "Les femmes et la Commune," *Europe* 29 (April–May 1951):136–46; Marie-Louise Coudert, "Il y a cent ans les femmes aussi...," *Cahiers du Communisme,* special issue "La Commune" (March 1971):110–15; Persis Hunt, "Feminism and Anti-Clericalism under the Commune," in John Hicks and Robert Tucker, eds., *Revolution and Reaction: The Paris Commune, 1871* (Springfield: University of Massachusetts Press, 1973), pp. 50–55; Kathleen B. Jones and Françoise Vergès, "Women of the Paris Commune," *Women's Studies International Forum* 14 (1991):491–503.

31. Studies of the Holocaust have also employed this technique, and as James Young points out, such understandings of the relationship between what was (the facts) and the telling of what was (texts) has a long history. James E. Young, *Writing and Rewriting the Holocaust: Narrative and the Consequences of Interpretation* (Bloomington: Indiana University Press, 1988), pp. 1–5.

Synopsis

1. For detailed information about the Commune's origins and history, see Lissagaray, *Histoire de la Commune,* which is also available in English translation: *History of*

the Commune of 1871, trans. Eleanor Marx Aveling (New York: International, 1898); Jellinek, _The Paris Commune;_ Edwards, _The Paris Commune;_ Robert Tombs, _The War against Paris, 1871_ (Cambridge: Cambridge University Press, 1981); Serman, _La Commune;_ or one of the many other histories of this period. In addition to these sources, details in the following account have been taken from Nathan Sheppard, _Shut Up in Paris_ (London: Richard Bentley, 1871), p. 9; the Reverend William Gibson, _Paris during the Commune: Being Letters from Paris and Its Neighbourhood Written Chiefly during the Time of the Second Siege_ (London: Whittaker, 1872); Goncourt, _Journal,_ vol. 2; _Cri du Peuple; Daily News;_ and _Times._

2. For analysis of this and other military decisions during this period, see Tombs, _War against Paris._

3. For information on the creation and evolution of Marianne, see Agulhon, _Marianne into Battle._

4. For a history of the Communes established briefly in Marseilles and Lyons in 1871, see Louis M. Greenberg, _Sisters of Liberty_ (Cambridge: Harvard University Press, 1971); Jeanne Gaillard, _Communes de Province, Commune de Paris, 1870–1871_ (Paris: Flammarion, 1971); and Julian P. W. Archer, "The Crowd in the Lyon Commune and the Insurrection of La Guillotière," in _1871: Jalons pour une histoire de la Commune de Paris,_ ed. Jacques Rougerie (Assen, Pays-Bas: Van Gorcum, 1973), pp. 183–90.

5. Gibson, _Paris during the Commune,_ pp. 130, 143.

6. Jules Vallès, _Cri du Peuple,_ March 30, 1871, p. 1.

7. Albert Boime, _Hollow Icons: The Politics of Sculpture in Nineteenth-Century France_ (Kent, Ohio: Kent State University Press, 1987), pp. 8–9.

8. Goncourt, _Journal,_ March 19, 1871, 2:747. Of the two Goncourt brothers, only Edmond wrote about the Commune; Jules had died on June 20, 1870.

9. "The frightful spectacle [of dead and captured Communards] will serve as a lesson, it is to be hoped, to the foolish people who dared to declare themselves partisans of the Commune." Official Government (Versailles) Dispatch, May 25, 7:00 A.M., quoted in Gibson, _Paris during the Commune,_ p. 267.

10. M. le Général Appert, _Rapport d'ensemble sur les opérations de la justice militaire relatives à l'insurrection de 1871_ (Paris: Assemblée Nationale, 1875), pp. 320–21.

11. V. I. Lenin, _The Paris Commune_ (New York: International, 1934); Karl Marx and V. I. Lenin, _The Civil War in France: The Paris Commune_ (New York: International, 1940).

12. The Communards, and especially the National Guard of Paris, were also referred to as the _fédérés,_ or the federals, since they espoused a federal form of government that would give more autonomy to individual departments than the centralized government of France did.

1. The Women of March 18

1. A correspondent for the London _Daily News_ witnessed the National Guard's seizure of the guns on February 27. While he and others stood on the street and watched anxiously, "National Guards, in various uniforms, and a confused mob of civilians, including many of the gamins and the voyous, for which Paris is famous, came running along, dragging and pushing about thirty large pieces of artillery. . . . At last a person standing near me" he reported, "caught hold of a National Guard and questioned him—retaining him by force. 'You shall tell us what you are doing with these cannon,' he exclaimed; and the National Guard, panting for breath, hastily replied, 'Those cannons are our cannons; we paid for them with the money collected among ourselves; they belong to us and not to the Government; and therefore we have a right to refuse to allow

them to be delivered up to the Prussians.' The word Prussian gave new strength to the man—he broke loose from the hands which imprisoned him and rejoined his cannon." *Daily News,* March 1, 1871, p. 6.

2. *La vérité sur la Commune par un ancien proscrit* (Paris: Louis Salmon, n.d.), pp. 222–23; Lissagaray, *Histoire de la Commune,* pp. 108–10; Da Costa, *La Commune vécue* 1:12; Lepelletier, *Histoire de la Commune* 1:396–98; Henri Lefebvre, *La proclamation de la Commune, 26 mars 1871* (Paris: Gallimard, 1965), p. 241; Tombs, *War against Paris,* pp. 43–44.

3. Georges E. B. Clemenceau, *Clemenceau: The Events of His Life as Told by Himself to His Former Secretary, Jean Martet,* trans. Milton Waldman (London: Longmans, Green, 1930), pp. 165–66. Clemenceau's account of March 18 was written in 1872 but not published until 1930. Edgar Holt, *The Tiger: The Life of Georges Clemenceau, 1841–1929* (London: Hamish Hamilton, 1976), p. 29.

4. Clemenceau, *Clemenceau,* p. 165, 170, 173, 182, 186; Assemblée Nationale, *Enquête parlementaire sur l'insurrection du 18 mars,* vol. 2: *Dépositions des témoins* (Versailles: Cerf, 1872), Jules Ferry, p. 64. General reports on these efforts and the difficulties involved in them can also be found in the *Times,* March 15 (p. 5), 16 (pp. 5, 10), and 17 (p. 5), 1871. Also see Tombs, *War against Paris,* pp. 34–35.

5. Clemenceau, *Clemenceau,* p. 166.

6. Readers should not confuse this street with the more famous rue des Rosiers in the fourth arrondissement.

7. Louise Michel, *La Commune,* 2d ed. (Paris: P.-V. Stock, 1898), pp. 139–40. Michel's and Clemenceau's accounts of their meeting and actions on the eighteenth concur.

8. *La vérité sur la Commune,* p. 229. This work was published anonymously and is undated, but Stewart Edwards identifies the author of it as Vergers d'Esboeufs and dates its publication as 1879–80. See Edwards, ed., *The Communards of Paris,* trans. Jean McNeil (Ithaca: Cornell University Press, 1973), pp. 56, 65, 175. Esboeufs was a member of the Revolutionary Committee in the seventeenth arrondissement.

9. Lepelletier, *Histoire de la Commune,* p. 400; *La vérité sur la Commune,* p. 229.

10. Clemenceau, *Clemenceau,* p. 168. Clemenceau felt insulted by the implicit accusation that he wanted to "parade the corpse." In his judgment, the crowd was calm and there was no danger. Turpin died a few days later. *La vérité sur la Commune* suggests that General Lecomte's callous disregard for the wounded Turpin was one of the reasons he was killed later in the day.

11. Clemenceau, *Clemenceau,* p. 169.

12. *La vérité sur la Commune,* p. 232.

13. Ibid.

14. Da Costa, *La Commune vécue* 1:15; *Daily News,* March 18, 1871 (dateline: Paris, March 17, evening), p. 6.

15. *La vérité sur la Commune,* p. 231.

16. *Times,* March 20, 1871 (dateline: March 18), p. 9.

17. For information on the events in Belleville, another working-class suburb of Paris, on March 18 and during the Commune, see Gérard Jacquemet, *Belleville au XIXe siècle du faubourg à la ville* (Paris: Editions de l'Ecole des Hautes Etudes en Sciences Sociales, 1984), pp. 178–83.

18. Tombs, *War against Paris,* p. 44. This was apparently a separate incident from the one I have already described.

19. Most historians and many participants in the events of March 18 believed that Lecomte did order his men to fire on the crowd. See *La vérité sur la Commune,* pp. 239–40; Michel, *La Commune,* pp. 140–41; and Paul Lanjalley and Paul Corriez, *His-*

toire de la révolution du 18 mars (Paris: A. Lacroix, Verboeckhoven, 1871), p. 27. Others have maintained that Lecomte knew his men would not fire on women and children and hoped merely to frighten the crowd by ordering his men to load their guns and fix their bayonets. See Tombs, *War against Paris*, p. 45. Da Costa reported that Lecomte ordered his men to charge the crowd, not to fire upon it. Da Costa, *La Commune vécue* 1:12–13. The decision to execute Lecomte later in the day was based at least partially on a deeply held conviction that he had ordered his men to fire on the crowd three times earlier in the day.

Regardless of how stalwart the crowd was at the beginning of this confrontation, Lecomte's soldiers refused to obey the orders to fire on their fellow Parisians. According to *La vérité sur la commune*, Lecomte then became so enraged that "he turned his revolver on [his own troops] and threatened to blow out the brains of those who refused to fire." Lecomte, in this version, was then surrounded by the people and almost lynched on the spot. *La vérité sur la Commune*, p. 240.

20. Michel, *La Commune*, p. 140.

21. Clemenceau, *Clemenceau*, p. 171.

22. *Times*, March 20, 1871 (dateline: March 18), p. 9.

23. *La vérité sur la Commune*, pp. 231, 234–36; Lefebvre, *La proclamation de la Commune*, p. 245.

24. *La vérité sur la Commune*, p. 235, 239–40; Michel, *La Commune*, p. 140; Arthur Chevalier in Da Costa, *La Commune vécue* 1:15.

25. Michel, *La Commune*, p. 140.

26. *La vérité sur la Commune*, pp. 239–40; Lissagaray, *Histoire de la Commune*, pp. 110–11. Also see Lefebvre, *La proclamation*, p. 254; Edwards, *The Paris Commune*, p. 139.

27. Lepelletier, *Histoire de la Commune*, p. 417. General Joseph Vinoy was the commander of Paris and was in charge of the attack on the cannons.

28. Da Costa, *La Commune vécue* 1:16–17; Lepelletier, *Histoire de la Commune* 1:422–23; Clemenceau, *Clemenceau*, p. 174; Lefebvre, *La proclamation*, pp. 257–58; Tombs, *War against Paris*, p. 46. Accounts of the number of casualties vary.

29. The *Times* correspondent, who had hurried off to Belleville and the buttes Chaumont while it was still early, was astonished to see the fraternizing of army troops and national guardsmen he had watched at Montmartre repeated there while the army waited for horses to pull the guns they had taken. *Times*, March 20, 1871 (dateline: Paris, March 18), p. 9.

30. Lissagaray, *Histoire de la Commune*, pp. 111–13; Edwards, *The Paris Commune*, pp. 144–45; Tombs, *War against Paris*, pp. 50–51.

31. Ernest Vizetelly, another English reporter who, like the *Times* correspondent spent the day wandering around the city, watched as soldiers "sold their weapons for a few francs, and then betook themselves to wine-shops where they soon got intoxicated." Vizetelly, *My Adventures in the Commune* (London: Chatto and Windus, 1914), p. 53. Susanna Barrows has demonstrated that late nineteenth-century analysts often attributed "irrational mob behavior" to alcoholism. Susanna Barrows, *Distorting Mirrors: Visions of the Crowd in Late Nineteenth-Century France* (New Haven: Yale University Press, 1981), pp. 43–72.

32. There is some disagreement over whether a message from the Central Committee was received by Mayer. Army Captain Comte Arthur-Jacques-Adolphe Beugnot, one of the prisoners, said that Mayer told them that they were being moved to where the committee was, but he did not believe the committee existed and thought they were going to be killed. See Da Costa, *La Commune vécue* 1:24.

33. Captain Beugnot, quoted in Le Comte d'Hérisson, *Nouveau journal d'un officier*

d'ordonnance: La Commune (Paris: Paul Ollendorff, 1891), pp. 51–52; and in Da Costa, *La Commune vécue* 1:25–26. Also see, Edwards, *The Paris Commune,* p. 140.

34. Beugnot, in d'Hérisson, *Nouveau journal,* p. 54; Edwards, *The Paris Commune,* p. 141.

35. Reports disagree about the behavior and bravery of the two generals. Anti-Commune writers represent them as brave, pro-Commune writers, as cowardly. Cf. Beugnot, in d'Hérisson, *Nouveau journal,* p. 55; Lissagaray, *History of the Commune,* p. 84. (This passage is missing from the 1983 reprint of the 1896 Dentu edition of Lissagaray's history.)

36. Clemenceau, *Clemenceau,* p. 184.

37. Ibid., pp. 185–87. That Clemenceau's life was in danger seems indisputable. See his own account and that of Beugnot in d'Hérisson, *Nouveau journal,* p. 56.

38. Edwards, *The Paris Commune,* pp. 147–48; Tombs, *War against Paris,* pp. 50–51.

39. See Armand Lanoux, *Une histoire de la Commune de Paris* (Paris: Bernard Grasset, 1971), 1:54; Gustave Lefrançais, *Etude sur le mouvement communaliste à Paris, en 1871* (Neuchâtel: G. Guillaume fils, 1871), p. 140. Lissagaray, in contrast, believed that Thiers acted out of contempt for the Parisians, whom he deemed "incapable of any serious action," and out of a desire to "play the part of a Bonaparte." Lissagaray, *History of the Commune,* p. 77. (This passage is missing from the 1983 reprint of the 1896 Dentu edition of Lissagaray's history.) Robert Tombs's analysis inherently supports the first part of Lissagaray's judgment. Tombs, *War against Paris,* p. 42.

40. General Vinoy so testified. Assemblée Nationale, *Enquête parlementaire* 2:98, 103.

41. Tombs, *War against Paris,* pp. 42–43.

42. Sheppard, *Shut Up in Paris,* pp. 3–12; *Times,* March 1, 1871 (dateline: February 27), p. 4.

43. Of these four, only Louise Michel and Edmond Lepelletier were clearly present in Montmartre. Da Costa quotes eyewitnesses extensively but does not appear to have been one himself. The author of *La vérité sur la Commune* writes as though he were present, but his anonymity makes it unverifiable.

44. Beugnot's 1888 account of his experience on the eighteenth is quoted at length in Da Costa, *La Commune vécue* 1:24–32, and d'Hérisson, *Nouveau journal,* pp. 46–58. Chevalier is quoted by Da Costa, 1:14–15, 32–35.

45. Clemenceau, *Clemenceau,* p. 166.

46. *Times,* March 20, 1871 (dateline: March 18), p. 9.

47. Da Costa, *La Commune vécue* 1:10.

48. Ibid., pp. 12–13, 20.

49. *Times,* March 20, 1871 (dateline: March 18), p. 9.

50. Lissagaray, *Histoire de la Commune,* p. 110.

51. Assemblée Nationale, *Enquête parlementaire* 2:434.

52. Lepelletier, *Histoire de la Commune* 1:411.

53. *La vérité sur la Commune,* p. 232.

54. Beugnot, in d'Hérisson, *Journal nouveau,* p. 52; and in Lepelletier, *Histoire de la Commune* 1:448–49.

55. *Times,* March 20, 1871 (dateline: March 18), p. 9.

56. E. B. Washburne, *Recollections of a Minister to France, 1869–1877* (New York: Charles Scribner's Sons, 1887), 2:37.

57. Beugnot, in d'Hérisson, *Journal nouveau,* p. 52; and in Lepelletier, *Histoire de la Commune* 1:448–49.

58. *Times,* March 20, 1871 (dateline: March 18), p. 9.

59. Catulle Mendès, *Les 73 journées de la Commune* (Paris: E. Lachaud, 1871), pp. 3–4.

60. Clemenceau, *Clemenceau,* p. 184.

61. Washburne, *Recollections* 2:36–7.
62. Alistair Horne, *The Fall of Paris* (New York: St. Martin's, 1965), p. 271.
63. Lepelletier, *Histoire de la Commune* 1:459.
64. Clemenceau, *Clemenceau*, p. 169.
65. *Times*, March 20, 1871 (dateline: March 18), p. 9.
66. Ibid.
67. Da Costa, *La Commune vécue* 1:20–22.
68. Ibid., 1:20. Also see Claretie, *Histoire de la révolution*, p. 598.
69. Lissagaray, *Histoire de la Commune*, pp. 109–10.
70. Lanjalley and Corriez, *Histoire de la révolution*, p. 27.
71. Clemenceau, *Clemenceau*, p. 166.
72. Rials, *Nouvelle histoire*, p. 252; Georges Bourgin, *La guerre de 1870–1871 et la Commune* (Paris: Flammarion, 1971), p. 167.
73. Serman, *La Commune de Paris*, p. 202.
74. Lefebvre, *La proclamation*, p. 243.
75. Lepelletier, *Histoire de la Commune* 1:399–400.
76. Lefebvre, *La proclamation*, p. 243.
77. Edwards, *The Paris Commune*, p. 138.
78. Bourgin, *Les premières journées de la Commune* (Paris: Hachette, 1928), pp. 53–54.
79. *La vérité sur la Commune*, pp. 239–40.
80. Michel, *La Commune*, p. 140.
81. Arthur Chevalier, guard of the 169th battalion, quoted in Da Costa, *La Commune vécue* 1:14–15, emphasis added. Chevalier, on the one hand, and Michel and the author of *La vérité sur la Commune*, on the other, may be describing different moments in the same action, or perhaps confrontations with at least two different generals. There is no way to be certain.
82. Da Costa, *La Commune vécue* 1:21.
83. Vizetelly, *My Adventures*, p. 38.
84. Lepelletier, *Histoire de la Commune* 1:400.
85. Claretie, *Histoire de la révolution*, p. 595.
86. For an example of each, see Bruhat, Dautry, and Tersen, *La Commune*, p. 109; Horne, *Fall of Paris*, pp. 270–71; Bourgin, *Les premières journées*, pp. 54–55.
87. Lepelletier, *Histoire de la Commune* 1:422–23. Lepelletier indicates that he was an eyewitness on p. 421 n. 1.
88. Tombs, *War against Paris*, p. 46.
89. Lepelletier, *Histoire de la Commune* 1:423 n. 1, emphasis added.
90. Clemenceau, *Clemenceau*, p. 174 n. 1.
91. William Pembroke Fetridge, *The Rise and Fall of The Paris Commune in 1871; with a Full Account of the Bombardment, Capture, and Burning of the City* (New York: Harper and Brothers, 1871), p. 34, is an exception to the rule. Vilifying fraternizing soldiers and guardsmen alike, he eliminated women from the story altogether and claimed that the horse "was cut up by the soldiers of the line who had mutinied, and sold on the Place, the proceeds of which they used for the purchase of liquor to cement their criminal union with the insurgents, who assured them the committee had plenty of money, or would soon have; and that the continuance of their pay, or better, was a certainty, with less to do and better food." This version of the story had no takers among later writers.
92. Claretie, *Histoire de la révolution*, p. 598, emphasis added.
93. Ibid. Claretie uses the word *fille* to describe the women. *Filles soumises* and *filles insoumises* were the terms used to describe prostitutes who had and had not registered with the police. In this context, the use of *filles*, even without an adjective, means prostitute.
94. Da Costa, *La Commune vécue* 1:22. Edith Thomas, the communardes' only histo-

rian to date, accepts Da Costa's distinction between the afternoon and morning crowds, although she emphasizes that the housewives, too, were capable of violent action, and points out that the harpies and the honest women of the people and the heroic citoyennes would fight and die together on the barricades. Thomas, *Les "pétroleuses,"* p. 70.

95. Da Costa, *La Commune vécue* 1:22.

96. Jellinek, *The Paris Commune,* p. 115, emphasis added. Jellinek also shortened Clemenceau's estimate that the dismembering of the horse took an hour: "Half an hour [after the horse was killed], there was not a trace of the animal left."

97. Ibid., p. 118.

98. Edwards, *The Paris Commune,* p. 140.

99. Rials, *Nouvelle histoire,* omits the entire place Pigalle incident; Serman, *La Commune de Paris,* pp. 205–6, includes the incident but omits the horse; Soria, *Grande histoire* 1:351, omits the butchering of the horse but includes Da Costa's representation of the women.

100. Lissagaray, *Histoire de la Commune,* p. 113; Da Costa, *La Commune vécue* 1:21–22.

101. Beugnot, in Da Costa, *La Commune vécue* 1:25–26.

102. Lepelletier, *Histoire de la Commune* 1:459–60.

103. Horne, *Fall of Paris,* p. 271.

104. In French, *le meurtre, la tuerie, l'exécution,* and *l'assassination.* See Bourgin, *La guerre de 1870–1871,* p. 174. For discussion of the political importance of other words applied to the Commune, see Paul Lidsky, *Les écrivains contre la Commune* (Paris: François Maspero, 1972), p. 152. Twentieth-century critics of the Commune have surpassed their nineteenth-century colleagues in their use of judgmental language. Rials, for instance, refers to the killing of the generals as a massacre. Rials, *Nouvelle histoire,* p. 258.

105. Lissagaray, *Histoire de la Commune,* pp. 414–15, 420; Edwards, *The Paris Commune,* p. 347; Jellinek, *The Paris Commune,* p. 377.

106. Da Costa, *La Commune vécue* 1:36; Lepelletier, *Histoire de la Commune* 1:463–64; *La vérité sur la Commune,* p. 245; Vizetelly, *My Adventures,* p. 45; Lissagaray, *Histoire de la Commune,* p. 114; Lanjalley and Corriez, *Histoire de la révolution,* p. 36; Edwards, *The Paris Commune,* p. 141. Although Vizetelly reportedly saw soldiers sell their "weapons" so they could buy wine (*My Adventures,* p. 53), there are no other reports of soldiers abandoning or surrendering their rifles when they fraternized with the national guardsmen, and hence no reason to believe that the men who shot the generals were national guardsmen armed with army rifles. The larger number of bullets found in the body of Clément Thomas lends credence to the belief that if he had not been taken prisoner and brought to the rue des Rosiers, Lecomte would have been saved.

107. See, Lissagaray, *Histoire de la Commune,* p. 114; Vizetelly, *My Adventures,* pp. 42–45; Bruhat, Dautry, and Tersen, *La Commune,* p. 113; and Edwards, *The Paris Commune,* pp. 141–42.

108. Da Costa, *La Commune vécue* 1:20.

109. Thomas, *Les "Petroleuses,"* pp. 69–70.

110. Claretie, *Histoire de la révolution,* p. 596; Beugnot implies the presence of women, since he says that the crowd that followed them up the hill filled the courtyard, and that crowd contained women. Beugnot, in d'Hérisson, *Nouveau journal,* p. 52.

111. Clemenceau, *Clemenceau,* p. 184.

112. Lanjalley and Corriez, *Histoire de la révolution,* p. 36.

113. *Journal Officiel,* March 19, 1871, p. 1.

114. Joanni d'Arsac, *La guerre civile et la Commune de Paris en 1871* (Paris: F. Curot, 1871), p. 15.

115. Claretie, *Histoire de la révolution,* p. 598. Claretie also claimed that seventy, not

forty, bullets were found in Clément Thomas's body, a figure repeated by Jellinek in *The Paris Commune,* p. 121.

116. Appert, *Rapport d'ensemble,* p. 23.

117. Clemenceau, *Clemenceau,* p. 185.

118. Bourgin, *Les premières journées,* p. 60.

119. Alphonse Daudet, "Le jardin de la rue des Rosiers," in *Lettres à un absent, Paris, 1870–1871* (Paris: Alphonse Lemirre, 1871), p. 128, reprinted in his *Souvenirs d'un homme de lettres* (Paris: C. Marpon et E. Flammarion, 1888); d'Arsac, *La guerre civile,* p. 16.

120. Vizetelly, *My Adventures,* p. 2.

121. Lepelletier, *Histoire de la Commune* 1:465; Lanjalley and Corriez, *Histoire de la révolution,* p. 39; *La vérité sur la Commune,* p. 256.

122. Claretie, *Histoire de la révolution,* pp. 596–98.

123. Washburne, *Recollections* 2:36–37.

124. *La vérité sur la Commune,* p. 255.

125. Goncourt, *Journal,* April 3, 1871, 2:757. This passage is omitted from some editions of the diary. Goncourt's failure to record the account for two weeks and his need to assure himself that the story was not a rumor make one wonder whether he was truly certain of this report.

126. D. W. Brogan, *The Development of Modern France, 1870–1939* (New York: Harper and Row, 1966), 1:58. Brogan also believed that the two generals "were shot down by unknown National Guardsmen" and that Clemenceau was "shattered by this revelation of his own impotence and of popular savagery."

127. Horne, *The Fall of Paris,* p. 272.

128. For discussion of crowd psychology later in the century, see Barrows, *Distorting Mirrors.*

129. Georges Clemenceau, letter, March 30, 1871, in *La vérité sur la Commune,* pp. 247–48. The letter was written to the editor of *Le Soir,* which had published Beugnot's memoir on March 24 and 25. The letter is also reprinted in Lanjalley and Corriez, *Histoire de la révolution,* pp. 38–39.

130. Clemenceau, *Clemenceau,* p. 184.

131. Claretie, *Histoire de la révolution,* pp. 596–98.

132. Beugnot in Da Costa, *La Commune vécue* 1:30.

133. Daudet, *Lettres,* p. 128.

134. Washburne, *Recollections* 2:36–37.

135. Da Costa, *La Commune vécue* 1:19–20.

136. Claretie, *Histoire de la révolution,* p. 598.

137. Appert, *Rapport d'ensemble,* p. 24.

138. *La vérité sur la Commune,* p. 255.

139. Beugnot in d'Hérisson, *Nouveau journal,* p. 55.

140. Clemenceau, *Clemenceau,* pp. 184–85. Clemenceau's account is self-serving but not necessarily wrong. The notion that a stupor fell over the crowd once its bloodlust was satisfied lingered on in histories, sometimes combined with Clemenceau's account, so that the crowd's interest in killing the prisoners fades quickly after its encounter with him. Edwards, *The Paris Commune,* p. 142; Jellinek, *The Paris Commune,* p. 121.

141. Adolphe Thiers, *Memoirs of M. Thiers, 1870–1873,* trans. F. M. Atkinson (New York: Howard Fertig, 1973), p. 124.

142. Mendès, *Les 73 journées,* p. 4; Clemenceau, *Clemenceau,* p. 184; Vizetelly, *My Adventures,* p. 2.

143. Jacques Chastenet, *Histoire de la Troisième République,* vol. 1: *Naissance et jeunesse* (Paris: Hachette, 1952), p. 72. Also see Jellinek, *The Paris Commune,* p. 121; Horne, *Fall of Paris,* p. 272.

144. Appert, *Rapport d'ensemble*, p. 24.
145. Jellinek, *The Paris Commune*, pp. 329–30.

2. Remembering and Representing

1. *Daily News*, March 21, 1871 (dateline: March 19), p. 5. Also see Lanjalley and Corriez, *Histoire de la révolution*, p. 54.
2. Lanjalley and Corriez, *Histoire de la révolution*, p. 58; Mendès, *Les 73 journées*, p. 12; Goncourt, *Journal*, March 19, 1871, 2:746–48; Da Costa, *La Commune vécue* 1:131–32; Lefebvre, *La proclamation*, pp. 289–90; Lissagaray, *Histoire de la Commune*, pp. 117–21; *Times*, March 21, 1871 (dateline: Paris, March 19, 4 P.M.), p. 8; *Daily News*, March 21, 1871 (dateline: March 19), p. 5. For photographs of the national guardsmen and their barricades, see Jean Braire, *Sur les traces des communards: Enquête dans les rues du Paris d'aujourd'hui* (Paris: Amis de la Commune, 1988).
3. I have placed quotation marks around "memories" and "remembered" to indicate that these are cultural not personal memories. Seventy-seven years had elapsed since the period of the French Revolution known as the Terror, too long for those who had personal memories to still be alive.
4. Gibson, *Paris during the Commune*, p. 120; *Daily News*, March 21, 1871 (dateline: March 19), p. 5.
5. Mendès, *Les 73 journées*, p. 13.
6. Goncourt, *Journal* 2:747; Lanjalley and Corriez, *Histoire de la révolution*, p. 57. Only four members of the Central Committee were generally known: Adolphe Assi, age thirty, who assumed the leadership of the committee, was a member of the International and had been one of the leaders of the steelworkers' strike at Le Creusot early in 1870. Charles Lullier, thirty-three, a naval officer whose enthusiasm for the republic was not matched by his competence, commanded the National Guard briefly and then was arrested by the Commune. Gabriel Ranvier was well known for his public speeches and for his participation in the October 31, 1870, revolt, for which the Government of National Defense was pursuing him. Eugène Varlin, age thirty-two, a bookbinder by trade and a member of the International, active in the strike movements of the 1860s, was a member of both the Central Committee and the Commune. Jean Maitron and M. Egrot, eds., *Dictionnaire biographique du mouvement ouvrier français*, part 2: *1864–1871* (Paris: Ouvrières, 1964–69).
7. Goncourt, *Journal*, March 19, 1871, 2:747.
8. *Times*, March 21, 1871 (dateline: Paris, March 19, 4:00 P.M.), p. 8.
9. Edwards, *The Paris Commune*, pp. 123–24; Jellinek, *The Paris Commune*, p. 94.
10. Those who might have taken decisive action were either not in the city or were not members of the committee. Most important, Auguste Blanqui, the veteran revolutionary of 1830 and 1848 who by 1871 was legendary in revolutionary and socialist circles, was once again in prison, this time for his activities during the failed uprising of October 31, 1870.
11. Lanjalley and Corriez, *Histoire de la révolution*, p. 53.
12. *Journal Officiel*, March 20, 1871, p. 1. Also see Jellinek, *The Paris Commune*, p. 134; Edwards, *The Paris Commune*, p. 161. This statement, widely believed to be true during the Commune (although parts of it now appear to be debatable), simply gave Thiers more reason to characterize the Central Committee as assassins in his communiqués with the provinces. The state prosecutor in the trial of the Communard leaders in August repeated this statement by the Central Committee in his opening statement to condemn the rebellion from the outset. See *Gaulois*, August 9, 1871, p. 3.

13. Lissagaray, *Histoire de la Commune,* pp. 118–33; Edwards, *The Paris Commune,* p. 165; Goncourt, *Journal,* March 20–21, 1871, 2:748–50.

14. Although Thiers pushed the National Assembly for quick ratification of the terms of the peace treaty with Prussia, which was the Prussian requirement for leaving Paris, in the eyes of the Parisians, his role in negotiating the treaty left him responsible for the Prussian occupation of the city. J. P. T. Bury and R. P. Tombs, *Thiers, 1797–1877: A Political Life* (London: Allen and Unwin, 1986), p. 199.

15. Jules Simon, *L'ouvrière,* 3d ed. (Paris: L. Hachette, 1861), p. v. Also see Gay L. Gullickson, "Womanhood and Motherhood: The Rouen Manufacturing Community, Women Workers, and the French Factory Acts," in *The European Peasant Family and Society: Historical Studies,* ed. Richard L. Rudolph (Liverpool: Liverpool University Press, 1995), pp. 206–32.

16. Joan Wallach Scott, "'L'Ouvrière! Mot Impie, Sordide . . .': Women Workers in the Discourse of French Political Economy, 1840–1860," in her *Gender and the Politics of History* (New York: Columbia University Press, 1988), pp. 139–63.

17. Eugène Varlin, one of the most politically radical members of the committee (he was also a member of the International), drew up the list. Varlin, himself, would have preferred a more radical set of demands, but he believed that the revolution had occurred too soon and that these demands were all the city could reasonably expect to win. The National Assembly and Thiers refused to accept even these demands when they were presented to them on March 20.

18. Jellinek, *The Paris Commune,* p. 137; Edwards, *The Paris Commune,* pp. 155–67.

19. Bury and Tombs, *Thiers,* pp. 52–55, 103–4, 117–19, 123–26.

20. *Journal Officiel,* March 19, 1871 (morning edition).

21. Goncourt, *Journal,* March 28, 1871, 2:753.

22. Jacobins and Blanquists looked back to the French Revolution and the constitution of 1793 for inspiration. Jacobins believed Parisians would lead the overthrow of the existing order and institute a republican, anticlerical government. Blanquists believed in a revolution led by a disciplined party of (radical bourgois) revolutionaries that would gain control of the government and institute social reforms. Proudhonists believed in workers' cooperatives and self-governing groups of producers, and distrusted all government. Communists (or Marxists) were members of the International Working Men's Association and believed in a working-class revolution that would create an economic revolution. Jellinek, *The Paris Commune,* pp. 19–39; Edwards, *The Paris Commune,* pp. 210–15; François Furet, *Revolutionary France, 1770–1880,* trans. Antonia Nevill (Oxford: Blackwell, 1992), pp. 500–504.

23. The salary of six thousand francs a year was actually a good bit higher than the average salary of skilled workmen, but it was considerably lower than the salary paid to politicians elsewhere. Perhaps most important, it was a democratic move away from a parliamentary system that paid no one and hence was restricted to the wealthy. See Jellinek, *The Paris Commune,* p. 391; Edwards, *The Paris Commune,* pp. 189–91, 207–8, 250–57.

24. The decree on rents was also very popular among the petite bourgeoisie.

25. Du Camp, *Les convulsions* 4:325.

26. Ibid., 4:326.

27. Gibson, *Paris during the Commune,* April 7, 1871, pp. 166–67.

28. Ibid., April 18, 1871, p. 198.

29. See, for instance, Appert, *Rapport d'ensemble,* p. 62; Barrows, *Distorting Mirrors.*

30. *Journal Officiel,* March 19, 1871, p. 1. The *Journal Officiel* was still under the control of the national government.

31. *Cri du Peuple,* April 20, 26, 1871; *Commune,* March 20, 1871; Vizetelly, *My Ad-*

ventures, p. 230; William Linton, *The Paris Commune: In Answer to the Calumnies of the "New York Tribune"* (Boston: N.p., 1871), pp. 13–17.

32. Gibson, *Paris during the Commune,* April 13, 1871, p. 186.

33. Ibid., April 22, 1871, p. 220.

34. Philibert Audebrand, *Histoire intime de la révolution du 18 mars* (Paris: E. Dentu, 1871), p. iv.

35. See, for instance, Jules Simon, *The Government of M. Thiers, from 8th February 1871 to 24th May 1873* (New York: Scribner's, 1879); Washburne, *Recollections* 2:163; Appert, *Rapport d'ensemble,* p. 87; Audebrand, *Histoire intime,* p. iv.

36. Appert, *Rapport d'ensemble,* pp. 59–62.

37. *Times,* March 22, 1871 (dateline: March 20), p. 5.

38. Lissagaray, *Histoire de la Commune,* pp. 137–40; Edwards, *The Paris Commune,* pp. 171–72; Jellinek, *The Paris Commune,* pp. 138–45.

39. *Times,* March 23, 1871 (dateline: Versailles, March 23, noon), p. 10; Edwards, *The Paris Commune,* pp. 178–79.

40. *Journal Officiel,* April 6, 1871; Lefebvre, *La proclamation,* pp. 371–72; Edwards, *The Paris Commune,* p. 200.

41. Gibson, *Paris during the Commune,* April 14, 1871, p. 188.

42. Vizetelly, *My Adventures,* p. 159; "A Victim of Paris and Versailles," *Macmillan's Magazine* 24 (September 1871):385.

43. Vizetelly, *My Adventures,* pp. 141, 165, 167; *L'Illustration,* May 6, 1871, p. 285.

44. Goncourt, *Journal,* May 7, 1871, 2:793–94.

45. See, for instance, *Standard,* April 8, 1871, editorial, p. 4.

46. *Journal de Bruxelles,* April 6, evening, quoted in *Standard,* April 7, 1871.

47. Edwards, *The Paris Commune,* pp. 284–85; *Times,* May 9, 1871; Vizetelly, *My Adventures,* pp. 262–63.

48. Gustave Courbet, quoted in Jellinek, *The Paris Commune,* p. 244.

49. Goncourt, *Journal,* May 7, 1871, 2:793.

50. Mendès, *Les 73 journées,* p. 135.

51. Dominique Godineau, *Citoyennes tricoteuses: Les femmes du peuple à Paris pendant la Révolution française* (Aix-en-Provence: Alinea, 1988), pp. 13–14; Gutwirth, *Twilight of the Goddesses,* pp. 322–24.

52. E. Lairtullier, *Les femmes célèbres de 1789 à 1795, et leur influence dans la Révolution* (Paris: chez France, à la Librairie Politique, 1840), 2:199–200.

53. Ibid., 2:200.

54. Mendès, *Les 73 journées,* p. 136.

55. *New York Herald,* May 5, 1871, p. 4.

56. *Journal Officiel,* April 10, 1871; Mendès, *Les 73 journées,* p. 140.

57. Goncourt, *Journal,* May 5, 1871, 2:789–90.

58. Charles Dickens, *A Tale of Two Cities* (1859; rpt. New York: Washington Square Press, 1960), pp. 452–53, emphasis added.

59. Washburne, *Recollections* 2:110.

60. John Russell Young, *Men and Memories: Personal Reminiscences,* ed. Mary D. Russell Young (New York: F. Tennyson Neely, 1901), 1:198. Young's memoir of the Commune is dated May 28, 1871.

61. Ibid.

62. [Charles] Bertall, *The Communists of Paris, 1871: Types, Physiognomies, Characters with Explanatory Text Descriptive of Each Design Written Expressly for This Edition* (London: Buckingham, 1873), text accompanying illustration no. 38, "Une Citoyenne (Préposée à la garde de la rue de Lille)." The reference to Communists in the title of the book reveals the anti-Commune bias of the writer at the outset.

63. Denis Arthur Bingham, *Recollections of Paris* (London: Chapman and Hall, 1896), 2:124. Bingham wrote daily reports for the *Pall Mall Gazette* and more occasionally for the *Army and Navy Gazette* and the *Scotsman*. During the Prussian siege and the Paris Commune, he kept a diary on which this book is based.

64. Ibid., 2:124n.

65. Horne, *Fall of Paris*, p. 99.

66. Lissagaray, *Histoire de la Commune*, p. 187.

67. See, for instance, Francisque Sarcey's column in *Gaulois*, April 5, 1871, p. 1; Augustine-Melvine Blanchecotte, *Tablettes d'une femme pendant la commune* (Paris: Didier, 1872), May 3, 1871, p. 130. Sarcey did not record the words of the women he observed, but he did perceive them as "more enraged than the men" and as "intoxicated from the joy of this festival."

68. Michel, *La Commune*, p. 206, emphasis added. I have translated *louve* as "she-wolf," but it also means "wanton woman."

3. The Symbolic Female Figure

1. Lissagaray, *Histoire de la Commune*, p. 306. The records of the Commune do not include the number of women killed and wounded.

2. For bourgeois Frenchmen in particular, personal courage was a crucial component of masculinity. The working-class National Guard stood largely outside this culture of honor which involved dueling and other acts of personal courage, but they were not the authors of the public speeches and articles that spoke of dead and wounded men as martyrs rather than as victims. Robert A. Nye, *Masculinity and Male Codes of Honor in Modern France* (New York: Oxford University Press, 1993), pp. 216–20.

3. See, for instance, *Mot d'Ordre*, April 8, 1871, p. 1, "Les martyrs de la Commune."

4. Charles Delescluze, "A la garde nationale," May 10, 1871, quoted in Lanjalley and Corriez, *Histoire de la révolution*, p. 441.

5. Daumier was a supporter of the Commune, but he made no drawings of the semaine sanglante. As a result, "Horrified by the Heritage" seems to speak for his reaction to the bloodshed of that and the following weeks as well as for the earlier Franco-Prussian War. See Ralph E. Shikes, *The Indignant Eye: The Artist as Social Critic in Prints and Drawings from the Fifteenth Century to Picasso* (Boston: Beacon, 1969), p. 193.

6. Linda Nochlin, "Women, Art, and Power," in her *Women, Art, and Power and Other Essays* (New York: Harper and Row, 1988), pp. 4–6.

7. Michel, *La Commune*, p. 163.

8. The early pro-Versailles histoires of the Commune include a scene in the garden in which General Lecomte pleads to be spared for the sake of his five children. Such texts emphasize the importance of women and children in the emotional pantheon of the bourgeois Frenchmen, even though Lecomte's wife is not explicitly mentioned in his lament. Alphonse Daudet's description is among the most detailed: "Falling on his knees and speaking of his children: 'I have five,' he said sobbing. The heart of the father had burst inside the soldier's tunic. There were fathers among this furious crowd. At his heart-rending appeal, a few weak voices responded; but the implacable deserters would hear nothing." Daudet, *Souvenirs*, p. 72. Also see Claretie, *Histoire de la révolution*, p. 598; Henri Rochefort, *The Adventures of My Life*, arranged for English readers by the author and Ernest W. Smith (London: Edward Arnold, 1896), 1:349.

9. Lanjalley and Corriez, *Histoire de la révolution*, p. 190; *Cri du Peuple*, April 4, 1871, p. 1.

10. Vizetelly, *My Adventures*, p. 202.

11. *New York Herald,* May 5, 1871 (dateline: Paris, April 19), p. 10.

12. Ibid.

13. Ibid., May 3, 1871, p. 7. The dispatch also appeared in the *New York Times,* May 3, 1871, p. 1.

14. Vizetelly, *My Adventures,* pp. 226–27.

15. Ibid., p. 227.

16. Bingham, *Recollections* 2:54. The reference to flour is obscure. It may have been used as a lubricant for chassepot cartridges to facilitate their removal from the gun after they had been fired, or perhaps it was used as a cushioning agent in packing crates.

17. For descriptions, see Goncourt, *Journal,* May 17, 1871, 2:801; Vizetelly, *My Adventures,* p. 283; *New York Times,* May 19, 1871 (dateline: Paris, May 18), p. 1; *Times,* May 20, 1871 (dateline: Paris, May 18), p. 5; Horne, *Fall of Paris,* p. 352.

18. For eyewitness accounts of the damage, see *Times,* May 20, 1871, p. 5 (dateline: Paris, May 18); Edwin Child, quoted in Horne, *Fall of Paris,* p. 352; Goncourt, *Journal,* May 17, 1871, 2:801; Gibson, *Paris during the Commune,* May 17, pp. 241–42.

19. *New York Times,* May 19, 1871 (dateline: Paris, May 18), p. 1.

20. Gibson, *Paris during the Commune,* (May 17, 1871), p. 241.

21. Child, quoted in Horne, *Fall of Paris,* p. 352.

22. Goncourt, *Journal,* May 18, 1871, 2:802.

23. *Times,* May 18, 1871 (dateline: Paris, Wednesday evening [May 17]), p. 5.

24. *Journal Officiel,* quoted in *Times,* May 19, 1871.

25. Gibson, *Paris during the Commune,* pp. 241–42; Lissagaray, *Histoire de la Commune,* p. 290.

26. Gibson, *Paris during the Commune,* p. 241.

27. *Times,* May 20, 1871 (dateline: Paris, May 18), p. 5.

28. *New York Times,* May 19, 1871 (dateline: Paris, May 18), p. 1. Also see *New York Herald,* May 19, 1871, p. 7.

29. Lewis Wingfield quoted in Horne, *Fall of Paris,* p. 352.

30. *New York Times,* May 19, 1871 (dateline: Paris, May 18), p. 1.

31. *New York Tribune,* June 2, 1871 (dateline: Paris, May 18), p. 1.

32. The text of the proclamation is published in Lanjalley and Corriez, *Histoire de la révolution,* p. 497.

33. Lissagaray, *Histoire de la Commune,* pp. 290–91, app. 15, pp. 485–86.

34. Gibson, *Paris during the Commune,* p. 242.

35. Vizetelly, *My Adventures,* p. 283.

36. *Times,* April 8, 1871 (dateline: Paris, April 7, 6:30 P.M.), p. 7. Also see *Vengeur,* April 12, 1871, p. 1; *Mot d'Ordre,* April 6, 1871, p. 1; *Cri du Peuple,* April 8, 1871, p. 1.

37. *Times,* April 6, 1871 (dateline: Paris, April 4), p. 10; *Vengeur,* April 12, 1871, p. 1 (reprinted from *Le Droit*).

38. Lissagaray, *Histoire de la Commune,* pp. 203–4. Also see *Mot d'Ordre,* April 8, 1871, p. 1; Lepelletier, *Histoire de la Commune* 3:310–15; Lanjalley and Corriez, *Histoire de la révolution,* pp. 224–29; Mendès, *Les 73 journées,* p. 108.

39. Lanjalley and Corriez, *Histoire de la révolution,* p. 224, emphasis added.

40. Lissagaray, *Histoire de la Commune,* pp. 203–4.

41. *Journal Officiel,* April 11, 1871; Lanjalley and Corriez, *Histoire de la révolution,* April 10, 1871, pp. 252–53. *Les murailles politiques françaises,* 2: *La Commune, 18 mars–27 mai 1871* (Paris: L. La Chevalier, 1874), n.p.

42. *New York Tribune,* May 25, 1871, p. 1; Mendès, *Les 73 journées,* p. 134, 162; John Leighton, *Paris under the Commune* (London: Bradbury Evans, 1871), p. 152; Vizetelly, *My Adventures,* p. 168.

43. Page duBois, *Centaurs and Amazons* (Ann Arbor: University of Michigan Press,

1982); Robert Graves, *The Greek Myths* (New York: George Braziller, 1957), 1:352–55; Abby Wettan Kleinbaum, *The War against the Amazons* (New York: New Press, 1983), p. 16; Wolfgang Lederer, *The Fear of Women* (New York: Grune and Stratton, 1968); Sarah B. Pomeroy, *Goddesses, Whores, Wives, and Slaves: Women in Classical Antiquity* (New York: Schocken, 1975), pp. 23–25; Guy Rothery, *The Amazons in Antiquity and Modern Times* (London: F. Griffiths, 1910); Pierre Samuel, *Amazones, guerrières, et gaillardes* (Grenoble: Presses Universitaires de Grenoble, 1975); Donald J. Sobol, *The Amazons of Greek Mythology* (London: Thomas Yoseloff, 1972); William Blake Tyrell, *Amazons: A Study in Athenian Myth-making* (Baltimore: Johns Hopkins University Press, 1984); Marina Warner, *Joan of Arc: The Image of Female Heroism* (New York: Knopf, 1981).

44. Warner, *Joan of Arc,* p. 215.

45. Graves, *The Greek Myths* 1:352–55; duBois, *Centaurs and Amazons,* p. 33.

46. See Warner, *Joan of Arc,* pp. 204–5; Heinrich von Kleist, *Penthésilée,* trans. Julien Gracq (Paris: Librairie José Corti, 1954).

47. Warner, *Joan of Arc,* pp. 7, 198–217.

48. AHG Ly22, Union des Femmes pour la Défense de Paris et les Soins aux Blessés, Statuts; Michel, *La Commune,* pp. 250–57; *La Sociale,* April 28, May 15, 1871; Thomas, *Les "Pétroleuses,"* pp. 83–100.

49. "Les Femmes au Combat," *Vengeur,* April 12, 1871, p. 1, reprinted from *Droit.*

50. Gibson, *Paris during the Commune,* March 20, 1871, p. 119.

51. "A Victim of Paris and Versailles," *Macmillan's Magazine* 24 (1871):386–87.

52. Du Camp, *Les convulsions de Paris* 2:60–61.

53. "A Victim of Paris and Versailles," p. 389.

54. Bertall, *Communists of Paris,* text for illustration no. 16.

55. Alix Payen, "Une ambulancière de la Commune de Paris," in *Mémoires de femmes, mémoire du peuple,* ed. Louis Constant (Paris: Maspero, 1979), pp. 61–87. Some of the letters are dated by the month only.

56. Ibid., pp. 62–63.

57. Victorine [Brocher/Brochon], *Souvenirs d'une morte vivante* (1909; rpt. Paris: Maspero, 1976), pp. 178, 182.

58. Payen, "Une ambulancière," April 24, 1871, p. 72.

59. Ibid., p. 71.

60. Ibid., pp. 64, 83.

61. Michel, *La Commune,* p. 220.

62. Payen, "Une ambulancière," pp. 84–87.

63. Rist (an engineer) and Julien (commandant of the 141st Battalion), quoted in Lissagaray, *Histoire de la Commune,* p. 260.

64. Brocher, *Souvenirs,* p. 178.

65. Elisée Reclus, *Correspondance* (Paris, 1911), vol. 2, quoted in Da Costa, *La Commune vécue* 1:373. Reclus reported that a vast, horrified silence fell among the soldiers.

66. *Sociale,* May 13, 1871; *Cri du Peuple,* May 21, 1871. At the daily meeting of the Commune on May 17, Raoul Urbain read a report to this effect from an officer of the National Guard and suggested that the Commune should execute ten hostages in reprisal, and then, for good measure, proposed that ten hostages should be executed every day to punish the attrocities of the Versaillais. As usual the commune declined to execute any hostages. See *Procès-verbaux de la Commune de 1871,* ed. Georges Bourgin and Gabriel Henriot (Paris: A. Lahure, 1945), 2:380; Lanjalley and Corriez, *Histoire de la révolution,* p. 493; Thomas, *Les "pétroleuses,"* p. 160; Jellinek, *The Paris Commune,* p. 292; Vizetelly, *My Adventures,* p. 289.

67. André Léo, "Aventures de neuf ambulancières à la recherche d'un poste de dévouement," *Sociale,* May 6, 1871, p. 1.

68. Ibid.

69. Ibid.

70. Louis Rossel, "Lettre," *Sociale*, May 7, 1871, p. 1.

71. *Cri du Peuple*, May 3, 1871.

72. Ibid., April 5, p. 2, and April 6, 1871, p. 1; *Sociale*, April 6, 1871, p. 1; *Mot d'Ordre*, April 5, 1871, p. 1; Vizetelly, *My Adventures*, p. 150. Some accounts describe meetings on April 4; some on April 5. Early histories followed suit. Lanjalley and Corriez, *Histoire de la révolution*, pp. 201–2; Lissagaray, *Histoire de la Commune*, p. 185.

73. "Les femmes," *Cri du Peuple*, April 4, 1871, p. 1. The article also appeared in *Action* on the same day.

74. Beatrix Excoffons, "Récit," in Michel, *La Commune*, pp. 459–60. Either Excoffons got the date wrong or there is a typographical error in the text. She says the meeting was on April 1; it seems most likely that she is talking about April 4, although Edith Thomas thought she was referring to April 3. Thomas, *Les "pétroleuses,"* p. 72.

75. *Sociale*, April 6, 1871, p. 1.

76. Blanchecotte, *Tablettes d'une femme*, April 5, evening, pp. 42–43.

77. Excoffons, "Récit," pp. 460–63.

78. Lanjalley and Corriez, *Histoire de la révolution*, pp. 201–2. William Shakespeare, *Julius Caesar* 3.2.79.

79. *Times*, April 6, 1871 (dateline: Paris, April 4), p. 10. Maillard, a member of the Parisian National Guard in 1789, was chosen by the women to lead their procession to Versailles to demand bread from the king in October.

80. R. C., "Les femmes," *Cri du Peuple*, April 5, 1871, p. 2; *Times*, April 6, 1871 (dateline: Paris, April 4), p. 10.

81. *Times*, April 6, 1871 (dateline: Paris, April 4), p. 10.

82. *Journal Officiel*, April 11, 1871; *Commune*, April 11, 1871; *Sociale*, April 12, 1871.

83. *Sociale*, April 12, 1871, p. 2.

84. Ibid.

85. *Journal Officiel*, April 14, 1871; *Cri du Peuple*, April 16, 1871.

86. "Women's Appeal for Peace," May 3, 1871, reprinted in Lanjalley and Corriez, *Histoire de la révolution*, p. 385; *Journal Officiel*, May 8, 1871.

87. Bingham, *Recollections* 2:17.

88. André Rossel, *1870: La première "grande" guerre, par l'affiche et l'image* (Paris: Les Yeux Ouverts, 1970), document 31; André Léo, "Toutes avec tous," *Sociale*, April 12, 1871, pp. 1–2; *Liberté*, October 3, 1870; Baron Marc de Villiers, *Histoire des clubs de femmes et des légions d'amazones, 1793, 1848, 1871* (Paris: Plon, 1910), pp. 383–85; Ernest A. Vizetelly, *My Days of Adventure: The Fall of France, 1870–71* (London: Chatto and Windus, 1914), pp. 134–37; Thomas, *Les "pétroleuses,"* pp. 55–56.

89. Quoted in Villiers, *Histoire des clubs*, p. 384.

90. Ibid.; Thomas, *Les "pétroleuses,"* p. 56.

91. Léo, "Toutes avec tous," p. 1. Léo declared that the female battalions had not been created because General Trochu, who was president of the Government of National Defense and in charge of the French forces during the siege of Paris, had opposed the idea.

92. It is possible to see sexual implications in the admiring glance between the last naked woman and the clothed amazon, especially since she holds the phallic bugle. Men's obsession with female sexuality in the nineteenth century seems to have been overwhelmingly heterosexual, however. Castration, not homosexuality, was the feared crime. It thus seems more likely that a nineteenth-century observer would have interpreted the glance as envious rather than lustful. See Josine Blok, "Sexual Asymmetry: A Historiographical Essay," in *Sexual Asymmetry: Studies in Ancient Society*, ed. Blok and Pe-

ter Mason (Amsterdam: J. C. Gieben, 1987), pp. 1–57; Neil Hertz, "Medusa's Head: Male Hysteria under Political Pressure," *Representations* 4 (Fall 1983):27–79.

93. Vizetelly, *My Days of Adventure*, p. 136.

94. As mayor of the eighth arrondissement, Allix also tried to institute a number of reforms in education and women's employment. Edwards, *The Paris Commune*, pp. 92, 379; Thomas, *Les "pétroleuses,"* pp. 53–54.

95. Edwards, *The Paris Commune*, pp. 92, 379.

96. Quoted in Horne, *Fall of Paris*, p. 133.

97. Jellinek, *The Paris Commune*, p. 74.

98. Mendès, *Les 73 journées*, pp. 160–61; Leighton, *Paris under the Commune*, pp. 176–77. Mendès's text appears almost verbatim in Leighton's. Most departures occur when Leighton decides to augment Mendès's already hyperbolic prose. What exactly is going on here is unclear. Leighton might be a pseudonym for Mendès, or Leighton might have plagiarized the French text. The translations of Mendès are mine, not Leighton's.

99. Léo, "Toutes avec tous," p. 1.

100. *Biographie universelle: Ancienne et moderne*, ed. J. François Michaud (Graz, Austria: Akademische Druck-u. Verlagsanstadt, 1967), 2:313.

101. Mendès, *Les 73 journées*, pp. 160–61; Leighton, *Paris under the Commune*, p. 174.

102. Mendès, *Les 73 journées*, pp. 162–63; Leighton, *Paris under the Commune*, p. 176.

103. Goncourt, *Journal*, May 1, 1871, 2:786.

104. "Les femmes au combat," *Vengeur*, April 12, 1871, p. 1, reprinted from *Droit; Cri du Peuple*, April 5, 14, 1871; *Journal Officiel*, April 10, 1871; *Sociale*, May 6, 1871.

105. Vizetelly, *My Adventures*, pp. 168, 272.

106. Commissaire, *Mémoires et souvenirs* 2:373.

107. *Times*, May 18, 1871, p. 5.

108. Malon, *La troisième défaite*, p. 279.

109. Simon, *Government of Thiers*, p. 466.

110. *Sociale*, April 12, 1871; *Commune*, April 14, 1871.

111. Malon, *La Troisième défaite*, p. 280.

112. Claretie, *Histoire de la révolution*, p. 651.

113. Mendès, *Les 73 journées*, pp. 136, 134–35; Leighton, *Paris under the Commune*, pp. 154, 152–53. (Leighton inserts a reference to a needle-gun and a bayonet. "What extraordinary beings are these who exchange the needle for the needle-gun, the broom for the bayonet.")

114. Mendès, *Les 73 journées*, p. 135; Leighton, *Paris under the Commune*, p. 153.

115. Mendès, *Les 73 journées*, p. 135; Leighton, *Paris under the Commune*, p. 153.

116. [P.-O.] Lissagaray, *Les huit journées de mai: Derrière les barricades* (Brussels: Bureau du Petit Journal, 1871; rpt. Paris: Editions d'Histoire Sociale, 1968), pp. 61–62; Michel, *La Commune*, p. 305; Edith Thomas, *Louise Michel; ou, La velléda de l'anarchie* (Paris: Gallimard, 1971), p. 99; Lissagaray, *Histoire de la Commune*, p. 327; Edwards, *The Paris Commune*, p. 318; Jellinek, *The Paris Commune*, p. 325. Other drawings, however, also show women and men defending the place Blanche together. See, for instance, "Women Defending the Barricade in the Place Blanche," *Penny Illustrated News*, reproduced in Bruhat, Dautry, and Tersen, *La Commune de 1871*, p. 192.

117. Paul Fontoulieu, *Les églises de Paris sous la Commune* (Paris: E. Dentu, 1873), pp. 15, 79, 113.

118. Thomas, *Les "pétroleuses,"* pp. 110, 114–16; Fontoulieu, *Eglises*, pp. 80, 163–65.

119. Fontoulieu, p. 159.

120. Ibid., p. 64.

121. Ibid., p. xxii.

122. Ibid., p. 49.

123. *Tribun du Peuple,* May 19, 1871; Gibson, *Paris during the Commune,* May 15, p. 239; Vizetelly, *My Adventures,* pp. 231–47.

124. Fontoulieu, *Eglises,* pp. 63–64; Edwards, *The Paris Commune,* p. 288; Bruhat, Dautry, and Tersen, *Commune de 1871,* p. 160.

125. Fontoulieu, *Eglises,* pp. 106, 79, 272; Villiers, *Histoire des clubs,* p. 399.

126. Fontoulieu, *Eglises,* p. 275; Edwards, *The Paris Commune,* p. 107.

127. Thomas, *Les "pétroleuses,"* pp. 109–17; Fontoulieu, *Eglises,* p. 16.

128. An article by Marius (the pseudonym of Maxime Villiers) in *Tribun du Peuple* on May 19, 1871, is the only extensive article on the clubs in the Commune press. For shorter pro-Commune accounts with very little information about women, see Lissagaray, *Histoire de la Commune,* p. 299; Michel, *La Commune,* p. 246.

129. Goncourt, *Journal,* May 7, 1871, 2:796.

130. *Daily News,* May 16, 1871, p. 3.

131. Bingham, *Recollections* 2:60.

132. Young, *Men and Memories* 1:198.

133. Washburne, *Recollections,* p. 110.

134. Young, *Men and Memories* 1:198.

135. Washburne, *Recollections,* p. 110. Gibson was also fascinated by discussions of divorce. Gibson, *Paris during the Commune,* May 15, 1871, pp. 240–41.

136. Young, *Men and Memories,* 1:198.

137. *Times,* May 6, 1871, (dateline: May 4), p. 10.

138. Fontoulieu, *Eglises,* pp. 105, 271.

139. Mendès, *Les 73 journées,* p. 272; Leighton, *Paris under the Commune,* p. 282. Mendès also commented on the "naturally hideous" faces of the men.

140. *Daily News,* May 16, 1871, p. 3.

141. Washburne, *Recollections,* p. 110; Young, *Men and Memories,* 1:198.

142. Mendès, *Les 73 journées,* p. 272; Leighton, *Under the Commune,* p. 283.

143. *Times,* May 6, 1871 (dateline: May 4), p. 10.

144. Fontoulieu, *Eglises,* pp. 16, 49, 63, 105, 106, 113.

145. The reference is to the Orleanist or July Monarchy which followed the Revolution of 1830. It was a change from the Bourbon monarchy, but it was still a monarchy. A "real" change would have been the institution of a republic.

146. Mendès, *Les 73 journées,* pp. 272–73; Leighton, *Under the Commune,* pp. 282–83.

147. The caricature is reproduced in James A. Leith, "The War of Images Surrounding the Commune," in *Images in the Commune/Images de la Commune,* ed. Leith (Montreal: McGill-Queen's University Press, 1978), p. 137, and see pp. 136, xiii.

148. Ibid., pp. 138, xiii.

149. *Times,* May 6, 1871, p. 10. Such statements were cited as proof of the Commune's intention to burn the city.

150. Edouard Manet, Constantin Guys, Honoré Daumier, and Pierre-Auguste Renoir painted the *amazone* "attired in black, in an outfit that included a tall, narrow, and rather masculine top hat, and a slim almost tubular black skirt." Kleinbaum, *War against the Amazons,* p. 191.

151. Moses, *French Feminism,* pp. 173–212.

152. Du Camp, *Les convulsions* 2:60–61.

153. Vizetelly, *My Adventures,* pp. 246–47.

154. Horne, *Fall of Paris,* p. 337.

155. Richard Cobb, "The Women of the Commune," in Cobb, *A Second Identity,* p. 232.

156. Warner, *Joan of Arc,* p. 274.

4. The Femmes Fortes of Paris

1. A[lexandre] de Mazade, ed., *Lettres et notes intimes, 1870–1871* (Beaumont-sur-Oise: Paul Frémont, 1892), pp. 598–99.

2. "Citoyennes," *Cri du Peuple,* April 4, 1871, p. 1.

3. Ibid.

4. "Les femmes," *Cri du Peuple,* April 6, 1871, p. 2.

5. Ibid. Both articles hold Versailles responsible "before all of France."

6. "Citoyennes," *Cri du Peuple,* April 4, 1871, p. 1.

7. "Les Femmes," *Cri du Peuple,* April 6, 1871, p. 2.

8. "Appel aux citoyennes de Paris," *Commune,* April 11, 1871, p. 2; also printed in *Sociale,* April 12, 1871, p. 2.

9. "Appel aux citoyennes."

10. Ibid.

11. Ibid.

12. Ibid.

13. Ibid.

14. Thomas, *Les "pétroleuses,"* pp. 83–100; Edith Thomas, *The Women Incendiaries,* trans. James Atkinson and Starr Atkinson (New York: George Braziller, 1966), pp. 70–87; Edwards, *The Paris Commune,* p. 266.

15. *Journal Officiel,* April 14, 1871. Eight women signed this open letter to the Executive Commission of the Paris Commune, Elizabeth Dmietrieff, Adélaide Valentin, Noémie Colleville, Marquant, Sophie Graix, Joséphine Prat, and Céline and Aimée Delvainquier.

16. Ibid.

17. Comité Central, Union des Femmes, to Commission de Travail et d'Echange, n.d., signed by Elizabeth Dmietrieff, in AHG, Ly 22. In addition to her proposals regarding women, Dmietrieff called for the creation of free producer associations in which workers would manage their own affairs, "the diversification of work in each trade, repetitive manual movements being deadly to the body and the mind," "the reduction of working hours, physical exhaustion leading inevitably to the extinction of the moral faculty," an organization to facilitate the movement and exchange of goods, and ultimately, membership in the International Working Men's Association for all workers in the producer associations.

18. Ibid.

19. See Olwen Hufton, "Women in Revolution, 1789–1796" *Past and Present,* no. 53 (1971): 90–108; Olwen H. Hufton, *Women and the Limits of Citizenship in the French Revolution* (Toronto: University of Toronto Press, 1992), pp. 89–130; and André Léo, "La révolution sans la femme," *Sociale,* May 8, 1871.

20. Women regularly denounced draft dodgers as cowards and traitors in the political clubs.

21. "République française: Liberté, egalité, fraternité," May 3, 1871, reprinted in Lanjalley and Corriez, *Histoire de la révolution,* p. 385.

22. "Manifeste du Comité Central de l'Union des Femmes pour la Défense de Paris et les Soins aux Blessés," *Journal Officiel,* May 6, 1871, signed by *La Commission exécutive du Comité central,* Le Mel, Jacquier, Lefèvre [*sic*], Leloup, Dmitrieff, reprinted in Lanjal-

ley and Corriez, *Histoire de la révolution,* pp. 410–11. Original handwritten manifesto is in AGH Ly 22.

23. Ibid.

24. For biographical information about André Léo, see Maitron and Egrot, *Dictionnaire biographique,* 7:52, 230; Thomas, *Les "pétroleuses,"* pp. 141–52; Thomas, *Women Incendiaries,* pp. 119–32.

25. Malon, *La troisième défaite,* pp. 273–74; Thomas, *Women Incendiaries,* p. 119; Thomas, *Les "pétroleuses,"* p. 141.

26. André Léo, *La femme et les moeurs: Liberté ou monarchie,* (Paris, 1869), pp. 130–31.

27. Ibid., pp. 138, 140, 139, 150–56.

28. Maitron and Egrot, *Dictionnaire biographique* 5:52. Maitron says Léo founded *La Sociale* with Mme Jaclard. Jules Lemonnyer (*Les journaux de Paris pendant la Commune: Revue bibliographique complète de la presse parisienne du 19 mars au 27 mai* [Paris: J. Lemonnyer, 1871], p. 72) says *La Sociale* was created by Vermesch and the other editors of *Père Duchêne.*

29. André Léo and Benoît Malon wrote a manifesto addressed to the "travailleurs des campagnes" in March, which was distributed to the countryside but not published in Parisian newspapers until the middle of May. They were convinced that the Commune could not survive if it did not counteract the false propaganda produced by Versailles and show the peasants that the revolution was for them too and not just for Parisians. "Aux Travailleurs des Campagnes," reprinted in Lanjalley and Corriez, *Histoire de la révolution,* pp. 248–50. Léo repeated this point in her address to the International Congress for Peace in Lausanne, Switzerland, September 27, 1871, published as *La guerre sociale: Discours prononcé au Congrès de la Paix à Lausanne (1871)* (Neuchâtel: n.p., 1871).

30. André Léo, "Toutes avec tous," *Sociale,* April 12, 1871. Also printed in *Commune,* April 14, 1871.

31. Ibid.

32. Ibid.

33. Ibid.

34. André Léo, "Les soldats de l'idée," *Sociale,* April 28, 1871.

35. André Léo, "Aventures de neuf ambulancières à la recherche d'un poste de dévouement," *Sociale,* May 6, 1871.

36. Ibid.

37. Léo, "La révolution sans la femme," *Sociale,* May 8, 1871.

38. Ibid.

39. Ibid.

40. Ibid.

41. Louis Rossel, Lettre à Citoyen [*sic*] André Léo," and subsequent announcement, *Sociale* May 7, 1871. Rossel, an army officer, was delegate of war for only the first nine days of May. He resigned on the ninth. The Commune wanted to arrest him for what it saw as his betrayal of the revolution when he resigned, but it failed to find him. Versailles found him, tried him, and executed him for his participation in the Commune.

42. Léo, "La révolution sans la femme"; André Léo, "Lettre à Citoyen Rossel, délégué à la guerre," *Sociale,* May 9, 1871.

43. Léo, "Lettre à Citoyen Rossel."

44. Ibid.

45. Léo, "La révolution sans la femme."

46. Léo, "Lettre à Citoyen Rossel."

47. Léo, "Toutes avec tous."

48. Léo, "Neuf ambulancières."

49. Léo, "Toutes avec tous."

50. Blanchecotte, *Tablettes d'une femme,* April 22, 1871, p. 104.

51. Ibid., April 14–25, pp. 75–113.

52. Ibid., March 19, p. 7.

53. Ibid., April 8, p. 50.

54. Ibid., May 3, p. 129.

55. Ibid., April 5, pp. 42–43, May 23, p. 259.

56. Ibid., April 7, p. 47.

57. Ibid., April 12, p. 60.

58. Ibid., April 13, p. 62.

59. Ibid.

60. Ibid., April 6, pp. 44–45.

61. Ibid., April 12, p. 59.

62. Ibid., May 6, pp. 133–36.

63. Ibid., April 5, pp. 42–43.

64. Ibid., May 6, p. 137.

65. Ibid., pp. 136–37.

66. Ibid., p. 137.

67. Ibid., April 5, p. 42.

68. Ibid., May 3, p. 130.

69. Ibid., May 8, p. 140.

70. Ibid., May 26, pp. 292–93. Blanchecotte was right to be incredulous in the case of the pétroleuses.

71. Ibid., May 8, p. 140.

72. Ibid., May 24, p. 265.

73. Ibid., June 17, p. 352. This was not an exclusively female reaction. Bourgeois men also found it painful to watch the convoys of prisoners and the crowds that taunted them.

74. Ibid., p. vii.

75. Ibid., p. viii.

76. Mazade, *Lettres.* To create a coherent narrative, Alexandre, who edited the volume, interspersed the letters with his own and other conservative descriptions of the Commune.

77. Ibid., Céline to Alexandre, April 6, 1871, p. 599.

78. *Journal Officiel,* April 5, 1871; Edwards, *The Paris Commune,* p. 222.

79. Mazade, *Lettres,* April 5, 1871, pp. 596–97. Alexandre reports on Céline's letter but does not print it. His account is not addressed to anyone and appears, perhaps, to be from a diary.

80. Ibid., Céline to Alexandre, April 6, 1871, pp. 598–99.

81. Ibid., Mme V. Pillon-Dufresnes to Victor Pillon-Dufresnes, April 26, 1871, p. 647.

82. Ibid., Céline to Alexandre, April 12, 1871, p. 608.

83. Ibid., Céline to Alexandre, April 18, 1871, pp. 618–19. Edouard was apparently concerned that she might not be allowed to return if she left Paris again.

84. Ibid., Céline to Alexandre, April 18, 1871, pp. 618–19.

85. Ibid., Céline to Alexandre, April 24, 1871, p. 639.

86. Ibid., Alexandre to Victor Pillon-Dufresnes, April 26, 1871, p. 644.

87. Ibid., Céline to Alexandre, April 26, 1871, p. 645.

88. Ibid., Alexandre to Céline, April 29, 1871, p. 648.

89. Ibid., Céline to Alexandre (Poste restante, Le Quesnoy), April 27, 1871, p. 650.

90. Ibid., Mme V. Pillon-Dufresnes to Victor Pillon-Dufresnes, April 27, 1871, p. 652; Roger L. Williams, *The French Revolution of 1870–1871* (New York: Norton, 1969), p. 138.

In fact, little pillaging occurred, and the furnishings of requisitioned dwellings were stored and protected by the Commune.

91. Mazade, *Lettres,* Alexandre to Céline, April 18 (p. 619), 19 (p. 621), 1871.

92. Ibid., Alexandre to Céline, April 29, 1871, p. 648. Either this letter is out of order in the correspondence or its date is a typographical error since it appears before letters dated April 27.

93. Ibid., Céline to Alexandre, April 20, 1871, pp. 626–27. Céline thought the *commissaire* seemed sympathetic to her when she told him that the lack of silk that she was sending could cut off the work of the entire population of a village. But he responded that "In such a moment no one ought to work, that each ought to be defending the *pays!!*"

94. Ibid., Céline to Alexandre, April 24, 1871, p. 639.

95. Ibid., Céline to Alexandre, April 26, 1871, p. 645.

96. Ibid., Alexandre to M. C. Amiard-Fromentin, May 12, 1871, p. 666.

97. Ibid., Céline to Alexandre, April 18, 1871, pp. 618–19.

98. Ibid., Céline to Alexandre, April 22, 1871, p. 635.

99. M. Pillon, père, to his children, May 13, 1871, p. 667, emphasis added.

100. Ibid., Céline to Alexandre, April 22, 1871, p. 635.

101. Ibid., Céline to A. M. Brent, May 30, 1871, p. 686.

102. Ibid., Berthe Amiard-Fromentin to M. Eugène Fromentin, May 29, 1871, p. 687.

103. Bingham, *Recollections of Paris* 2:121.

104. Gaston Cerfbeer, "Une nuit de la semaine sanglante," *La Revue Hebdomadaire,* May 23, 1903, p. 423.

105. Du Camp, *Les convulsions,* 2:299.

106. Smith, *Ladies of the Leisure Class,* esp. p. 53.

107. Other examples include Elizabeth Dmitrieff and Olympe de Gouges. Thomas, *Louise Michel,* pp. 13–14; Thomas, *Les "pétroleuses,"* p. 103; Joan Wallach Scott, "'A Woman Who Has Only Paradoxes to Offer': Olympe de Gouges Claims Rights for Women," in *Rebel Daughters: Women and the French Revolution,* ed. Sara E. Melzer and Leslie W. Rabine (New York: Oxford University Press, 1992), pp. 107–8.

108. For biographical information on Louise Michel, see Louise Michel, *Mémoires* (1886; rpt. Paris: Maspero, 1979); Thomas, *Louise Michel;* Louise Michel, *The Red Virgin: Memoirs of Louise Michel,* ed. and trans. Bullitt Lowry and Elizabeth Ellington Gunter (University: University of Alabama Press, 1981); Xavier de La Fournière, *Louise Michel: Matricule 2182* (Paris: Perrin, 1986); Marie Marmo Mullaney, "Sexual Politics in the Career and Legend of Louise Michel," *Signs 15* (1990):300–322; Lepelletier, *Histoire de la Commune* 1:401–5.

109. Michel, *Mémoires,* p. 130; Thomas, *Louise Michel,* pp. 65–70.

110. Michel, *La Commune,* p. 156; Thomas, *Louise Michel,* p. 70.

111. The Montmartre Vigilance Committees held nightly meetings, provided food and shelter for people, and searched out what they regarded as the food hoards of "reactionaries." Because the men's meeting began one hour after the women's, women like Louise Michel could join the men's meeting after their own had adjourned. Michel, *Mémoires,* pp. 121–22.

112. Thomas, *Louise Michel,* pp. 65–82.

113. Goncourt, *Journal,* January 18, 1871, 2:720.

114. Ibid., January 21, 1871, 2:723.

115. Michel, *La Commune,* pp. 102–3.

116. Ibid., pp. 163–64.

117. Thomas, *Louise Michel,* p. 96.

118. Ibid., p. 90; Michel, *La Commune*, p. 188.

119. *Vengeur,* April 12, 1871 (reprinted from *Droit*).

120. Thomas, *Louise Michel,* pp. 83–102.

121. Léo, "Aventures de neuf ambulancières."

122. Thomas, *Louise Michel,* p. 94; Michel, *Mémoires,* p. 166.

123. Thomas, *Louise Michel,* pp. 100–101; Michel, *La Commune,* pp. 337–39.

124. Michel, *Mémoires,* p. 134.

125. Ibid., pp. 111, 113. For a fuller analysis of Louise Michel's grief over her mother's death, see Thomas, *Louise Michel,* pp. 264–76.

126. Michel, *The Red Virgin,* p. 59.

127. Michel, *Mémoires,* p. 106.

128. Ibid., pp. 106, 109. I have assumed this was Louise Michel's decision and not that of her publisher.

129. Michel, *La Commune,* p. 284.

130. Michel, *Mémoires,* p. 275.

131. Ibid.

132. Ibid., p. 85.

133. Ibid., p. 109.

134. Ibid., p. 121.

135. Ibid., p. 106.

136. Michel, *La Commune,* p. 154.

137. Michel, *Mémoires,* p. 83.

138. Blanchecotte, *Tablettes,* pp. 44–45.

139. Mazade, *Lettres,* M. Pillon, père, to his children, May 13, 1871, p. 667.

140. Michel, *Mémoires,* pp. 274–75.

141. Thomas, *Louise Michel,* pp. 191–93; *Français,* November 23, 1880; *Journal du Soir,* November 30, 1880; Lepelletier, *Histoire de la Commune* 1:401.

142. Lepelletier, *Histoire de la Commune* 1:401; Horne, *The Fall of Paris,* p. 270; Edward S. Mason, *The Paris Commune: An Episode in the History of the Socialist Movement* (1930; rpt. New York: Howard Fertig, 1967), p. 291; Soria, *Grande histoire de la Commune* 3:128; Bourgin, *La guerre,* p. 298.

143. Félicien Champsaur, "Louise Michel," *Contemporains,* no. 3 (1880):1–3.

144. Agulhon, *Marianne into Battle,* p. 142.

145. Ibid.

146. Thomas, *Louise Michel,* p. 10.

147. For example, see Soria, *Grande histoire,* 3:128; Bourgin, *La guerre,* p. 298.

148. For example, André Falk, "Louise Michel, la vierge rouge," *Paris-presse—Intransigeant,* November 13–26, 1957; Carl Freiherr von Letetzow, *Louise Michel (la vierge rouge): Eine Charakterskisse* (Leipzig: F. Rothbarth, 1906); André Lorulot, *Louise Michel: La vierge rouge* (Herblay: Editions de l'Idée Libre, 1930); Edith Sellers, "The Red Virgin of Montmartre," *Fortnightly Review,* February 1, 1905, pp. 292–304; Edith Thomas, "Louise Michel, la vierge rouge," *Miroir de l'Histoire* (April 1958):509–15.

149. Michel, *The Red Virgin.*

150. Clovis Hugues, "La muse du peuple: Sérénade à Louise Michel," *Intransigeant,* January 15, 1882; Françoise Moser, *Une héroïne, Louise Michel* (Paris: Vigneau, 1947); Maurice Barrès, *Mes Cahiers, 1896–1923* (Paris: Plon, 1963), pp. 392–94; Thomas, *Louise Michel,* p. 10; Lepelletier, *Histoire de la Commune* 1:401.

151. Alistair Horne, *The Terrible Year: The Paris Commune, 1871* (New York: Viking, 1971), pp. 116, 99, 98, 84.

152. Thomas, *Louise Michel,* p. 188.

153. Ibid., p. 189.

5. Les Pétroleuses

1. Tombs, *War against Paris*, pp. 119, 171–93. The first executions of prisoners by Versailles soldiers during the semaine sanglante took place on May 22.

2. Charles Delescluze, "Au peuple de Paris," *Journal Officiel*, May 22, 1871, reprinted in Lanjalley and Corriez, *Histoire de la révolution*, pp. 522–23.

3. Lanjalley and Corriez, *Histoire de la révolution*, p. 524.

4. For discussion of the barricades as a defensive system, see Lepelletier, *Histoire de la Commune* 3:375–77.

5. Mark Traugott, "Barricades as Repertoire: Continuities and Discontinuities in the History of French Contention," in *Repertoires and Cycles of Collective Action*, ed. Traugott (Durham, N.C.: Duke University Press, 1995), p. 51.

6. See the forty photographs in Braire, *Sur les traces des communards*.

7. Archibald Forbes, "What I Saw of the Paris Commune," *Century (Illustrated) Magazine* 44 (1892):815; *Daily News*, May 26, 1871 (dateline: Paris, Tuesday [May 23]), p. 5; Mendès, *Les 73 journées*, p. 296.

8. Goncourt, *Journal*, May 22, 1871, 2:805; Mendès, *Les 73 journées*, p. 295.

9. Blanchecotte, *Tablettes*, pp. 257–59.

10. Ibid., pp. 265–66.

11. *Tribun du Peuple*, May 24, 1871.

12. *Vengeur*, May 24, 1871, p. 2.

13. *Journal Officiel*, May 24, 1871, p. 2.

14. In addition to the examples I give, see Lanjalley and Corriez, *Histoire de la révolution*, p. 524; Lepelletier, *Histoire de la Commune* 3:375; Malon, *La troisième défaite*, pp. 400–401.

15. Blanchecotte, *Tablettes*, pp. 266, 279–80.

16. Thomas, *Louise Michel*, pp. 97–100; Michel, *La Commune*, p. 265; Michel, *Mémoires*, pp. 267–68. Lissagaray, *Histoire de la Commune*, pp. 324–25, reported that "a detachment of twenty-five women, under the conduct of citoyennes Dimitrieff and Louise Michel" helped defend the barricades in Montmartre. Michel, *La Commune*, pp. 303–10.

17. As the Versailles forces moved resolutely forward, Elizabeth Dmitrieff issued an appeal to the Women's Committee of the Eleventh Arrondissement: "At this moment, the supreme battle has been joined in the last arrondissements held by the insurrection. . . . Assemble ALL THE WOMEN and the committee itself, and come immediately TO THE BARRICADES." Citoyenne E. Dmitri[eff], "Appel Aux Femmes," reprinted in Claretie, *Histoire de la révolution*, p. 703.

18. Elizabeth Dmitrieff, Nathalie Lemel, Malvina Poulain, Blanche Lefebvre, and Beatrix Excoffons were among the women who defended the place Blanche. André Léo was at Batignolles. Michel, *La Commune*, p. 305; Thomas, *Michel*, p. 99; Lissagaray, *Histoire de la Commune*, pp. 327, 339; Lissagaray, *Les huit journées*, p. 63.

19. Lissagaray, *Histoire de la Commune*, p. 336.

20. Ibid., p. 353.

21. Commissaire, *Mémoires et souvenirs* 2:374–75.

22. Louis Jezierski, *La bataille des sept jours*, quoted in Vizetelly, *My Adventures*, p. 316.

23. Forbes, "What I Saw," p. 56.

24. Lissagaray, *Histoire de la Commune*, p. 352.

25. Edwards, *The Paris Commune*, p. 337.

26. Ibid., pp. 328–29.

27. The hostages had been held in the Prefecture of Police until that building was abandoned on May 22. At that point, they were transferred to La Roquette.

28. Lissagaray, *Histoire de la Commune*, pp. 343–44; Edwards, *Paris Commune*, pp. 329–30.

29. Jules Vallès, *The Insurrectionist*, trans. Sandy Petrey (Englewood Cliffs, N.J.: Prentice-Hall, 1971), pp. 212–16; Lissagaray, *La Commune*, pp. 363–64; Edwards, *The Paris Commune*, pp. 336–37; Jellinek, *The Paris Commune*, pp. 333–36, 348–50, 358–60.

30. Jellinek, *The Paris Commune*, pp. 329–30.

31. Lissagaray, *Histoire de la Commune*, p. 359.

32. The Versailles troops examined men's hands for signs of dirt and powder that would indicate they had participated in the battle, and their clothing for signs that National Guard insignia had been ripped off.

33. See Tombs, *The War against Paris*, pp. 166–93, for an account of the terror instituted by the army during and after the week of fighting.

34. Lissagaray, *Histoire de la Commune*, p. 356.

35. *Daily News*, Friday, May 26, 1871 (dateline: Paris, Tuesday, May 23), p. 5. Forbes is identifiable as the correspondent because the text parallels his later account of the same events. See Forbes, "What I Saw."

36. Lissagaray, *Histoire de la Commune*, pp. 320–21.

37. Blanchecotte, *Tablettes*, May 24, 1871, p. 277.

38. *Daily News*, May 26, 1871 (dateline: Paris, May 23), p. 5.

39. Edmond de Goncourt, *Paris under Siege, 1870–1871: From the Goncourt Journal*, ed. and trans. George J. Becker (Ithaca: Cornell University Press, 1969), May 25, 1871, pp. 304–5; Goncourt, *Journal* 2:812–13.

40. See Bruhat, Dautry, and Tersen, *La Commune*, p. 289; Lissagaray, *Histoire de la Commune*, pp. 370–81; Edwards, *The Paris Commune*, p. 346; Tombs, *War against Paris*, pp. 188–91; Maitron and Egrot, *Dictionnaire biographique* 4:82. An additional 38,000 prisoners were marched to Versailles and imprisoned.

41. Paul A. Gagnon, *France since 1789*, revised edition (New York: Harper and Row, 1964), pp. 118, 154–55.

42. *New York Tribune*, June 1 (dateline: Paris, May 31), p. 1; June 10, 1871, p. 1.

43. *New York Herald*, May 25, 1871 (dateline: St. Denis, May 24), p. 7.

44. *Daily News*, May 26, 1871 (dateline: Paris, May 22), p. 6.

45. *New York Times*, May 27 (dateline: May 25), p. 1; May 29, 1871 (dateline: May 28), p. 1.

46. *Standard*, June 1 (dateline: Paris, May 30), p. 5; June 5 (dateline: Paris, June 2), p. 5; June 7, 1871 (dateline: Paris, June 5, evening), p. 5.

47. *Vengeur*, May 24, 1871, p. 2; *Journal Officiel*, May 24, 1871, p. 2.

48. Mendès, *Les 73 journées*, p. 295. This scene occurred on May 22, the first morning of the invasion.

49. Vizetelly, *My Adventures*, p. 316.

50. Forbes, "What I Saw," p. 56.

51. Vizetelly, *My Adventures*, p. 316.

52. Lissagaray, *Histoire de la Commune*, pp. 368, 353.

53. Commissaire, *Mémoires et souvenirs* 2:374–75.

54. For accounts of the causes of the fires, see Jellinek, *The Paris Commune*, pp. 331–32; Tombs, *The War against Paris*, p. 152; Horne, *The Fall of Paris*, pp. 390–91; Edwards, *The Paris Commune*, pp. 323–28.

55. Gibson, *Paris during the Commune*, May 24, 1871, p. 263. Gibson's letters were originally published in the *Watchman*.

56. *Daily News*, May 26, 1871 (dateline: Paris, May 24); *New York Times*, May 26, 1871 (dateline: Paris, May 24, night).

57. "What an American Girl Saw of the Commune," *Century (Illustrated) Magazine*, 45 (n.s. 23) (November 1892):66.

58. Cerfbeer, "Une nuit de la semaine sanglante," p. 421.

59. Goncourt, *Journal*, May 24, 1871, 2:812.

60. *Standard*, May 27, 1871 (dateline: Versailles, May 24, 1:00 P.M.).

61. Ibid., June 1, 1871 (dateline: Paris, May 30), p. 5; also see *Times*, May 26, 1871 (dateline: Versailles, Thursday night, May 25), p. 5.

62. *Times*, May 25, 1871, editorial, p. 9.

63. *Standard*, May 27, 1871, editorial, p. 4.

64. *New York Herald*, May 31, 1871, editorial, p. 6.

65. Mazade, *Lettres et Notes Intimes*, May 30 (p. 686), May 29 (p. 687), 1871.

66. Even the most conservative historians no longer credit the rumor of the pétroleuses. See, for instance, Mason, *The Paris Commune*, 281–82; Horne, *The Fall of Paris*, 391–93. For the similar views of a more liberal historian, see Edwards, *The Paris Commune*, pp. 322–27.

67. Assemblée Nationale, sitting of May 24, 1871, reported in *Gaulois*, May 25, 1871, 2d edition, p. 1. Also reported in *Times*, May 25, 1871, p. 5.

68. *Times*, May 25, 1871, editorial, p. 9.

69. *Figaro*, May 31, 1871.

70. *New York Herald*, June 4, 1871, editorial, p. 6.

71. *Times*, Friday, May 26, 1871, p. 5, emphasis added.

72. *Monde Illustré*, June 3, 1871, p. 343.

73. Washburne, *Recollections* 2:223.

74. Wickham Hoffman, *Camp, Court, and Siege* (New York: Harper and Bros., 1877), p. 283. William Gibson also recorded the "information" about the fire fighters as well as about the women incendiaries in his journal on May 25, 1871. Gibson, *Paris during the Commune*, p. 285.

75. See, for instance, the reports in Joanna Richardson, ed., *Paris under Siege: A Journal of the Events of 1870–1871 Kept by Contemporaries and Translated and Presented by Joanna Richardson* (London: Folio Society, 1982), pp. 180–98.

76. Washburne, *Recollections* 2:155. One of the most amazing aspects of Washburne's account of the pétroleuses is that it appears in a memoir rather than in an unedited or unpublished diary. By the time Washburne's memoirs were published in 1887, many, including Colonel Hoffman, no longer believed the rumors. Either time had done nothing to alter Washburne's belief in the rumors, or his notes and letters were published virtually unedited. For Hoffman's views, see his *Camp, Court, and Siege*, pp. 282–83.

77. *Gaulois*, May 28 (p. 28), 29 (p. 1), 1871. The story of the incendiary boxes was repeated on May 29.

78. Chastel, letter, May 24, 1871, quoted in Gibson, *Paris during the Commune*, p. 283.

79. Washburne, *Recollections* 2:222.

80. Ibid., 2:222–23. Washburne's account of the amount of money paid to the pétroleuses differs from that of *Le Gaulois*.

81. Hoffman, *Camp, Court, and Siege*, p. 281; Washburne, *Recollections* 2:155. Hoffman reported six deaths; Washburne, eight.

82. Georges Renard, "Mes Souvenirs, 1870–1871," *La Révolution de 1848 et les révolutions du XIXe siècle, 1830, 1848, 1870* 28 (1931):78.

83. Goncourt, *Journal* 2:815.

84. Quoted in Gibson, *Paris during the Commune*, p. 290. The Versailles government took 650 children aged sixteen or under prisoner. The number killed in the streets of

Paris or on the forced marches from Paris to Versailles is unknown. See Appert, *Rapport d'ensemble,* p. 180.

85. *Journal des Débats,* May 30, 1871.

86. *Times,* May 27, 1871, p. 5; Edwin Child, letter, May 28, 1871, published in Richardson, *Paris under Siege,* p. 197.

87. *Times,* May 26 (dateline: May 23), p. 12, May 29, 1871 (dateline: Paris, Thursday, May 25), pp. 9–10; Goncourt, *Journal,* May 26, 1871, 2:814.

88. *Times,* May 26, 1871 (dateline: Versailles, May 23), p. 12; *Daily News,* May 26, 1871 (dateline: Paris, Wednesday, May 24), p. 6.

89. *Daily News,* May 26, 1871 (dateline: Paris, Wednesday, May 24), p. 6.

90. Chastel, letter, May 28, 1871, quoted in Gibson, *Paris during the Commune,* p. 290.

91. Bingham, *Recollections of Paris* 2:121.

92. *Times,* May 27, 1871, p. 5.

93. *New York Tribune,* June 7, 1871, p. 2.

94. *Gaulois,* April 5, 1871, p. 1.

95. *Times,* May 26, 1871, p. 12; Goncourt, *Journal,* May 28, 1871, 2:816; Blanchecotte, *Tablettes,* June 17, 1871, p. 352.

96. Goncourt, *Journal,* May 26, 1871, p. 814.

97. Child, letter, in Richardson, *Paris under Siege,* p. 197.

98. *Paris-Journal,* Wednesday, May 31, 1871, quoted in Mason, *The Paris Commune,* p. 291. Only the conservative newspapers were still publishing at this point.

99. Gibson, *Paris during the Commune,* May 27, 1871, p. 270.

100. Bingham, *Recollections* 2:124.

101. Reported by Vizetelly, *My Adventures,* p. 316.

102. *New York Tribune,* May 26, 1871, p. 1.

103. *Figaro,* June 2, 1871, p. 1.

104. Goncourt, *Journal* 2:814.

105. *Figaro,* June 1, 1871, p. 1.

106. *Times,* May 29, 1871 (dateline: Paris, May 25), p. 10.

107. Ibid., May 26, 1871 (dateline: Versailles, May 23), p. 12.

108. Goncourt, *Journal,* May 26, 1871, 2:815. The African infantrymen (*chasseurs d'Afrique*) Goncourt mentions are probably *Zouaves,* an elite infantry of North African origins recruited by the French. Tombs, *War against Paris,* p. xii.

109. Francisque Sarcey, "Les aliénistes," *Gaulois,* May 28, 1871, p. 1.

110. Francisque Sarcey, *Gaulois,* June 13, 1871.

111. *The New York Herald,* May 28, 1871, p. 7.

112. Appert, *Rapport d'ensemble,* p. 214.

113. *New York Tribune,* June 7, 1871, p. 2.

114. "Le râle des pétroleuses," *Gaulois,* June 14, 1871, p. 2.

115. *Times,* May 29, 1871, editorial, p. 9.

116. *Standard,* May 30, 1871, editorial, p. 4.

117. *New York Herald,* May 28, 1871, editorial, p. 7.

118. Jules Bergeret, *Le dix-huit mars,* p. 25.

119. Ibid., p. 25.

120. Sarcey, "Les aliénistes."

121. Jean-Baptiste Millière, a Parisian deputy to the National Assembly who had condemned Versailles for fighting a civil war against Paris but had not been involved in the Commune, was forced to kneel on the steps of the Panthéon, then shot. Edwards, *The Paris Commune,* p. 341; Lissagaray, *Histoire de la Commune,* pp. 492–94.

122. Child, letter, in Richardson, *Paris under Siege,* p. 197.

123. *Times,* May 27, 1871, p. 5.

124. Bergeret, *Le dix-huit mars,* p. 24.

125. Georges Jeanneret, *Paris pendant la Commune révolutionnaire de 71* (1871; rpt. Paris: Editions d'Histoire Sociale, 1968), p. 250.

126. Lissagaray, *Histoire de la Commune,* p. 378.

127. Goncourt, *Journal,* May 26, 1871, 2:815.

128. Ibid., 2:816.

129. *Times,* May 27, 1871.

130. Forbes, "What I Saw of the Paris Commune," p. 54; *Daily News* (London), May 26, 1871, p. 5. Articles in the *Daily News,* as was generally the case in this era, were unsigned. The identities of the correspondents were well known in journalistic circles, however, and Forbes notes in his 1892 article that he went to Paris as the *Daily News*'s reporter. The wording of the 1871 and 1892 articles is identical.

131. Cerfbeer, "Une nuit," p. 423.

132. Du Camp, *Les convulsions* 2:299.

133. A variety of liberal and conservative men and at least one woman, Augustine-Melvine Blanchecotte, criticized the bourgeoises' attacks on prisoners from the time the first captured guardsmen were taken to Versailles in early April.

134. *New York Tribune,* May 31, 1871, p. 1.

135. For a more complete analysis of the role of female nudity in art, see Warner, *Monuments and Maidens;* and Hollander, *Seeing through Clothes.* During this period of war and civil war, it was common for artists to depict both France and Paris as semiclad goddesses being raped or stabbed in the back by evil men. For examples, see Leith, "The War of Images," p. 111.

136. Goncourt, *Journal,* May 26, 1871, 2:815.

137. The Bibliothèque Nationale's collection of drawings from the period of the Commune contains many representations of *pétroleuses,* all of whom are depicted in skirts or dresses.

138. See, for instance, Coventry Patmore, *The Angel in the House,* (1854–56; rpt. London: G. Bell and Sons, 1920), excerpted in Hellerstein, Hume, and Offen, *Victorian Women,* pp. 134–40:

> To the sweet folly of the dove,
> She joins the cunning of the snake,
> To rivet and exalt his love;
> Her mode of candour is deceit;
> And what she thinks from what she'll say,
> (Although I'll never call her cheat,)
> Lies far as Scotland from Cathay.

139. Gibson, *Paris during the Commune,* p. 293.

6. Women on Trial

1. Memoirs that contain no references to the trials include Mendès, *Les 73 journées;* Blanchecotte, *Tablettes d'une femme;* and Goncourt, *Journal.* For early histories that contain no reference or only brief mention, see Claretie, *Histoire de la révolution,* pp. 723–28; Malon, *La troisième défaite,* none; Lanjalley and Corriez, *Histoire de la révolution,* none. Lissagaray devoted a chapter to the trials and executions of Communards. See Lissagaray, *Histoire de la Commune,* pp. 409–27.

Later histories are often almost as brief. Those who wrote from a pro-Commune perspective generally included longer accounts of the trial than pro-Versailles writers did. For pro-Commune historians, see Jellinek, *The Paris Commune,* pp. 373–86; Georges Laronze, *Histoire de la Commune de 1871 d'après des documents et des souvenirs inédits* (Paris: Payot, 1928), pp. 575–671; André Decouflé, *La Commune de Paris (1871): Révolution populaire et pouvoir révolutionnaire* (Paris: Cujas, 1969), none; Bruhat, Dautry, and Tersen, *La Commune de 1871,* pp. 292–94; Bourgin, *La guerre,* pp. 399–408; Lepelletier, *Histoire de la Commune,* none. For neutral but Commune-leaning historians, see Edwards, *The Paris Commune,* pp. 346–50; Jacques Rougerie, *Procès des Communards* (Paris: Collection Archives, 1967). For anti-Commune historians, see Mason, *The Paris Commune,* pp. 288, 291–92; Horne, *The Fall of Paris,* pp. 422–26.

2. John Knox, *The First Blast of the Trumpet against the Monstrous Regiment of Women* (1558; rpt. New York, AMS Press, 1967).

3. Appert, *Rapport d'ensemble;* Tombs, *The War against Paris,* pp. 191–92, 219.

4. Jellinek, *The Paris Commune,* p. 366. For general descriptions of prison conditions, see "A Visit to Satory," *Standard,* May 30, 1871 (dateline: May 28), p. 5; Lissagaray, *Histoire de la Commune,* pp. 385–88, 395–98; Edwards, *The Paris Commune,* pp. 346–48; Jellinek, *The Paris Commune,* pp. 366–68. For accounts by prisoners, see Elisée Reclus, *La Commune de Paris au jour le jour* (Paris: Schleicher frères, 1908); Paul Ferrat, quoted in Jellinek, *The Paris Commune,* p. 367; Michel, *Mémoires,* pp. 133–36; Mme C. Hardouin, *La détenue de Versailles en 1871* (Paris: author, 1879), pp. 26–45; Malon, *La troisième défaite* pp. 490–502.

5. Lissagaray, *Histoire de la Commune,* pp. 385–86.

6. Ibid., p. 386; Jellinek, *The Paris Commune,* p. 366.

7. Jellinek, *The Paris Commune,* p. 367.

8. Ibid., p. 367; Lissagaray, *Histoire de la Commune,* p. 386.

9. Account of the unnamed wife of a *chef de légion,* in Lissagaray, *Histoire de la Commune,* pp. 386–87.

10. Ibid., p. 387; Fetridge, *Rise and Fall of the Paris Commune,* pp. 487–89. Fetridge quotes an unnamed "noted journalist." Michel, *Mémoires,* p. 133.

11. Michel, *Mémoires,* p. 133.

12. "A Visit to Satory," *Standard,* May 30, 1871 (dateline: May 28), p. 5. Benoît Malon includes excerpts from other press accounts of prison conditions in *La troisième défaite,* pp. 490–503.

13. "A Visit to Satory."

14. *New York Times,* May 31, 1871 (dateline: Versailles, May 29), p. 1.

15. *New York Tribune,* June 10, 1871, p. 1.

16. Michel, *Mémoires,* pp. 134–35.

17. Jan Goldstein, *Console and Classify: The French Psychiatric Profession in the Nineteenth Century* (Cambridge: Cambridge University Press, 1987), pp. 242, 264, 154, 232–33. See pp. 240–75 for an analysis of the tenets and popularity of physiology in nineteenth-century France.

18. *Standard,* May 30, 1871, p. 5.

19. Ibid.

20. Quoted in Fetridge, *Rise and Fall,* p. 489.

21. *Standard,* May 30, 1871, p. 5.

22. Quoted in Fetridge, *Rise and Fall,* pp. 491–93.

23. In this regard the trials conformed to nineteenth-century notions of female criminality. See Patricia O'Brien, *The Promise of Punishment: Prisons in Nineteenth-Century France* (Princeton: Princeton University Press, 1982), pp. 64–70. O'Brien maintains that nineteenth-century criminologists regarded women as biologically destined for marriage

and motherhood. "Those who tried to overturn this [destiny] were likely to become criminals" (p. 67).

24. Quoted in Fetridge, *Rise and Fall,* pp. 491–93.

25. Edouard Dangin, "Les prisonnières," *Gaulois,* June 28, 1871, p. 2.

26. *Gazette des Tribunaux,* September 6, 1871, p. 508.

27. Francisque Sarcey, "Les aliénistes," *Gaulois,* May 28, 1871, p. 1.

28. Ibid. This was a common nineteenth-century assumption. See O'Brien, *Promise of Punishment,* pp. 64–69.

29. *Monde Illustré,* May 20, 1871, p. 312.

30. Francis Marnard, "La femme libre," *Figaro,* June 2, 1871, p. 1.

31. The French word is *libre,* which is difficult to translate because of its multiple meanings in English. I have chosen to translate it with the contemporary feminist term "liberated," which has similar connotations.

32. Marnard, "La femme libre."

33. Ibid. At this time, Louise Michel was not famous enough to make Marnard's list of undesirable women, even though she fit into his category of *institutrices déclassées.*

34. Ibid.

35. He was like the men whose writings would intrigue Virginia Woolf in 1929 when she looked up "woman" in the card catalog of the British Museum. Virginia Woolf, *A Room of One's Own* (1929; rpt. New York: Harcourt Brace Jovanovich, 1957), pp. 26–27.

36. Marnard, "La femme libre." Recognizing that men might refuse to submit to their wives, *Le Figaro* declared that women's role then was to pray "in silence to the God who judges and restores."

37. AHG, Conseil de Guerre Dossiers, 1871. Dossiers were compiled for all prisoners, but only those of the women and men who were convicted still exist in the archives.

38. Appert, *Rapport d'ensemble,* pp. 219, 227.

39. Ibid., p. 246.

40. Ibid., p. 214.

41. Ibid., p. 215.

42. See, for instance, Blanchecotte, *Tablettes,* pp. 257–59; Mendès, *Les 73 journées,* p. 296; Lepelletier, *Histoire de la Commune* 3:375; Malon, *Troisième défaite,* pp. 400–401; Lanjalley and Corriez, *Histoire de la révolution,* p. 524.

43. See, for instance, *Monde Illustré,* June 1871, p. 343.

44. Appert, *Rapport d'ensemble,* pp. 222–23.

45. *Figaro,* September 6, 1871, p. 3.

46. Ibid.

47. Ibid. The second day, there were fewer spectators and those who were there were mostly women. *Figaro,* September 7, 1871, p. 3.

48. Léonce Dupont, *La Commune et ses auxiliaires devant la justice* (Paris: Didier, 1871), pp. 234–37.

49. *Figaro,* August 8, 1871, p. 2.

50. Claretie, *Histoire de la révolution,* p. 724.

51. Da Costa, *La Commune vécue* 3:207.

52. Dupont, *La Commune,* pp. 234–36.

53. *Figaro,* September 7, 1871, p. 3.

54. Ibid.

55. AHG, Conseil de Guerre Dossiers.

56. The transcript for this and the other trials was published in the *Gazette des Tribunaux.* For this trial see September 4–5 (pp. 503–4) and 6 (pp. 507–8), 1871.

57. *Standard,* September 8, 1871 (dateline: September 6), p. 5.

58. AHG Conseil de Guerre Dossiers; *Gazette des Tribunaux,* September 4–5, 1871, p. 503.

59. AHG Conseil de Guerre Dossiers.

60. See *Figaro,* September, 1871, p. 3; *Standard,* September 8, 1871, p. 5.

61. Claretie, *Histoire de la révolution,* p. 727.

62. *Figaro,* September, 1871, p. 3.

63. Armand Audiganne, *Les populations ouvrières et les industries de la France,* 2 vols. (1860; rpt. New York: B. Franklin, 1970); Julie V. Daubié, *La femme pauvre au XIXe siècle* (1866; rpt. Paris: Côté-femmes, 1992); Jules Michelet, *La femme,* 5th ed. (Paris: Calmann Lévy, 1885); Simon, *L'ouvrière;* Louise A. Tilly and Joan W. Scott, *Women, Work, and Family* (New York: Holt, Rinehart, and Winston, 1978); Lenard R. Berlanstein, *The Working People of Paris, 1871–1914* (Baltimore: Johns Hopkins University Press, 1984); Joan W. Scott, "'L'ouvrière! Mot impie, sordide . . .': Women Workers in the Discourse of French Political Economy, 1840–1860," in her *Gender and the Politics of History,* pp. 139–63; Gullickson, "Womanhood and Motherhood," pp. 206–32.

64. AHG, Conseil de Guerre Dossiers.

65. *Figaro,* September 7, 1871, p. 3.

66. Ibid.

67. Ibid. Writing about the trial of the five pétroleuses and before Louise Michel's trial, Léonce Dupont referred to her as Madame Michel and "cette mère Michel," an indication that he knew very little about her. Dupont, *La Commune,* p. 245.

68. Transcripts of Louise Michel's trial can be found in *Gazette des Tribunaux,* December 17, 1871, p. 862; *Figaro,* December 18, 1871, p. 3; Louise Michel, *Devant le 6e Conseil de Guerre; son arrestation par elle-même dans une lettre au Citoyen Paysant* (Paris: Nouvelle Association Ouvrière, 1880); Michel, *Mémoires,* pp. 313–21. All the following quotations can be found in all these sources.

69. Michel, *La Commune,* p. 188.

70. Thomas, *Louise Michel,* pp. 103–21.

71. Mullaney, "Sexual Politics," p. 314.

72. *Standard,* December 19, 1871, p. 5.

73. *Gazette des Tribunaux,* December 17, 1871, p. 862.

74. Ibid., *Figaro,* December 18, 1871, p. 3.

75. *Gazette des Tribunaux,* December 17, 1871, p. 862; *Figaro,* December 18, 1871, p. 3; *Standard,* December 19, 1871, p. 5.

76. Ibid.

77. Warner, *Joan of Arc,* pp. 139–61, 170–73. Unlike Michel, George Sand and Madeleine Pelletier wore men's clothing, at least on occasion.

78. *Gazette des Tribunaux,* December 17, 1871, p. 862.

79. Michel, *Mémoires,* p. 321.

80. *Gazette des Tribunaux,* December 17, 1871, p. 862.

81. *Figaro,* December 18, 1871, p. 3.

82. Despite their best efforts, the government's investigators found no evidence of sexual activity on her part. She appeared to be a *célibataire* in all senses of the word. AHG, Conseil de Guerre Dossier, Louise Michel.

83. *Standard,* December 19, 1871, p. 5.

84. Ibid.

85. Ibid.

86. Bruhat, Dautry, and Tersen, *La Commune de 1871,* p. 441.

87. Da Costa includes a transcript of his trial and an account of his private conversations with his lawyer in *La Commune vécue* 3:227–39.

88. The French term is *pédérastie.*

89. T. J. Clark, *The Painting of Modern Life* (Princeton: Princeton University Press, 1984), pp. 204–14; Boime, *Art and the French Commune,* pp. 115–20.

90. Da Costa, *La Commune vécue* 3:228.

91. A cursory two-minute examination by an *aide-major* confirmed the judge's accusation. Gatineau demanded a second examination by a physician from the military hospital at Versailles. Da Costa reported that the doctor "asked questions and examined him." This examination "proved" Da Costa was not a homosexual. Da Costa, *La Commune vecue* 3:236–39.

92. Ibid., 3:239, 245.

93. Ibid., 3:232.

94. Lissagaray, who followed the press accounts of the trials closely, obliquely referred to the accusation against Da Costa but made no reference to any other attacks on the men's sexuality. "The squalid imagination of some soldiers . . . taxed itself to taint the accused," he declared. Lissagaray, *Histoire de la Commune,* p. 241. There may be other accusations of homosexuality in the dossiers compiled on the male prisoners, but they remain to be revealed.

7. The Unruly Woman and the Revolutionary City

1. Goncourt and Goncourt, *Journal,* August 21, 1862, 1:1121. A femininist reading of the Goncourts' distress over Rose's deception might see it not as male fear of women's duplicity but as male fear that women could outwit them, that is, of women's superiority.

2. Moses, *French Feminism in the Nineteenth Century,* pp. 151–89.

3. Warner, *Monuments and Maidens,* pp. 280–81; Warner, *Joan of Arc,* pp. 198–217; Kleinbaum, *War against the Amazons;* Samuel, *Amazones;* Tyrrell, *Amazons;* duBois, *Centaurs and Amazons;* Graves, *The Greek Myths.*

4. Hollander, *Seeing through Clothes,* pp. 184–203.

5. Goncourt and Goncourt, *Journal,* August 16, 21, 1862, pp. 1:1111, 1119.

6. For a discussion of other female representations of French revolutions, see Hertz, "Medusa's Head."

7. Warner, *Monuments and Maidens,* p. 37; De Lauretis, *Alice Doesn't;* Gutwirth *Twilight of the Goddesses,* pp. 255–59.

8. Holt, *The Tiger,* p. 31.

9. For more on this issue, see Joan W. Scott, "Gender: A Useful Category of Historical Analysis," in Scott, *Gender and the Politics of History,* pp. 46–48.

10. See Lederer, *Fear of Women,* for a psychological exploration of male fear of the unruly woman.

Selected Bibliography

ARCHIVAL AND OFFICIAL SOURCES

Appert, M. le Général. *Rapport d'ensemble sur les opérations de la justice militaire relatives à l'insurrection de 1871.* Paris: Assemblée Nationale, 1875.

Archives Historiques de Guerre (AHG)

 Ly 7. Rapport sur les jeunes prevenus de 16 ans et au dessus, compromis dans l'Insurrection parisienne

 Ly 22. Operations judiciaires concernant les femmes: Rapport d'ensemble.

 ——. Rapport sur les conseils de guerre

 ——. Union des Femmes. Statutes

 Ly 140. Papers of the Union des Femmes, including membership list, officers, members of committees

 Conseil de Guerre Dossiers:

  Femme Bocquin

  Marie Augustine Gaboriaud

  Josephine Marché or Marchais

  Lucie Maris

  Louise Michel

  Eulalie Papavoine

  Elisabeth Retiffe

  Leontine Suetens

Archives Nationales (AN)

 AB XIX 3353. Dessins accompagnés de légendes représentant des femmes de la Commune

 BB27, 107–9. Fichier des Grâces de la Commune

 BB 24. Dossiers des Grâces

Assemblée Nationale. *Enquête parlementaire sur l'insurrection du 18 mars.* 3 vols. Versailles: Cerf, 1872. See especially Vol. 2: *Pièces Justificatives.* "Du rôle des femmes pendant la lutte de la Commune," (Rapport du capitaine Briot), pp. 309–13; and

"Du rôle des enfants dans l'insurrection" (Rapport du capitaine Guichard), pp. 313–20.
Bibliothèque Historique de la Ville de Paris (BHVP)
    F.M. 6347-IX. Caricature collection
    F.M. 6347-IX. Première liste des femmes prisonnières à Versailles
    F 10495. 1872 Enquête
    Fol. 10037 *Memorial Illustrée des Deux Sièges de Paris, 1870–1871*, texte de Loredan Larchey. Paris: Librairie du Moniteur Universel, 1872.
Bibliothèque Nationale (BN)
    Collection de Vinck (Cabinet des Estampes) caricatures
Les murailles politiques françaises. Vol. 2: *La Commune, 18 mars–27 mai 1871.* Paris: L. La Chevalier, 1874.
Le procès de la Commune: Compte rendu des débats du Conseil de Guerre. Paraissant tous les jours par livraison de huit pages, avec illustrations. Paris, 1871.
Proces-verbaux de la Commune de 1871. 2 vols. Edited by Georges Bourgin and Gabriel Henriot. Paris: A. Lahure, 1924, 1945.
Les 31 séances officielles de la Commune de Paris. Paris: Revue de France, 1871.

CONTEMPORARY NEWSPAPERS

General

La Commune
La Gazette des Tribunaux
L'Illustration
Le Monde Illustré

Communard

L'Avant-Garde
Le Cri du Peuple
Le Droit
Le Journal Officiel de la République Française
La Mère Duchêne
Le Mot d'Ordre
La Sociale
Le Tribun du Peuple
Le Vengeur

Versaillais

Le Figaro
Le Gaulois

Foreign

Daily News (London)
New York Herald
New York Tribune
New York Times

Standard, later *Evening Standard* (London)
Times (London)

Compilations

Dupuy, Aimé. *1870–1871: La guerre, la Commune, et la presse.* Paris: Coline, 1959.
Lemonnyer, Jules. *Les journaux de Paris pendant la Commune: Revue bibliographique complète de la presse parisienne du 19 mars au 27 mai.* Paris: J. Lemonnyer, 1871.

MEMOIRS, DIARIES, LETTERS

Adam, Juliette. *Mes illusions et nos souffrances pendant le siège de Paris.* 1906.
Allemane, Jean. *Mémoires d'un Communard.* Paris: F. Maspero, 1981.
Andrieu, Jules. "The Paris Commune: A Chapter towards Its Theory and History." *Fortnightly Review,* November 1, 1871, no. LIX.
Barrès, Maurice. *Mes Cahiers, 1896–1923.* Paris: Plon, 1963.
Barron, Louis. *Sous le drapeau rouge.* Paris: A Savens, 1889.
Bergerand, Charles. *Paris sous la Commune en 1871.* Paris: A. Lainé, 1871.
Bergeret, Jules. *Le 18 mars: Journal hebdomadaire.* London: n.p., August 21–September 6, [1871].
Bingham, Denis Arthur. *Recollections of Paris.* 2 vols. London: Chapman and Hall, 1896.
Blanchecotte, Augustine-Melvine. *Tablettes d'une femme pendant la Commune.* Paris: Didier, 1872.
B[rocher/Brochon], Victorine. *Souvenirs d'une morte vivante.* Lausanne: At her own expense, 1909. Rpt. Paris: Maspero, 1976.
C. de B. *Letters from Paris, 1870–1875.* Translated and edited by Robert Henrey. London: J. M. Dent and Sons, 1942.
Cerfbeer, Gaston. "Une nuit de la semaine sanglante." *Revue Hebdomadaire* 6 (1903): 417–24.
Clemenceau, Georges E. B. *Clemenceau: The Events of His Life as Told by Himself to His Former Secretary, Jean Martet.* Translated by Milton Waldman. London: Longmans, Green, 1930.
Commissaire, Sébastien. *Mémoires et souvenirs.* Paris: Garcet et Nisius, 1888.
Compiègne, Marquis de. "Souvenirs d'un Versaillais pendant le second siège de Paris." *Correspondant,* August 10, 1875, pp. 589–633.
Constant, Louis, ed. *Mémoires des femmes, mémoir du peuple: Anthologie.* Paris: Maspero, 1979.
Daudet, Alphonse. *Lettres à un absent, Paris, 1870–1871.* Paris: Alphonse Lemirre, 1871.
———. *Souvenirs d'un homme de lettres.* Paris: C. Marpon et E. Flammarion, 1888.
Deraismes, Maria. *Ce que veulent les femmes: Articles et conférences de 1869 à 1891.* Paris: Syros, 1980.
Desmoulins, Auguste. "The Paris Workmen and the Commune." *Fortnightly Review* 42 (September 1871): 308–20.
Dumas, fils, Alexandre. *Une lettre sur les choses du jour.* Paris: Michel Lévy Frères, 1871.
Dupont, Léonce. *La Commune et ses auxiliaires devant la justice.* Paris: Didier, 1871.
———. *Souvenirs de Versailles pendant la Commune.* Paris: E. Dentu, 1881.
An Englishman. *The Insurrection in Paris, Related by an Englishman, an Eye-Witness of That Frightful War and of the Terrible Evils Which Accompanied It.* Paris: A. Lemoigne, 1871.
Excoffons, Béatrix. "Récit." In Louise Michel, *La Commune.* Paris: P.-V. Stock, 1898.

Forbes, Archibald. *My Experiences of the War between France and Germany.* London: Hurst and Blackett, 1871.

——. "What I Saw of the Paris Commune." *Century (Illustrated) Magazine* 44 (1892): 803–17; 45 (1892): 48–61.

Galliffet, General Gaston de. "Mes souvenirs." *Journal des Débats,* July 19, 22, and 25, 1902.

Gautier, Théophile. *Tableau de siège, Paris, 1870–1871.* Paris: Bibliothèque-Charpentier, 1894.

Gibson, the Reverend William. *Paris during the Commune: Being Letters from Paris and Its Neighbourhood Written Chiefly during the Time of the Second Siege.* London: Whittaker, 1872. (Letters originally appeared in the *Watchman.*)

Gobineau, [Joseph] A[rthur] de. *Lettres à deux Athéniennes (1868–1881).* Athènes: Kauffmann, 1936.

Goncourt, Edmond de, and Jules de Goncourt. *Journal: Mémoires de la vie littéraire.* Edited and annotated by Robert Ricatte. 2 vols. Paris: Fasquelle and Flammarion, 1956.

——. *Paris under Siege, 1870: From the Goncourt Journal.* Edited and translated by George J. Becker. Historical introduction by Paul H. Beik. Ithaca: Cornell University Press, 1969.

Guéniot, A. *Souvenirs parisiens de la Guerre de 1870 et de la Commune.* Paris: J.-B. Baillière et fils, 1928.

Halévy, Ludovic. *Notes et souvenirs, de mai à septembre 1871.* Paris: Calmann, 1889.

Hardouin, Mme C. *La détenue de Versailles en 1871.* Paris: author, 1879.

Harrison, Frederic. "The Fall of the Commune." *Fortnightly Review* 41 (August 1871): 129–55.

——. "The Revolution of the Commune." *Fortnightly Review* 53 (May 1871): 556–79.

Hegermann-Lindencrone, Lillie de. *In the Courts of Memory.* 1925. Rpt. New York: Da Capo, 1980.

Hérisson, Le Compte d'. *Nouveau journal d'un officier d'ordonnance: La Commune.* 17th edition. Paris: Paul Ollendorff, 1891.

Hoffman, Wickham. *Camp, Court, and Siege.* New York: Harper and Bros., 1877.

Lefrançais, Gustave. *Etude sur le mouvement communaliste à Paris en 1871.* Neuchâtel: G. Guillaume fils, 1871.

——. *Souvenirs d'un révolutionnaire.* Paris: Société Encyclopédique Française, 1872. Rpt. Brussels: Les Temps Nouveaux, 1902.

Leighton, John. *Paris under the Commune.* London: Bradbury Evans, 1871. (Translation and embellishment of Mendès.)

Léo, André. *La guerre sociale: Discourse prononcé au Congrès de la Paix à Lausanne (1871).* Neuchâtel: n.p., 1871.

Linton, William. *The Paris Commune: In Answer to the Calumnies of the "New York Tribune."* Boston: n.p., 1871.

Malet, Sir Edward. *Shifting Scenes.* London: Murray, 1901.

Mazade, A[lexandre] de, ed. *Lettres et notes intimes, 1870–1871.* Beaumont-sur-Oise: Paul Frémont, 1892.

Mendès, Catulle. *Les 73 journées de la Commune.* Paris: E. Lachaud, 1871.

Michel, Louise. *Devant le 6e Conseil de Guerre; Son arrestation par elle-même dans une lettre au Citoyen Paysant.* Paris: Nouvelle association ouvrière, 1880.

——. *Mémoires.* 1886. Rpt. Paris: Maspero, 1979.

——. *The Red Virgin: Memoirs of Louise Michel.* Edited and translated by Bullitt Lowry and Elizabeth Gunter. University: University of Alabama Press, 1981.

Payen, Alix. "Une ambulancière de la Commune de Paris." In *Mémoires de femmes, mémoire du peuple,* edited by Louis Constant, pp. 61–87. Paris: Maspero, 1979.

Renard, Georges. "Mes souvenirs, 1870–1871." *La Révolution de 1848 et les révolutions du XIXe Siècle, 1830, 1848, 1870* 28 (1931): 13–35, 57–81, 117–126.

Richardson, Joanna, ed. *Paris under Siege: A Journal of the Events of 1870–1871 Kept by Contemporaries and Translated and Presented by Joanna Richardson.* London: Folio Society, 1982.

Rochefort, Henri. *Les aventures de ma vie.* Paris: P. Dupont, 1896.

———. *The Adventures of My Life.* Vol. 1. Arranged for English readers by the author and Ernest W. Smith. London: Edward Arnold, 1896.

Sheppard, Nathan. *Shut Up in Paris.* London: Richard Bentley, 1871.

Thiers, Adolphe L. *Memoirs of M. Thiers, 1870–1873.* Translated by F. M. Atkinson. New York: Howard Fertig, 1973.

———. *Notes et souvenirs (1870–1873).* Paris: Calmann-Lévy, 1903.

La vérité sur la Commune par un ancien proscrit. Paris: Louis Salmon, n.d.

"A Victim of Paris and Versailles." *Macmillan's Magazine* 24 (1871): 384–408, 487–96.

Veuillot, Louis. *Paris pendant les deux sièges.* Vol. 2. Paris: Librairie de Victor Palmé, 1871.

Vuillaume, Maxime. *Mes cahiers rouges au temps de la Commune.* Paris: Société d'éditions littéraires et artistiques, 1971.

Washburne, E. B. *Franco-German War and Insurrection of the Commune: Correspondence of E. B. Washburne.* Washington, D.C.: Government Printing Office, 1878.

———. *Recollections of a Minister to France, 1869–1877.* 2 vols. New York: Charles Scribner's Sons, 1887. (Quotes liberally from his letters, with alterations.)

"What an American Girl Saw of the Commune." *Century (Illustrated) Magazine* 45 (n.s. 23) (November 1892): 61–66.

Willard, Mrs. F. (An American Lady). *Pictures from Paris: In War and in Siege.* London: Richard Bently and Son, 1871.

Young, John Russell. *Men and Memories: Personal Reminiscences.* Vol. 1. Edited by May D. Russell Young. New York: F. Tennyson Neely, 1901.

Histories by Eyewitnesses, Participants, Opponents, and Contemporaries

Arnould, Arthur. *Histoire populaire et parlementaire de la Commune de Paris.* 3 vols. 1878. Rpt. New York: AMS Press, 1972.

Arsac, Joanni d'. *La guerre civile et la Commune de Paris en 1871.* Paris: F. Curot, 1871.

Audebrand, Philibert. *Histoire intime de la révolution du 18 mars.* Paris: E. Dentu, 1871.

———. *Nos révolutionnaires: Pages d'histoire contemporains, 1830–1880.* Paris: L. Frenzine, 1886.

Barbey d'Aurevilly. *1871: La Commune de Paris.* Paris, 1903.

Brokett, Linus Pierpont. *Paris under the Commune; or, The Red Rebellion of 1871, a Second Reign of Terror, Murder, and Madness.* New York: H. S. Goodspeed, 1871.

Champsaur, Félicien. "Louise Michel." *Les Contemporains*, no. 3 (1880): 1–3.

Claretie, Jules. *Histoire de la révolution de 1870–71.* Paris: Bureaux du Journal *L'Eclipse*, 1872.

Clère, Jules. *Les hommes de la Commune: Biographie complète de tous ses membres.* Paris: E. Dentu, 1871.

Da Costa, Gaston. *La Commune vécue.* 3 vols. Paris: Ancienne Maison Quantin, 1903–5.

Darlet, A. *La guerre et la Commune, 1870–1871: Dessins par les principaux artistes.* Paris: Michel Lévy Frerès, 1872.

Daudet, Ernest, *L'agonie de la Commune: Paris à feu et à sang (24–29 mai 1871).* 2d ed. Paris: E. Lachaud, 1871.

Du Camp, Maxime. *Les convulsions de Paris.* Vols. 1–4. Paris: Librairie Hachette, 1881. 5th edition. Rpt. AMS, 1978.

Fetridge, W. Pembroke. *The Rise and Fall of the Paris Commune in 1871; with a Full Account of the Bombardment, Capture, and Burning of the City.* New York: Harper and Brothers, 1871.

Fontoulieu, Paul. *Les églises de Paris sous la Commune.* Paris: E. Dentu, 1873.

Guerre des communeux de Paris, 18 mars–28 mai, 1871; par un officier supérieur de l'armée de Versailles. Paris: Firmin Didot Frères, fils, 1871.

Hommes et choses du temps de la Commune: Recits et portraits pour servir à l'histoire de la première révolution sociale. 1871. Rpt. Paris: Editions d'histoire sociale, 1968.

Hugues, Clovis. "La muse du peuple: Sérénade à Louise Michel." *L'Intransigeant.* January 15, 1882.

Jeanneret, Georges. *Paris pendant la Commune révolutionnaire de 71.* Neuchâtel: chez les principaux librairies, 1871.

Lanjalley, Paul, and Paul Corriez. *Histoire de la révolution du 18 mars.* Paris: A. Lacroix, Verboeckhoven, 1871.

Lepelletier, Edmond. *Histoire de la Commune de 1871.* 3 vols. Paris: Mercure de France, 1911–13.

Lissagaray, P.-O. *Histoire de la Commune de 1871.* 1896. Rpt. Paris: Maspero, 1983. Originally published in 1876.

———. *History of the Commune of 1871.* Translated by Eleanor Marx Aveling. New York: International, 1898.

———. *Les huits journées de mai: Derrière les barricades.* Brussels: Bureau du Petit Journal, 1871. Rpt. Paris: Editions d'Histoire Sociale, 1968.

Malon, Benoît. *La troisième défaite du prolétariat français.* Neuchâtel: G. Guillaume fils, 1871.

Marx, Karl, and Friedrich Engels. *Writings on the Paris Commune.* Edited by Hal Draper. New York: Monthly Review Press, 1971.

Michel, Louise. *La Commune.* Second edition. Paris: P.-V. Stock, 1898.

Molinari, Gustave de. *Les clubs rouges pendant le siège de Paris.* Paris: Garnier frères, 1871.

Mottu, John. *Les désastres de Paris ordonnés et causés par la Commune dans la seconde quinzaine de Mai 1871.* Paris: Chez l'auteur et à la librairie internationale, 1871.

Patry, Léonce. *La guerre telle qu'elle est (1870–1871).* Paris: Montgredien, 1897.

Pelletan, Camille. *La semaine de mai.* Paris: Dreyfous, 1880.

Reclus, Elisée. *La Commune de Paris au jour le jour.* Paris: Schleicher fréres, 1908.

Simon, Jules. *The Government of M. Thiers, from 8th February 1871 to 24th May 1873.* New York: Scribner's, 1879.

Vizetelly, Ernest A. *My Adventures in the Commune.* London: Chatto and Windus, 1914.

———. *My Days of Adventure: The Fall of France, 1870–71.* London: Chatto and Windus, 1914.

LATER HISTORIES AND BIOGRAPHIES

Adamov, Arthur. *La Commune de Paris, 18 mars–28 mai 1871.* Paris: Sociales, 1959.

Azéma, Jean-Pierre and Michel Winock. *Les Communards.* Paris: Seuil, 1970.

Baldick, Robert. *The Goncourts.* New York: Hillary House, 1960.

Bourgin, Georges. *La Commune.* Paris: Presses Universitaire de France, 1953.

———. *La guerre de 1870–1871 et la Commune.* Paris: Flammarion, 1971.

———. *Histoire de la Commune.* Paris: Bibliothèque Socialiste, nos. 41–42, 1907.

———. *Les premières journées de la Commune.* Paris: Hachette, 1928.

Braire, Jean. *Sur les traces des communards: Enquête dans les rues du Paris d'aujourd'hui.* Paris: Amis de la Commune, 1988.

Brogan, D. W. *The Development of Modern France, 1870–1939.* Vol. 1: *From the Fall of the Empire to the Dreyfus Affair.* New York: Harper, 1966.

Bruhat, Jean, Jean Dautry, and Emile Tersen. *La Commune de 1871.* 2d edition. Paris: Sociales, 1970.

Bury, J. P. T., and R. P. Tombs. *Thiers, 1797–1877: A Political Life.* London: Allen and Unwin, 1986.

Chastenet, Jacques. *Histoire de la Troisième République.* Vol. 1: *Naissance et jeunesse.* Paris: Hachette, 1952.

Cobb, Richard. *A Second Identity: Essays on France and French History.* London: Oxford University Press, 1969.

La Commune de Paris, 1871–1971. Paris: Institute Maurice Thorez, 1971.

Coudert, Marie-Louise. "Il y a cent ans les femmes aussi . . ." *Cahiers du Communisme,* special issue, "La Commune." (March 1971): 110–15.

Decouflé, André. *La Commune de Paris (1871): Révolution populaire et pouvoir révolutionnaire.* Paris: Cujas, 1969.

Dommanget, Maurice. *Blanqui, la guerre de 1870–71, et la Commune.* Paris: Domat, 1947.

Doré, Gustave. *Versailles et Paris en 1871.* Paris, 1907.

Dubois, Jean. *La vocabulaire politique et sociale en France de 1869 à 1872; à travers les oeuvres des écrivains, les revues, et les journaux.* Paris: Librairie Larousse, 1962.

Durand, Pierre. *Louise Michel: La passion.* Paris: Messidor, 1987.

Edwards, Stewart. *The Paris Commune, 1871.* Chicago: Quadrangle, 1971.

——, ed. *The Communards of Paris.* Translated by Jean McNeil. Ithaca: Cornell University Press, 1973.

Experiences et language de la Commune de Paris. Paris: La Nouvelle Critique (special issue), 1971.

Fabre, Marc-André. *Les drames de la Commune, 18 mars–27 mai 1871.* Paris: Librairie Hachette, 1937.

Falk, André. "Louise Michel, la vierge rouge." *Paris-presse—Intransigeant.* November 26, 1957.

Faucher, Jean-André. *L'agonie de la Commune.* 3 vols. Paris: Atlantic, 1960.

Fournière, Xavier de La. *Louise Michel: Matricule 2182.* Paris: Perrin, 1986.

Gaillard, Jeanne. *Communes de province, Commune de Paris, 1870–1871.* Paris: Flammarion, 1971.

Grant, Richard B. *The Goncourt Brothers.* New York: Twayne, 1972.

Greenberg, Louis M. *Sisters of Liberty.* Cambridge: Harvard University Press, 1971.

Guérin, André. *1871: La Commune.* Paris: 1966.

Gullickson, Gay L. "*La Pétroleuse:* Representing Revolution." *Feminist Studies* 17 (1991): 240–65.

——. "The Unruly Woman of the Paris Commune." In *Gendered Domains,* edited by Dorothy Helly and Susan Reverby, pp. 135–53. Ithaca: Cornell University Press, 1992.

Holt, Edgar. *The Tiger: The Life of Georges Clemenceau, 1841–1929.* London: Hamish Hamilton, 1976.

Horne, Alistair. *The Fall of Paris.* New York: St. Martin's, 1965.

——. *The Terrible Year: The Paris Commune, 1871.* New York: Viking, 1971.

Hunt, Persis. "Feminism and Anti-Clericalism under the Commune." In *Revolution and Reaction: The Paris Commune, 1871,* edited by John Hicks and Robert Tucker, pp. 50–55. Springfield: University of Massachusetts Press, 1973.

Jellinek, Frank. *The Paris Commune of 1871.* 1937. Rpt. New York: Grosset and Dunlap, 1965.

Jones, Kathleen B., and Françoise Vergès. "Women of the Paris Commune." *Women's Studies International Forum* 14 (1991): 491–503.

Kranzberg, Melvin. *The Siege of Paris, 1870–1871: A Political and Social History.* Ithaca: Cornell University Press, 1950.

Lanoux, Armand. *Une histoire de la Commune de Paris.* Paris: Bernard Grasset, 1971.

Laronze, Georges. *Histoire de la Commune de 1871 d'après des documents et des souvenirs inédits.* Paris: Payot, 1928.

Lefebvre, Henri. *La proclamation de la Commune, 26 mars 1871.* Paris: Gallimard, 1965.

Leith, James A., ed. *Images of the Commune/Images de la Commune.* Montreal: McGill-Queen's University Press, 1978.

Lenin, V. I. *The Paris Commune.* New York: International, 1934.

Levy, Yves. "Communards et pétroleuses." *Contrat Social,* 9 (July–August 1965): 242–53.

Lidsky, Paul. *Les écrivains contre la Commune.* Paris: François Maspero, 1972.

Lorulot, André. *Louise Michel: La vierge rouge.* Herblay: Editions de l'Idée Libre, 1930.

Maitron, Jean, and M. Egrot, eds. *Dictionnaire biographique du mouvement ouvrier français.* Part 2: 1864–1871. Paris: Ouvrières, 1967–71.

Marx, Karl, and V. I. Lenin. *The Civil War in France: The Paris Commune.* New York: International, 1940.

Mason, Edward S. *The Paris Commune: An Episode in the History of the Socialist Movement.* 1930; rpt. New York: Howard Fertig, 1967.

Moser, Françoise Moser. *Une héroïne, Louise Michel.* Paris: Vigndau, 1947.

Mullaney, Marie Marmo. "Sexual Politics in the Career and Legend of Louise Michel." *Signs* 15 (1990): 300–322.

Noel, Bernard. *Dictionnaire de la Commune.* Paris: Fernand Hazan, 1971.

Parmelin, Hélène. "Les femmes et la Commune." *Europe* 29 (April–May 1951): 136–46.

Price, Roger. "Conservative Reactions to Social Disorder: The Paris Commune of 1871." *Journal of European Studies* 1 (1971): 341–52.

Rials, Stéphane. *Nouvelle histoire de Paris: De Trochu à Thiers, 1870–1873.* Paris: Hachette, 1985.

Rossel, André. *1870: La première "grande" guerre, par l'affiche et l'image.* Paris: Les Yeux Ouverts, 1970.

Rougerie, Jacques. "La Commune de 1871: Problèmes d'histoire sociale." *Archives Internationales de Sociologie de la Coopération,* no. 8 (1960).

———. *1871: Jalons pour une histoire de la Commune de Paris.* Assen, Pays-Bas: Van Gorcum, 1973.

———. *Paris libre.* Paris: Seuil, 1971.

———. *Procès des Communards.* Paris: Collection Archives, 1967.

Schulkind, Eugene W. "The Activity of Popular Organizations during the Paris Commune of 1871." *French Historical Studies* 1 (1960): 394–415.

———. "The Historiography of the Commune: Some Problems." In *Images of the Commune/Images de la Commune,* edited by James A. Leith, pp. 319–32. Montreal: McGill-Queen's University Press, 1978.

———. "Le rôle des femmes dans la Commune de 1871." *1848: Revue des Révolutions Contemporaines* 42 (February 1950).

———. "Socialist Women during the 1871 Paris Commune." *Past and Present,* no. 106 (February 1985): 124–63.

———, ed. *The Paris Commune: The View from the Left.* London: Jonathan Cape, 1972.

Sellers, Edith. "The Red Virgin of Montmartre." *Fortnightly Review.* February 1, 1905.

Serman, William. *La Commune de Paris (1871).* Paris: Librairie Arthème Fayard, 1986.

Soria, Georges. *Grande histoire de la Commune.* 5 vols. Paris: Livre Club Diderot, 1970.

Soukhomline, Vasili. "Deux femmes russes combattantes de la Commune." *Cahiers Internationaux* 16 (May 1950): 53–62.

Thomas, Edith. "Louise Michel, la vierge rouge." *Miroir de l'Histoire*, 1958.

——. *Louise Michel; ou, La velléda de l'anarchie.* Paris: Gallimard, 1971.

——. *Les "pétroleuses".* Paris: Gallimard, 1963.

——. *The Women Incendiaries.* Translated by James Atkinson and Starr Atkinson. New York: George Braziller, 1966.

Tombs, Robert. "Paris and the Rural Hordes: An Exploration of Myth and Reality in the French Civil War of 1871." *Historical Journal* 29 (1986): 795–808.

——. *The War against Paris, 1871.* Cambridge: Cambridge University Press, 1981.

Villiers, Baron Marc de. *Histoire des clubs de femmes et des légions d'Amazones, 1793, 1848, 1871.* Paris: Plon, 1910.

Williams, Roger L. *The French Revolution of 1870–1871.* New York: Norton, 1969.

Wright, Gordon. "The Anti-Commune: Paris, 1871." *French Historical Studies* 10 (Spring 1977): 149–72.

CARICATURE, ALLEGORY, AND REPRESENTATION

Agulhon, Maurice. *Marianne into Battle: Republican Imagery and Symbolism in France, 1789–1880.* Translated by Janet Lloyd. Cambridge: Cambridge University Press, 1981.

——. "On Political Allegory: A Reply to Eric Hobsbawm." *History Workshop,* no. 8 (1979): 167–73.

Bertall, [Charles]. *The Communists of Paris, 1871: Types—Physiognomies—Characters with Explanatory Text Descriptive of Each Design Written Expressly for This Edition.* London: Buckingham, 1873.

Boime, Albert. *Art and the French Commune: Imagining Paris after War and Revolution.* Princeton: Princeton University Press, 1995.

——. *Hollow Icons: The Politics of Sculpture in Nineteenth-Century France.* Kent, Ohio: Kent State University Press, 1987.

Clark, T. J. *The Painting of Modern Life.* Princeton: Princeton University Press, 1984.

DeGroat, Judith. "Representative of Her Class: Images of Working Women in the July Monarchy." Unpublished paper delivered at the Thirty-Fourth Annual Meeting of the Society for French Historical Studies, 17–19 March 1988.

De Lauretis, Teresa. *Alice Doesn't: Feminism, Semiotics, Cinema.* Bloomington: Indiana University Press, 1984.

Feld, Charles. *Pilotell: Dessinateur et communard.* 2d edition. Paris: Livre Club Diderot, 1970.

Goldstein, Robert Justin. *Censorship of Political Caricature in Nineteenth-Century France.* Kent, Ohio: Kent State University Press, 1989.

Gutwirth, Madelyn. *The Twilight of the Goddesses: Women and Representation in the French Revolutionary Era.* New Brunswick, N.J.: Rutgers University Press, 1992.

Hertz, Neil. "Medusa's Head: Male Hysteria under Political Pressure." *Representations* 4 (Fall 1983): 27–79.

Hollander, Anne. *Seeing through Clothes.* New York: Viking, 1978.

Lambert, Susan. *The Franco-Prussian War and the Commune in Caricature, 1870–1871.* London: Her Majesty's Stationery Office, 1971.

Leith, James A. "The War of Images Surrounding the Commune." In *Images of the Commune/Images de la Commune,* edited by Leith, pp. vii–xv, 101–50. Montreal: McGill-Queen's University Press, 1978.

Miles, Margaret R. *Carnal Knowing: Female Nakedness and Religious Meaning in the Christian West.* Boston: Beacon, 1989.

Money, E. "La caricature sous la Commune." *Revue de France* (April–May 1872): 33–54.

Nochlin, Linda. "Women, Art, and Power." In her *Women, Art, and Power and Other Essays,* pp. 1–36. New York: Harper and Row, 1988.

Pagels, Elaine. *Adam, Eve, and the Serpent.* New York: Random House, 1988.

Reshif, Ouriel. *Guerre: Mythes et Caricature.* Paris: Presses de la Fondation Nationale des Sciences Politiques, 1984.

Rifkin, Adrian. "No Particular Thing to Mean." *Block* 8 (1983): 36–45.

Rossel, André. *1871: La Commune; ou, L'experience du pouvoir, par l'affiche et l'image.* Paris: Les Yeux Ouverts, [c. 1970].

Schor, Naomi. "Triste Amérique: Atala and the Postrevolutionary Construction of Woman." In *Rebel Daughters: Women and the French Revolution,* edited by Sara E. Melzer and Leslie W. Rabine. New York: Oxford University Press, 1992.

Shikes, Ralph E. *The Indignant Eye: The Artist as Social Critic in Prints and Drawings from the Fifteenth Century to Picasso.* Boston: Beacon, 1969.

Shikes, Ralph E., and Steven Heller. *The Art of Satire: Painters as Caricaturists and Cartoonists from Delacroix to Picasso.* New York: Pratt Graphics Center and Horizon Press, 1984.

Warner, Marina. *Alone of All Her Sex: The Myth and the Cult of the Virgin Mary.* New York: Random House, 1983.

——. *Monuments and Maidens: The Allegory of the Female Form.* New York: Atheneum, 1985.

Wiener, Jon. "Paris Commune Photos at a New York Gallery: An Interview with Linda Nochlin." *Radical History,* no. 32 (1985): 59–70.

Young, James E. *Writing and Rewriting the Holocaust: Narrative and the Consequences of Interpretation.* Bloomington: Indiana University Press, 1988.

AMAZONS AND OTHER UNRULY WOMEN

Bachofen, J. J. *Myth, Religion, and Mother Right: Selected Writings of J. J. Bachofen.* Translated by Ralph Manheim. Princeton: Princeton University Press, 1967.

Blok, Josine. "Sexual Asymmetry: A Historiographical Essay." In *Sexual Asymmetry: Studies in Ancient Society,* edited by Blok and Peter Mason, pp. 1–57. Amsterdam: J. C. Gieben, 1987.

duBois, Page. *Centaurs and Amazons.* Ann Arbor: University of Michigan Press, 1982.

Eckstein-Diener, Berta [Diner, Helen]. *Mothers and Amazons: the First Feminine History of Culture.* Translated and edited by John Philip Lundin. New York: Julian Press, 1965.

Graves, Robert. *The Greek Myths.* 2 vols. New York: George Braziller, 1957.

Harding, M. Esther. *Women's Mysteries, Ancient and Modern: A Psychological Interpretation of the Feminine Principle as Portrayed in Myth, Story, and Dreams.* New York: G. P. Putnam's Sons, 1971.

Hartman, Mary S. *Victorian Murderesses: A True History of Thirteen Respectable French and English Women Accused of Unspeakable Crimes.* Stanford: Stanford University Press, 1981.

Hufton, Olwen H. *Women and the Limits of Citizenship in the French Revolution.* Toronto: University of Toronto Press, 1992.

Kerber, Linda K. "Separate Spheres, Female Worlds, Woman's Place: The Rhetoric of Women's History." *Journal of American History* 75 (July 1988): 9–39.

Kestner, Joseph A. *Mythology and Misogyny: The Social Discourse of Nineteenth-Century British Classical-Subject Painting.* Madison: University of Wisconsin Press, 1989.

Kleinbaum, Abby Wettan. *The War against the Amazons.* New York: New Press, 1983.

Lederer, Wolfgang. *The Fear of Women.* New York: Grune and Stratton, 1968.

Lefkowitz, Mary R. "Influential Women." In *Images of Women in Antiquity*, edited by Averil Cameron and Amélie Kuhrt, pp. 49–64. Detroit: Wayne State University Press, 1983.

Merck, Mandy. "The Patriotic Amazonomachy and Ancient Athens." In *Tearing the Veil: Essays on Femininity*, edited by Susan Lipshitz, pp. 95–115. London: Routledge and Kegan Paul, 1978.

Pomeroy, Sarah B. *Goddesses, Whores, Wives, and Slaves: Women in Classical Antiquity*. New York: Schocken, 1975.

Rothery, Guy. *The Amazons in Antiquity and Modern Times*. London: F. Griffiths, 1910.

Samuel, Pierre. *Amazones, guerrières, et gaillardes*. Grenoble: Presses Universitaires de Grenoble, 1975.

Sobol, Donald J. *The Amazons of Greek Mythology*. London: Thomas Yoseloff, 1972.

Tiffany, Sharon W., and Kathleen J. Adams. *The Wild Woman: An Inquiry into the Anthropology of an Idea*. Cambridge, Mass.: Schenkman, 1985.

Tyrell, William Blake. *Amazons: A Study in Athenian Myth-Making*. Baltimore: Johns Hopkins University Press, 1984.

Warner, Marina. *Joan of Arc: The Image of Female Heroism*. New York: Knopf, 1981.

Nineteenth-Century Women's History

Bell, Susan Groag, and Karen Offen, eds. *Women, the Family, and Freedom: The Debate in Documents*. Vol. 1: *1750–1880*. Stanford: Stanford University Press, 1983.

Gullickson, Gay L. "Womanhood and Motherhood: The Rouen Manufacturing Community, Women Workers, and the French Factory Acts." In *The European Peasant Family and Society: Historical Studies*, edited by Richard L. Rudolph, pp. 206–32. Liverpool: Liverpool University Press, 1995.

Hellerstein, Erna, Leslie Hume, and Karen Offen, eds. *Victorian Women: A Documentary Account of Women's Lives in Nineteenth-Century England, France, and the United States*. Stanford: Stanford University Press, 1981.

Hufton, Olwen. "Women in Revolution, 1789–1796," *Past and Present*, no. 53 (1971): 90–108.

Léo, André. *La femme et les moeurs: Liberté ou monarchie*. Paris, 1869.

Levy, Darlene Gay, Harriet B. Applewhite, and Mary D. Johnson, eds. *Women in Revolutionary Paris, 1789–1795: Selected Documents Translated with Notes and Commentary*. Urbana: University of Illinois Press, 1979.

Melzer, Sara E., and Leslie W. Rabine, eds. *Rebel Daughters: Women and the French Revolution*. New York: Oxford University Press, 1992.

Mink, Paule. *Le travail des femmes*. Paris: Chez Mary, 1868.

Le Moniteur des Citoyennes: Journal du droit et de l'intérêt des femmes, November 6, 1870.

Moses, Claire Goldberg. *French Feminism in the Nineteenth Century*. Albany: State University of New York Press, 1984.

Poovey, Mary. *Uneven Developments: The Ideological Work of Gender in Mid-Victorian England*. Chicago: University of Chicago Press, 1988.

Riley, Denise. *"Am I That Name?" Feminism and the Category of "Women" in History*. Minneapolis: University of Minnesota Press, 1988.

Scott, Joan Wallach. *Gender and the Politics of History*. New York: Columbia University Press, 1988.

Simon, Jules. *L'ouvrière*. 3d ed. Paris: L. Hachette, 1861.

Smith, Bonnie G. *Ladies of the Leisure Class: The Bourgeoises of Northern France in the Nineteenth Century*. Princeton: Princeton University Press, 1981.

Tilly, Louise A., and Joan W. Scott. *Women, Work, and Family.* New York: Holt, Rinehart, and Winston, 1978.

Vicinus, Martha, ed. *Suffer and Be Still: Women in the Victorian Age.* Bloomington: Indiana University Press, 1973.

Welter, Barbara. "The Cult of True Womanhood, 1820–1860." *American Quarterly* 18 (Summer 1966): 151–74.

FRENCH HISTORY AND OTHER WORKS

Agulhon, Maurice. *Marianne into Battle: Republican Imagery and Symbolism in France, 1789–1880.* Translated by Janet Lloyd. Cambridge: Cambridge University Press, 1981.

Alexander, Marc Daniel. "The Administration of Madness and Attitudes toward the Insane in Nineteenth-Century Paris." Ph.D. dissertation, Johns Hopkins University, 1976.

Barrows, Susanna. "After the Commune: Alcoholism, Temperance, and Literature in the Early Third Republic." In *Consciousness and Class Experience in Nineteenth-Century Europe,* edited by John M. Merriman, pp. 205–18. New York: Holmes and Meier, 1979.

———. *Distorting Mirrors: Visions of the Crowd in Late Nineteenth-Century France.* New Haven: Yale University Press, 1981.

Berlanstein, Lenard R. *The Working People of Paris, 1871–1914.* Baltimore: Johns Hopkins University Press, 1984.

Brogan, D. W. *The Development of Modern France.* New York: Harper and Row, 1966.

Ferguson, Priscilla Parkhurt. *Paris as Revolution: Writing the Nineteenth-Century City.* Berkeley: University of California Press, 1994.

Furet, François. *Revolutionary France, 1770–1880.* Translated by Antonia Nevill. Oxford: Blackwell, 1992.

Geertz, Clifford. "Centers, Kings, and Charisma: Reflections on the Symbolics of Power." In *Rites of Power: Symbolism, Ritual, and Politics since the Middle Ages,* edited by Sean Wilentz, pp. 13–38. Philadelphia: University of Pennsylvania Press, 1985.

Godineau, Dominique. *Citoyennes tricoteuses: Les femmes du peuple à Paris pendant la Révolution française.* Aix-en-Provence: Alinea, 1988.

Goldstein, Jan. *Console and Classify: The French Psychiatric Profession in the Nineteenth Century.* Cambridge: Cambridge University Press, 1987.

Hunt, Lynn. "Hercules and the Radical Image in the French Revolution." *Representations* 1 (1983): 95–117.

Jacquemet, Gérard. *Belleville au XIXe siècle du faubourg à la ville.* Paris: Editions de l'Ecole des Hautes Etudes en Sciences Sociales, 1984.

Lairtullier, E. *Les femmes célèbres de 1789 à 1795, et leur influence dans la Révolution.* 2 vols. Paris: chez France, à la Librairie Politique, 1840.

Michelet, Jules. *La femme.* 1860. 5th edition. Paris: Calmann Lévy, 1885.

———. *Histoire de la Révolution française.* Paris: C. Marpon et E. Flammarion, n.d.

Nye, Robert A. *Masculinity and Male Codes of Honor in Modern France.* New York: Oxford University Press, 1993.

O'Brien, Patricia. *The Promise of Punishment: Prisons in Nineteenth-Century France.* Princeton: Princeton University Press, 1982.

Orr, Linda. *Headless History: Nineteenth-Century French Historiography of the Revolution.* Ithaca: Cornell University Press, 1990.

Poulot, Denis. *Question sociale: Le sublime ou le travailleur comme il est en 1870 et ce qu'il peut-être.* Paris: A. Lecroix, Verboeckhoven, 1870.

Sewell, William H., Jr. *Work and Revolution in France: The Language of Labor from the Old Regime to 1848.* Cambridge: Cambridge University Press, 1980.

Traugott, Mark. "Barricades as Repertoire: Continuities and Discontinuities in the History of French Contention. In *Repertoires and Cycles of Collective Action,* edited by Traugott, pp. 43–56. Durham, N.C.: Duke University Press, 1995.

——. *The French Worker: Autobiographies from the Early Industrial Era.* Berkeley: University of California Press, 1993.

LITERATURE

Dickens, Charles. *A Tale of Two Cities.* 1859. Rpt. New York: Washington Square Press, 1960.

Henty, George A. *A Girl of the Commune.* New York: R. F. Fenno, 1895.

Hugo, Victor. *L'année terrible.* In *Les chatiments—L'année terrible,* edited by Pol Gaillard. Paris: Bardas, 1967.

Kleist, Heinrich von. *Penthésilée.* Translated by Julien Gracq. Paris: Librairie José Corti, 1954.

Vallès, Jules [Jacques Vingtras]. *L'insurge.* Paris: Les Editeurs Français Réunis, 1968.

——. *The Insurrectionist.* Translated by Sandy Petrey. Englewood Cliffs, N.J.: Prentice-Hall, 1971.

Verlain, Paul. *Confessions of a Poet.* Translated by Joanna Richardson. 1950. Rpt. Westport, Conn.; Hyperion, 1979.

Zola, Emile. *The Debacle.* Translated by Leonard Tancock. London: Penguin, 1972.

Index